LONDON FALLING

ALSO BY PATRICK RADDEN KEEFE

Rogues

Empire of Pain

Say Nothing

The Snakehead

Chatter

LONDON FALLING

A MYSTERIOUS DEATH IN A GILDED CITY AND A FAMILY'S SEARCH FOR TRUTH

PATRICK RADDEN KEEFE

PICADOR

First published 2026 by Doubleday
an imprint of Penguin Random House LLC, New York

First published in the UK 2026 by Picador
an imprint of Pan Macmillan
The Smithson, 6 Briset Street, London EC1M 5NR
EU representative: Macmillan Publishers Ireland Ltd, 1st Floor,
The Liffey Trust Centre, 117–126 Sheriff Street Upper,
Dublin 1 D01 YC43
Associated companies throughout the world

ISBN 978-1-0350-5627-9 HB
ISBN 978-1-0350-5629-3 TPB

Copyright © Patrick Radden Keefe 2026

The right of Patrick Radden Keefe to be identified as the
author of this work has been asserted in accordance with
the Copyright, Designs and Patents Act 1988.

Extract from 'The Boy Who Became a River' taken from *Adam* © Estate of
Gboyega Odubanjo, 2024. Reprinted by permission of Faber and Faber Ltd.

All rights reserved. No part of this publication may be reproduced,
stored in a retrieval system, or transmitted, in any form, or by any means
(including, without limitation, electronic, mechanical, photocopying, recording
or otherwise) without the prior written permission of the publisher.

Pan Macmillan does not have any control over, or any responsibility for,
any author or third-party websites (including, without limitation, URLs,
emails and QR codes) referred to in or on this book.

1 3 5 7 9 8 6 4 2

A CIP catalogue record for this book is available from the British Library.

Title page photograph: Chrysa DaCosta
Part I photograph: Mattia Balsamini
Part II photograph: Instagram, @safiyashamji
Part IV photograph: David Barrie

Book design by Michael Collica
Printed and bound in the UK using 100% Renewable Electricity
by CPI Group (UK) Ltd

This book is sold subject to the condition that it shall not, by way of
trade or otherwise, be lent, hired out, or otherwise circulated without
the publisher's prior consent in any form of binding or cover other than
that in which it is published and without a similar condition including this
condition being imposed on the subsequent purchaser. The publisher does not
authorize the use or reproduction of any part of this book in any manner
for the purpose of training artificial intelligence technologies or systems.
The publisher expressly reserves this book from the Text and Data Mining
exception in accordance with Article 4(3) of the European Union
Digital Single Market Directive 2019/790.

Visit **www.picador.com** to read more about all our books
and to buy them.

For Jennifer Radden and Frank Keefe

the boy shocked to see
what could so easily be himself in the river bent to greet it.

—Gboyega Odubanjo

London, after all, is a city of tombs.

—Virginia Woolf

CONTENTS

Prologue — 1

PART I THE FALL

1. The Big I Am — 9
2. A Fast Life — 29
3. An Edifice of Lies — 50
4. Missing Persons — 68
5. River of Death — 76
6. The Night in Question — 84

PART II COINCIDENCES

7. A Family of Braves — 95
8. Prodigal Son — 119
9. Suspicion of Murder — 132
10. The Great Sham — 140
11. A Jigsaw in the Dark — 148
12. Lights Out — 161
13. The Little Fella — 168

PART III THE BALANCE OF PROBABILITIES

14. The Cipriani Five — 197
15. Private Investigations — 218
16. Pocket Dial — 238

17	A Different Light	250
18	Hornet's Nest	258

PART IV   SURVIVORS

19	A Chance Encounter	271
20	The Black Box	286
21	Undertow	297
22	The Kid's Home Safe	305
	Epilogue	317
	Acknowledgements	323
	A Note on Sources	327
	Notes	333

What follows is a true story. The book contains lengthy stretches of verbatim dialogue. None of this language is invented or imagined. Longer conversations come directly from transcripts or recordings that were made available to the author. Some shorter snatches are drawn from the recollections of people who took part in a conversation or from their contemporaneous notes. The book also cites numerous text messages and emails, which have been edited only to correct for typos.

LONDON FALLING

PROLOGUE

THE HEADQUARTERS OF BRITAIN'S Secret Intelligence Service, MI6, occupies an imposing edifice of concrete and green glass on the south bank of the River Thames, in London. It was erected in the early 1990s, alongside Vauxhall Bridge, under circumstances of such secrecy that when the architect was commissioned to design the building, he did not know who he was designing it for.

The Thames is a tidal river, its powerful currents ebbing and surging twice each day with salt water from the North Sea. Occasionally a bottlenose whale will veer off course, separated from its pod, and wander downriver, dangerously far from the ocean. When the tide recedes, the Thames shrinks, its level plummeting by as much as twenty feet, exposing a muddy shoreline. Urban beachcombers – 'mudlarks', as they're known – have unearthed artefacts of previous civilizations from the silt along the riverbanks: Bronze Age daggers and Iron Age coins.

It was the Thames that first drew the Romans, two thousand years ago, to establish a walled entrepôt, which they gave the name Londinium. By the heyday of the British Empire, London had colonized a quarter of the globe. In 1860, half of all exports from Asia, Africa and Latin America were sent there; the Thames was the busiest port in the world. Hundreds of ships arrived each week, and towering cranes unloaded tobacco, ivory, spices, wool, rice, tea and other treasures. The river was teeming, thrumming with commerce, jostling with all manner of vessels and tradesmen and stevedores and mariners from strange lands, hinting at the existence of other civilizations over the horizon.

But the riverbank could be a frightening place as well. In the Victorian era, the waterfront was rife with crime. People had an alarming tendency to die in the Thames, whether voluntarily, in a moment of despair, or because somebody pushed them. If you misstepped on a slick cobble after a night out drinking, the black water could suck you under in an instant. In the work of Charles Dickens, the river was often depicted as a malignant force, grimy and malodorous, 'lapping at piles and posts and iron rings, hiding strange things in its mud, running away with suicides and accidentally drowned bodies'. This was the paradox of the Thames: it was the pulsing artery of London's industrial boom, with vast factories and warehouses swarming with labourers and belching smoke along its banks. But at the same time, Dickens saw in the river 'an image of death', a ribbon of danger coiling through 'the midst of the great city's life'.

The design of the MI6 building was meant to evoke Britain's industrial era, echoing the monolithic power stations, like Battersea and Bankside, which stood nearby. But by 1994, when Queen Elizabeth II presided over the opening of the new spy headquarters, the power stations had long since been decommissioned and now seemed like artefacts themselves, relics of London's vanished past as a factory town. The city had shuttered most of its factories; between 1960 and 1990, jobs in the manufacturing sector declined by 80 per cent.

Shipping, too, had disappeared. In 1955, an American trucking executive from North Carolina invented the modern stackable shipping container. The standardization of these twenty- and forty-foot steel boxes during the 1960s sparked a revolution in global commerce, enabling a more integrated transportation infrastructure in which containers could be transferred fluidly from truck to ship to train. Suddenly big waterfront warehouses for the storage of goods were obsolete, and a new class of gigantic container ships could accommodate ever-larger loads. These vessels were so big that they could no longer navigate the narrow docks lining the Thames. So between 1960 and 1980, nearly all of London's docks shut down and a whole commercial sector that had sustained the region virtually disappeared. For hundreds of years, London had been a port city. Then, quite abruptly, it wasn't.

At least the air was clear. The word 'smog' had been invented in

London, to describe the smoke from coal fires and factories, mingled with English fog, that often enshrouded the city. But new regulations on such fires, combined with the closure of so many factories, meant that suddenly London had clean air. By the time MI6 headquarters opened, the old Dickensian industrial city had been supplanted by a glistening new metropolis. London might not be a centre of shipping or manufacturing anymore, but it was reinventing itself as a financial capital. The waterfront was experiencing an astonishing revitalization: in 1988, a group of young British art students had converted a derelict warehouse in the Surrey Docks into a temporary gallery for an exhibition called *Freeze*. Cool restaurants soon followed, and eventually new housing and high-tech trading floors. Having shed any trace of its old grit or menace, London's waterfront had become a sanitized playground for tourists and young professionals. In 2000, Bankside Power Station reopened as the Tate Modern museum. Battersea Power Station would eventually find new life as a shopping centre.

To many, this new London was hugely exciting: the city had been reimagined as a preferred destination for money and people who had it. Suddenly there were good restaurants for what felt like the first time in history, and world-class shopping and deluxe hotels with chauffeured Bentleys idling out front. Once again, cranes dominated London's skyline, but now they were not unloading cotton or nutmeg but throwing up glass-and-steel skyscrapers and glossy residential complexes with staggering prices. In fact, a lot of Londoners found themselves priced out of this new version of their city, forced to relocate and commute from distant suburbs. Much of the real estate speculation was driven by foreign buyers, who regarded property in London as an investment rather than a place to live. So the buildings were full of amenities – but curiously devoid of residents, because the international owners were mostly out of town. Clocks in lobbies displayed the times in Moscow, Hong Kong and Abu Dhabi. 'You have people with five, ten apartments all around the world,' a staffer at one new luxury tower remarked. 'They come and go.'

London was an attractive second home for 'potentates, monarchs, chiefs, sultans and diplomats,' Trevor Abrahmsohn, a veteran real estate agent with a billionaire clientele, observed. But many of these foreign-owned properties remained unoccupied for much of the year. A former deputy mayor of London, Nicky Gavron, complained that overseas investors 'want to buy a luxury flat in a skyscraper to treat as a safety deposit box'. In fact, there is a statistical correlation between the value of a property and the likelihood that it will be occupied: the higher the price, the greater the chance it is empty. As a consequence, parts of London that had once thronged with local people now often seemed eerily depopulated. The effect was unsettling; in fashionable neighbourhoods after sundown, the windows of the multimillion-dollar dwellings were all dark. The press gave a nickname to these vacant palaces: ghost mansions.

In 2016, one of these luxury buildings was constructed on the north bank of the Thames, directly across from MI6, on a site that had once housed a nineteenth-century prison. It was a residential complex called Riverwalk and consisted of a pair of sleek towers, one tall and one short, connected by a low-slung lobby and fronted by a cascade of curved balconies. Riverwalk had been conceived by a buccaneering property impresario, Sir Gerald Ronson, who was convicted in 1990 on charges of conspiracy, false accounting and theft in connection with a stock fraud case; did a stint in prison; and then, in 2012, was made a Commander of the British Empire for his philanthropic work. 'Imagine the parties you could throw here,' Ronson told an interviewer when construction was complete. From the £25 million penthouse, you could see as far away as Wembley Stadium. The building's wealthy residents were rumoured to include Tom Jones, the Welsh crooner who was famous for songs like 'It's Not Unusual' and 'Help Yourself'. But it was hard to say for sure, because people who purchased units at Riverwalk tended to register them through offshore trusts and shell companies, to preserve their anonymity. And anyway, much of the time the place seemed empty.

In the early hours of 29 November 2019, a surveillance camera on MI6 headquarters registered movement on the fifth floor of the taller tower at Riverwalk, just across the water. The night was cold. The Thames was running high, and the reflected illumination of the lamps lining Vauxhall Bridge danced on the surface of the water. Riverwalk was almost entirely dark, but one apartment blazed with light: unit 504.

At 2:23 a.m., the MI6 camera captured a dark figure walking out of the apartment and onto the narrow balcony overlooking the Thames. It was a slender silhouette against the brightly lit windows: a young man. He made his way to one corner of the balcony and seemed to peer over the ledge, before crossing to the other corner and briefly pausing there. Then, returning to the centre of the balcony, he jumped.

PART I
THE FALL

Chapter 1

THE BIG I AM

AFTER ZAC BRETTLER DIED, his parents tried to decode the mystery of what had happened to him, endlessly revisiting specific moments from his short life. When Zac was born, on a rainy evening in September 2000, his head was crowned with a soft tuft of red hair. This was unexpected: neither his mother, Rachelle, nor his father, Matthew, could remember anyone on either side of their family having ginger colouring. At first it looked like it might not be hair at all but a smudge of dried blood, so they tried to wipe it away. But it was hair all right. From the start, your own children can surprise you.

Matthew had been in his London office that afternoon when he received a call from Rachelle, to say that her contractions had started. The couple had another child, Joe, who was not yet two, so Rachelle's brother, David, came over to watch the baby while she raced off to the hospital, in St John's Wood. Matthew met her there, and as he cradled his tiny newborn in his arms, he was struck by the peculiar expression on the baby's face. There was something wizened about it, something knowing. One of the nurses noticed, too. 'He looks like he's been here before,' she said.

The Brettlers had selected a name in advance: Louis. But the baby had such a distinctive nature that Louis no longer seemed quite right. Instead they chose Zachary – Zac for short. As Matthew would later remark, 'The *zing* of that first letter together with the *click* of the second consonant combined to encapsulate the force of his personality.'

In any family, the birth of a child is grounds for celebration, but one unusual bond that Rachelle and Matthew shared was that both of their fathers had survived the Holocaust. So there was a pronounced feeling, in this particular family, that to create new life and continue the bloodline represented a triumph over long odds, and a way to answer the unspeakable loss of an earlier generation. Rachelle's father, Hugo Gryn, had arrived in the United Kingdom in 1946, at the age of fifteen, having survived Auschwitz and lost nearly all of his family in the camps. In London, Hugo had started a new life, eventually becoming a beloved rabbi and a well-known broadcaster on the BBC. According to family lore, when Rachelle's older sister Gaby gave birth to Hugo's first grandchild, the rabbi was so overcome by enthusiasm that he had to be restrained from entering the delivery room himself. 'Who would have thought, in those dark days in a concentration camp, that he would live to the next day?' Rachelle pointed out. 'Never mind that he would have children, and his *children* would have children.'

Matthew's father, who was born Baruch Brettler, went by Benny. In 1939, he had left Germany on the last of the so-called *Kindertransports* out of that country, arriving in England as a refugee, completely alone at thirteen. During the war, Benny's entire family was murdered. But he, too, managed to forge a new existence for himself. He learned English by going to the cinema, until he could speak it with hardly any trace of an accent, and he made a new life in the northern city of Manchester, entering the textile business and eventually marrying Matthew's mother. Matthew attended an elite private school, Manchester Grammar, and went on to university at the London School of Economics. He studied political science and contemplated a career in journalism or law, before going into finance.

Matthew graduated in 1983, as London was on the brink of a sweeping transformation. In October 1986, Margaret Thatcher deregulated the banking industry in what is known as the City of London, the traditional centre of British finance and commerce, which lies east of St Paul's Cathedral in an area that is sometimes referred to as the Square Mile. Up to that point, London's banking sector had been something of an old boys' club, full of English gentlemen who went to the right schools, commuted from genteel outer suburbs, indulged in boozy lunches at private clubs or local chophouses, then tottered off to catch the 5:15 home. The 'Big Bang', as deregulation became known, cracked open this rarefied bastion, ushering in a horde of American brokers and traders who operated at a more rapacious tempo. Foreign banks swept into London, acquiring some smaller English firms and poaching the best talent from others. Recognizing London's potential as a gateway to both Asia and Europe, this new breed of bankers got to work early and stayed late. The older generation, confronted for the first time possibly ever by something that looked like meritocracy, had no choice but to work longer hours or retire. 'These guys are taking trains they never knew *existed*,' one observer marvelled in 1986. The young bankers worked incessantly, fuelled by coffee, ambition and cocaine. The drug became so pervasive on trading floors that *The Sunday Times* ran a story headlined 'The Big Snort'.

The Big Bang also prompted the greatest wave of new construction London had ever seen. In 1985, a bank chairman, on a visit to the Isle of Dogs, in a desolate stretch of East London that had once been the heart of the shipping industry, had the idea of converting an abandoned banana warehouse into a back office for Credit Suisse. At the time, the notion of expanding London's financial sector beyond the Square Mile and into the poorer East End was unthinkable. But over the next decade and a half, a consortium of banks developed Canary Wharf into a sprawling seventy-acre complex of office towers, trading floors and upscale apartments.

As a young graduate, Matthew held entry-level jobs at a couple of big accounting firms. It felt thrilling to be in London during that period: you could sense the city experiencing this metamorphosis, practically in real time. The standard of living was improving. The price of flats in central London jumped by 30 per cent – then kept climbing. The city seemed finally to be rousing itself from the long hangover of postwar austerity and recession. Even Thatcher acknowledged that pay packages for London's young professionals were enough to 'make one gasp'. And it wasn't just the bankers, because so many other ancillary industries were bolstered by the great tide of money flowing in. Conspicuous consumption was suddenly in vogue. People Matthew knew started acquiring the accoutrements of a certain lifestyle: the ski chalet in France, the high-performance automobile. BMW was the car of choice for London yuppies, to the point where the German carmaker felt the need to artificially restrict inventory, lest the product lose its air of exclusivity. Wine bars started popping up, offering a more sophisticated alternative to London's pubs. For Matthew, who had a very analytical sensibility, it was difficult to pinpoint whether all these changes could be attributed to the influx of money unleashed by the Big Bang or whether deregulation had just accelerated deeper structural mutations that might already have been underway. But what he knew for certain was that during the second half of the 1980s, London underwent a stark evolution in a short period of time. As one BBC report suggested, it was as if the city had vaulted directly from the nineteenth century into the twenty-first.

Matthew did not meet Rachelle until 1997, when they were both in their mid-thirties. He had eventually come to specialize in structured finance. He was not a high-flying, flashy banker, by any means, but he made a comfortable living. Nor was he a corporate drone: he loved live music and theatre, and he tried to make the most of London's abundant cultural offerings. At a gallery opening one evening, he got to talking with a man who thought that Matthew might be a good match for a friend of his – and gave him Rachelle's phone number.

'It was sort of a blind date,' Rachelle recalled. 'He phoned me up, and he had such a lovely voice.' Matthew was calling from a flat that he had bought, in a gentrifying area near Regent's Canal in King's Cross. As they spoke on the phone, Rachelle could hear gulls squealing in the background. They arranged to meet in person, at a wine bar in St John's Wood. Rachelle was petite and stylish, with lively eyes, curly brown hair and a wry sense of humour. Matthew was slim, balding and athletic. He was extremely genial, but he had a quiet intensity about him. 'We just talked and talked,' Rachelle recalled. 'And he said, "I would like to see you again." And I thought, "How wonderful."'

Though their fathers were both Holocaust survivors, Rachelle's upbringing had been different from Matthew's. She had grown up in London, in a cosmopolitan family. Like Matthew's father, Hugo Gryn had married an Englishwoman, Jacqueline Selby, and they had lived in Cincinnati while he was a rabbi in training, then moved to Bombay, before returning to London, where he was eventually appointed senior rabbi of the West London Synagogue. This was a prominent position with a large congregation, and Hugo became a public intellectual, featuring in documentaries about history, ethics and faith. He had a wonderfully sonorous speaking voice ('chocolate stained with nicotine' is how Rachelle's sister Naomi described it), and he was a fixture on BBC Radio, as one of the regular panelists on a weekly programme called *Moral Maze*. Rachelle and her brother and two sisters were artistically inclined and shared a beatnik urbanity. In her teens, Rachelle had been more interested in London's punk scene than in studying, and she never went to university. By the time she met Matthew, she was working as an assistant to the film director Oliver Parker, at a little production company in Soho. Matthew, with his educational pedigree, stable income and grown-up wardrobe, seemed almost exotic. 'People I knew didn't generally wear suits,' she recalled with a laugh. But Matthew had so many of his own enthusiasms – he loved to cycle and to travel, and he loved the Grateful Dead – and he was so open to hers. If she proposed that they go to see some exhibit, Matthew would happily come along, and he wouldn't do it just to humour her, either; he would take a genuine interest.

They married in September 1998, surrounded by friends and family, in the garden of Peacock House, a lovely old mansion in Holland Park. There was one conspicuous absence: Hugo Gryn had died, of brain cancer, at sixty-six, not long before Rachelle and Matthew met. It was difficult for Rachelle to imagine being married by a rabbi who was not her father. But it was a beautiful ceremony, elegant yet informal. She wore a simple dress of cream silk, care of a friend who was a costume designer, with a sheer green shawl around her shoulders. Matthew wore a dark suit and a blue-green tie. The whole thing felt spontaneous, in a way that was pleasing to Rachelle. And in at least one important respect it *was* spontaneous: as her brother, David, walked her down the aisle, Rachelle was already six months pregnant.

Joe was born in early 1999, a sweet, serious-eyed little baby, and not long after Joe turned one, Rachelle was pregnant again. Initially, the family of three had been living in Matthew's bachelor flat in King's Cross. But before Zac was born, they moved to a larger place, a spacious three-bedroom unit that occupied the ground-floor and basement levels of a late-Victorian mansion block on Lauderdale Road, a pretty street lined with London plane trees in the quietly prosperous neighbourhood of Maida Vale.

When Zac started speaking, his first word was not 'Mama' or 'Dada', but 'DoDo', his name for Joe. As the brothers grew, they looked quite similar. Both were slim and pale, with delicate features, full lips and intense eyes. But Joe had brown hair that, when he grew it out, exploded into corkscrew curls, and Zac had that distinctive auburn colouring. If Rachelle and Matthew were in some respects quite different – she more emotional, he more cerebral – their sons likewise developed distinct personalities. Whereas Joe was more subdued and thoughtful by comparison, Zac established himself, from an early age, as a joker. Even as a child he had a surprisingly deep, gravelly voice, and he was extremely quick-witted. Rabbi Hugo had been famous for his sense of humour, and though he died before Zac was born, his grandson seemed to have inherited his talent for entertaining. Zac could deliver note-perfect imitations of family friends that would quickly get everyone laughing. He was also a good mimic of foreign accents.

'He was the funniest little boy,' one cousin, Adam Massey, recalled. The son of Rachelle's sister Gaby, Adam was eleven when Zac was born. 'He had this facility for language, and for *bullshit*,' he said. When Zac was scarcely out of nappies, he memorized the lyrics to the Notorious B.I.G. song 'Going Back to Cali', and anytime he saw Adam and his sister, Zac would launch into a rendition, knowing it would have them in hysterics. He was uninhibited and chatty and seemed to relish the jazzy improv of good conversation. Once, at a family function when Zac was about five, Joe witnessed an interaction in which an older girl handed Zac some piece of reading material and asked pointedly, 'Can you read this, Zac?'

'I didn't bring my glasses,' Zac replied. (He did not wear glasses and could not read.)

Benny Brettler was known within the family for his extraordinary memory, which he passed down to Matthew, and Matthew, in turn, passed it to Zac. This trait manifested itself in curious ways. As a child, Zac would study the Argos catalogue, memorizing the consumer electronics on offer, their brand names and prices, then recite them in fantastic detail to anyone who would listen. He became the person in the family who relatives would consult when they were in the market for a new Kindle or some other device. Long before Zac was old enough to drive, he developed a fascination with cars, and he liked to narrate family jaunts around the city with a recitation of the models and prices of passing vehicles. London was a good city for that: in the right neighbourhood, an afternoon stroll could turn into a supercar safari. Zac was always on the lookout for his favourite sports car – the elusive, curvaceous, eye-wateringly expensive Bugatti Veyron.

Rachelle and Matthew were baffled to hear their ten-year-old advising random family friends about the merits of upgrading to a Mercedes. Neither of them had ever been particularly materialistic. They had little interest in the Argos catalogue, or in high-end vehicles, for that matter. Their family car was a Mazda. But as juvenile passions went, this seemed harmless enough, and they were amused and impressed by their son's encyclopedic tendencies. Zac was quirky, but he was clearly bright, and unpredictable in a way that made him fun to be around.

It was a happy life. Matthew made enough money that the family could live comfortably in a city that was getting more expensive every year. Rachelle became a freelance journalist, writing articles and books mostly about crafts and design. But she did not feel the kind of financial pressure that would oblige her to work full time. The Brettlers travelled, taking family trips to Italy, Portugal, France, Germany, Spain. Along with two partners, Matthew founded a boutique firm devoted to structured finance, which afforded him a pleasant degree of professional autonomy; he preferred to make his own schedule and liked not having a boss. A lot of the firm's clients were in the United States, and eventually the family bought a second apartment in New York City. They would spend a few weeks together there each summer and take long bike rides around Manhattan.

Both Joe and Zac were athletic, and as the boys reached adolescence, they became increasingly competitive with each other. In addition to skiing and biking and Rollerblading, they played cricket, football, squash and tennis. 'A lot of sports Zac followed me into,' Joe recalled. 'And there would be that younger-brother chip on his shoulder, like he's always comparing, always looking up, and not feeling quite good enough.' The family apartment on Lauderdale Road was just around the corner from a tennis centre, the Paddington Sports Club. For years, Joe was the better tennis player. But one summer, when Zac was about twelve, he devoted all his time to getting better at the sport. He played every day at the club and studied YouTube videos to improve his technique. Zac could be quite single-minded when he developed a fixation, and that summer he got so much better at tennis that for the first time he was able to beat his big brother. It was around this time that Joe lost interest in tennis and stopped playing.

Matthew and Rachelle were aware that their boys, so close in age, felt this sense of rivalry, but they were not overly troubled by it. Some degree of sibling competition is hardly unusual. And if Zac could occasionally be testy with his older brother, he was a well-liked fixture in the neighbourhood. Not having a younger sibling himself, Zac became a sort of informal camp counsellor to a gaggle of kids who would gather on summer days in a communal garden nearby. Matthew would see him out there, trailing a congregation of eager little children, and think that Zac looked like a pied piper. He would organize games of cricket and football and deliver little sermons on the importance of eating healthily. When Zac outgrew a pair of football boots, he would give them away to younger children in the neighbourhood. 'He was like a kind big brother,' the mother of two of these kids remembered. 'People loved him, because he had a great sense of fun.' He was also 'at ease talking to adults', she noted, adding, 'He was quite charismatic.'

When Joe was twelve, he was accepted at University College School (UCS), a selective private school in Hampstead that put a strong emphasis on academics. Studying had always come easy to Joe, and he seemed to gain admission without much trouble. When he started at UCS, he was happy, and Rachelle and Matthew took it for granted that when the time came, Zac would join him there. The application process was intense, however; it entailed several tests and a group interview on campus with other children and administrators. Zac struggled with the maths portion of the entrance exam. But given his natural gift for conversation, the Brettlers assumed the interview would go well. Parents were excluded from the group session, though, and when Zac rejoined Rachelle afterwards, he told her that he had fumbled. One of the grown-ups had posed a question about abstract art, and Zac (being eleven) had not been able to muster an edifying answer. His application was rejected.

Zac was distraught, and so were Matthew and Rachelle. With his usual determination – and encouragement from his parents – Zac applied again, taking the tests once more. But again he was turned down. The Brettlers appealed to the school, trying to explain how demoralizing it was for two siblings to be split apart in this manner, and for Zac to be denied an educational opportunity that had been extended to his brother. But the administrators were unsympathetic, explaining that UCS did not have a 'sibling policy', in which favourable treatment might be extended to children from the same family, and that it was paramount that they maintain a 'level playing field'.

Rachelle felt particularly wounded on behalf of her son, to the point that Matthew sometimes worried that his wife's sense of grievance might be making it harder for Zac to simply let it go and move on. Rachelle was aware that some people thought she was being an overanxious mother, but she also feared that the emotional toll on Zac had been colossal. 'I knew there was something so big for that little boy in that rejection,' she said. Education mattered a great deal to the Brettlers, as it did in their wider social milieu, in which families were often quietly judged by other families over where their children went to school. Zac was old enough, and socially perceptive enough, to grasp this, and it must have stung. Eventually he found a place at another private school in London, called Mill Hill, and it was there that he started to change.

When a group of merchants and ministers founded Mill Hill, in 1807, they chose to establish the school a safe distance from central

London because of the 'dangers both physical and moral' that young people might be exposed to in such a 'crowded and corrupt city'. Located on the northern outskirts of London and surrounded by manicured athletic fields, the 150-acre campus is leafy and bucolic and features a mix of creaky old buildings and fancier new structures. By the time Zac Brettler was admitted to study at Mill Hill, it had the same sort of hefty tuition price that UCS and other leading private schools did, but a less academic reputation. Zac was thirteen when he arrived, in the autumn of 2013, and he was obliged to wear a school uniform with a tie and a crested blazer. There were dormitories at Mill Hill, but he started as a day student. On weekday mornings, Rachelle would drive him from Maida Vale, and each afternoon she would bring him home. Because traffic coming in and out of the city was often horrendous, this commute could take more than an hour each way.

Zac was miserable, at least initially. He didn't want to be there. In the high-achieving, bourgeois environment he had grown up in, to say that you attended Mill Hill was, in effect, to acknowledge that you had been rejected by other, better schools. There was a 'pecking order', Rachelle conceded, and everybody knew it: if you didn't get into Westminster or St Paul's or Highgate or UCS, then maybe you ended up at a place like Mill Hill. Zac had a proud streak, and his new school, rather than help him shake off the indignity of the UCS rejection, instead seemed only to remind him of it. The demographic at Mill Hill was also somewhat different from the one Zac was accustomed to. There was more money, and more *new* money, specifically. 'All the girls are *orange*,' Zac said to his mother when he came home from school, remarking on the fondness of some of his female classmates for heavy makeup in shades of butterscotch, even in the dead of winter.

Whatever his misgivings, Zac had always been outgoing. He joined the cricket and tennis teams, and he used his formidable memory to turn casual encounters into friendships. 'Zac came into meeting me already knowing things about me, which I thought was kind of interesting,' Andrei Lejonvarn, who befriended him at Mill Hill that autumn, remembered. One of Zac's cousins had played tennis with Andrei, and Zac must have filed the name away, because when Andrei introduced himself, Zac exclaimed, 'Oh – you play tennis.'

As they got to know each other, Andrei found that Zac possessed a wealth of arcana about various sports teams and players and statistics, which he would draw upon to get a conversation going. 'Zac was entertaining,' he said. 'He was never someone who would just sit quietly.' He carried himself as if he were older and more worldly.

'I remember there was a girl I liked,' another classmate recalled. 'And I was always getting advice from him about that. He framed himself as the master of getting girls, and we were maybe thirteen.'

Zac was not exactly a disciplined student, but between his self-assurance and his ability to retain information and talk off the cuff, he coasted to decent grades. He would sit at the back of the class, laptop open on the desk in front of him, fully absorbed in some story on a sporting news website, only to be asked a question by the teacher and pipe up with a riff that was just plausible enough to keep him out of trouble. More than one Mill Hill classmate suggested that Zac's memory was almost photographic and that this enabled him to get by with minimal effort. 'Like, he would *never* do his homework,' Andrei said, chuckling. After the setback at UCS, he seemed to be fashioning a new identity for himself as a brilliant if unmotivated class clown. But then, Andrei said, 'Zac got obsessed with money.'

London has been a hospitable destination for foreign money for centuries. Voltaire marvelled, in 1733, that people of many different creeds flocked to the city to 'transact together', as if 'they all professed the same religion, and give the name of infidel to none but bankrupts'. In the 1960s, an influx of wealthy Greeks arrived, fleeing political instability in their country. In the 1970s, it was oil-rich Arabs. With the Big Bang in 1986 came the Americans. Around the time of the First Gulf War, in the early 1990s, the Saudi royal family purchased ten properties on The Bishops Avenue in Hampstead, which became known as 'Billionaires' Row'. There were well-heeled Iranians and Nigerians and Japanese, and eventually Chinese, but the dominant arrivals, starting in the mid-1990s, came from the former Soviet Union.

The dissolution of the USSR in 1991 sparked one of the most dramatic wealth transfers in the history of the world, as large swaths of formerly state-owned industry were rapidly privatized, in a quick and messy fashion, under circumstances that were anything but transparent. If you were young, savvy and unscrupulous, it was an amazing time to be a capitalist. Vast fortunes were accumulated practically overnight as a handful of canny operators managed effectively to repossess for themselves a series of lucrative assets that had previously belonged, at least in theory, to the whole Soviet public. 'They steal and steal and steal,' Anatoly Chubais, Russia's privatization czar, who oversaw this process, told a friend in the mid-1990s. 'They are stealing everything and it is impossible to stop them.'

The thieves in this case were a group of men who would become known as the oligarchs, a small, fractious fraternity of free-market bandits who amassed outsized fortunes at the expense of their countrymen. In 1996, one oligarch – a squat, balding, flamboyantly brilliant mathematician and engineer named Boris Berezovsky – boasted that he and six other men controlled 50 per cent of Russia's economy. It was the massive upheaval of a collapsing empire that enabled these men to obtain their wealth. But if political instability can be great when you're trying to make a fortune, it's less attractive when you're trying to hold on to one. So having acquired their riches in the hurly-burly of the former Soviet Union, the oligarchs started looking for safe havens abroad where law and order prevailed and they could securely park their money – and, if necessary, themselves. After the diminutive ex-KGB agent Vladimir Putin was elected president of Russia for the first time, in 2000, he set about trying to bring the oligarchs to heel, reminding them that their fortunes were vulnerable and their power was subordinate to his own. Some, like Berezovsky, resisted, trying to unseat Putin, from exile. Others, like Roman Abramovich, a lanky orphan with a boyish aspect who took over a state oil company in 1995 in a rigged auction, chose to placate Putin, showing deference to him, and in exchange were granted the freedom to enjoy their riches unmolested. Whichever posture one adopted vis-à-vis Moscow,

London offered a highly attractive second home. Berezovsky was granted political asylum in the UK. Abramovich became the owner of an English football team, Chelsea Football Club, purchasing it for £140 million in 2003.

If Chelsea fans welcomed their new Russian overlord, celebrating the dawn of a 'Roman empire' in which Abramovich would spend lavishly on the team, their unguarded embrace of this mysterious arriviste with his dodgy riches and aspirations to legitimacy was typical of London's obsequious hospitality when it came to the oligarchs. This wasn't a case of the English political and financial establishment holding its nose and tolerating a few vaguely unsavoury interlopers. Quite the opposite: there was a recognition at the highest levels of government and society that if the oligarchs were looking for a commodious sanctuary, this could be a lucrative opportunity for London. In 2008, the UK introduced a new visa programme in which foreign nationals who were willing to invest millions of pounds in the local economy could effectively buy status as permanent legal residents. In the first seven years of the programme, roughly three thousand people took advantage of it – a quarter of them from Russia – injecting more than £3 billion into the British economy. 'London is to the billionaire as the jungles of Sumatra are to the orangutan,' Boris Johnson, who at the time was the city's mayor, boasted in 2014. 'We're proud of that.'

Zac Brettler was born the year Putin won his first term, and by the time Zac arrived at Mill Hill, this influx of oligarchs and their money had noticeably transfigured the city in which he lived. Wealthy foreigners with a foothold in London were drawn by the real estate, the financial markets and the shopping – but also by the schools. In 1994, Russians made up only 3 per cent of the foreign students in British private schools; within five years that number had jumped to 20 per cent. 'I want my children to go to school in England,' Roman Abramovich remarked in 2003. 'I'm satisfied they will get the best education in the world.' Private schools started actively recruiting the children of oligarchs. In 1994, an administrator who oversaw some of this recruitment told *The Guardian*, in a moment of impolitic candour, 'We don't screen the mafia out because you can't. You don't know where the money is coming from.'

Mill Hill School offered a particularly attractive option to the children of foreign plutocrats. It might not be Eton or Harrow, but it had the same fusty air of aristocratic tradition, it was close to central London and it was a lot easier to get into. In the 1990s, a sharp-featured Russian boy named Evgeny Lebedev enrolled at Mill Hill. He was the son of an oligarch – his father, Alexander Lebedev, was an ex-KGB colonel who bought a bank in 1995 and went on to make billions – and in that respect, Evgeny was a pioneer. In a *Town & Country* article, one of his former teachers described him as 'a quiet, almost anonymous boy'. But his classmates would remember him differently. 'As best I recall, Lebedev was the first Russian oligarch's child at Mill Hill,' one member of his graduating class said. 'He never, and I do mean never, wore the school uniform, which everyone else had to wear,' preferring his own elegant suits and ties, as if he were attending a board meeting rather than third-period geography. 'None of the teachers ever said anything,' the classmate added. 'Which I found odd.' Evgeny would eventually grow up to become Lord Lebedev, friend of Boris Johnson, owner of the *Independent* and the *Evening Standard*, and member of the House of Lords, a veritable advertisement for the kind of enthusiastic acceptance that money can buy from the British establishment. (His full title is Baron Lebedev of Hampton in the London Borough of Richmond upon Thames and of Siberia in the Russian Federation.)

By the time Zac Brettler arrived at Mill Hill, he was surrounded by the next generation of aspiring Lebedevs. 'It was the children of oligarchs,' Andrei Lejonvarn said of the international students. Of course, there were a lot of English students and foreign students whose families did not come from the former Soviet Union, and there were students who might be Russian or Georgian or Kazakh but whose families were merely very wealthy and not billionaires. But there did seem, to Zac and to Andrei, to be an overrepresentation of a certain kind of entitled, ex-Soviet scion. 'These guys had serious money, and they walked around the school like, "I don't give a shit, I will do exactly what I want",' Andrei recalled. Like Lebedev, they dressed in conspicuously expensive designer clothes. On weekends they partied in London's nightclubs and swanky hotels.

On cold winter mornings, some of the boarding students, rather than make the eight-minute walk from the dormitory to class, would summon Ubers.

Zac was intrigued by these kids – not just by their riches but by their swagger. To his parents, it seemed that part of his attraction must have stemmed from how different that whole lifestyle was from their own. Rachelle and Matthew had come of age in an England in which showing off one's wealth was regarded as deeply unclassy. Moreover, there had been fewer *opportunities* to flaunt wealth even if you wanted to, because the ubiquity of luxury consumer goods in England was really a post-Big Bang phenomenon. 'This world of Porsches and cosmetic surgery and Ibiza, it's everything we're not,' Rachelle said. 'Matthew is stable, but he's not flash. He's a very decent fellow, living a decent life.' That had always been what they wanted for themselves – stability, modesty, decency – and had tried to impart to their children.

But Zac was coming of age not just in a city that was drunk on foreign lucre but in an era of social media. Instagram had been founded just a few years before he entered Mill Hill, and the culture at large was becoming transfixed by a new mode of gaudy ostentation. Another close friend Zac made at Mill Hill was a sweet-natured kid with a croaky voice named Dimitris. When they first encountered each other, Zac reminded Dimitris that they had actually met once before, at a football match – when they were seven. 'He said, "I remember you",' Dimitris recalled. 'And I was like, "Wow, six years ago..."' Zac and Dimitris liked to watch movies together and had a particular fondness for true stories about young men on the make. They loved *The Wolf of Wall Street*, the 2013 Martin Scorsese film that chronicles the rise and fall of a stock fraudster named Jordan Belfort, who made tens of millions of dollars through his firm, Stratton Oakmont, before ending up in federal prison. Another favourite was *War Dogs*, a 2016 movie about a couple of buddies in Florida who, when they were barely out of their teens, went into business as international arms dealers, before one of them wound up in federal prison. Zac and Dimitris watched *War Dogs* over and over, and Dimitris thought that

Zac bore some resemblance to Efraim Diveroli, the antihero, who is played in the movie by Jonah Hill. A fast-talking, morally vacuous hustler, Diveroli tempts fate by taking on ever-larger scams, seeing just how far he can get on his own charisma. 'Efraim's genius,' the narrator of the movie observes, is that he could 'figure out who someone wanted him to be, and he would become that person.'

Dimitris got a kick out of *War Dogs*, but he sometimes felt Zac might be deriving something more from it. 'He wanted to *be* like Efraim,' he said. Zac seemed gripped by a kind of aspirational fantasy – and a lifestyle of splashy, macho flamboyance. Such predilections were only inflamed by the presence at Mill Hill of all these real-life rich kids whose families had, in some cases, amassed their fortunes quite quickly, via uncertain means. 'You know, they say, "Oh, we're *property developers*..."' Dimitris chuckled. 'But behind the scenes, we don't know *what* they do. So, to Zac, that was like, "This is where the money is."'

At one point, Zac told Dimitris that he admired his own father – that Matthew had done well for his family – but that Zac wanted more. 'It's not enough. I want to be bigger,' he said. He seemed hungry and restless. '*We* should start a business,' he proposed. But Dimitris wasn't interested. 'I was only sixteen, you know?' he said. 'I just wanted to hang out with my friends.'

When Zac turned fifteen, he started boarding at Mill Hill. The daily commute from Maida Vale had become onerous for both Zac and Rachelle, so they decided that he would stay at school during the week and return home on weekends. Andrei Lejonvarn was already a boarder, and as it happened, they would share the same dorm, a drafty brick house on the edge of campus called Burton Bank. Zac was excited by the prospect of independent living. 'He was a happy-go-lucky kid who could get along with a lot of people,' Andrei said. Half of the boys in the dorm were foreign, and the other half were English. 'We formed our own little gang,' Andrei recalled. The 'BB Boys', people called them, after Burton Bank. They played sports and hung out, and a camaraderie was forged in cold showers and strict curfews. Within this little fraternity, Zac established himself as something of a prude: he didn't drink alcohol, and he was particular about what he ate. He wouldn't smoke cigarettes, much less cannabis. He also continued to fixate, more so than the other BB Boys, on the lifestyles of his wealthy classmates.

Matthew and Rachelle were conscious of this change in Zac, and it made them uncomfortable. Rachelle felt like she had a bit of insight into her son's experience, because during her own childhood she had attended a fancy private school called Queen's College, on Harley Street in Marylebone. Her older sisters were students there as well, but unlike their classmates, the Gryn girls did not pay the expensive tuition. As a rabbi, Hugo Gryn made a modest salary, but the West London Synagogue covered the school fees of his kids, as well as the cost of the family's spacious apartment, which was also in Marylebone. So Rachelle could relate to that peculiar sensation in which, as she put it, 'you look like others, but you're not actually of the same class'. The unspoken taxonomy of social class is one of the defining features of British life, and the Gryns were not exactly middle class or upper middle class. They were this weird anomaly: clergy class.

Though he spoke with no trace of a Manchester accent, Matthew identified, in some fundamental ways, with the proud industrial city of his youth. In Manchester, there had always been a fierce sense of proletarian solidarity, a workman's view that anyone who might presume to put on airs is faintly ridiculous and deserving of mockery. This ethos was exemplified by the Manchester artist L. S. Lowry, who was famous for his paintings of industrial scenes and was forever being offered titles and honours (Commander of the British Empire, Officer of the British Empire), only to turn them all down. When he was approached about a knighthood, he explained – to the prime minister – that he was 'against social distinction of any kind'.

Like Lowry, Matthew had little time for 'the big "I am"'. It wasn't just that such grandiloquence was distasteful; it felt like tempting fate. As the son of a refugee, Matthew had been taught to be sceptical of borrowing money to buy things one can't afford. Even purchasing his own apartments, he preferred to put down as much cash as possible, rather than leverage himself too much. It's not as though the Brettlers were socialists: Matthew worked in finance, and Rachelle regularly wrote for a *Financial Times* publication called *How to Spend It*, a glossy magazine spotlighting luxury goods and leisure activities, which another *FT* journalist once characterized as 'the Argos catalogue for rich people'. The couple were spending roughly £50,000 a year just on secondary education for their children. But they made a point of living within their means and had little interest in the status markers of consumption, even when they could afford them.

So Matthew and Rachelle were perplexed when Zac began to suggest that they should get a nicer car or buy a bigger home. They lived in a two-thousand-square-foot apartment in an attractive neighbourhood in central London. By any reasonable standard, they were extremely well off. How much more could he *want*? But something seemed to have taken hold of Zac, and it only intensified when he started boarding at Mill Hill. One day not long after he moved into Burton Bank, the Brettlers received a phone call from an administrator who informed them that Zac had just left the campus in a chauffeured limousine. Questioned by his parents when he got home, he confessed that he had paid for this extravagance himself.

'I wanted to see what it would feel like,' he said.

To make money, he had started to devise his own little entrepreneurial schemes, reselling trainers and other clothing to fellow students and on the internet. Zac may have disdained cigarettes himself, but he started dealing them on campus, enlisting an older friend to purchase packs for him, then selling loosies to underage students. Like the ambitious, amoral antiheroes of his favourite movies, Zac seemed ready to try any scheme that might turn a profit. There was a storage room in the boarding house full of discarded items left behind by previous students. 'We ended up just selling a lot of that crap,' Dimitris recalled. Zac was 'really into that', he said. 'He was into the whole money aspect of life in general.'

At seventeen, Zac was undergoing what Matthew would later characterize as a 'profound change'. Over time, he had become increasingly surly with his family. He still had occasional moments when he could be sweetly childlike and affectionate, particularly with Rachelle. But much of the time, it seemed as if he had transformed into a person his parents and his brother scarcely recognized, as if some powerful spell had come over him. He even *carried* himself differently. He wore a sharp suit to school and would eventually take to storing his classwork in a briefcase. In a photo Rachelle took to mark his seventeenth birthday, he sticks his chest out, thrusts his shoulders back, juts his chin provocatively and glowers at the camera. Zac the goofy smart aleck had been eclipsed by this ambitious, self-serious young man.

As his relationship with his family grew strained, Zac's friendships at school were beginning to feel more transient. 'He would be friends for a certain moment, and then disappear,' Dimitris said. Engaged and present one day, he could seem like a stranger the next. Zac had a few fleeting encounters with girls during his time at Mill Hill, but there were no sustained romantic relationships. Increasingly, he appeared to want to move past the whole charade of secondary school altogether, become a grown-up and launch a business.

To his brother, Joe, all of this was confounding – and annoying. Joe could certainly appreciate that sometimes siblings, especially competitive siblings, can feel as though it might be best if each selects a different lane in life. Perhaps Zac, perceiving his older brother to have laid claim to the traditional path of academic achievement, was trying to distinguish himself by finding some alternative avenue in which to realize his ambitions. But was *this* what he wanted to become? Some kind of preening gangster capitalist? Joe hoped it was a phase: the temporary renunciation of family that many kids go through in adolescence. But he did worry. He would imagine family lunches, years in the future, 'where Zac rocks up in a flash way with some, you know, fake-boobed model or whatever. And just the dynamic, I could foresee it being difficult, moving forwards, because I'm not that way at all,' he said. 'Those aren't my aspirations.'

Adam Massey, the older cousin who had known Zac since his birth and been so entertained by him as a child, lived in New York, but he would see the Brettlers once or twice a year. On one occasion in 2017, he encountered Zac at a family birthday party in London and was taken aback by the extreme shift in his cousin's personality. Zac wore a suit, which felt at odds with the informality of the occasion, and he started talking about how much he admired the unfathomably rich, unfathomably corrupt, casually homicidal kleptocrat who ruled Russia, Vladimir Putin. At first Adam laughed, figuring that Zac was doing what he had always done – a gag to keep everyone entertained. But then Zac didn't break character. 'He's earnestly talking about how wonderful Putin is, in this fanboy, internet edgelord way,' Adam recalled. Democracy was overrated, Zac proclaimed. All that really mattered in the world was money and power. Adam was deeply unsettled. He wanted to cast out this hard-eyed stooge and bring back the irreverent kid he knew and loved.

Chapter 2

A FAST LIFE

RACHELLE HAD BEEN A bit of a wild child herself. The household she grew up in was warm, boisterous – and permissive. Hugo, the polymathic rabbi, was busy with the synagogue and his many other commitments. Jacqueline, Rachelle's mother, was an exceptional rebbetzin, or rabbi's wife. There were lunches and dinners in the Marylebone apartment, often with twenty or more people crowded around the table and fascinating, notable figures drifting in and out. The adults seemed mostly to be focused on their stimulating adult life, and while the Gryn children were always welcome at the table, they were otherwise treated with a form of benign neglect that was hardly unusual for a London family in the 1960s and '70s. The kids were left to figure life out for themselves. Whereas Matthew had been raised to place enormous value on the sort of formal education that his own refugee father had been denied, Rachelle and her siblings enjoyed a more free-range upbringing. 'There was no "Have you done your homework?"' Rachelle observed. 'I could do whatever I wanted, because my parents weren't paying attention to me.'

By the time she was sixteen, she had started skipping school to spend time at a pub on the King's Road, the Roebuck, where the Sex Pistols and other formative punk acts hung out. It was the era of The Clash. 'Every American girl who came into the pub said she was a member of The Runaways, which obviously wasn't true, because they couldn't *all* be members of The Runaways,' she said dryly. This was not a scene in which it was considered particularly hip to profess any sort of professional aspiration, which was convenient, because Rachelle didn't have one. They were 'wild years', she says now, and when it came time to apply for university, she lacked the necessary drive to believe she could succeed as an undergraduate.

One of the many remarkable aspects of Hugo Gryn's biography was that after surviving the war and arriving in the UK as a refugee in 1946, he had ended up at Cambridge University, where he received a special two-year scholarship to study mathematics and biochemistry. He had become proficient in maths, he would later explain, after befriending a Catholic priest who gave him lessons in the death camps. Academic life at Cambridge is organized around residential colleges, and when Rachelle and her siblings were growing up, their father still had the purple-and-white scarf of King's, one of the oldest and most prestigious Cambridge colleges, which had produced such illustrious graduates as Alan Turing and John Maynard Keynes. When Rachelle's big sister Naomi, who was more academically inclined, was applying to university, Hugo visited Cambridge with her and pointed out his old rooms at the college.

Naomi, like Matthew, ended up attending the London School of Economics. But at this crucial juncture in Rachelle's life, when she felt insecure about her academic prospects and unsure of how to chart a path from her teen years into her twenties, her parents did not intervene to offer guidance or support. This was the downside of laissez-faire parenting. Rachelle had an interest – still tentative, but real – in design and the arts. What she needed was somebody to step in and help her find a sense of direction. But nobody did. 'I now would be a great mother to that girl, aged seventeen, named Rachelle,' she reflected wistfully. 'I would have said, "Why don't you go and learn design? Or learn to be a shoemaker. Or do *something*." But instead my parents said, "Go and learn to type." Because that's what they knew.' So she enrolled in clerical school, learned shorthand and became a typist.

Three decades later, when Rachelle had established herself, after years of odd jobs, as a freelance writer and had children of her own, the norms of parenting had changed. In affluent Maida Vale, benign neglect could practically get you arrested. For the Brettlers and many of their peers, just *being* a parent could feel like an all-consuming full-time job: you were cook, cleaner, tutor, cheerleader, chauffeur, friend and shrink. Both Matthew and Rachelle adored their own parents and wanted to emulate aspects of their respective upbringings, yet they were also well attuned to the shortcomings of the parenting models that generation provided. So they strove to be more perfect caregivers, like the latest version of some technology that promises to fix all the bugs of the last one.

Before Zac began to change, it all seemed to be working. Joe had always been an easy child, loving and considerate, gifted academically and athletically. For the most part, Zac had been, too, until his mid-teens. But now the Brettlers were faced with a dilemma: how interventionist should they be? Perhaps this *was* just a phase, a bit of adolescent rebellion. Neither Joe nor Zac had ever gone through a rebellious period before. Maybe this was just what it looked like. It might even be healthy; after all, it is a necessary function of maturity for a child to create some distance between himself and his parents. If Zac was professing to admire wealthy thugs and autocrats, that could just be a particularly cheeky way of differentiating himself from a family that found such figures abhorrent. 'How do you reject liberal parents?' Rachelle wondered out loud. 'He'd do anything to get a rise from us, perhaps.' When Zac started suggesting that he wished his father were Roman Abramovich, the oligarch owner of Chelsea Football Club, it was hurtful and confusing. But what teenager hasn't lashed out at a parent with words intended to draw blood?

There were also plenty of moments when Zac showed signs of being his same old self. Brusque and unpleasant as he might be with the family, he was still a nurturing presence for the kids in the neighbourhood. Rachelle wondered if perhaps this was because they looked up to him and regarded him as the kind of figure he wanted to be: the big man. Zac got certified as a tennis coach, which he was very proud of. And on Thursday evenings he would sometimes join Matthew's football club, which was composed mostly of local dads and known as the Paddington Wrecks. He would play for an hour, then chat amiably with Matthew as they strolled home.

But a number of events conspired to intensify Zac's sense of estrangement. Having appeared finally to have made peace with Mill Hill, he announced that he wanted to transfer for his last two years of school. Rather than aim for some other institution where he might stand a better chance of being admitted, Zac wanted to apply to Harrow – one of the most selective secondary schools in the UK. Harrow was more difficult to get into than UCS, which had twice rejected him. Once again, the Brettlers found themselves in a tricky position. When Zac was determined to do something, it could be difficult to dissuade him, and in parenting him they had opted for a default setting of gentle encouragement. But parents can be so invested in their children that it is difficult to see them in a clear light, and Rachelle and Matthew came to share Zac's conviction that he might be a plausible candidate for Harrow. His academic performance had improved over his time at Mill Hill, and he was such an accomplished athlete. Their love for Zac may have left them unable to recognize the degree to which this impulse to apply to Harrow was likely to end up being self-destructive.

Zac was rejected before he could even make it to the final round of applications. Harrow 'did not think that he was quite good enough', an administrator wrote to Rachelle, adding that the competition was fierce and 'coming from all over the world'.

Zac was despondent and angry, and his general hostility only intensified when Joe graduated from UCS and departed for a gap year in South America. The relationship between the brothers had been tense lately, yet Joe's departure seemed to leave Zac feeling dislocated, and he increasingly took his anger out on his mother and father. He would stomp around the apartment, slamming doors and raising his voice. 'I felt sorry for Rachelle as a mother,' a longtime friend of hers said. 'Her little boy was pulling away quite quickly.' The Brettlers were fairly private, even with their friends, and they did not share much about their troubles with Zac, in part because they hoped that whatever he was going through would soon pass. 'It looked from a distance as if Matthew and Rachelle might be having a very tricky time navigating the maze of finding a way to communicate with him without pushing him away,' the friend continued. 'It's impossible to be a parent,' she added. 'It's an impossible job.'

One night, when Zac and Rachelle were alone at home, the antagonism reached a new level. They had been bickering: a familiar argument over whether the family should buy a nicer car or a bigger home. Rachelle made a sharp remark, to the effect that Zac sounded like a 'spoiled brat', and suddenly his hands were around her throat.

'I'm five foot four and he's nearly six foot, and I don't feel good and I don't feel safe,' she recalled. The moment was over before it started, and Rachelle would later insist that Zac had throttled her 'more in rage than in earnest'. He was lashing out impulsively, she felt, and had not actually wanted to choke her. Even so, she was deeply rattled. She had grown fearful of her own child, and after that altercation she insisted that Zac see a psychiatrist.

One day in January 2018, Zac visited Roger Howells, a kindly doctor in private practice with an office near Sloane Square. When Howells entered the waiting room, he found Zac dressed in athletic clothes, giving off the air of someone who had more important places to be. As the session commenced, Zac maintained 'a somewhat defiant manner', the doctor wrote in his notes. But gradually his natural chattiness took over. When Howells wondered if he was bullied at school, Zac scoffed at the notion and boasted that nobody would 'mess' with him. Asked about his family, Zac complained that his parents were 'narrow-minded and restrictive'. But he also conceded that they could be capable and funny.

In the weeks leading up to the appointment, Rachelle had been frantically doing online research, wondering whether her son might be suffering from some serious affliction. Could he be bipolar? Did he have borderline personality disorder? Or *narcissistic* personality disorder? Or intermittent explosive disorder? To search for answers in the bottomless abyss of the internet could feel like its own sort of insanity. But she was desperate. She explained to Howells that Zac had 'always been a loved and loving son until approx. six months ago', when there had been 'a stark behavioural change with sporadic rage, contempt and extreme disdain'. He had been 'influenced by a Russian set at school', Rachelle said. She did not know if this was just 'a 17-year-old pushing hard for independence' or something more complicated and exotic. 'I really am at my wit's end and need help,' Rachelle pleaded. 'He is very attracted towards power and danger and consequently quite vulnerable.'

In the doctor's office, Zac sat slumped in his chair, too cool for the whole routine. Yet he was candid with Howells about his ambitions. 'He explained that he is focused on being very wealthy,' the doctor wrote, noting that Zac 'enjoys crime documentaries' and 'has a passion for exceptional cars'. Howells was tentative in his diagnosis, concluding that Zac showed no signs of depression, mood elevation, cognitive impairment or psychotic thought disorder. He did show traits of a 'strong asocial narcissistic flavour', however, and 'a potentially dangerous lack of insight and skewed norms of behaviour'.

Howells recommended that Zac go through a course of therapy with the National Health Service, and that Matthew and Rachelle join him for family counselling. But Zac consented only to attend one session of his own therapy, explaining, according to a report from the physician who saw him, that he did not trust the NHS, because they were compelled to 'report to the government'. As for the family therapy, this was an area in which, as it turned out, Zac was not the only sceptic. Rachelle had been seeing a therapist for many years and found the treatment to have been extremely helpful in her own life. But rational, systematic Matthew had always been a bit dismissive of the idea of therapy and dubious about its value – at least where he was concerned. He attended one session of family therapy, and thereafter both he and Zac refused to go. Instead, Rachelle attended each of the six remaining sessions on her own.

One reason that Zac and Matthew were disinclined to give therapy a go may have been that, after the session with Dr Howells, things appeared to be improving on their own. It was as if that terrible moment of violence in the kitchen had 'lanced something', Rachelle thought, as if some sort of fever had broken. Zac seemed to calm down somewhat, and he did end up transferring schools in 2018, enrolling for his final year and a half at Ashbourne College, a private secondary school in the wealthy neighbourhood of Kensington. This transition seemed to agree with him. Even though he was living at home full-time again, he had autonomy in the city, the freedom to move around London like an adult.

Matthew and Rachelle were determined to present their son with options, to help him navigate some path to a happy and productive life. If he was intent on being different from them, then so be it: they could accept that he had different goals and aspirations. They could even, on some level, accept his rejection of them. They just wanted, desperately, to help him. Zac spoke to Matthew about perhaps becoming a sports agent, which seemed like it could be a good match for his skills and interests. During the summer of 2018, he found an internship working for a man named Adam Bawany, who was an associate of a cousin of his old friend Dimitris. Bawany ran a chauffeur service, and Zac loved learning about how the business worked. His new boss found him impressive. 'Zac is a phenomenal guy,' Bawany told Dimitris. 'He's got amazing ideas.' In fact, Bawany even suggested that he and Zac start their own company together, which they did, calling it Omega Stratton and incorporating it that September, the week Zac turned eighteen and became a legal adult.

Bawany later told Dimitris that Omega Stratton 'never really did anything', but it certainly looked official on paper, and Zac set up a company email address. One night, as a gesture of thanks for helping him land the internship, Zac took Dimitris out to dinner at a branch of the hibachi chain Benihana. This was an inside joke: Benihana makes a cameo in *The Wolf of Wall Street*. In fact, the name of Zac's new company owed a debt to the movie as well. While 'Omega' was presumably a reference to the high-performance Swiss watch favoured by James Bond, 'Stratton' was almost certainly a salute to Stratton Oakmont, the crooked brokerage house featured in Scorsese's film. It was an ironic choice, to put it mildly: in the movie, Leonardo DiCaprio invents the name Stratton Oakmont because it sounds just blue-blooded and starchy enough to lure unsuspecting investors. It's an illegitimate business using a fake name to sound legitimate. Now Zac, at age eighteen, was starting a real business, which presumably would be legitimate, but naming it after another business which famously was not.

Dimitris had been seeing less of his old friend since Zac left Mill Hill, but they both had fun that night. Zac dressed up and insisted on paying for dinner. He arranged for a chauffeur to drive them, because he did not yet have his licence.

In the family apartment on Lauderdale Road, things had grown more peaceful, which was a great relief. But Zac also seemed more remote and secretive. He did not appear to be spending much time on his studies and came and went at all hours. Matthew and Rachelle began to worry that he might be doing drugs – or selling them. In a fit of suspicion, Rachelle arranged for Zac's paediatrician to draw blood at a routine appointment and surreptitiously test it for drugs. But it came back clean. When the parents took a holiday for several days in Oman and Zac stayed home alone, Matthew installed a hidden video camera to secretly monitor the flat. But when he checked the feed afterwards, it just showed Zac hanging with friends from the tennis club, watching TV.

Rachelle also began to suspect that Zac might be carrying on a clandestine romantic relationship with an older woman who lived across the street. Her name was Zamira, and she was a single mother in her thirties, Russian, quite voluptuous, Rachelle thought, and beautiful. She also drove a Bentley, the only one on the street, which was the sort of detail that would surely appeal to Zac. He started to disappear from time to time in the evenings, saying, 'I'm going over the road', and when he came home he would tell Rachelle that he'd been visiting Zamira. But occasionally Rachelle would be out in the neighbourhood, running an errand, and she would pass her son's new friend on the street, only to have Zamira continue by without acknowledging her. Rachelle did not know what to make of this, or what to make of the notion that a woman close to twice her son's age was hanging out with him in the first place. Perhaps Zac was fibbing about how old he was? He'd always been good at talking to adults.

In early 2019, Zac made another new friend, with whom he started to spend a great deal of time: Akbar Shamji. Akbar was a wealthy businessman, Zac told his parents. He was in his forties and resided in one of London's poshest districts, Mayfair. A graduate of Cambridge University, he lived with his wife and two children in a £10 million apartment on Mount Street, a short thoroughfare off Park Lane that is lined with pricey boutiques. Apparently, Akbar had extensive business connections in India. The website for a company he ran, a renewable energy concern called CPEC, featured a photo of him receiving an award from Narendra Modi, India's prime minister. Akbar's son, Akbar Jr, attended St Paul's School, one of the most elite private schools in London, and his daughter, Safiya, was a student at Ashbourne College, where Zac went. They were beautiful, glamorous kids. Akbar's wife, Daniela Karnuts, who was originally from Germany, was a fashion designer with her own London atelier. She made tasteful eveningwear for famous women such as Gwyneth Paltrow, Michelle Obama and Meghan Markle. The company was named Safiyaa, after her daughter. On his iPad, Zac showed the Safiyaa collection to Rachelle, saying, 'You should get one of her dresses.' Rachelle replied politely that she liked the look of the clothing but felt that it might not be her style.

Zac was spending so much time in Akbar's neighbourhood that he could sometimes sound as though he lived there himself, applying his old encyclopedic tendencies to a whole new dataset. Once, when Matthew and Rachelle had plans to see a movie at the Curzon cinema in Mayfair, Zac launched into a spontaneous rundown of all the dining options nearby.

Akbar and Daniela maintained an office just a short walk from the Mount Street apartment on Berkeley Square, which, even by the fashionable standards of Mayfair, was an address with unimpeachable pedigree. In 1673, Lord Berkeley of Stratton, who had fought in the first English civil war and helped found a British colony that would later become the state of New Jersey, built a mansion north of Piccadilly. After his death, his widow, Lady Berkeley, who was the daughter of an early chairman of the East India Company, envisioned an Italian-style piazza that would extend beyond the grounds of her home. In the eighteenth century, this became an elegant quadrangle, surrounded by grand buildings, known as Berkeley Square. 'Many a successful British business man in days past has gratified a lifelong ambition by living in Berkeley Square,' one press account noted in 1919. The square became home to viscounts, duchesses and families who made their fortunes in the colonies. Winston Churchill spent the first years of his life at No. 48. Lord Clive, the so-called Conqueror of India, who presided over the violent looting of Bengal, killed himself at No. 45, haunted, or so Samuel Johnson contended, because his fortune derived from monstrous crimes. No. 18 housed a Bentley dealership.

The handsome Georgian townhouse at No. 46 was home to a legendary private nightclub named Annabel's, which had recently relocated from two doors down at No. 44. In the early 1960s, a vivacious gambler named John Aspinall had established an exclusive private casino at No. 44, calling it the Clermont Club. Aspinall was an eccentric: he had spent his early years in India and flunked out of Oxford, and his two great passions were gambling and wild animals. He developed a grand ambition to 'close the gulf between the species', and though he boasted about not possessing a degree in any zoological discipline, he liked the idea of English gentlemen breeding wild animals on their estates. So he opened a private zoo at his mansion outside Canterbury, where he encouraged friends and employees to mingle freely with the tigers and bears. He published a coffee table book called *The Best of Friends*, which featured photos of warm interactions between humans and wild animals, and he once said of his own children, 'I'd rather leave them with gorillas than with a social worker.' Five of his assistants were killed over the years, trampled by elephants or mauled by tigers. A young boy had his arm ripped off by a chimpanzee.

The basement of the Clermont Club had its own entrance and featured a coal cellar comprising a warren of interconnected rooms. Aspinall wanted to install a high-class nightclub there, with live music, so he approached a man named Mark Birley. Six foot five and impeccably tailored, Birley was an old Etonian known for his superior taste who had opened the first Hermès boutique outside of France, on Jermyn Street. Birley had come of age during the austerity of the postwar years and resented every minute of it. With Annabel's he would create a temple of decadence, with stiff drinks, a sunken dance floor and beautiful lighting. The club should 'smell of exclusivity and sex', he said. A parade of celebrities partied at Annabel's over the decades: Frank Sinatra, Princess Diana, Naomi Campbell, Tom Cruise. Ella Fitzgerald played Annabel's. Tina Turner, too. Lady Gaga once commenced an acoustic set at the club by murmuring, 'Hello, rich people.'

Annabel's was named after Birley's wife, Lady Annabel, though the nightclub ended up outlasting the marriage. One day in 1970, on a visit to John Aspinall's private zoo, their twelve-year-old son, Robin, entered the enclosure of a pregnant tiger, and the animal lunged at him, placing his whole head in her mouth. He survived but was permanently disfigured by the ordeal and would grow up to manage Annabel's himself. For many years the club retained its reputation as a den for dissolute aristocrats. But by the 1990s, Annabel's was no longer cool. Young people steered clear, it was said, because it was the kind of place where you might bump into your father with his mistress.

Fortuitously, however, there was a new demographic that was eager to gain entry to the club: wealthy foreigners. For a certain kind of person, the English upper classes still retained the allure of a silver spoon fairy tale – pinched accents, double-barrelled names, fancy educations, country homes, Barbour jackets, Savile Row suits, horseback riding, Range Rovers, gin and tonics, and a jaded atmosphere of withering politeness. For a long time, Annabel's catered to actual British aristocrats, but by the 1990s, it was already becoming something different. For new arrivals to London who had money and wanted class, a membership at Annabel's offered a chance to buy in. For Londoners who had class but needed money, this presented an opportunity. People started to joke that Annabel's was where 'the middle-aged meet the Middle East'. The club actively catered to the international set, organizing themed 'Russia' weeks. In earlier eras, English aristocrats would occasionally throw Orientalist costume parties at which they dressed up as sultans, maharajas and other grand foreign types. Now, at Annabel's, rich foreigners could dress up as English aristocrats.

It was to this incarnation of Annabel's that Zac Brettler's new friend Akbar Shamji took him one evening. Matthew and Rachelle had never been to the club, but they knew about it. Everybody did. It seemed wild to picture their eighteen-year-old son in such a milieu. But Zac was rolling with Akbar now, and Akbar was the sort of jet-setting businessman who hung out at places like Annabel's. It was only natural; he lived just up the road.

Akbar had a big, beautiful dog, a black Weimaraner he was very devoted to, named Alpha Nero. The whole family was active on Instagram, and Alpha Nero had his own dedicated account, featuring photos of the dog posing with fashion models and rearing up on his hind legs to greet an ice cream van. Sometimes Zac would join Akbar when he walked the dog around Mayfair. Eventually he volunteered to walk Alpha Nero himself. His parents felt okay about this, all things considered. It was somewhat weird that their son was hanging out with a man who was so much older, but Akbar seemed like a benign influence – next to Vladimir Putin, anyway – a successful entrepreneur with a stable family. With any luck, he might end up becoming a mentor.

On one occasion, Rachelle joined Zac for one of his walks. First he went up to retrieve the dog from the office at No. 52 Berkeley Square, in a handsome black-brick building fronted by a wrought iron railing. When Zac emerged with Alpha Nero on a leash, he and his mother set off for Green Park. Zac seemed pleased to be 'in Akbar's orbit', Rachelle thought. Akbar was a man of the world, clearly very rich, and a bit showy – but in a way that would appeal to Zac. It was painful for her to think that her son might require some surrogate family. But if that was what he desired – if his own family, for whatever reason, was not enough for him – she still wanted him to be happy. As they walked that day, Rachelle noticed that Zac seemed to carry himself with a sense of pride, strolling around Mayfair with this big, elegant, obviously expensive dog, as if it were his own.

When Zac and Akbar took their walks with Alpha Nero, they sometimes arranged to meet in front of One Hyde Park, an outsized residential complex of four blocky glass towers in Knightsbridge. One Hyde Park offered a superluxury housing option that even by the standards of postmillennial London seemed extravagant. Trumpeted by its own developers as 'the most expensive residential development ever built anywhere on earth', it featured eighty sprawling, climate-controlled units, an in-house security detail of men in bowler hats who had been trained by British Special Forces, and acres of bulletproof glass. The clientele was rich and secretive, with apartments registered to companies in Liechtenstein, the Cayman Islands and Liberia. The twenty-five-thousand-square-foot penthouse triplex sold to a Ukrainian billionaire who had a reputation for suing media outlets that suggested he had a criminal past.

Part of the building's allure was undoubtedly its location, in the heart of Knightsbridge, overlooking Hyde Park – and just around the corner from London's sprawling, overpriced mecca of retail ostentation, Harrods. The famous department store had long been a magnet for the city's wealthy transplants. For some customers, the high prices might have been prohibitive, but for others, the exorbitant cost of everything at Harrods was part of the appeal. According to court papers, one well-to-do Azerbaijani woman spent £16 million at the shop over a ten-year period. When the first generation of oligarchs from the former Soviet Union arrived in London in the 1990s, some of them instructed their advisers to acquire property sight unseen – just as long as it was close to Harrods.

One Hyde Park was the brainchild of a pair of London brothers who got their start as entrepreneurs when they were not much older than Zac was now. Nick and Christian Candy had grown up in Surrey and been educated at private school. Like Zac and Joe, they were less than two years apart. In 1995, when Christian was still living in a residence hall at King's College and Nick was an entry-level employee at the accounting firm KPMG, the brothers borrowed £6,000 from their grandmother to make a down payment on an apartment in Fulham. They bought the place for £122,000, fixed it up, and sold it for £172,000. Using their profits from this transaction, they bought another apartment, this one for £236,000, and sold it for £345,000. The brothers had ventured into the London property market at a very lucky time, as the rising tide of housing prices created opportunities to make millions through judicious flipping. But the Candys were not content to flip apartments.

They established a firm, Candy & Candy, and pioneered a special niche: helping rich Russians find and decorate London properties. Boris Berezovsky, the billionaire who had once remarked that he and six other men controlled half of Russia's economy, hired the pair to refurbish an office for him, then, in 2001, enlisted them to find him an apartment in Belgrave Square. London's oligarchs, both real and aspiring, tended to define themselves through acts of consumption, so others took notice, and soon every wealthy Russian in town had to have a Candy & Candy residence. The brothers, who were still in their early twenties, became multimillionaires. They took pride in catering not just to the standard demands of your average obscenely rich, security-conscious, status-anxious consumer, but also to the more exotic whims of the buyer who will pay almost any price for something that might distinguish him from his peers. A Jacuzzi on a private jet? A helicopter with its own boardroom? This was the sort of candy that the Candys' clients demanded. The brothers boasted that they were in the business of satisfying outlandish demands. The whole thrust of their sales pitch was that the true measure of success is when you are liberated once and for all from the indignity of owning conventional stuff. Nick once scoffed that the normal-sized bathtub one might expect to find in the average English home was simply unfit for his clients, 'like a puddle for a dog'.

Of course there were naysayers, prigs who sniffed at the tastelessness of the Candy aesthetic. A Cambridge architectural historian condemned their showpiece at One Hyde Park as 'a vulgar symbol of the hegemony of excessive wealth'. The writer Peter York summed up the general vibe of the new building as 'junior Arab dictator'. But whatever their detractors might say, Nick and Christian Candy were, indisputably, men of their moment, and the press anointed them 'the Brothers Bling'. Some commentators pointed out, disapprovingly, that many of the wealthy owners at One Hyde Park used offshore shell companies to purchase their apartments and weren't paying income tax in England. But this hardly offended the Candys. Part of what made London such an attractive destination for affluent internationals was so-called non-dom status, a legal fiction, dating back to 1799, in which someone could be a resident of Britain but not 'domiciled' there for tax purposes. This arrangement had been very useful in helping British aristocrats to avoid being taxed on money they made in the colonies. But now it was mostly taken advantage of by people who lived and worked in London but claimed to be domiciled elsewhere, and thus paid no taxes in England on any income or capital gains ostensibly made outside the UK. Nick Candy once described London as 'the best tax haven in the world', and when Christian's children were born, he appears to have taken the unusual step of actually *naming* his offspring after tax havens. His daughter, Isabella Monaco, shared a name with the Mediterranean principality in which Christian's family had become 'domiciled', for tax purposes. His son's name was Cayman. (A family spokesman insisted that the boy was not in fact named after the Caribbean tax haven – but after a German sports car, the Porsche Cayman.)

Zac Brettler surprised his parents one day by informing them that he himself had recently been involved in a transaction relating to One Hyde Park. He had happened to overhear that there was a unit in the building that might soon become available, and, through one of his contacts, he brought this information to a potential buyer named Marina Granovskaia. A Russian Canadian businesswoman and longtime confidante of Roman Abramovich, Granovskaia was the chief executive of Chelsea Football Club. Though she was notoriously press-shy and almost never granted interviews, she was invariably described in media accounts as 'the most powerful woman in football'. When Zac told Rachelle and Matthew that he had managed to alert her to this apartment in One Hyde Park, which she went on to buy for herself, they were startled. He had received a commission on the purchase, he said proudly: a finder's fee.

The Brettlers didn't know what to make of Zac's sudden foray into the world of high-end real estate, but he did appear to possess some inside connection at Chelsea. At one point, he told his parents that at a recent match at Stamford Bridge, the team's stadium, he had ended up in conversation with Abramovich's daughter. On another occasion, he confided to Matthew a bit of gossip about the Portuguese coach José Mourinho, saying it would soon be announced that he was moving to Tottenham Hotspur FC. Nothing of the sort had been reported publicly, at least as far as Matthew had seen, but several weeks later, the story broke, and Zac turned out to have been right.

Zac had always spent a lot of time on Instagram. In the family apartment, a high interior window separated his bedroom from the hallway so that light could circulate. Passing by late at night, Rachelle would sometimes look up through that window and see the pale glow of her son's phone on the ceiling. Without entering, she would call to him that it was time to go to sleep, then see the light wink out as he complied. But these days, when Zac was on his phone at home, he seemed increasingly to be doing deals. He had started to wear a chic gilet, made by the Italian skiwear brand Moncler, which gave him the appearance of a young finance bro. In fact, he reported to his parents that he was collaborating with Akbar Shamji on a variety of business ventures. There was a transaction involving cars from Romania and talk of a mining project in Kazakhstan. They were also collaborating on a line of CBD-infused skin-care products, and at one point a shipment of samples arrived at the apartment on Lauderdale Road and sat for several weeks in the living room. Matthew and Rachelle found this somewhat irritating, but it also seemed like concrete evidence that Zac's relentless entrepreneurial bluster might actually be coming to fruition.

By chance, Matthew had an acquaintance, Antony Buck, who had established his own skin-care company and sold it to Unilever. Zac asked his father if he'd arrange a meeting. 'Investment into R&D is approaching $20mn across two unconnected facilities,' Zac wrote to Buck in advance of their appointment, saying that his 'partner' Akbar would be joining them. The three of them did meet, and though Buck simply offered advice and had no further involvement in the project, he came away impressed by Zac's presentation. Akbar had not contributed much, allowing Zac to do most of the talking. But the boy seemed older than his years, Buck thought, self-possessed and persuasive, not like some kid 'turning up in his dad's suit'. He had a credibility about him.

To Joe Brettler, this new incarnation of his brother as some kind of successful wheeler-dealer was perplexing. After a comparatively straightforward experience in secondary school, followed by his gap year in South America, Joe had moved to the picturesque medieval city of Utrecht, in the Netherlands, for university. His programme was in English and full of international students, and there were aspects of the city and the university that he enjoyed. But Joe found that he was unhappy there, lonely and disengaged academically. Having had such a clear sense of direction for years, he now felt like he was floundering. And just as he was encountering this period of instability, his little brother seemed suddenly to be thriving, forsaking the humdrum game plan of university and conventional achievement for a career as a high roller.

Zac appeared to savour 'the adrenaline of a fast life', Joe thought. He bought a pair of Gucci shoes, which Joe found pretentious. 'He'd often have a wad of cash on him,' Joe recalled. 'And he'd make remarks like "It means nothing to me, you know, twenty quid here and there."' On one occasion, he brandished a thick stack of fifties at Rachelle and said that he was off to play blackjack at a casino near Berkeley Square. Another time, when Joe was home for the summer after his first year in Utrecht, Rachelle had an assignment from the *Financial Times* to write about a hotel in Sussex, on England's south coast. She suggested that Joe and Zac come along and asked if Zac would like to bring a friend. In addition to Akbar, Zac had been spending time lately with a young Londoner named Archie Craddock, who had been a couple of years ahead of him at Mill Hill. Archie was stocky, with close-cropped blond hair. He was an amiable fellow. His father had been a successful television producer who died when Archie was quite young, and his mother was a prominent media executive. He didn't go to university, and apart from knocking about with Zac, it wasn't clear what exactly he was doing with his life. Though he was older than Zac, Archie was not as clever or as charismatic, and he could seem to be a bit in Zac's thrall. Matthew joked privately that he acted like Zac's 'bagman'. Archie had his driver's licence and often drove Zac around. Some days, as a favour to Akbar, they would borrow the Shamjis' Mercedes and pick Akbar Jr up from school.

Zac told his mother that he and Archie would come along for the weekend in Sussex but rather than take the train, they would drive. Rachelle and Joe had already arrived at the hotel when Zac and Archie pulled up in a Maserati. They had an air of smug exhilaration about them, cruising around in an expensive Italian sports car. In a way that wasn't all that unusual for a twenty-first-century teenager, Zac could sometimes comport himself as if he were auditioning for a rap video, strutting about like a badass, affecting a scowling pose. But when Rachelle and Joe wondered who exactly this car belonged to and how they had come to be driving it, the boys just mumbled something indistinct about having 'access' to high-end machines.

'They were very vague about where they got it from,' Joe said. Unlike his brother, Joe actually had his licence. But when he asked if he could try driving the Maserati, Zac said no.

Joe was back in Maida Vale for the summer holidays, living with the family. But Zac wasn't. In July, Zac had announced to his parents that he was moving out. He had been introduced by Akbar to a man named Verinder Sharma, who was a rubber tycoon, Zac explained. Verinder lived in a new luxury building in Pimlico, by Vauxhall Bridge, right on the Thames. The building was called Riverwalk. It was just opposite MI6. Verinder owned three different units in the complex, Zac told Matthew and Rachelle. One of them was currently unoccupied, and he had offered Zac a place to stay.

The Brettlers were caught off guard by this development, but not unduly alarmed. Their son seemed to be pulling together real deals in adult London. He was beginning to think that he might not go to university at all, and instead jump right into business as a full-time entrepreneur. And why not? The Candy brothers got their start when they were his age. Mark Zuckerberg founded Facebook when he was nineteen. When Zac was at home on Lauderdale Road, he would pace around the apartment, having phone calls with people about real estate prospects and commodities transactions. Sometimes, when discussing sensitive matters, he would step outside, and Matthew and Rachelle could see him through the window, talking intensely on the street. He seemed to be earning enough income to be financially independent, so it wasn't unnatural to presume that at a certain point he might move out. As for Joe, he was so fatigued by Zac's volatility that he was content not to ask too many questions. 'I was kind of unclear on the exact details as to what the property was and how he got there,' Joe said later. 'But I think part of it was like *"He's gonna be out of the house..."'*

When Rachelle and Matthew asked, repeatedly, if they could visit Riverwalk and see the new apartment, Zac said no. But on a video call, he gave them a virtual tour and they were able to glimpse a sleek, white, sparsely furnished space, with stunning views out over the river. Rachelle wanted to know more about Zac's new landlord, Verinder Sharma. Zac had mentioned that Verinder was somehow involved with Pirelli, the Italian tyre manufacturer. But when she searched online, she couldn't find anyone with that name listed as working at the company. As Zac became more ensconced in Mayfair circles, however, he had spoken to his parents about the great premium placed on privacy by some of his new friends – and suggested that people of real means often kept a deliberately low profile on the internet.

Zac had also begun to intimate that he personally was now making quite a lot of money. At one point he showed Matthew, on his iPad, the balance in his HSBC account. It was £850,000. Matthew was astounded. It seemed impossible that his son could have accumulated that much cash, whatever deals he might be doing. But it wasn't as if Zac had printed off some crudely photoshopped bank statement: Matthew had helped Zac set up the HSBC account; he was an HSBC customer himself, and what Zac was showing him on the iPad appeared, as far as Matthew could tell, to be identical to the interface he used on his own account. So where had the cash come from?

'Tell me the three main component elements of what has generated that money,' Matthew demanded. Zac replied that he had got into the oil and gas business through a Nigerian contact and some Kazakhs he knew. He was doing real estate deals, which Matthew already knew about. And the third main component was cars: he and Akbar had a car importation scheme, in collaboration with an associate in Georgia.

Matthew and Rachelle often found themselves in this curious, liminal zone with Zac, in which they did not know what exactly to believe. Zac had a penchant for embroidery in his stories, and a reflexive braggadocio. 'He's always had this BS element to him,' Matthew acknowledged. 'I kind of take a lot of what he says with a pinch of salt.' But there had also been plenty of occasions in Zac's life when he claimed something that sounded improbable, but it would turn out to be true. If Zac was exaggerating or trying to mislead his father in some way, it was likely in an effort to impress him. It might even be a gesture to reassure Matthew, because Zac was emotionally astute enough to recognize how much both of his parents were worried about him. So Matthew wanted to select his words carefully and use the delicate register that he so often did with Zac: he didn't want to accuse his son of lying, but he also didn't want to seem unduly gullible; he didn't want to offer wholesale approval of Zac's mysteriously lucrative new lifestyle, yet he also didn't want to completely withhold approval from a child who might be desperately seeking it.

Both parents had been nursing a gnawing apprehension that some of Zac's enterprises might not be strictly legal. They had no hard evidence to support this intuition; it was more just a sense of foreboding. Truly, it was hard *not* to wonder, given all of Zac's admiring talk about gangsters and oligarchs. Could he be dealing drugs? Or guns, like Efraim Diveroli in *War Dogs*? Matthew and Rachelle had both questioned him about this directly, stressing that it was very important that whatever business he became involved in, he should not do anything illegal or dangerous – and Zac had always sworn to them that he wouldn't. But even if they chose to take him at his word, in the face of this mammoth bank balance, Matthew did feel obliged to raise the delicate matter of tax considerations. Zac did *not* have non-dom status, which meant that he would owe quite a lot in taxes on an income of that size. 'People won't listen to excuses,' Matthew told him. Was he setting money aside for taxes? Zac assured his father that he was.

When Zac spoke to Dr Howells, the psychiatrist, he had complained that his parents were 'controlling'. But really, the opposite seems to have been true. The Brettlers gave their son enormous latitude to live his life. From their perspective, they had little choice: Zac was eighteen now, almost nineteen, and there was only so much control they could exert over him. He had money, and he came and went as he pleased. As the boy they had raised matured into a young man who was almost unrecognizable, they engaged in a kind of emotional triage, in which the paramount objective was to keep Zac in their sphere of influence, to keep him engaged. 'Sometimes it almost seems that it is a mismatch of parents to child,' Rachelle wrote to another psychiatrist at the end of 2018. 'However much we love him, Zac is sometimes wanting something very different from us – bling, power, action-packed. And he doesn't quite get that he can be that person, and have that lifestyle if he wants, and without judging us. And then we can get on harmoniously for a while.'

The Brettlers did make clear to Zac the distaste and disapproval they felt when it came to the false gods he now looked up to and the aspirations he professed. But their fear was that if they really cracked down, trying to legislate whom he spent time with and where he could live and how he made money, all that would do is drive him away. Dr Howells had cautioned that if Zac perceived 'a parental reaction as unreasonable or unwarranted', it might cause him to 'escalate his behaviour'. The more they tried to parent him, the more he would pull away.

In any case, Zac's stay at Riverwalk didn't last long. By the end of the summer, he had returned to Maida Vale. The building had been nice, he told Matthew and Rachelle – he had enjoyed the independence and liked taking long runs along the river – but he felt isolated in Pimlico, and he missed home.

Joe had been missing home, too. When he returned to Utrecht at the end of that summer, he felt lonely in the city and unhappy at university. At one point, aimless and depressed, he spoke to Zac on the phone, and Zac was uncharacteristically sweet and reassuring. 'Don't worry,' he said to Joe. 'Come home.' The irony was not lost on Joe that their roles seemed to have reversed, and the younger brother was delivering a consoling pep talk to the older one. But perhaps Zac had a special insight into what it can feel like for a young person who finds himself unable to forge ahead on the traditional route that is expected of him.

So Joe left university and came home that October, and for a while all four Brettlers were living under the same roof again. It seemed as if together they might find a way, however messy and unconventional, to move forwards. Then, at the end of November, Zac disappeared.

Chapter 3

AN EDIFICE OF LIES

MATTHEW WAS GONE THAT week, on a trip to the United States, and Joe was in and out of the apartment. On Thursday morning, Rachelle stuck her head into Zac's bedroom before leaving for the day. He was sleeping in, and when he woke long enough to speak with her, he did not look well. He seemed tired and agitated and had dark rings under his eyes, so Rachelle thought it was probably best if he relaxed and tried to catch up on sleep. He told her that he was going to take a 'phone detox' that weekend. He and Akbar had been having trouble with a Romanian partner on one of their deals who had been 'annoying' them, he said. So they were going to chill out over the weekend and stay off their phones. He would go to Riverwalk that evening, he said, and might stay with his friend Verinder for a couple of days. It was 28 November.

Rachelle went out to get her hair cut. She phoned Zac from St John's Wood to see if he wanted her to pick up any food for him. 'No, I'm fine,' he said.

Late that afternoon, Rachelle made her way to a gallery on Cork Street, to see a talk by the artist Albert Paley. She was excited. She liked Paley's metal sculptures and had recently interviewed him by phone for a column she wrote for *How to Spend It*. It would be fun to have the opportunity to say hello in person. By the time she left the gallery, it was early evening and already dark. As Rachelle made the short walk from Cork Street to Piccadilly Circus to catch the Tube home, the shops were festooned with Christmas displays and there was a sense of merriment in the air. The curving thoroughfare of Regent Street was aglow, lit by a procession of angels – giant LED light sculptures, their wings spanning fifty feet, their arms raised to the heavens – which hovered, suspended on cords, between the old stone buildings. Regent Street is famous for its Christmas lights, and as she neared Piccadilly, Rachelle noticed a pair of illuminated angel's wings that had been embedded in a wall, so that people could be photographed standing in front of them. On a cheerful impulse, she stopped a passing stranger, handed over her phone and posed against the wall, bundled in her puffy coat, the delicate wings branching out on either side of her. Rachelle did not know it in that moment, but it was the last time for a long time that she would feel happy.

Before arriving home that evening, Rachelle received an email from Zac. He'd sent it at 7:21 p.m., from his Omega Stratton email address. He wanted her to know that he had used her credit card, because it was preloaded on his iPad, to purchase an app that would help him prepare for an upcoming exam to obtain his driver's licence. 'I hope that is okay,' he wrote.

'I don't mind as long as you study for it,' Rachelle wrote back.

Zac's bedroom was a neat, narrow space just off the kitchen, which had the minor luxury of its own bathroom. Rachelle often went in and out of the room when Zac was not around, picking up laundry when it was dirty or dropping it off when it was clean. Recently, in moments of worry or suspicion, she would occasionally linger and snoop. When she entered the room that evening, she noticed something unusual: Zac had left his credit cards and house keys on the bedside table. She also discovered that he had left behind the Moncler gilet, which he wore so often that it had come to feel like a de facto uniform. At 10:49 that night, she emailed Zac again, this time with the subject line 'darling'. 'I am a wee bit worried about you,' Rachelle wrote, 'are you seriously ok? and you have left your jacket and coat and credit cards here – how does that work for a few days?' She signed off, 'Sending you much much much love x.'

At 2:03 a.m., Zac replied: 'All good x.'

The following morning, Friday, just after nine o'clock, Joe was out and Rachelle was preparing to leave the apartment and head to a class at her gym when the doorbell rang. Curious because she wasn't expecting anyone, she walked out of the apartment and into the building's vestibule, where, through the windows of the front door, she could see a tall Black man she did not know, waiting. He had a shaved head and was dressed in a tailored blue coat, a button-down with a stiff white collar and a purple tie that was cinched in a fat Windsor knot.

'Is Zac here?' the man said. He was holding a phone in his right hand and appeared to be talking to someone on it over the speaker.

'No, he's not,' Rachelle said. 'Who are you?'

'Who are *you*?' the man shot back, aggressively enough to startle her.

'I'm his mum,' Rachelle replied.

Whoever was on the other end of the man's telephone had clearly been following this exchange, because now Rachelle heard a deep voice, through the phone, exclaim, 'That can't be his mum. His mum's in Dubai.'

Rather than offer Rachelle any explanation of what that could possibly mean, the man abruptly turned and, climbing into a Range Rover, drove away, leaving her alone on her doorstep, feeling panicked and confused. There had been something intimidating about the whole encounter, particularly the rough bark of that voice on the other end of the phone, and now quite suddenly Rachelle became very worried about Zac. She tried calling him, but his phone went straight to voicemail. She emailed, demanding to know who these 'aggressive' men were and saying, 'I really don't feel comfortable about them and what is going on?' But he didn't reply. Rachelle's fears about Zac becoming entangled with dangerous people came rushing back: what if he had got mixed up in some bad business and owed the man on the other end of the phone money? What if the men came back?

Matthew was in Charlotte, North Carolina, about to board a flight to return to New York, when he received a call from Rachelle. 'Zac's gone missing,' she said. She told him about her encounter with the elegantly dressed visitor and said she was worried that 'somebody nasty' might be looking for their son. Matthew suggested that she call around to Zac's friends and associates to see if she could track him down. Meanwhile, he would catch his flight and check in with her when he landed. Rachelle tried Zac's friend and acolyte Archie Craddock, but he was out of the country, in Amsterdam, and she couldn't get through to him. She texted Dimitris and a few of Zac's other friends, but none of them had heard from him or knew where he might be. She called Roger Howells, the doctor, who, sensing her alarm, suggested that Zac needed to see a forensic psychiatrist. *Fine*, she thought. *Great idea. But first we have to find him.* That afternoon, Rachelle missed a call on the landline in the apartment, and when she listened to the voicemail, she was unnerved. It was a man speaking in a deep baritone, which sounded very much like the voice she'd heard that morning. He spoke slowly, the words seeming almost to slur. 'Zac, it's Dave...' Who was *Dave?* The man paused. 'Come and see me, Zac...' Another pause. 'Give me a call...'

When Rachelle finally got through to Archie Craddock in Amsterdam, he didn't know anything about Zac's whereabouts. But he was able to give her a phone number for Akbar Shamji. Rachelle had heard a great deal about Akbar, and had walked his dog with Zac, but she had never met or spoken to him. When he answered the phone, he sounded gentle, posh and deeply concerned. Zac had spent the previous night at Riverwalk, Akbar said. But in the morning he had vanished.

As soon as Matthew landed in New York, he called Rachelle again. He was scheduled to fly home on Sunday, and in the meantime, they decided that Rachelle should call the police and officially report Zac missing. He had not even been gone for twenty-four hours, but it was as if the simmering anxiety the Brettlers had been living with for the past two years had all at once come to a boil.

'Please call me,' Rachelle emailed Zac that night. 'Please come home.'

People go missing every day in London. The Metropolitan Police receive tens of thousands of calls each year, often involving young people. On Friday and Saturday nights, the numbers spike. Some weekends, as many as fifty calls reporting missing people come in every hour. Most of the missing have a tendency to turn up after a day or two. So the report that Zac Brettler had not been seen for eighteen hours and wasn't responding to emails from his mother was not greeted by the authorities with any great sense of alarm. It probably did not help that on the particular day Zac went missing, the city happened to be seized by a more spectacular and immediate crisis.

As Rachelle was frantically telephoning Zac's friends in Maida Vale that Friday morning, five miles to the east, a twenty-eight-year-old man from Stoke-on-Trent walked into a handsome stone building known as Fishmongers' Hall, on the northern end of London Bridge. The man had a bushy black beard and thick eyebrows and was wearing an oversized winter coat. His name was Usman Khan, and he had come to London that morning to attend a conference sponsored by a programme at Cambridge University called Learning Together, which was devoted to the idea that people with criminal convictions should not be excluded from educational opportunities and should be given the chance to reintegrate into society.

Khan had been convicted in 2012 on terrorism charges along with a ring of men who had been planning to bomb the London Stock Exchange. (Khan himself was charged not with that actual plot but with a separate offence of attempting to set up a terrorist training centre.) He had served several years in prison, and upon his release, he was closely monitored. But the authorities responsible for supervising Khan had granted him permission to travel to London for the day so that he could attend the Learning Together conference on rehabilitation.

As it turned out, Khan was not as thoroughly rehabilitated as the organizers might have hoped, and just before 2 p.m. he produced two large knives and started stabbing people. The spontaneity of the violence was awful; at first people didn't know what was happening. But several brave men joined forces to suppress the attacker: a Polish porter armed himself by pulling an ornamental spear from the wall, while a South African-born civil servant grabbed a decorative narwhal tusk. They were assisted by a convicted murderer who was serving a life sentence but had been released for the day to attend the conference. Khan managed to stab five people, killing two recent Cambridge graduates, Saskia Jones and Jack Merritt, before he was chased out onto London Bridge, where he was shot to death by police.

Because this bloody debacle transpired on the day Zac disappeared, the Metropolitan Police were distracted. London had a painful history of terrorist attacks, and the newspapers were dominated by dramatic photos of the showdown on the bridge. Three days later, the city was still on edge when Matthew and Rachelle entered the plush lobby of Le Méridien, a five-star hotel on Piccadilly Circus. They had still heard nothing from Zac. Matthew had flown home from New York over the weekend, and Rachelle had been checking in by phone periodically with Akbar Shamji. Some of the things he said had alarmed her. In fact, she now wished that she and Matthew had been able to get to know Akbar much sooner. He seemed extremely worried about Zac, and eager to help, so they agreed to meet in person. Akbar had proposed the Méridien; a friend of his was staying there, he explained, so he had access to an exclusive club lounge where they would be able to talk privately.

When they encountered Akbar in the lobby, there was something immediately reassuring about him. He was forty-seven, though he looked younger, and he wore a trim three-piece suit. Tall, slim and conspicuously handsome, he had a full head of rakishly coiffed black hair and an easy confidence. Ushering the Brettlers into the club lounge, Akbar explained that he had last seen Zac on Thursday night. The two of them had spent much of that day together, driving around London in Akbar's Mercedes. Then, in the evening, after Zac had stopped off at the apartment in Maida Vale for a while, Akbar had picked him up and they had gone to Riverwalk to see Verinder Sharma. Around midnight, Akbar had departed, leaving Zac to spend the night there. But in the morning, Verinder had telephoned to say that when he woke up, Zac had vanished.

The strangest thing that Akbar reported, however, was that he and Verinder had known the missing boy not as Zac Brettler – but as Zac Ismailov, the son of a Russian oligarch.

Akbar had first met Zac roughly eight months earlier, he told the Brettlers, in March or April of 2019. They were introduced by a man named Mark Foley. This was not a name that was familiar to Matthew or Rachelle, but Akbar explained that Foley was an executive at Chelsea Football Club who worked closely with the Russian billionaire Roman Abramovich. Foley had introduced Zac for a specific reason: at the time, Akbar and a friend of his were in the process of raising funds for a real estate venture, a pair of luxury residential towers in Lisbon. Foley said that he happened to be acquainted with a young man who lived in London and came from a wealthy Russian family. His name was Zac Ismailov. His father was a billionaire, and Zac had been entrusted to help his family 'make investments'.

This Ismailov kid might be a 'perfect candidate' to help underwrite the Portugal project, Foley suggested. So he arranged a meeting at a coffee shop in St John's Wood. Akbar brought along his partner in the venture, a London businessman named John Connies-Laing.

'We pitched it all to Zac,' Akbar recalled. 'And he said, "Let me take it back to my family."'

The Brettlers were thunderstruck. What was this man telling them? What did any of this mean? Akbar explained that he was equally dumbfounded to be learning that Zac's last name was Brettler and not Ismailov, and that his parents were English and not billionaires.

'So I'm . . . Georgian?' Rachelle said in total bewilderment.

'No, you're Swiss,' Akbar corrected. The father was Russian. Or possibly Kazakh? It was a little unclear. But the mother was definitely Swiss. With the ruefulness of someone just waking up to what an idiot he's been, Akbar murmured, 'You're a Swiss model. With six kids.'

But this all seemed so outlandish to Matthew. What about Safiya – Akbar's daughter? he wondered. She went to *school* with Zac, at Ashbourne College. 'Didn't she know him as Zac Brettler?'

Safiya and her schoolmates had known him only as Zac, Akbar said. 'Zac who had quite a thick Russian accent,' he added, certainly 'not a Londoner'. He paused. 'Which apparently he was.' He paused again. 'Which is astounding.'

After the initial meeting with Akbar and John Connies-Laing, Zac had supposedly presented a prospectus for the Lisbon project to his family, and 'the family liked the plan', Akbar recounted. But before they could consummate any actual investment, Zac had got in touch with terrible news. His father had suddenly died. 'Heart attack,' Akbar explained.

That was early May. Zac disappeared for a stretch, to attend to family matters, but eventually he re-emerged and told Akbar that he now stood to inherit roughly £200 million from his father's estate. Even as the prospect of Zac investing in the Lisbon project seemed to fall by the wayside, he and Akbar were developing a more enduring rapport. Meeting Akbar, Rachelle could see how this would have happened. Like Zac, he was an uninhibited, sociable, chatty creature. Akbar seemed to enjoy the very sort of deluxe life that Zac so wanted for himself – and to Akbar it must have appeared that *Zac* was the richer of the two. Zac had started spending time with Akbar's family, and Akbar, in his words, tried to be a 'mentor' to his new young friend.

'He was obviously taken with you,' Rachelle said.

'He described you as his business partner,' Matthew added. Zac had often talked about the many business deals he had going with Akbar. Was that just pure fantasy?

'Strangely, a lot of that is true,' Akbar said. They *had* been doing business together. Those were real deals. There was the scheme trading cars between Romania and Georgia, and a transaction involving 'rare earth mineral mining', Akbar volunteered. The two of them had been engaging with some high-level business partners, including 'the former head of the Kazakh wealth fund' and 'the former head of the CIA for the Middle East'.

Listening to Akbar, Matthew and Rachelle were starting to experience a kind of woozy vertigo, as what had previously seemed to be the solid factual underpinnings of their family's existence began to shudder and torque. Zac had never been a particularly reliable narrator of his own life, but even in the darkest moments of the past two years, neither Matthew nor Rachelle had ever guessed that he could be running around adult London pretending to be somebody else altogether – much less doing so in a manner that real adults, people of substance, might actually fall for. 'Zac quite brilliantly talked his way into everyone's favour,' Akbar said. He seemed to know 'a great deal about wealth in Kazakhstan', having absorbed a lot from his father, who had been 'involved in uranium, and all sorts of other mining and processing businesses with Putin'.

Akbar did not appear to be a particularly credulous person. Far from it: he seemed sophisticated and urbane, a Cambridge graduate, an affluent businessman. Yet he didn't make it sound as though he'd been indulging the pretensions of an ambitious young protégé whose reach might have exceeded his grasp. On the contrary, he seemed genuinely impressed by Zac's knowledge and savvy. 'He knew quite a lot,' Akbar said. 'About a lot of subjects.'

'Did you and Zac help sell the property to Marina at One Hyde Park?' Rachelle asked.

'No,' Akbar said. He'd had nothing to do with that. But with Zac there *was* always a lot of talk about One Hyde Park, he noted, and for a more obvious reason: 'He lived there.'

In his guise as the scion of a billionaire family, Zac had pretended to reside in a luxe Candy & Candy apartment in One Hyde Park. Each time Akbar picked him up outside the complex for their walks with Alpha Nero, he was under the impression that Zac had just descended in the lift. It was only upon reflection that he realized he had never actually seen Zac exit the lobby; instead he would always be waiting outside the building by the time Akbar arrived. One ironic by-product of all the secrecy enshrouding the ownership of high-end property in London was that *anybody* could claim to be a resident of One Hyde Park, and there was no public record you could consult to determine whether they were telling the truth.

Even so, it seemed bizarre to Rachelle and Matthew that Akbar might have taken all these details at face value. Most businesspeople entertaining a real estate investment (to say nothing of a mining venture in Kazakhstan) might be expected to conduct some minimum amount of due diligence on a prospective partner. Even a cursory Google search would have revealed that Zac Ismailov did not exist. There *was* a prominent oligarch named Ismailov: an Azerbaijani tycoon, Telman Mardanovich Ismailov, who was infamous for throwing lavish parties and paying celebrities such as Sharon Stone, Mariah Carey and even Tom Jones to attend them. An account of one such bash described the oligarch cavorting in a flurry of hundred-dollar bills dropped from the ceiling. But the scant biographical details Zac had provided to Akbar about his supposed oligarch father were not a precise match for Telman Mardanovich. Nor was there any trace on the internet of an oligarch who had died that year and fit the general description Zac had offered.

Yet just as Zac had informed his parents that people with real status and power often keep a low profile, Akbar intimated that privacy was such a fetish for certain well-off Londoners that if somebody didn't show up in a Google search, that didn't mean anything. In fact, it might even count, paradoxically, as a form of prestige: to be so rich there was no trace of you on the web. Besides, Zac had another email account that his parents didn't know about: a Russian address ending with the .ru domain extension. What London teenager would go to the trouble of obtaining such a thing if he wasn't Russian himself?

According to Akbar, the most salient proof that Zac Ismailov was the person he claimed to be was that Mark Foley had vouched for him in the first place. Foley didn't just work for Chelsea Football Club, Akbar pointed out. He worked directly for the most famous oligarch of them all, Roman Abramovich. It would be unbelievably risky to put on a thick accent and pose as a well-to-do Russian in the presence of Mark Foley, because he was precisely the sort of person who might see through the ruse. 'We never thought to do due diligence beyond "Well, we've got Mark Foley",' Akbar said.

The more they talked, the more Rachelle worried. It wasn't just foolish for Zac to have concocted this elaborate subterfuge; it was dangerous. Rachelle didn't know a great deal about the world of London's oligarchs, but she knew enough to be scared. Akbar seemed genuinely sweet. He could have been angry for having been so thoroughly duped by Zac, but instead he kept stressing to the Brettlers that his main goal was to find their son and get him home safely. What frightened Rachelle was that Zac had misled other people as well, and some of them might not be so forgiving. She had lived in London her whole life, with only a dim awareness of this other dimension to the city, a realm of money and intrigue that could be intoxicating but also treacherous. 'It's a scary world,' Rachelle said softly.

'Very,' Akbar agreed. 'And a world which I'm constantly trying to explain to my children – it's not *real*.' It didn't help, he confided, that many of his wife's clients at her atelier came 'from exactly that world'. For a moment they commiserated, as parents. 'Managing my own kids on this is already a challenge,' Akbar said. Even he could feel alienated by the decadence of the city. 'Just *leave* London,' he said. 'It's a constant thought.'

After the supposed death of the Ismailov family patriarch, Zac had clashed with his mother, who was living with his siblings in Dubai, Akbar said. There was a dispute, apparently, over the allocation of the late oligarch's fortune. One day in early summer, Zac had telephoned Akbar and announced that he was homeless. The family had moved out of One Hyde Park, and for a time Zac had been reduced to staying in a more modest apartment, a rental property the family owned on Lauderdale Road in Maida Vale. But tensions over the disposition of his father's multibillion-dollar estate had eventually grown so acute that the widow Ismailov kicked her own son out of the apartment – and barred him from the family's other properties in London. 'I've got literally nowhere to stay,' Zac said.

'For a few days I put him up in hotels,' Akbar told Matthew and Rachelle. 'And I said, "Come on, Zac, let's talk to your mother, it can't be too bad."' But Zac seemed very reluctant to let his new friend speak directly to his mother, saying, 'No, Akbar. You absolutely can't.'

It was at this point, Akbar told the Brettlers, that he had an idea. A close friend of his, Verinder Sharma, was living by himself in a large apartment next to Vauxhall Bridge. Verinder was a few years older than Akbar, in his mid-fifties. His kids didn't live with him, and he had 'a big heart', Akbar explained. So Akbar outlined for him the whole Ismailov family saga, and Verinder generously told Zac, 'I'll look after you until you're sorted out.' He did not own three units in the building and offer up a vacant one, as Zac had claimed to his parents. He lived in a three-bedroom apartment and allowed Zac to stay in one of the rooms.

'The two of them hit it off, I mean brilliantly,' Akbar said. To Akbar and Verinder, Zac seemed like a privileged young man who was in turmoil, cut off from his family and on his own for the first time. Motivated not just by their sense of compassion but by a genuine affection for Zac, they welcomed him into their lives, offering him a place to stay but also business opportunities and moral support. Zac and Verinder grew 'very close', Akbar continued. But the living arrangement was 'not tenable in perpetuity', and Verinder felt that Zac should achieve some sort of détente with the family and sort out the details of his inheritance. So at the end of the summer, Zac moved back to Lauderdale Road, having received grudging permission to do so from his mother in Dubai. Akbar and Verinder had no inkling that he shared the flat with his actual parents, who were English and both very much alive. They thought he lived alone.

The fashion line of Daniela Karnuts, Akbar's wife, operated a production facility in Turkey, and the week of Zac's disappearance, Akbar had travelled to Istanbul on a business trip. But while he was there, he told Matthew and Rachelle, Zac had started to call him incessantly, claiming that he was having emotional problems and that he felt depressed and possibly even suicidal. Akbar was irritated by this needy badgering, but he grew worried enough about Zac that he cut his trip short and flew back to London to see if he could help.

Zac *had* seemed a bit depressed when Rachelle saw him the previous Thursday, she reflected. But not enough to cause any alarm, and he certainly hadn't seemed suicidal. If she had been under the impression that he was in any sort of dire emotional state, she wouldn't have left the house for a hair appointment. After Rachelle headed out that morning, Akbar had swung by the apartment in his Mercedes and picked Zac up. The two of them drove around the city, Akbar told the Brettlers, and in the car Zac made a startling confession. He was addicted to heroin.

Rachelle had continued writing to Zac over the weekend, sending a series of increasingly desperate emails. 'You may be having a whale of a time somewhere, not knowing the chaos and distress left by your absence, or you may be in a very difficult position,' she wrote on Monday morning before leaving for the meeting with Akbar. 'Zac – I need to know you are alive. My motherly heart is aching, as is Dad's. Somehow send me a clue. If you need help, we can get it. If you are broken, we can help fix it. If you are in trouble, whatever, we can sort it out – with doctors, lawyers, new country, restart.'

Increasingly, Rachelle was becoming convinced that her son might have got himself into trouble with unscrupulous people. When a pair of officers from the Missing Persons unit of the Metropolitan Police visited the flat on Saturday morning and carried out a perfunctory search of Zac's room, she had stood by in silent terror, fearing that they might unearth a stash of drugs or other contraband. But they found nothing. The Brettlers were prepared to accept the idea, in other words, that their son might have made rash and illegal choices, putting himself in severe jeopardy. But heroin? That seemed unlikely. For one thing, they had been living with Zac, and he had shown no signs whatsoever of heroin use: no drug paraphernalia, no stupor-like disengagement, 'not a pinned eye in sight', as Rachelle put it. Zac was still fairly sporty, bopping out of bed for early-morning runs, and he was so ambitious and impatient. Now, *cocaine* – that was a drug they could see him taking. What is *The Wolf of Wall Street* if not a three-hour ode to its pleasures? But heroin was a vice of a different flavour. And the clandestine drug test on Zac's blood had come back entirely clean.

The Brettlers had been shocked by the big revelation from Akbar about Zac's secret alter ego. But they believed it. Neither of them was prepared to believe the heroin story. Zac might have *told* Akbar he was addicted to heroin; they just didn't think it was true. Instead, this was yet another invention, they were certain, and both Matthew and Rachelle thought that it was also probably a cry for help. Since childhood, Zac had occasionally feigned illness or injury when he was looking for compassion. He was the kid who claimed a migraine on the day of the exam. The best way to understand the heroin story, they thought, was as part of that pattern.

Akbar, too, had initially been sceptical, he told them. How could he have failed to notice over the eight months he and Zac spent hanging out? But Zac was adamant that he'd been secretly abusing heroin for five years, having started at the age of fourteen. Akbar drove him to Riverwalk that evening so that Zac could unburden himself to Verinder. Both men were 'furious' that he had kept this secret from them, Akbar told the Brettlers. But they were also determined to get Zac into treatment. Akbar found a programme run by the Church of Scientology, which he thought seemed promising. At about midnight he headed home to Mayfair, with the understanding that Zac would sleep at Riverwalk and the next day they would bring him to rehab. But early the next morning, Verinder called. 'Zac's not here,' he said. He must have snuck out of the building at some point during the night. The most likely explanation, Akbar said gently to the Brettlers, was that he had 'gone off to get some drugs'.

As distressed as the Brettlers were by this story, their main fear was not that Zac might have scored a bad batch of heroin and overdosed. What terrified them was that he would be exposed as a fraud. 'If I tell one lie – a *white* lie – I find that really hard,' Matthew exclaimed. But it was becoming clear that his nineteen-year-old had constructed 'a whole life that was just an edifice of lies'. Now it was collapsing – and people were going to find out. Had anyone told Mark Foley and others at Chelsea Football Club that Zac was not really an oligarch's son?

Not yet, Akbar said, suggesting that it might be better to 'just keep our mouths shut'.

'I have certain fears,' Rachelle said, choosing her words carefully. 'I don't know who Verinder's contacts are, but...' She hesitated. 'Abramovich is clearly powerful.'

Akbar tried to reassure her that even if Zac had angered powerful people, he had a measure of protection because of his friendship with Verinder. 'He's kind of looking after Zac,' Akbar said. 'Anywhere in London can be a bit dangerous if you're a kid with lots of money,' he remarked. And it was true that Zac had been telling lies in 'dangerous circles'. But Verinder was pretty powerful himself, he pointed out. Now it was Akbar who seemed to be selecting his words with care. He didn't say precisely what it was that Verinder Sharma did for a living, but Rachelle was getting the distinct impression that it wasn't a job at Pirelli rubber, as Zac had claimed. All it took to guarantee Zac's safety, Akbar suggested, was for Verinder to say, 'This guy's with me.'

After Zac went missing on Friday morning, Akbar said, Verinder had sent a man he knew – a driver, named Carlton – to see if Zac might have gone home to Maida Vale. This was the smartly dressed man who had spoken to Rachelle at the front door. It was Verinder's deep voice she had heard on the phone, saying that she couldn't be Zac's mum because his mum was 'in Dubai'. Verinder was sometimes known as 'Dave', Akbar said. And Dave had been the name of the man who left the voicemail on Friday, telling Zac to call him back. So that was Verinder, too.

'Is he . . . in business?' Rachelle ventured gingerly. 'Or does he work on . . . the dark side?'

'He's on . . . the line,' Akbar said. But what they needed to know was that Verinder was going to protect Zac, so nobody would mess with him. 'Verinder's the top dog,' Akbar proclaimed.

This was strangely comforting for Rachelle. 'Top, top, top,' she repeated quietly, like a little incantation to ward off evil. Of course, it was dismaying to learn that the man their son had stayed with the previous summer was not a rubber tycoon but someone who made his living 'on the line', whatever that might mean. But at least Verinder didn't appear to be too angry about the lies of his former houseguest, so hopefully he could help them locate Zac.

'The question is, where has he gone?' Rachelle said.

'Where's he gone,' Akbar agreed. 'That's the top question.'

It was still hanging in the air when Akbar's phone rang. It was Verinder.

'When Zac came into my life,' Verinder Sharma began, 'it was a kind of blessing.' Akbar had put his phone on speaker, and Matthew and Rachelle hovered over it to hear. It was clear from the way Akbar and Verinder spoke to each other that the two men were close.

Yet they sounded remarkably different. The Brettlers had never laid eyes on Verinder and had no idea what he looked like, but he really did have a distinctive voice: deep, resonant and slow as molasses, a rich and slightly cockney drawl. He almost sounded hungover, or still drunk, as if he'd been awakened by the call and was speaking to them from bed, though it was the middle of the afternoon and he had called them.

In the past year, Verinder told them, he had lost two of his closest friends, so Akbar had introduced Zac at a fortuitous moment, when he needed companionship, and the two of them had quickly forged a bond. Verinder seemed entirely discombobulated by the revelation that Zac's father was alive – and not a billionaire – and that his mother had never set foot in Dubai. 'I didn't think someone could *lie* to that extent,' he murmured slowly, sounding almost in awe.

Matthew replied, with a self-admonitory chuckle, that he and Rachelle hadn't, either.

'Now Akbar says Zac Ismailov is not his name,' Verinder continued, doing a mental inventory of the fabrications. Then a thought occurred to him. Zac had a 'mark on his back', he said. A scar. 'He said it was shrapnel from a bullet wound?'

Both Brettlers burst into laughter. 'It was a skin tag,' Rachelle said. A mole he'd had removed by the dermatologist.

Verinder did not seem amused about having been so gullible. 'All these things are very, very strange to me,' he said.

'It's strange to all of us,' Rachelle agreed, pointing out that Zac had 'run rings' around everyone. What was abundantly clear, she now realized, was that her son needed a serious psychological intervention. And he would get one, she vowed. 'If we can find him.'

For both parents, fear about Zac's whereabouts and discomfort at the idea that Verinder might be some kind of underworld crime boss were mingling with an acute sense of embarrassment about the months-long con that their son had perpetrated upon these unsuspecting, middle-aged men. 'Oh dear, this is just so upsetting,' Matthew fretted. 'I'm sorry for you guys,' he said earnestly. 'You've been sort of ensnared in this.'

'Yeah, it's not ideal,' Akbar acknowledged with a sigh. 'But none of it matters until he turns up and you get him back.'

Rachelle wasn't the only one who'd been sending messages to Zac. 'I sent him an email today and said, "Look, Zac, we all love you, we're here to support you,"' Verinder told them. '"We don't care what lies you've told."'

'That's very kind of you,' Matthew said.

'But it's the truth!' Verinder exclaimed.

'No, I understand that,' Matthew stuttered. 'It's very kind of you, having been spun this whole web, to be so magnanimous towards him.'

'He was so thrilled to be part of your family,' Rachelle chimed in. 'So thrilled to be part of *Akbar's* family.' Now that she finally had a chance to speak to these men, she could see why Zac had found them so appealing. He was 'looking for these sorts of *strong figures*', she told them. He had been seeking a life that was 'different from ours'.

'We're not ultra-wealthy,' Matthew explained.

Rather than politely protest that Zac's birth family might have had other virtues to offer, Akbar and Verinder seemed ready to concede the premise that Zac had turned to them in search of role models. 'All I says to Zac was, "Zac, you be you. I want you to be the best you. Don't compare yourself to me",' Verinder recounted.

'Which is such the right parental advice,' Rachelle said appreciatively.

As the conversation wound down, Rachelle emphasized again her fear that Zac could be in danger from some *actual* oligarch he might have duped. Verinder and Akbar might 'have a fondness and a kindness towards Zac', she pointed out, but 'there are people who will feel...betrayed. And they could be really, you know...' Her voice trailed off, as if she were too nervous even to speak the words. 'The Chelsea people could be quite vicious,' she said.

'Yeah,' Verinder said, not disagreeing.

What Rachelle wanted was to pull her son out of that world, to get him 'out of the Abramovich arena'. But 'if we find him – *if* we find him', she said, 'I need to get him straight to a forensic psychiatrist and then into a clinic. For months.'

Verinder said that they would sort it out 'once we get him back under our wing', adding, 'Hopefully it will be sooner rather than later.'

To that end, the Brettlers asked if the men might be willing to speak to the police.

'I absolutely will hide nothing from them,' Akbar said. 'Because with all the stories that Zac has been telling, I don't want to get myself implicated in anything. I want him found and put into a place where he can get treated. Before he gets us all in trouble.'

Chapter 4

MISSING PERSONS

THE LOBBY OF RIVERWALK was decorated for Christmas on the morning of Tuesday, 3 December, when a private investigator named Clive Strong entered the building. Strong, who was in his late fifties and solidly built, had the calm demeanour of a man who has seen everything. As a Scotland Yard detective, he'd spent his police career investigating organized crime, drug cases, firearms and human trafficking. Now he ran his own detective agency, and he had been hired by Matthew and Rachelle Brettler to help them find their son.

Riverwalk's interior was fitted out in the antiseptic fashion of today's superrich, with gleaming surfaces, velvet sofas and generic accent sculptures. Real wealth, this aesthetic seemed to imply, meant living full-time in the featureless splendour of a corporate hotel. The lobby was positioned between two glass walls, one facing north onto the building's circular driveway, the other south onto the Thames. Approaching the reception desk, Strong flashed his ID, explained that he was investigating a disappearance and asked to consult the building's CCTV footage from the early hours of 29 November. Zac had sent his final email to Rachelle ('All good x') at 2:03 a.m. that Friday, and Verinder Sharma said that he had awoken at 8 a.m. to find Zac gone. So Strong requested everything in the early-morning hours, hoping to pinpoint the precise moment Zac walked out.

The building's manager seemed reluctant. With a clientele that fetishized personal privacy, any employee might hesitate before complying with such a request. Strong explained that he understood any concerns about 'collateral intrusion' and assured the manager that building staff could review the footage before turning anything over to him. This was not some idle fishing expedition, he stressed: the 'safety of a young man' was at stake.

The manager, still noncommittal, asked to make a copy of Strong's identification card and disappeared with it. Another employee brought him a coffee, and he waited. Strong had been sitting in the lobby for twenty minutes when a short, sharp-featured man appeared. He was sweaty and dressed in athletic clothes, and he was holding Strong's ID in his hand. The man appeared to be of South Asian extraction, with closely cropped grey hair. He introduced himself as Verinder Sharma. Scrutinizing the little picture on the ID card, then looking up at Strong, he said, 'You're a bit fatter than in the photo.'

This was a revealing gambit, Strong thought. Verinder was trying to knock him off balance, to establish dominance. Saying that he had just come from the gym, Verinder mentioned that he'd been sparring with his boxing trainer. He was not a large man, but he seemed fit and unpredictable. Strong had spent enough time over the decades interviewing a certain kind of belligerent macho aggressor that, rather than be intimidated, he simply made a mental note of the fact that this fellow clearly wanted him to be. He explained that he had been hired by the family of Zac Brettler, who had now been missing for five days.

The Brettlers hadn't derived much comfort from their initial encounters with Scotland Yard. The officers who visited their apartment on Saturday had not seemed unduly concerned. It may have been the case that the whole department remained distracted after Friday's terrorist attack on London Bridge. Or the officers might not have been ready to sound the alarm about a privileged nineteen-year-old boy who had been missing for scarcely a day.

One thing the Brettlers could have done to elevate the urgency of the case was inform the cops about what they had learned from Akbar Shamji and Verinder Sharma: that Zac was not just some kid who disappeared but that he had been hoodwinking powerful Londoners into believing he was the son of a Russian oligarch. But for now, Rachelle and Matthew had decided to keep that dimension of the story to themselves. They wanted, as much as possible, to contain the fallout from their son's deceptions, to make sure that once they got him back, he would be able to go on with his life. So they'd enlisted Strong, who seemed as though he might be more proactive than Scotland Yard – and, if necessary, more discreet. 'I have a feeling Zac has got very much involved in an underworld,' Rachelle told Strong, adding, 'The last thing I want is my son to end up in prison.'

Matthew expressed some discomfort that Rachelle might disclose even to a private investigator the full extent of Zac's misadventures. The stress they were under could occasionally erupt in sharp moments of marital disagreement. Matthew, imposing a kind of emotional discipline, felt that they should focus on the most pressing objective: finding Zac. But Rachelle couldn't help but worry about how best to protect him once they had got him back. 'If he burns every bridge, there is no future,' she told Strong. 'What I'm really scared of is that we are lifting up stones and there are going to be big snakes underneath.' There were some dangerous people, she said, who now might have 'egg on their face, because they were duped by a nineteen-year-old pathological huckster'.

When they articulated this fear, the Brettlers were not thinking about Verinder Sharma. Verinder and Akbar had taken Zac 'into the centre of their families', Rachelle told Strong. Verinder seemed distraught, she thought, almost 'like a father who has lost his child'. Strong had been cautioned by Matthew and Rachelle that Verinder might be uncomfortable with the idea of engaging directly with the police. But he had been the last person to see Zac, so it was important for Strong to get his full account.

Verinder settled into a comfy chair in the Riverwalk lobby with the regal languor of a lion on the veldt. Clive Strong, with his little investigator's notebook, would have to assume the role of supplicant. Verinder was not wearing shoes and had been padding around the building in his socks. He was in his element. In control. He announced, munificently, that he had authorized the building staff to allow Strong to see whatever video he might need. The employees were highly deferential to Verinder, and the overall impression he created, Strong thought, was 'I'm running the show.' It appeared to be a very fancy building, and Strong had never heard of Verinder Sharma. But he was developing a definite impression that whatever Verinder might have done to be able to afford this place, it probably wasn't legal. As Strong would later put it, 'Everything about the guy seemed sinister.'

While Strong scribbled notes, Verinder repeated the story he had told the Brettlers: Akbar and Zac had come over on Thursday night. When Akbar left, Zac stayed. But in the morning Zac was gone. 'I was told his father was an oligarch,' Verinder added. When they had first met, Zac was 'sleeping rough', the child of a billionaire forced to camp in London parks. 'I felt sorry for the young man,' he told Strong. 'I said he could stay at my flat.'

Zac took one of the spare bedrooms, and they became friends. Zac was fascinated by 'gangsters and violence', Verinder said. But he had warned the boy to steer clear of such 'negative energy'. When Zac moved out of Riverwalk at the end of the summer, he claimed that the Lauderdale Road apartment was one of twenty-five units his family owned on that block. It was only on Friday morning – when Verinder dispatched Carlton, the driver, to check on Zac's whereabouts, and Carlton spoke to Zac's real mother – that 'his lies began to unravel'.

As Verinder talked, the building's staff had been combing through footage from Riverwalk's CCTV cameras. The deputy manager showed Strong a screenshot of Zac entering the building with Akbar at around nine o'clock that Thursday night. A different camera showed them exiting the lift on the fifth floor and disappearing into Verinder's apartment. Later, there was footage of Akbar leaving. But, surprisingly, he was not alone. He exited the apartment and entered the lift at 1:25 a.m., accompanied by a young, dark-haired woman.

'That's my daughter,' Verinder said.

This was a new detail. Verinder Sharma had three children. The oldest was a woman in her early twenties named Dominique Sharma Clarke. She had been friendly with Zac and had come to the apartment that evening, before leaving at the same time as Akbar, Verinder said. All of this was helpful context, but what Strong really needed was footage of Zac leaving the building. The staff had not been able to locate it yet, but they were still reviewing the various feeds. As Strong sat with Verinder and continued their conversation, a handsome man with an angular face strolled into the lobby and approached them. It was Akbar Shamji.

Clive Strong was not the only investigator who wanted to check out Riverwalk that day. While he was inside talking with Verinder Sharma, a police officer named Gemma Scott had arrived at the building along with a colleague, Judith McCabe, and the two of them had commenced a slow walk around the perimeter. Scott was a constable with the Missing Persons unit. She'd been with the Met for nearly twelve years and worked out of Kensington Police Station. Both she and McCabe were dressed in civilian clothes, and they took photographs and notes while they circumnavigated the complex. As they stood outside the building, facing the river, Vauxhall Bridge was to their right. There were cranes in front of MI6, where some sort of construction was underway. There was a little coffee shop facing the Thames, on the ground floor of Riverwalk, called Café Society. A few people were sitting outside in the brisk morning air, having coffees. Scott noted a number of dome-shaped CCTV cameras around the building.

After finishing their survey of Riverwalk's exterior, Scott and McCabe entered the warmth of the lobby, where Clive Strong was sitting with Verinder Sharma and Akbar Shamji. Everyone said hello politely, but there was a degree of awkwardness. Police don't generally welcome the presence of private investigators, even if they're ex-cops. Worst-case scenario, they get in the way, obstructing or inadvertently sabotaging your investigation. Best-case scenario, they outwork you, which makes you look bad. The officers did not seem 'particularly interested with my take on the situation', Strong reflected, so he receded, respectful of their authority and ready to defer to it. He said he would leave them to go about whatever business they had with Sharma.

Gemma Scott noticed that Verinder had a cut on the bridge of his nose. She did not ask how he got it. But she said that she and

McCabe would like to take a look inside apartment 504. Leaving Akbar with Strong in the lobby, the policewomen rode the lift up with Verinder.

The apartment was bright, spacious and immaculate. The walls were white and mostly undecorated. There was very little in the way of clutter or personal effects. Some papers and a Dan Brown novel on a glass-topped table. A big-screen TV. A shag carpet. The kitchen and living room were one continuous space, with floor-to-ceiling glass doors looking out over the river. Scott asked Verinder if they could go out onto the balcony, so he turned a key on a little panel on the wall and the door slid open, letting in a rush of cold air. Scott and McCabe stepped out onto the balcony. It was a shallow space, curving around the facade like a sickle moon. There were a couple of stray chairs. The view was sensational. They gazed down at the water, which was now at low tide. Traffic whizzed across Vauxhall Bridge.

Walking back into the apartment, Gemma Scott examined the balcony door. It was on runners and slid back and forth automatically. 'I asked Verinder if you close the doors the same way,' she wrote in a subsequent report. He explained that there was no key on the exterior, so the door could be controlled only from inside. She inquired whether Sharma had happened to notice when he woke up on Friday morning whether the doors were open or closed.

'Closed,' he said.

McCabe asked Verinder if she could take a formal statement. He seemed to have reservations about dealing with the police. He had already provided a statement to the private investigator, he said. Was it really necessary to do another? McCabe persisted, and Verinder, who may have been reluctant to openly defy her, grudgingly agreed. He and McCabe stood at the breakfast bar, and he started to relate once again the events of Thursday evening. But he now seemed conspicuously anxious. His voice sounded 'quite shaky', McCabe wrote in her notes.

As McCabe and Verinder were talking, Constable Scott's attention was elsewhere. She kept staring at the balcony, and the balcony door.

Then suddenly she spotted something she hadn't noticed before. In the gutter of the rail for the sliding door, she saw a dark object: a telephone. It was black and had been camouflaged there. Scott picked it up and upon doing so realized that it was only half of a phone, the back half. After hunting around, she discovered the other half wedged beneath a sofa. The device had broken in two, as if it had landed on the floor with some force. It was not an iPhone but a slim, exotic-looking model. She asked Verinder if it belonged to him. It didn't, he said. It was Zac's.

One of Zac's peculiar affectations was an abundance of concern for his digital privacy. In reality, he was just a teenager. But he carried on as though he might at any moment be the subject of hostile surveillance by a sophisticated foreign power. He invested in a particular type of phone that was said to be more secure than regular phones. Made by a Swiss company called Punkt, it had a simple design. It could call and text and had strong encryption, but no web functionality. The phone had a retro appearance, like a burner phone. It was this sort of detail that had made Matthew and Rachelle wonder if their son might be dealing drugs. But the truth was that the Punkt phone may have been more of a fashion statement than anything else. Zac had purchased it at Harrods.

And now it emerged that when Zac departed Riverwalk, he had left his secure phone behind. Though it was Tuesday and Zac had been missing since Friday, Verinder had apparently not noticed it, either. When Constable McCabe tried to resume her interview, Verinder announced that he was done talking and would say nothing further until he had a lawyer present.

The officers made their way back down to the lobby. Clive Strong was still there, and he looked concerned, because he had received an alarming piece of news. The building staff had sorted through hours of CCTV from multiple cameras around Riverwalk, and they had printed out stills of Zac and Akbar arriving, and Akbar and Dominique leaving. But they could now say conclusively, having gone through everything on the building's system, that there did not appear to be any footage of Zac Brettler exiting Riverwalk.

Upon hearing this, Strong had stepped away from the desk,

mystified, and walked through the lobby doors onto the waterfront. When he got outside, he spotted Akbar Shamji by the river wall. He was alone, apparently deep in thought, and he had something in his hand: one of the printed CCTV stills. Akbar stood there, in the afternoon cold, and gazed down into the Thames.

Chapter 5

RIVER OF DEATH

ANOTHER BOY HAD GONE missing twelve years earlier, on Christmas Eve in 2007, seven miles east along the Thames in the borough of Greenwich. Joshua Beasley was seventeen, a promising young actor who was a member of the National Youth Theatre and hoped to study drama at university. He had gone to a local pub with friends that afternoon, then departed on his own and was last seen outside the Hoy Inn, a pub in Deptford, at around 6 p.m. After that he seemed to vanish without a trace. Unlike Zac Brettler's parents, the Beasley family quickly went public, and soon the press was feverishly covering his disappearance. 'He is incredibly vulnerable out there,' his mother said when he had been gone for nearly a week. 'We don't understand how he could just disappear.' Greenwich was plastered with MISSING posters, and the police launched an urgent investigation to determine whether there had been any foul play.

Their attention soon turned to a young man named Baxter Willis, who had been an acquaintance of Joshua's. This was an alarming turn of events for Baxter, who was not yet eighteen himself. He had not had anything to do with Joshua's disappearance, and in fact had known the missing boy only in passing, as a friend of friends. But Baxter had recently thrown a house party that Joshua was rumoured to have attended some days before he disappeared. In truth, Baxter had no memory of actually seeing Joshua there – it was a rowdy party – but the police seemed convinced that there was a connection. For weeks they questioned Baxter and his family, telephoning again and again, telling him that they thought he was being less than honest. 'I was proper harassed, for days,' he recalled. 'They turned up at my work, at my school, at my house.' They implied that he was being viewed as a suspect. It was a nightmare.

Nearly a month later, a passing bargeman spotted Joshua's body floating in the Thames, seven miles downriver from Greenwich in Barking. At a subsequent inquest, it emerged that the boy had consumed a great deal of alcohol that evening: a pathologist testified that at the time of his death, his blood alcohol level had been four times the legal limit. What appeared to have happened is that he drunkenly stumbled into the river, alone and unseen by anyone in the winter darkness, and drowned.

After the body was discovered, the police promptly stopped calling Baxter Willis. But they never made any acknowledgement that they'd been mistaken in their tenacious effort to implicate him in Joshua's disappearance. This irked Baxter. But in fairness, there had been an enormous amount of pressure on the authorities to crack the case. 'I guess they just had no clues,' he reflected. 'Because he was in the river, right?'

Any number of people in London have a story like this – about a body in the Thames. Every year, thirty or so bodies are retrieved from its waters. For centuries, the river has been a preferred dumping ground for the corpses of people who have died violently. As Peter Ackroyd observes in *Thames: The Biography*, 'The vast majority of these crimes remain unsolved, no doubt because the Thames itself acted as a great dissolvent of motive and locality.' In 1977, the corpse of an unidentified woman was discovered next to Vauxhall Bridge, on a set of stairs leading down to the water, just across from where Riverwalk stands today. She came to be known as the 'Lady in the Thames', and people are still trying to figure out her real identity.

But the great majority of deaths in the Thames are suicides. In a short story from 1853, Dickens describes the preference of jumpers for Waterloo Bridge, 'the favourite bridge for making holes in the water'. After the body of one young man was discovered in the Thames at Lambeth Reach in 2003, his mother told *The Guardian*, 'The river is haunted – it draws people in.' There are so many of these fatalities that few of them make headlines. But you occasionally hear tales about Londoners who brush up against this macabre phenomenon of riverine death, and so Baxter Willis, after the police stopped calling him, just figured that this was his story, a grim memory he would carry with him but try not to think about too much. He moved on with his life, heading off to the University of York and eventually starting a career as a tech consultant.

On the morning of Friday, 29 November, 2019, Baxter woke early. Nearly thirty now, he lived in an apartment on London's south bank, near the Oval Cricket Ground. The office where he worked was in Victoria, and in the mornings he liked to walk all the way there, a straight shot along Vauxhall Bridge Road, which usually took him about forty minutes. On that Friday morning, he put his earbuds in to listen to a podcast and set off in that direction. It was cold outside and still dark. As Baxter walked past the MI6 building, Vauxhall Bridge stretched out ahead of him, illuminated in yellow lamplight. The tide was low, and beneath the bright lights of the bridge, the river was swathed in shadow. But as Baxter made his way across the bridge, absorbed in his podcast, dawn broke and the sky started to brighten. He was walking on the pedestrian path along the right side of the roadway, and as he approached the far end of the bridge, he looked down and saw something on the exposed riverbank below, something that only a few minutes earlier would have been concealed by darkness. A body.

The river had receded, exposing a wide stretch of grubby shoreline, and this was where the body lay, bright and pale and ghostly against the charcoal-coloured mud. A young man, of slight build. He was shirtless, in sweatpants and athletic socks, lying facedown in the muck with one arm curled beneath him. Baxter stood there looking down at him for a second. Then he stopped his podcast and called the police.

The dispatcher asked if the man was breathing. It was too far away for Baxter to judge. She suggested he go down and approach the body. But over the phone, she may not have appreciated how significant a drop it was from the bridge to the riverbank. Baxter looked for some stairway or ladder, but there was no way down. When he reached the north bank of the river, he saw a set of stairs that led down from the bridge to a pedestrian footpath by the Riverwalk complex, allowing him to get a bit closer to the body.

The police arrived almost immediately. A small crowd had

assembled. It was mostly morning commuters stopping to gawk, but there was a homeless man there as well. The proprietor of the little café on the ground floor of Riverwalk, a voluble Italian man named Pino D'Amore, came out. He could see that Baxter was shaken and brought him a cup of hot tea to steady his nerves. The first police officers who arrived faced the same dilemma Baxter had: they couldn't safely get down to the riverbank. So they stood in front of Café Society and tried shouting to the prone figure below, in the hope that perhaps he was simply asleep or passed out. A zonked-out raver. A napping drunk. But to Baxter it seemed obvious the young man was dead.

'It happens more than you would think,' one of the officers informed the little group of onlookers. This was almost certainly a 'jumper', he said – some poor soul who had made the decision to end it all at some other point along the river, perhaps miles away, and been borne here by the tide. It was Baxter's second close encounter with a person who had died in the river. What were the chances? While he was waiting for the police, he had held up his phone, more out of instinct than for any particular reason, and taken a picture of the body. It was only later that Baxter Willis would reflect on the fact that as they all stood there in front of Riverwalk, staring down at the body and assuming it must have washed in from far away, nobody thought to turn around and look up at the balconies above them.

By seven thirty that morning, several emergency responder boats had arrived, and members of the London Ambulance Service were approaching the body. 'My patient was cold to the touch and extremely stiff,' a paramedic later reported. 'Life was recognized to be extinct at 7:36 a.m.' When one of the first responders rolled the body over, the onlookers gathered above gasped at the sight of the young man's face, which appeared to have sustained some sort of terrible blow. 'It was obvious that a very traumatic injury had happened,' Baxter said. 'Like someone had whacked a massive dent into his face.'

A young police officer approached Baxter and asked to take his statement. Baxter thought he looked like he could be new to the job and wondered if this might be his first dead body. As the officer took notes, Baxter could see that his hands were shaking. An older policewoman with an air of authority approached and laid a quiet hand on the young cop's shoulder, which seemed to calm him. Among the rubberneckers, only the homeless man displayed any scepticism about the intentions or general competence of law enforcement. As they watched the paramedics attend to the body, one of the officers said again that this was likely just a suicide who had jumped off some distant bridge.

'Then why is he missing half his face?' the homeless man said.

The corpse was transported by boat to Wapping Police Station, then to Poplar Public Mortuary, near Canary Wharf, for examination by a pathologist. There was no identification: no wallet, no credit cards, no driver's licence, no tattoos. Police endeavoured to take fingerprints, but they were useless for identification purposes, because the body had been submerged in water for too long. London is a city of roughly nine million people, and the Met has more than thirty thousand police officers. As such, it can sometimes be the case that police in one part of the city are racing to find a missing person while police in another part of the city are trying to identify a John Doe, and neither contingent of officers recognizes that it has the answer to the other's investigation. So even though a team of officers had assembled outside Riverwalk after Baxter Willis spotted the body that Friday morning, none of them thought to enter the building and make inquiries – because they assumed the body had washed in from somewhere else. Instead, it took four days before Gemma Scott and Judith McCabe visited Riverwalk, spoke to Verinder Sharma and put the pieces together, on Tuesday, 3 December.

That afternoon, Rachelle was alone in the family apartment, talking to Joe on the phone, when through the window she saw a police car pull up out front. She knew instinctively why they had come. A pair of sombre policewomen entered. They sat in the living room and one of them held Rachelle's hand while they told her that Zac's body had been found.

Of the many things Rachelle had feared over the past two years, this was the inconceivable worst. 'I cannot describe how I felt at that moment,' she reflected later. 'No one can prepare you to be told your son is dead.' The first thing Rachelle had to do was inform Matthew. He was at the office when she reached him, talking with one of his business partners, Stephen Barratt. The exchange was brief and awful. In a kind of stupor, Matthew started gathering his things to go home. During moments of high trauma, people sometimes enter a dissociative state in which it's still possible to access ordinary emotions but not to cope with the extraordinary ones. What Matthew was thinking about, in the office, was that he felt sorry for Stephen, because it must have been so awkward for him to witness the moment in which Matthew learned about the death of his son.

Rachelle called Joe, who registered the news with a dreadful sensation of finality: all the ups and downs of the past few years, the perpetual uncertainty and anxiety and frustration surrounding Zac, had abruptly culminated in this moment. His little brother was not coming back. Over the days since Zac had gone missing, Rachelle had been in touch with his friends, in hopes that they might hear from him. Now she had to tell them, one by one. Dimitris was in a lecture when she reached him, and he was in such shock that for a couple of hours he couldn't speak.

Matthew caught an Uber. On his way home in the car, he got a call from Akbar Shamji, who had just heard the news and wanted to express his condolences. Both he and Verinder were in a 'state of shock', he told Matthew. In a reassuring tone, he said that he hoped Matthew did not blame himself in any way, because he had been a good father to his son.

Hoop Lane Cemetery is a picturesque Jewish burial ground in Golders Green that dates to the late nineteenth century and serves both the Reform and Sephardic communities. Many well-known figures are buried there, among them Hugo Gryn. 'My lovely friends I have the saddest news,' Rachelle wrote in a post on her Facebook page. 'Our beautiful Zac died, age 19, this weekend.' She included a recent photo of Zac, staring straight into the camera, his reddish curls swept back, his expression serious and rather dashing. The photo was ever so slightly out of focus, which gave it a spectral aspect, as if even before he died Zac already had one foot in the afterlife. The funeral would be at Hoop Lane, Rachelle said. 'All welcome.'

On the afternoon of 15 December, hundreds of people filed into the cemetery. Zac may have lied about being the scion of a Russian dynasty, but in real life, as Hugo's grandson, he was something like London Jewish royalty, and he was buried in a prime location in the cemetery, close to the entrance, alongside his grandfather. The death seemed to reverberate far beyond the Brettler family and Zac's small circle of friends. The Paddington Wrecks, Matthew's football club, which Zac had joined for games, suspended two weeks of matches as a show of respect. The children who had trailed Zac around the neighbourhood in Maida Vale were 'completely devastated', one of the mothers recalled. Many young people turned up at the funeral who had known Zac only distantly at school, if they had known him at all. Dimitris was amused to observe people he knew Zac had 'hated' now showing up for his funeral. Yet, interestingly, neither Akbar Shamji nor Verinder Sharma made an appearance.

Like any ethnic enclave, London's Jewish community could be gossipy, and having grown up as the daughter of a famous rabbi, Rachelle was hoping to avoid any press coverage of Zac's death. This was a private matter, and the Brettlers were aware that it had ingredients that might appeal to tabloid editors, prompting sensationalistic coverage that would only prolong their ordeal. With no public account of the death, an atmosphere of uncertainty hung over the funeral, and none of the mourners could say with any confidence what had actually happened.

'As some of you may be aware, the circumstances of Zac's death are complicated,' Matthew said in a eulogy that he delivered in the prayer hall. 'For Rachelle, Joe and me, this makes things even more difficult.' There were rumours at the funeral that Zac had died by suicide, having thrown himself from the balcony. But for many people who knew him, the notion seemed too incredible. 'There is no way he would have done that,' Dimitris declared. One of Zac's newer friends from Ashbourne College agreed, saying, 'Bro, Zac is not one to kill himself. I'm telling you for sure.'

One person who attended the funeral was a thin old man who was about to turn ninety-four. He was completely bald and wore tinted glasses, and his movements were slow and deliberate. It was Benny Brettler, Matthew's father. He had already lost a son, earlier that year, when Matthew's brother Jonathan died of cancer. And now, through some grotesque accident of fate, he had outlived one of his own grandchildren. Benny Brettler had a notion about how Zac must have died, and it definitely wasn't by suicide, he told Matthew.

'I think he was murdered,' he said.

Chapter 6

THE NIGHT IN QUESTION

ON THURSDAY, 5 DECEMBER, one week after Zac's final night and two days after his body was identified, Akbar Shamji presented himself at Charing Cross Police Station for an interview. He was accompanied by a lawyer, and at nine o'clock that night the questioning commenced. 'I know Zac Brettler very well, I thought,' he began. 'I mean, he was very disturbed and kind of slightly schizophrenic, we've come to learn.'

'What were your first impressions of Zac when you met?' a detective named Daniel Cook asked.

'He talked the life of a very rich young kid,' Akbar replied. 'He had fancy watches, fancy cars, planes, all the stuff that is very aspirational wealth in London.'

Akbar never actually *saw* the watches or cars or planes, but it is not uncommon for wealthy people to maintain a low profile. Zac preferred a 'laid-back, tracksuit, T-shirt sort of dress, you know, relaxed,' he said. The first time they met in person, at a coffee shop in St John's Wood, Akbar recalled, Zac mentioned that he had just put down an offer on a mansion around the corner, on Hamilton Terrace.

Reiterating the explanation he had provided to the Brettlers at the Méridien hotel several days earlier, Akbar told the cops that he had first been introduced to Zac by Mark Foley, who worked for Roman Abramovich. Akbar and his partner John Connies-Laing were told by Foley that Zac was the son of an oligarch, and they had been under the impression that he might want to invest in their real estate venture in Lisbon. But the money never materialized, he said, and they hadn't wanted to be 'too pushy'. After the ostensible death of Zac's father, Akbar had started to explore other business ventures with the boy.

The announcement that Zac had become homeless prompted genuine compassion. 'He's a kid that's had nothing but wealth his whole life, based on the fact that he's been living at One Hyde Park and, you know, this fabulously expensive school,' Akbar said, referring to Ashbourne College, where his own daughter was also a student. Suddenly Zac had been 'living on the street, and this is obviously not... tenable'. That was why he had introduced Zac to his good friend Verinder.

On social media, Akbar's family presented an image of glamorous harmony. But in his police interview, he made it sound as though there might be discord in his marriage to Daniela Karnuts. Asked why he had not just let Zac stay with him, Akbar replied, 'I live with my wife and kids in Mayfair, but I don't really have much voice over decision-making.' He had recently lost all his money, he said, and was 'kind of rebuilding'. As for the £10 million family home on Mount Street, that was 'not my place', he said. 'It's hers.'

'How old are you?' Cook asked.

'Nearly forty-eight.'

'How old was Zac?'

'Nineteen.'

When Cook ventured that he seemed to have spent 'a lot of time' hanging out with a nineteen-year-old, Akbar said that really it was Verinder who spent more time with Zac.

'What does Verinder do for a living?'

'He's now, to the best of my understanding, semi-retired,' Akbar said. 'He's quite well-connected, so he tries to put people together in deals and stuff. I'm not that deep inside his business affairs, to be honest,' he added, explaining that Verinder 'is a supremely private person'. He had first got to know Verinder six years earlier, at a gym where they both trained.

'And what is your relationship?'

'Mates,' Akbar said, who occasionally did 'bits of business together'.

'Was there anything ever more than friendship between you and Zac?' Cook asked.

'No way, nothing like that,' Akbar said. 'Nothing, ever.'

'As far as you're aware, there was no relationship sexually between Verinder and Zac?'

'Listen, I'd be shocked beyond belief,' Akbar replied. Zac was all about the birds, he said.

'Did you ever *see* him with a girl?'

There had been one occasion, Akbar said. It was the evening that he took Zac to Annabel's, the famous nightclub on Berkeley Square. The two of them were downstairs at the club and spotted a woman on the dance floor whom Zac appeared 'to know very well'. Zac didn't introduce her but went over by himself to talk to her. When he returned, he mentioned to Akbar that she was his ex-girlfriend.

While the officers spoke to Akbar, in a separate interview room elsewhere in the station, a different team of detectives was interrogating Verinder Sharma. Or trying to. 'I believe that Zac Brettler, who I knew as Zac Ismailov, killed himself by jumping from the balcony in my apartment,' Verinder asserted in a statement. When he fell asleep that night at around 12:30 a.m., he had been 'drinking Jack Daniel's' and had also taken temazepam – a sleeping pill – so his memory of the evening was impaired. He recalled Zac 'crying', and apologizing for 'lying' by concealing his heroin addiction. He remembered that at the end of the night they had reconciled, and 'we all hugged'. When Verinder woke the next morning, Zac was gone. He concluded: 'I would like to state for the record that I was not responsible for Zac's death in any way.'

But he refused to answer any questions beyond what was in his statement. When the detectives asked if Verinder was the owner of the Riverwalk apartment, he said, 'No comment.'

'Do you pay the rent?'

'No comment.'

'Did you have access to Zachary's iPad?'

'No comment.'

'We don't know Zachary,' one of the interrogators said. 'There might be information you know which might help us.'

But Verinder wouldn't give them a thing.

'Is this some old-school, "I don't wanna be a grass" sentiment?' the other detective asked.

'No comment,' Verinder said. They kept questioning him, and he kept replying 'No comment.' All told, he said it nearly two hundred times.

In Akbar's interrogation room, the conversation was flowing more freely. Gregarious by nature and reflexively well-mannered, Akbar had the agreeable demeanour of a people pleaser. After arriving in Istanbul the previous week, he told the detectives, he had received 'frantic' calls from Zac, in which he said, 'Akbar, I'm not feeling great. I'm feeling suicidal.' So Akbar flew back to London to see if he could help, only to have Zac reveal that he had become addicted to heroin. According to Akbar, Zac had wanted to get out of the apartment on Lauderdale Road, saying, 'Every time I go into that flat, all I think of is drugs, and it triggers me.' This was why Zac had been eager to stay at Riverwalk that night, Akbar explained: to avoid temptation.

'I'm in a red Mercedes GLA,' Akbar told the cops. It was actually a 'replacement car' from the dealership, he elaborated, because his Mercedes had been broken into a week earlier and was being repaired. Akbar and Zac entered Riverwalk, accompanied by Alpha Nero, the Weimaraner. 'The dog usually stays with me,' he said, adding, 'He's a good boy.' Verinder had put Zac's name on a list of people who could freely enter the apartment without the concierge having to call up for permission, so Zac and Akbar made their way directly upstairs. In the apartment, the three of them sat and talked, Akbar recalled. Then Verinder's daughter Dominique arrived, and eventually Akbar, Dominique and the dog all left together. That was some time after 1 a.m., he said.

'I'm trying to be quite specific here about comings and goings,'

Detective Cook said. 'It's extremely important for you to try and remember as much as possible about that night.'

Akbar had been drinking, he acknowledged, but he clarified that it wasn't enough to impair his driving.

'Were you taking any drugs at all?'

'No.'

'Do you take drugs?'

'As rarely as possible.'

'Cocaine?'

'Rarely.'

'When was the last time you took cocaine?'

'The thing about cocaine is, you don't always remember when you've taken it,' Akbar said, before qualifying, 'But not recently.' Then, qualifying again, 'Not in the last week, for sure.'

Initially, Akbar told the police that when he left the apartment, he had returned home to Mount Street. Then he amended this account to say that after going downstairs with Dominique to see her off, he'd gone back upstairs 'to say goodbye to Verinder and Zac and make sure that Zac was okay'. *Then* he'd gone back down and driven home.

But as Akbar stumbled his way through the interview, the detectives were growing impatient. 'Zac is *dead*, okay?' Cook said. 'Every question I'm asking you now about the night in question is extremely important – about your movements, what you did, what you drank, what you ate – so you need to rack your mind and answer.'

'I'm definitely trying to be as helpful as possible,' Akbar said defensively. 'I left and went back to Mount Street.'

'That's your family address?'

'That's my wife's address,' Akbar corrected. 'When I'm in London, I stay there. I would like it to be our family address. I'm working towards that.'

When he arrived back at Mount Street late that night, Akbar said, he parked directly in front of the apartment. But when Daniela saw him, she was 'absolutely livid', because he had been 'out so late on a school night'. Daniela took Alpha Nero into the apartment but barred her husband from entering, saying that he could sleep in the car. So he did. Initially, he stayed parked where he was, in front of the family flat, but then he decided to move, because it might be embarrassing if someone should walk by the following morning and recognize him. So he drove to a quiet side street nearby, took a diazepam, and tried to fall asleep.

Why not just go back and sleep at Verinder's? Cook wondered.

'Well, it was late, and it would have been a strange and unnecessary journey,' Akbar said. Besides, before he left Riverwalk earlier, he had already 'kind of put them to bed'.

When Zac went missing in the morning, Akbar said, they 'didn't contemplate that he'd jumped off the balcony'. Instead, they were certain that he must have run away during the night. 'I'm still very curious as to what triggered this,' he told the police, meaning the fact that they were questioning him. 'It's fine. I know you're all doing your jobs. But everyone's in mourning... I thought we were working through more with the mum and dad and just life issues, and... being *arrested*... I just kind of find it a bit weird.'

Cook concluded the interview at 10:41 p.m., but Akbar was not free to leave. The problem the cops had was that he was lying, and they knew it – because they had obtained all the CCTV footage from Riverwalk on the night Zac died. So later that evening they began questioning Akbar again, and this time they wanted to focus on one critical respect in which the video they had gathered diverged from his account.

At 1:25 a.m. on 29 November, Akbar could be seen leaving apartment 504 along with Dominique Sharma Clarke and Alpha Nero. They descended in the lift to the building's underground garage and climbed into Dominique's car. They sat in the car, talking, until Dominique drove above ground and dropped Akbar and the dog off at his Mercedes, which was parked in the driveway, at 1:46. At this point, the cameras recorded Akbar doing precisely what he told the police he'd done: he loaded Alpha Nero into the car and drove away.

Zac's plunge from the fifth-floor balcony did not register on any of the building's cameras, but it was picked up by the MI6 camera directly across the river. At 2:23, he walked out onto the balcony, moved to one corner and then the other, returned to the centre, then jumped into the Thames. But the minute before Zac left the balcony and entered the water, on the other side of Riverwalk, the CCTV cameras captured a car pulling up to the building. It was a red Mercedes. Akbar had come back.

He entered the lobby, Alpha Nero by his side, then ascended in the lift to the fifth floor, where a camera registered him walking back into Verinder's apartment. Twenty minutes later, Akbar and Alpha Nero left the apartment, rode down in the lift, passed through the lobby, and went back out to the Mercedes. But this time, rather than climb into the driver's seat, Akbar loaded the dog into the car, then shut the door and started walking around the perimeter of the building. It was 2:48 a.m. For a moment he seemed to disappear, in a blind spot between cameras. When he re-emerged, it was on the other side of Riverwalk, heading in the direction of the Thames.

A camera captured Akbar approaching the concrete wall overlooking the river. He craned his body to lean over the wall, then peered into the water at precisely the spot where Zac had just plunged into it. Then Akbar straightened, returned to his car, and drove away.

PART II
COINCIDENCES

Chapter 7

A FAMILY OF BRAVES

ONE FRIDAY IN AUGUST 1972, in the East African nation of Uganda, General Idi Amin Dada announced an audacious new policy initiative. Amin was a flamboyant military dictator who had seized power in a coup eighteen months earlier, and now he vowed to expel from the country the entirety of Uganda's Asian population. The inspiration had come to him in a dream, he said. But in the light of day, he had decided it was a good idea. For any demographic, the prospect of such a sweeping ethnic purge would be cruel and complicated; Amin had already expelled most of the Israelis living in Uganda earlier that year. But the idea of banishing Uganda's Asian community was particularly fraught. 'Asian', in this case, generally meant South Asian, and a substantial population of people who traced their roots to that part of the globe were already firmly entrenched in Uganda. Merchants from the subcontinent had been crossing the Indian Ocean to trade in the ports of East Africa for thousands of years. But the population movement that really created the community had come at the end of the nineteenth century, on an imperial whim of Great Britain, which had ruled Uganda as a colony.

In the 1890s, the Imperial British East Africa Company launched an ambitious and immensely complex new infrastructure project, the Uganda Railway, to facilitate the movement of goods and people from the port of Mombasa, on the Kenyan coast, to the interior of Kenya and Uganda. The actual work of laying down hundreds of miles of railway through highly inhospitable terrain would be difficult and hazardous, so the company imported so-called coolies – low-wage indentured servants from colonial India – to do it. Recruiting agents got to work in Karachi and Lahore, in what is today Pakistan. They drafted labourers who were willing to sign a three-year contract at a rate of twelve rupees per month. Over a six-year period, nearly forty thousand of these recruits made the journey from the British Raj in India to the British protectorate of Uganda. The project was incredibly dangerous. The workers were laying track through swampland, desert, dense jungle and the foothills of snowcapped mountains. Crews erected high-altitude viaducts that spanned deep ravines, and most of the food for this expedition had to be transported from the coast. People died of disease and exhaustion. In what sounds like a fantastical detail from a Kipling story, a pair of voracious man-eating lions stalked the work crews over a nine-month period, killing dozens of them. Ultimately, some twenty-five hundred labourers perished while constructing the Uganda Railway, nearly four people for each mile of track.

'The Gateway to British East Africa', an advertisement trumpeted, after the railway was completed in 1901, describing it as the 'Brightest Gem in Britain's Cluster of Colonies'. In the end, the Uganda Railway extended all the way to Kisumu, on the eastern shore of Lake Victoria, in what was Uganda at the time but today is Kenya. Once construction was complete, most of the labourers who had built it returned to India. But thousands chose to stay, establishing the seeds of a community that, over the course of the twentieth century, would come to thrive. They found work as shopkeepers and traders; one account in 1912 noted that Uganda's mercantile sphere was 'filled with Indians'.

In the strict racial hierarchy of the Uganda protectorate, the British colonial overlords tended to favour South Asians over the indigenous population, and to suggest that they were culturally and genetically superior to Black people (though still inferior to white Europeans). Many Asian families prospered under these circumstances, occupying a precarious role as both subjugated minority and imperial collaborator. After Uganda achieved independence from Britain in 1962, the privileges of this community were thrown into starker relief: by the time Idi Amin took power, Uganda's tiny Asian minority – roughly eighty thousand people in a country of more than ten million – controlled 90 per cent of the economy.

Now they had ninety days to leave. Amin framed this forced evacuation in the language of national self-determination. It did not matter that many of Uganda's Asians had been living in the country for generations: they were an outdated relic of British imperial rule. This would be a 'war of economic liberation', Amin declared.

In practice, this triumphant reclamation of Uganda's national wealth could often look a lot like theft. Uganda's Asian population was informed that those fleeing would not be permitted to take any of their assets with them. Homes they had lived in, businesses they had built – everything would have to be left behind. You could leave the country with up to £55 in cash and two suitcases – but nothing more. Everything that remained in Uganda would be expropriated by the state, Amin decreed. Black Ugandans were encouraged to take over abandoned farms and move into homes that had previously been occupied by Asian families. In some cases, household servants simply took possession of the grand residences in which they had previously been employed. Asian families pulled their children out of school and scrambled to gain legal entry to other countries. In Uganda's capital, Kampala, people waited overnight in queues outside the British High Commission, anxiously clutching their passports. In three months, nearly the entire Asian population left.

One of them was Akbar Shamji. Born 22 January, 1972 almost a year to the day after the coup that placed Idi Amin in power, Akbar was six months old when his family was forced to leave. His father, Abdul Shamji, was an intensely focused businessman with an outsized personality who was so successful that he had become one of the richest men in Uganda. Abdul ran the Gomba Group, a sprawling conglomerate with interests in trading, mining, manufacturing and property. He had two thousand people working for him. Gomba took its name from the remote district in central Uganda where Abdul had been born, in 1932. His roots in East Africa went back two generations: Abdul's grandfather had come to Uganda from Gujarat, in India, in the nineteenth century. Like many of his fellow Ugandan Asians, Abdul was a member of the Ismaili community, a transnational sect of Shia Muslims with some fifteen million members scattered around the globe. The Ismailis followed a spiritual leader known as the Aga Khan, a hereditary imam who was purported to be a direct descendant of the Prophet Muhammad.

Abdul was a small man bursting with Napoleonic energy. He had a toothbrush moustache reminiscent of Charlie Chaplin and arresting light eyes. As a seasoned narrator of his own origin story, Abdul loved to recount the tale of how his father had died when he was just a child, leaving him no choice but to get an early start in business. At first, he helped his mother in the shop the family operated. He would set off on his bicycle and sell ice cubes to the people of Gomba on a hot summer day. Eventually he moved to Kampala, where he struck out on his own, launching a little business that supplied kerosene to outlying villages. Abdul drove a van on his rounds. One day, a man offered to purchase the van from him. So he sold it and, using the proceeds, bought a bigger van. After he sold the bigger van, again for a profit, he decided that maybe he should ditch the kerosene business and start selling vans.

By 1964, Abdul had become Uganda's biggest importer and assembler of foreign cars. Though he was still in his early thirties, he began to branch out: textiles. Hotels. Marinas on Lake Victoria. He married a woman named Zarina, who was quietly supportive of her dynamic husband but so overshadowed by him that she could seem at times almost to disappear. The family had two boys and two girls – and then Akbar, the fifth and final child. It was shortly after Akbar's birth, Abdul would later remark, that 'everything blew up'.

One aspect of the 1972 expulsion that was particularly unfair for people like Abdul Shamji was that they felt, on some intrinsic level, very Ugandan. General Amin likened the country's Asian population to an invasive parasite, 'bloodsuckers', in his words, who 'milked the cow but did not feed it'. But however much an individual like Abdul Shamji might have thrived in Uganda, and whatever comforts he enjoyed that were beyond the reach of the average Black Ugandan, it was simply inaccurate to characterize him as some sort of foreign interloper. He wasn't an immigrant. He wasn't even the *child* of immigrants: his parents had been born in Uganda. The Aga Khan, whom Abdul revered, had encouraged the loosely dispersed members of his Ismaili flock not to nurture any ongoing sense of dual loyalties to the countries of origin their families had left behind, but to put down durable roots wherever they had transplanted and to assimilate. Addressing his followers in East Africa specifically, he said that they should think of that part of the world as their 'permanent home'.

Abdul Shamji was a full Ugandan citizen. Even the act of naming his company after the provincial Ugandan district where he'd been born reflected a kind of nationalistic pride. But as it turned out, none of this meant anything. After the expulsion was announced, Amin had him thrown in jail. With his stupendous wealth and extensive corporate empire, he made a suitable poster child for the contention that Uganda's Asians were nothing but rapacious neocolonial profiteers. After eleven days in confinement, Abdul managed to escape, with the assistance of friends in Kampala and presumably some well-placed bribes. People were starting to leave in large numbers, navigating the roadblocks that had sprung up around the city to reach Entebbe International Airport, where flights were departing for the UK, Canada and other countries where fleeing Ugandans had managed to secure asylum. A harrowing atmosphere was setting in. A report from America's Central Intelligence Agency described conditions on the streets as 'just short of anarchy'. Gangs of uniformed soldiers preyed on the civilian population, harassing Asian people even as they scrambled to leave. There were fears that the ethnic cleansing could turn into a massacre. As families fled to the airport, troops stopped them and searched them to make sure they were not leaving with more than their permitted allowance. Many were stripped of the watches on their wrists and the cash in their pockets. Even as the planes taxied to the runway for departure, the passengers were gripped by anxiety. It was only when the wheels finally left the ground and they could feel the plane enveloped in the gentle embrace of the air that the fleeing Ugandans could exhale and erupt into cheers.

'Every colonial child grew up with the notion that the motherland was the greenest pasture on earth, that the English tree had the sweetest fruit,' the Ugandan Asian scholar Mahmood Mamdani, who himself made the flight from Entebbe to England, wrote in his account of the exodus, *From Citizen to Refugee*. Approximately twenty-eight thousand of the expelled Ugandan Asians ended up resettling in Britain. When the Shamjis arrived in the autumn of 1972, they encountered a climate that was greyer and colder than the tropical one they had known all their lives. The welcome extended by the English people was not much warmer. Prime Minister Edward Heath had argued that Britain had a 'moral duty' to accept the refugees. But this sudden influx of tens of thousands of Asian immigrants from a former African colony happened to coincide with a moment of intensifying anti-immigrant hysteria in Britain. The country was in the throes of economic anxiety, headed towards recession, and some English politicians had been stoking the fires of resentment. Four years before the Shamjis arrived, the Conservative Member of Parliament Enoch Powell had delivered his famous 'Rivers of Blood' speech, in which he contended that for Britain to allow non-white immigrants into the country was tantamount to 'heaping up its own funeral pyre'. Invoking a conversation with one of his constituents, Powell warned that before long 'the black man will have the whip hand over the white man'.

Powell and many of his fellow Conservative politicians vehemently opposed the decision to offer safe harbour to Uganda's refugees, arguing, as one MP put it, that they had 'no connection with Britain either by blood or residence'. In London, angry porters from Smithfield Meat Market took to the streets in protest, holding banners and signs that read BRITAIN FOR THE BRITISH and ENOCH WAS RIGHT. The fascist political party known as the National Front hung posters in Tube stations featuring malevolently caricaturish Asian faces and the slogan WE'RE AFTER YOUR JOBS. WE'RE AFTER YOUR HOMES. WE'RE AFTER YOUR COUNTRY. Skinheads – marauding gangs of white youths with buzz-cut hair and Doc Martens boots – descended on immigrant neighbourhoods, looting businesses and throwing bricks through shop windows. Physically assaulting Asian people became a kind of recreational sport. 'Paki bashing', the press called it. This violence slowly intensified until 1976, when a Sikh boy named Gurdeep Singh Chaggar was stabbed to death in Southall by a gang of teen assailants. The fear of Ugandan Asians grew so pronounced that the city of Leicester resorted to the unconventional tactic of taking out press advertisements back in Uganda to warn those who had not yet departed that if they were going to come to England, they shouldn't come to Leicester, because Leicester had too many Ugandan Asians already. (This gambit backfired rather spectacularly, according to Mamdani, when Asians in Uganda who had not yet departed learned from the ads about the existence of this English city full of their fellow countrymen and started 'making arrangements to go to Leicester'.)

If Abdul Shamji was extremely sensitive to British racism, and often confronted with it upon his arrival, he also possessed a fierce determination to overcome it. He came from 'a family of braves', he liked to say, and he was not inclined to let the ignorance or xenophobia of some people in his adopted country stand in the way of his ambitions. On the contrary, the rejection Abdul encountered in those initial years in England seems only to have solidified his will to succeed. Besides, the English were a bit soft, he thought. 'For an Asian man, his enjoyment is not his pub or his TV,' Abdul once observed. 'It's his work.'

The British state created sixteen refugee camps for the Ugandan arrivals. These were spartan facilities located on decommissioned military bases, and thousands of people ended up in them. In later years, Abdul Shamji would occasionally imply that he, too, had been forced to seek shelter with his family in such grim accommodations. But the truth was that before he left Uganda, Abdul had made arrangements, squirrelling away large sums of money in bank accounts in Switzerland. He did not actually arrive in England with 'virtually nothing', as he would later claim, but with more than $1 million in these accounts. The Shamji family never spent so much as a night in a refugee camp. Instead, they moved into an apartment in Kensington.

It was nevertheless true that Abdul had arrived in England, as he put it, having 'lost much of my empire'. Now, with his family safely ensconced in London, he was ready to rebuild. Almost immediately, Abdul began trading with another African country in which he had contacts: Zaire. At first it was crockery, cutlery and Johnnie Walker whisky. Moving quickly, he reinvested his profits and diversified, branching into shipping, property and manufacturing. Abdul loved to play the board game Monopoly, and at times he could seem almost like the top-hatted mascot of the game, buying up one enterprise after another, forever augmenting his portfolio.

Within four years of arriving in England, Abdul presided over a thriving export operation, a chain of supermarkets, a small fleet of cargo ships, and a factory in Blackburn that made handbags. Michael Hendry, an executive who worked closely with him in England, remarked that Abdul was 'the best salesman I've ever seen'. Having built a diversified conglomerate back in Uganda, Abdul saw no reason to confine himself to any one industry in England. He invested in a metalworks in the Midlands and in a crocodile farm in Malaysia. He bought a 176-room hotel in Maida Vale and a slew of other hotels from Birmingham to Dallas to Kathmandu. He started getting press coverage, lots of it, and one sentiment that was often repeated in articles about his business prowess was that 'Uganda's loss was Britain's gain'. This appeared to be true in a fairly literal sense for Uganda: after Amin expelled so many of the people who had been running the country's formal economy, the economy collapsed. As for Britain, a later prime minister, David Cameron, would observe that the Ugandan Asians who resettled in the United Kingdom turned out to be 'one of the most successful groups of immigrants anywhere in the history of the world'.

In 1981, a troubled Scottish truck manufacturer, Stonefield Vehicles, based in the town of Cumnock, south of Glasgow, was looking for a bailout. The Scottish Development Agency had pumped £5 million into the company, but it was floundering. A number of established commercial vehicle makers expressed an interest in acquiring Stonefield, but they wanted to shift production out of Scotland, because it would be more efficient to manufacture the trucks in England. Out of nowhere, in swept Abdul Shamji, praising the 'determination of the Scottish worker' and announcing that if Stonefield were to accept his bid, he would keep production right where it was, preserving the jobs of fifty people who worked at the plant. Abdul offered to pay £300,000 for the beleaguered company, and when the deal went through, workers at the factory poured champagne into coffee mugs and raised a toast. The press hailed Abdul as a 'saviour'. In a publicity photo, he looked benevolent and determined, with his glossy black hair and sharply clipped moustache.

After he took over the company, Abdul managed to orchestrate an extraordinary public relations coup. Margaret Thatcher had recently been elected to her first term as prime minister, and Abdul persuaded her to make an official visit to the plant in Cumnock. The purpose of the trip was to highlight how well Scottish enterprise was doing after two years of Conservative rule. The plan was for Thatcher to visit a denim factory and then stop in at the Stonefield plant nearby. But even at that time, Thatcher was not a universally beloved figure. Cumnock was a mining town. Organized labour loathed the new prime minister, and hundreds of thousands of Scottish people were on the dole. When Thatcher, on the floor of the denim factory, resplendent in a royal-blue suit and pearls, approached random employees and purred ridiculous questions ('Do you *enjoy* your work?'), the sour-faced workers turned their backs on her. By the time she got outside, a crowd of protesters had assembled. Fifteen hundred of them. They were chanting, 'Maggie, Maggie, Maggie! Out, out, out!' Someone had brought a supply of eggs, and the protesters began hurling them at the prime minister. A member of her security detail lunged, valiantly, to intercept one of these projectiles before it could detonate on her famous coif.

A hasty decision was made that it might not be a great idea for Thatcher to push her luck by visiting the Stonefield plant as planned. She couldn't get to the plant, in any case, because it was physically blocked by an egg-wielding mob of hostile constituents. But Abdul Shamji, who was a master of improvisation, realized that if you can't bring the dignitary to the trucks, you bring a truck to the dignitary. Someone drove one of the Stonefield trucks over to where Thatcher was sheltering, and she gamely climbed aboard just long enough for a photographer to snap a picture of her posing behind the wheel. No matter that she hadn't actually visited the factory, or that just off camera embittered protesters were baying for her head. Abdul had the picture framed and displayed it prominently in Stonefield's office.

Within just a few years of his arrival in England, Abdul had begun cultivating political connections in London. It may simply be the case that one lesson he learned in Uganda was that sometimes economic power is not enough: you can be the richest person in the country and, if you get on the wrong side of the political establishment, you're still vulnerable. But it is interesting to consider that when Abdul began donating money to a political party in his new home, it was to the party of Enoch Powell, who had opposed the resettlement of the Ugandan Asians. In the late 1970s, Abdul befriended an Eton-educated Conservative fixer named Andrew Rowe. Reedy and tweedy, Rowe had a plummy accent and wore ascots. Recognizing that there was a new generation of successful Asian businessmen who coveted the validation of politicians, and that politicians would covet the money of Asian businessmen, Rowe established a new group called the Anglo Asian Conservative Society. With his help, Abdul hosted a dinner in March 1978 at the mansion he had recently purchased for his family in Kingston upon Thames, creating a forum in which he and some of his fellow Asian businessmen could mingle with Conservative Party grandees. Thatcher, who was party leader at the time but not yet prime minister, attended, in a powder-blue dress with long white gloves, and posed alongside Abdul, who looked debonair in a dinner jacket with a pocket square. As Rowe remarked, rather forthrightly, 'Whenever anybody swims into one's ken as a politician who seems to be both sympathetic politically and rich, one's eyes reflect pound signs.'

By 1981, Thatcher was prime minister and Abdul had recently been named vice president of the Small Business Bureau, a group she championed. If Abdul was attracted to the cultural acceptance and reflected political power that these relationships seemed to confer, his new friends had designs of their own, and it wasn't just his money they were after. In the wake of the flagrant xenophobia spouted by Conservative leaders like Powell, there was often an implied note of self-congratulation, on the part of Thatcher and her allies, in boosting Asian immigrant success stories like Abdul Shamji. When Abdul vowed to save the Stonefield factory in Cumnock, Thatcher's secretary of state for Scotland said he was a 'miracle man'. Abdul's own lawyer described him as 'a prototype of the Asian immigrant who rose to prominence'. There may have been some comforting satisfaction, at a time of racial and economic strife, in the idea that a model minority could succeed in prospering so magnificently in England. Abdul grew so close to the Conservative leader Norman Tebbit that after Tebbit was injured in a 1984 bombing by the Irish Republican Army, Abdul was one of the few people permitted to visit him at the hospital.

⌇

As religious leaders go, the Aga Khan was no ascetic. Though technically imam to a flock of fifteen million Ismaili Muslims, he enjoyed the sybaritic lifestyle of a playboy from a royal family. This particular branch of lineal descendants of the Prophet Muhammad had become extraordinarily prosperous over the decades. With billions of dollars in assets and business interests ranging from insurance to airlines to hospitality, the Aga Khan had a staff of 150; split his time between a château in France, a villa on Lake Geneva, a private island in the Bahamas, and other properties around the globe; and ferried between these homes in a fleet of Mercedes and a Gulfstream jet. He owned some six hundred horses, which he stabled at estates in Ireland and Normandy. Though he shunned publicity, he was a fixture in gossip columns because of his colourful family (his father, a famous lothario, married Rita Hayworth) and his tendency to mingle with the rich and glamorous in places such as Ascot, St Moritz and the Costa Smeralda.

To outsiders, it was occasionally perplexing that such a beacon of profligacy could double as a pillar of moral instruction for religious Muslims. But there's no accounting for faith. Millions of Ismailis paid a tithe to the Aga Khan of up to 12 per cent of their income, which he then redistributed to the religion's many charitable endeavours. For members of the faith who were more entrepreneurially inclined, the Aga Khan could be regarded as an aspirational role model. He was certainly a source of great inspiration to Abdul Shamji, who installed a portrait of the religious leader in every bedroom of his new home in Kingston upon Thames.

Unlike many of his fellow transplants from Uganda, who built new lives in the UK on a foundation of frugal self-restraint, Abdul seemed to take his lifestyle cues from the Aga Khan. The home he purchased for his family was a rambling Tudor-style mansion on a leafy plot of land. On the grounds he installed a miniature train that travelled on a track around the garden and was sturdy enough to carry small children. The house was furnished with English antiques, and the many pictures of the Aga Khan were joined by shots of Abdul with his close friend Mrs Thatcher. There were big Alsatian dogs, and servants. By Abdul's own account, he worked incessantly. As a parent, he was stern, demanding and formal. When it came to spending time with his children, his preferred activity was to play Monopoly. 'We play that a lot,' he acknowledged to an interviewer. But he rarely went in for more frivolous forms of popular entertainment. Akbar later told a friend that his father had taken him to the movies on only one occasion; it was *Big*, the 1988 film in which Tom Hanks plays a boy who is so impatient to be an adult that he makes a wish and suddenly becomes one overnight. Both Akbar and his father wore a suit and tie for the excursion.

The Gomba Group occupied a handsome building that Abdul had purchased at 97 Park Lane, directly facing Hyde Park. This was the sort of London address that really announced itself: Park Lane is a short street with only so many buildings, a number of which are hotels. Abdul didn't even use the whole building: there were empty apartments upstairs. But just saying the name or emblazoning it on letterhead conferred an air of irreproachability. Like a lot of successful entrepreneurs, Abdul Shamji was not a person who was overburdened by introspection. But there were hints, in the flamboyantly aristocratic manner in which he chose to live his life, that his revenge would be success – and that he was desperate to win over the very same racist and elitist establishment that had so coldly rejected his people.

Shortly after Margaret Thatcher first moved into 10 Downing Street, a British gangster film was released that would offer a prescient glimpse of the culture of Thatcherism. In *The Long Good Friday*, Bob Hoskins played Harold Shand, a London mobster who wants to reinvent himself as a property impresario. Shand is a zesty dynamo, bursting with the ravenous energy that fuels both worlds he is trying to straddle: old-school crime and 1980s capitalism. He is also a creature of East London, where by 1980 the once thriving docklands had become an eight-mile wilderness of disused gantry cranes and derelict wharves and warehouses. But early in the film, Shand articulates a dream: where others see a forgotten zone of urban decay, he sees the future home of luxury housing, office spaces and casinos – precisely the sort of development, in other words, that in real life would soon come to occupy Canary Wharf and the surrounding area. 'This is the decade,' Shand vows. 'No other city in the world has got, right in its centre, such an opportunity for profitable progress.' Framed by Tower Bridge, speaking with a sense of manifest destiny, he says that it is time for 'a new London'.

Shand spends much of *The Long Good Friday* on the deck of a sleek white pleasure boat of a sort you might find navigating the Grand Canal in Venice or bobbing at a marina in Cap d'Antibes. Accompanied by the movie's groovy soundtrack, the vessel sails along forlorn stretches of the post-industrial Thames. It looks like a shimmering white space capsule that is visiting from a brighter future. In real life, the name of the boat was the *Fatimah*, and it had been rented to the filmmakers, at what one of them described as a 'humongous' price, by its owner – Abdul Shamji.

Like Harold Shand, Abdul had discovered that if you act like you are already a success, people tend to treat you like a success, which in turn can lead to real success. To be an entrepreneur is, on some level, to engage in a confidence game – to show people a business prospectus or an architectural model and persuade them that it is not just your idle fancy but a reality that you will soon birth into existence. When Abdul welcomed Margaret Thatcher into his mansion, he did not mention that he had purchased the property with the help of a jumbo mortgage. In truth, he had financed much of his lifestyle and his ever-expanding business portfolio with debt. He borrowed heavily from a number of banks, which were quite happy to lend to him, because they understood that his holdings now exceeded £125 million. In pre-Big Bang London, the banking sector was still very much a relationship business. When the chairman of the merchant bank Lazard Brothers was asked in the mid-1970s about his lending philosophy, he said, 'Quite simple. I only lent money to people who had been at Eton.' Just as Shand used his boat to entertain London movers and shakers, Abdul found that it could be helpful, in securing the allegiance of his bankers, to wine and dine them. 'He was entertaining them lavishly,' Michael Hendry, Abdul's colleague during this period, recalled. 'And obviously he would invite them on the yacht.'

Thatcher's visit to Cumnock was a good example of the importance of image in selling a business or an individual. Abdul secured his photo opportunity, and afterwards the photo would matter more than anything that might or might not have actually happened that day. At the time, the visit had seemed like a good omen for the employees at Stonefield. But eventually the workers at the plant started to grow dubious about Abdul's true intentions. Occasionally he would fly up to Scotland on an executive jet, for brief visits. But he never seemed to make any of the capital investments in the plant that he had promised. Then, in 1983, he abruptly announced that he was closing the factory and moving production south, to Kent. This was the precise thing Abdul had pledged *not* to do when he acquired the company. All fifty employees lost their jobs. 'The man arrived on the scene like a saviour,' George Foulkes, an MP who represented Cumnock, said. 'He was the ultimate patter merchant, frequently referring to his contacts in the Tory Party, including Mrs Thatcher. But all he did was leave behind broken promises and shattered dreams.'

Officials in Scotland were irate, and not just because the Scottish government had invested £5 million in the company with the intention of supporting Scottish industry, but because, as it transpired, Abdul had never delivered the full £300,000 he agreed to pay for Stonefield. Attempts at legal action proved difficult, because Abdul's accounts turned out to be bewilderingly convoluted. Gomba Stonefield, the new entity he had created when he purchased the company, was a subsidiary of Gomba Motors, which was a subsidiary of Gomba UK. But Gomba UK was *itself* a subsidiary, of Gomba Holdings, which was incorporated in the Channel Island of Jersey. And the true owners of Gomba Holdings were difficult to identify. When newspaper reporters tried to figure out whether any human being existed who could actually be held liable for the money owed in Scotland, they were informed that Abdul Shamji was not available, because he was 'on holiday in India'.

None of this seemed to trouble the Shamji family. Years later, Akbar would describe 1983 as the 'peak' of his father's career. *Tatler* ran a laudatory feature in early 1985 on what it referred to as Britain's 'Upper Crust Asians'. The subhead for the piece was 'The Empire Strikes Back'. This was a useful bit of press, at a moment when the unpleasantness in Stonefield seemed largely to be forgotten. In fact, Abdul was in the process of finalizing a deal that had all the hallmarks of a capstone achievement: he was going to purchase Wembley Stadium, the storied home of English football.

Built in 1923 and originally known as the Empire Stadium, Wembley was the most iconic sporting ground in Britain. Its twin towers were as familiar to many English schoolchildren as Buckingham Palace or the Houses of Parliament. It was at Wembley that England had hosted the opening of the first post-war Olympic Games, in 1948, and won the World Cup in 1966. Wembley Stadium was hallowed ground, in other words, and for Abdul the deal seemed not merely to be an important benchmark of his vertiginous ascent but a sign that he had won the acceptance he had been working for since arriving in England thirteen years earlier. In a self-glorifying, privately published history of the Gomba Group, Abdul described himself as a 'Phoenix Who Rose from Ashes to Recreate an Industrial Empire of Unsurpassed Splendour'.

Abdul said nothing about his daughters in the *Tatler* article, but he revealed an ardent hope that his three sons would continue his legacy. Ryaz (who was twenty at the time) and Alim (who was nineteen) were both off studying at the University of Texas, in Austin. Akbar was thirteen and a student at King's College School, in Wimbledon. The Shamji brothers would 'take over the business', Abdul predicted. His ambition, he said, was to 'create a dynasty'.

One of the biggest heists in British history took place on the morning of 26 November 1983. A gang of thieves converged on a warehouse on the industrial outskirts of Heathrow Airport that was managed by a security and transportation company called Brink's-Mat. The robbers had cultivated an inside man: a security guard named Anthony Black, who worked for Brink's-Mat. From Black they had obtained a copied key to the warehouse and a preview of when the place would be filling up with cash, precious stones and other valuables that were destined to be flown onwards to locations such as Tokyo, Johannesburg and Dubai. They carefully selected the right day to strike. Before the morning of the robbery, Black had tipped them off that the warehouse vault would contain cash and goods worth as much as £3 million.

The ringleader of this ambitious criminal enterprise was a seasoned South London crook named Micky McAvoy. Fit and flinty, McAvoy came from a family of Irish immigrants in Camberwell and had got his start as a schoolboy, stealing items from the docks and, later, carcasses of beef from a meat warehouse. He was cunning, organized and violent and had been planning the Brink's-Mat job for a year. After letting themselves into the building, McAvoy and his crew quickly restrained the guards. The real prize they were after was in the vault: £1 million in used banknotes. To get into it, they would need a numeric code, and they had been told in advance that, as an added security precaution, each of the two head guards on duty that day would know half of the numbers – meaning that only together could they open it. McAvoy and his men pointed guns at the guards, doused them with gasoline and threatened to set them on fire if they didn't turn over the codes.

Both guards proved eager to cooperate. The only hitch was that one of them could not remember his portion of the code. The thieves rattled a matchbox in his face, but he couldn't remember. They produced a nasty-looking serrated knife and threatened to castrate him. Still nothing. After all of Micky McAvoy's careful planning, it was beginning to look as if this robbery might be a bust. If the crew couldn't get into the vault, there would be no cash; they would have to make do with some scrap silver, traveller's cheques, and whatever else was lying around. In one corner they spotted two pallets piled with neat stacks of cardboard boxes, which did not look especially promising. Desperate to find anything of value, the thieves opened the first box, which was roughly the size of a shoebox, and found that it contained a dozen bars of pure gold.

Rushing to check the other boxes, the robbers realized that they all had the same contents. In total, there were sixty-eight hundred gold bars. Unbeknownst to McAvoy's crew, the gold had recently been collected from a business headquartered in London called Johnson Matthey. In the early 1980s, roughly twenty tonnes of gold passed through the United Kingdom every week. Johnson Matthey, which traced its origins to 1817, was a banking-and-metals concern, with offices in Hatton Garden, London's gold district. It had served as the official refiner for the Bank of England. Surveying this mountain of gold, one of the thieves said, 'We're going to need another van.'

Working quickly and quietly, the Brink's-Mat robbers loaded over two tonnes of gold into a pair of vans. Then, loosening the guards' restraints but warning them not to alert the authorities, they made a very slow getaway. Multiple eyewitnesses would later report having noticed one of the vans creeping through the streets of Hounslow, riding dangerously low on its suspension because it was so overladen with precious metal.

The value of the gold McAvoy and his crew stole that day turned out to be £26 million. Or rather, that is what it was worth at the moment they stole it. After news of the heist broke, it sent shock waves through the bullion market, driving up the price of gold. So by the end of the day, the loot was worth £1 million more. After their clean getaway, however, the thieves were quickly apprehended. When an elite unit of the Metropolitan Police, the Flying Squad, started questioning Brink's-Mat security guards, they quickly zeroed in on Anthony Black. McAvoy had warned Black in advance, 'The only way you're gonna get arrested is if you open your mouth.' But that's exactly what Black did, and soon he had given up McAvoy and the other members of the crew. McAvoy ended up standing trial at the Old Bailey in 1984, along with two of his accomplices. He arranged for several people to provide a false alibi, testifying that he couldn't have committed the robbery because he was elsewhere at the time. It didn't help: he was convicted.

But that was hardly the end of the Brink's-Mat saga. For one thing, the authorities never managed to recover the gold. A haul of that magnitude would necessitate a small army of co-conspirators to hide or move or launder it, so even as McAvoy served his sentence, a wider community of unindicted facilitators undertook the slow and complex process of sanitizing the money and filtering it back into the licit financial system. Each Johnson Matthey bar had distinctive markings, but that was easily fixed by a smelter, which could render the gold completely untraceable. In this manner, much of the Brink's-Mat plunder ended up being sold right back into the gold market in Hatton Garden. Incredibly, a lot of it was purchased, unwittingly, by the very company it had been stolen from, Johnson Matthey. The laundering of the money would be a more complex process involving crooked lawyers and unscrupulous bankers and a variety of fixers willing to lend a hand. Nearly a decade after the robbery, a London woman who ran a modest cigarette shop was convicted of depositing plastic bags full of cash at her local bank, which ended up in a high-interest account in Dublin.

In a turn of events straight out of *The Long Good Friday*, a lot of the laundered Brink's-Mat gold was channelled into London real estate – and, in particular, into the redevelopment of the Docklands. Because McAvoy and many of his associates had grown up around East London, they knew the area intimately and may have liked the idea of devoting the proceeds of a notorious heist to the revitalization of their home turf. Brink's-Mat funds that passed through shell companies and accounts in Liechtenstein, Switzerland and the Channel Islands were later traced to the early development of New Caledonian Wharf, Globe Wharf and Cyclops Wharf, though the criminals did not hold on to any of these interests for long. They got in and out quickly, flipping their holdings and walking away with a nice profit.

Micky McAvoy languished in prison for nearly two decades. But over time he grew anxious that his friends on the outside might not be honouring their fiduciary duties as reliable custodians of his share. In a letter from prison, he promised dire consequences to anyone who crossed him, writing, 'I have no intention of being fucked for my money.' And for whatever reason, beginning not long after the robbery, people connected with the heist started to die. In 1985, a detective investigating the case was stabbed ten times outside the home of one of the co-conspirators. Two years later, an ex-cop looking into what had become of the loot was found in a southeast London car park with an axe in his head. Three years after that, a crook who had allegedly mishandled some of the Brink's-Mat cash was shot dead at his home near Marbella, Spain. In 1993, a businessman who was said to have laundered some of the money was walking with his girlfriend on Marylebone High Street when an assassin pulled up on a motorcycle and shot him in the head. A few years later, a suspected money launderer whose home had been searched during the investigation was shot dead on his yacht off Corfu. Two years after that, a North London jeweller suspected of fencing some of the gold was shot four times on his doorstep in Finchley. Of course, there were always other plausible explanations: many of these men spent long careers in the underworld, where misunderstandings are occasionally settled with violence. But all told, more than a dozen people who were allegedly connected to the robbery turned up dead. The press called it 'the curse of Brink's-Mat'.

It wasn't just the robbers and their accomplices who seemed cursed, either. Since the 1960s, Johnson Matthey had operated a successful banking subsidiary, Johnson Matthey Bank, which was part of a small circle of banks that fixed the price of gold in London. Over the centuries, the Johnson Matthey pedigree had become synonymous with dependability. The loss of the Brink's-Mat gold was not the sort of story that any bank would want to see receiving blanket coverage in the newspapers. It was an embarrassment. But on the heels of the robbery, Johnson Matthey became embroiled in an even greater scandal, and in 1984 the bank collapsed altogether. It turned out that Johnson Matthey had become seriously overextended, racking up hundreds of millions of pounds in bad debts. Some of the senior bankers, it emerged, had been quite careless in making outsized loans to certain clients who proved to be less than reliable. One of those clients was Abdul Shamji.

From his earliest days in the UK, Abdul had evinced a belief that if you have to spend money to make money, and you have to borrow money to spend money, then you had better develop good relationships with your bankers. In private, he would sometimes joke that all you needed to make a fortune in England was to persuade a bank to lend you money. Over the years, Abdul had cultivated an especially close relationship with Johnson Matthey Bank. Like the address of the Gomba Group, on Park Lane, or the Rolls-Royce in which Abdul now commuted from his baronial home, the very name Johnson Matthey, with its fusty aura of British exclusivity, seemed to solidify Abdul's standing as a blue-chip establishment player. This, in turn, helped him cultivate new business, which added to his bottom line, which enabled him to borrow more. A virtuous cycle – or so it appeared. Over the years, Abdul managed to persuade a handful of banks to lend him £35 million. Gomba owed £20 million to Johnson Matthey alone.

When Johnson Matthey collapsed in 1984, the Bank of England stepped in to rescue it, and the Chancellor of the Exchequer decried Johnson Matthey's 'appalling and bizarre record of incompetence and mismanagement'. Soon questions arose about how Abdul Shamji had managed to borrow such a formidable sum. Part of the answer was that his business empire was so international, so diversified and so swathed in corporate secrecy that it had been difficult to audit the many claims he made about his holdings or to suss out what was puffery and what was real. But it seemed also to have been a factor that Abdul had developed an unusually close relationship with one of his bankers: a Johnson Matthey director named Ian Fraser, who happened to head up the loan department. Fraser had a lumbering walk and a comb-over, and he wore oversized tinted glasses. Even by the wayward standards of the 1980s, his general presentation did not inspire a surge of confidence in his integrity.

In the House of Commons, the case came to the attention of a tenacious Labour MP named Brian Sedgemore. Six foot four and a former rugby player, Sedgemore had a reputation for approaching his job as an elected representative with the kind of antagonistic brawn normally reserved for the rugby pitch. Having attended night school to train as a barrister, he had a notably prosecutorial sensibility. Against the backdrop of the Johnson Matthey meltdown, the fraud squad of the Metropolitan Police had started to investigate the dealings between Abdul Shamji and Ian Fraser, and on the floor of the House of Commons, Sedgemore revealed some of the more shocking findings of this inquiry. According to Sedgemore, Abdul Shamji had made one of the spare apartments in the Gomba Group building on Park Lane available to Ian Fraser as a love nest for trysts with young women. The scenario he outlined was tawdry: recognizing that there might be upside in compromising the judgement of the chief loan officer at his bank, Abdul had corrupted him with inappropriate favours, and in exchange, Fraser had been all too ready to authorize outsized loans. The London tabloids, which were not known for their love of banking stories, thrilled to this one, running breathless (and highly conjectural) accounts of quid pro quo 'sex romps' behind the staid facade of 97 Park Lane.

This publicity seems only to have intensified Sedgemore's zeal. There were three ways to account for Ian Fraser's role in this sordid affair, he asserted: 'The first is that he might be a simpleton, the second is that he has turned a blind eye to fraud, and the third is that he is a party to fraud.' Approached for his reaction, Fraser did not exactly offer the kind of comprehensive rebuttal that might have laid the matter to rest. 'While possible errors of judgement can, with hindsight, be identified, I have done nothing dishonest or crooked,' he said vaguely. But even as he left the allegation of 'sex romps' basically undisputed, Fraser insisted that his decisions about whether to issue loans had not been influenced by any 'improper considerations'.

If Sedgemore was tough on Fraser, he was even more withering when it came to Abdul Shamji, whom he described as a 'crook'. Abdul was more of a counterpuncher than Fraser, however, and he categorically denied the accusations, saying that the whole story was 'baseless' and that he had been made a scapegoat for the collapse of Johnson Matthey Bank. In the midst of the investigation, he requested a meeting with an associate of Sedgemore, perhaps hoping that he could explain his position and persuade the MP to call off this inquisition. They met at the Pavilion bar of the Grosvenor House Hotel, a short walk down Park Lane from the Gomba building. What actually transpired between the two men at this rendezvous would become a matter of dispute, but suffice it to say that the encounter did not go as Abdul had hoped. After the meeting, Sedgemore announced, with great indignation, that Abdul had tried to 'buy' him – offering a bribe to call off his crusade. Abdul furiously denied this accusation, calling it a 'load of rubbish'. He was a family man, he pointed out, and 'very saddened' by this impugning of his integrity.

Having spent so many years and so much money trying to cultivate an aura of well-to-do English respectability, Abdul suddenly found his eligibility for the club being openly questioned. 'I have always understood that Victorian values were about respect for family life and a fear of God,' Sedgemore declared. 'But according to Mr Abdul Shamji, they are about bribery, corruption, fraud, and tarts for bankers.'

To repay his debts, Abdul was forced to sell his interest in Wembley Stadium. It must have stung, to hold such a prize in his hands for a brief moment before having to relinquish it. As the receivers appointed by Johnson Matthey searched for other assets that they could repossess, their attention turned to the family mansion in Kingston upon Thames. But they discovered that ownership of the house had been transferred to a company that was registered offshore and itself owned by a trust. The trust permitted the Shamjis to live in the house, but legally speaking the house did not belong to any of them and thus could not be repossessed. In a court proceeding, Abdul asserted that, though he had once boasted of a net worth of more than £100 million, and may have trotted out such figures in persuading banks to let him borrow from them, he actually possessed *no* significant assets that could now be used to satisfy his debts. All that he owned, Abdul said in court, was 'champagne, clothes and jewellery'.

It was around this time that the pillars of Britain's Conservative Party rather abruptly stopped taking Abdul's calls. When Margaret Thatcher was questioned about her long-standing friendship with him, she responded, with her usual facility for syntactical obfuscation, that it would 'be neither practicable nor reasonable for me to answer questions about where and when I meet private named individuals', and refused even to acknowledge that she knew Abdul outside of a few passing encounters at official events, much less to offer any defence of his character.

In the autumn of 1986, the programme *World in Action*, which aired on ITV, devoted two whole episodes to an investigation of Abdul, exploring his questionable business practices and his close ties with the Tories. 'This is the story of Abdul Shamji's house of cards,' the narrator intoned. 'How he managed to build a business empire of ships and apartments, offices and factories, hotels and theatres, and even Wembley Stadium – almost entirely on other people's money.' The former executive Michael Hendry was interviewed. 'The appearance of the Gomba Group was evidenced by the chauffeur-driven Rolls-Royce, the yachts, the executive jet charters, the Park Lane offices,' he said. 'The reality was wages not getting paid... suppliers not being paid... writs being issued. That was the reality.' The programme cited a high court judge who had described Abdul as 'a lonely trader who played his cards very close to his chest, using prevarication and falsehoods to advance his business interests'. Because Abdul refused to be interviewed, a reporter ambushed him outside his office, accompanied by a cameraman, and proceeded to chase him down Park Lane.

'Are you still in contact with Mrs Thatcher?' the reporter asked.

'Bastards!' Abdul shouted, lunging at the camera. 'I'll grab that damn thing!'

As it turned out, Abdul had personally guaranteed £5 million of the loans that Johnson Matthey made to Gomba. In the ensuing fight to shelter his own assets, he hired one of the most famous barristers in England, George Carman. Abdul had promised that Gomba would ultimately pay back any debts that were owed, but he continued to maintain that he possessed nothing that could be seized as security. In a related proceeding, his legal team insisted that he had 'few assets, lives in a house which is not his own, has no personal bank account, and has no income at all'. It may be that after his experience in Uganda, Abdul had adopted a reflexive furtiveness, a disinclination to let anyone see all of what he had, for fear that they might try to confiscate it – a tendency to claim that £55 and two suitcases was really all he owned. Asked in court whether there might be other funds outside of England, hiding in a Swiss bank account, perhaps, he testified that he had no Swiss bank account. But this was untrue. He did have a Swiss bank account. Six of them.

Eventually the truth came out, and after his lies were exposed, in 1989, Abdul was convicted in the Old Bailey for committing perjury. The judge in the case sounded almost impressed when he described Abdul's 'ability and determination both in hiding your assets and concealing the truth'. When it came to those secret bank accounts, the judge said, 'You lied like a trooper.'

As he received his sentence – fifteen months in prison – Abdul looked stricken and incredulous. George Carman immediately requested bail pending an appeal, but the judge denied it, and Abdul Shamji was escorted out of the courtroom and directly to the cells. The headlines were stark: 'Millionaire Jailed for Lying'. At the time, his youngest son, Akbar, was seventeen.

Chapter 8

PRODIGAL SON

MUHAMMAD ALI WAS STILL a formidable presence when he visited London in the summer of 1993, tall and broad and solid as an oak. But he moved slowly, with a stiffness in his gait, and when he spoke, his words could slur. A decade earlier, the three-time heavyweight champion of the world had been diagnosed with Parkinson's disease. By his own acknowledgement, he probably had not helped matters by taking what he estimated to be a million punches over the course of his boxing career. But he continued to live a full and joyful life, even as he was ravaged by the disease. A year earlier he had turned fifty and been feted onstage at a televised bash, where he was serenaded by Diana Ross and Whitney Houston. His limbs, which had once moved at hummingbird speed, didn't work the way they used to. His face, which had previously been almost cartoonishly animated, was now often expressionless for long periods of time. It could occasionally seem as if he might not be following what was going on around him – until suddenly his eyes would narrow and he would break into that famous smile.

The boxer had come to London for the premiere of *Ali*, a one-man show featuring the actor and writer Geoffrey C. Ewing, which depicted a series of moments from Ali's life: the surprise victory over Sonny Liston in 1964; the decision to jettison his 'slave name', Cassius Clay, and reinvent himself as Muhammad Ali; getting stripped of his title after he refused to be drafted for the Vietnam War. The play had enjoyed a successful run off-Broadway in New York, and now it was transferring to the Mermaid, a theatre next to Blackfriars Bridge on the north bank of the Thames.

In Shakespeare's day, this part of London had been a vibrant theatrical hub, anchored by the original Blackfriars Theatre, where plays were performed by candlelight, indoors. The Mermaid Tavern, where a fraternity of Elizabethan dramatists and poets are believed to have congregated, was nearby, and in 1613 Shakespeare himself purchased a house 'abutting upon a street leading down to Puddle Wharf'. A place called Puddle Dock still existed by the time Ali visited nearly four hundred years later, but the area's fortunes had changed. By the eighteenth century, the centre of gravity for theatre in London had already shifted to the West End, and the area around Puddle Dock was more associated with commerce than the arts: with the rise of the British Empire, this whole stretch of the river had become dominated by shipping. In the Blitz, during the Second World War, the area was heavily bombed, and after the war, it lay mostly derelict for decades, still pockmarked with bomb sites that had never been cleaned up. Puddle Dock was one of them: a warehouse had stood on the little dock jutting out into the river, but it was decimated by a German bomb, and only the ghostly skeleton of the ruined outer walls remained. In between was a kind of junkyard that was open to the elements. Stuff washed up there from the river, and scavengers would sort through the flotsam, searching for lost treasure or for driftwood to burn. 'Puddle Dock is no romantic riverside pleasance. It's a dump,' the *Daily Mirror* observed in 1956. 'It sprawls muddily by the Thames Bank, shadowed by Blackfriars Bridge, just inside the City. Discriminating bums, hoboes and tramps avoid it.'

The only reason the *Mirror* saw fit to remark on Puddle Dock in the first place was that a well-known London thespian named Bernard Miles had decided to build a new theatre there. Miles was a charismatic, Oxford-educated dreamer who had found success on the stage and on television and initially launched what would become the Mermaid Theatre company as a scrappy troupe that held productions in the back garden of his home. The notion of building the first new theatre in centuries in this part of London – as opposed to the West End – was radical on its own, never mind the fact that Miles intended to construct it on a bomb site. But he loved the idea of creating a new theatre destination on the hallowed ground where Shakespeare once walked. To raise money, he sold bricks (a symbolic novelty – own a little piece of the building) and enlisted celebrity friends, including Laurence Olivier, to help persuade people to buy them. By early 1959, the building was finally complete: a brand-new theatre with a single, steeply raked tier of seating that could accommodate an audience of six hundred. It was an innovative space built directly into the shell of the old bombed-out warehouse, with a concrete barrel vault ceiling.

After it opened, the Mermaid was home to many successful productions, and great actors of the day, from Julie Walters to Ian McKellen, performed there. But in 1981, Bernard Miles oversaw a costly redevelopment of the theatre. Once again he sold novelty bricks, this time for a tenner apiece. But it was not enough. Miles was an inspired showman, but he had never been particularly good with money, and now, to finance the renovation, he and his wife ploughed their own savings into the theatre. He was bitter about this. He had helped bring new life to the area, and he had watched as the City of London grew and flourished as a financial centre, anchored – at least in his view – by this cultural polestar he had created. 'The richest square mile in the world,' he complained, couldn't look after one of its 'most precious children'. In a biography of Miles, Alan Strachan writes that the City had changed around him and was 'now ruled by a breed utterly removed from the values of 1959. It was a much more venal world.'

Miles was desperate, and close to destitution, when in 1983 he finally sold the Mermaid to Abdul Shamji. At the time, Abdul seemed very much on the ascendant, his scandals and court battles still a couple of years away. What exactly possessed him to want to own a theatre at all was unclear; he was too maniacally focused on work to be much of a theatregoer. And he already had two storied West End theatres – the Duchess and the Garrick – in his portfolio. Perhaps, like the Monopoly player he was, Abdul just couldn't resist the idea of augmenting his holdings. Or he may simply have smelled a bargain. Because the Mermaid still had outstanding debts of £650,000, it was effectively a distressed asset. Though Bernard Miles had spent more than £2 million to upgrade the whole facility, Abdul was able to purchase the Mermaid for just £675,000.

Technically, Abdul would not own the land upon which the theatre sat, which belonged to the City: what he was purchasing from Miles was a rent-free ninety-seven-year lease. After the theatre's founder was cast out and the Gomba Group took over, the Mermaid had a few ups and downs. It staged a series of shows, some of them modestly successful, but also cycled through a succession of management companies. Between changes of management, the theatre would go dark for long periods, with no shows at all. But in 1993, the Mermaid announced that Gomba Holdings had appointed a new general manager who would oversee a bold resurgence of the theatre: it was the boss's youngest son, Akbar Shamji. He was twenty-one years old. His big inaugural production would be *Ali*.

In a press interview on the occasion of his ascendance to the job, Akbar said that his father had purchased the Mermaid not with the thought that it would be any sort of profit-making venture but as an expression of his commitment to England. Whereas the two older Shamji brothers, Ryaz and Alim, had gone to university in the United States, Akbar had earned a spot at one of the most exclusive training grounds for the British elite: the University of Cambridge. He was a student at Sidney Sussex College, a cluster of manicured courtyards and ornate halls that traced its origins to 1596 and counted Oliver Cromwell among its notable alumni.

Akbar studied history, but according to people who knew him at university, he was not a diligent student. Instead, he was a bit of a playboy. 'He was very pretty,' a woman who was briefly involved with him at Cambridge recalled. Rich, entitled and charming, he tried to cultivate an air of mystery that could at times seem silly to his classmates. 'He was sort of a posh boy who wanted to be a gangster,' the woman said. 'He would say things like "There's stuff about me you don't want to know."' Akbar might very well have been referring to the recent incarceration of his father, but the woman did not know about that at the time. At any rate, she dismissed such talk as Akbar 'just being a kind of slightly shit teenage fantasist'. Akbar dabbled in theatre, acting in a Christmas pantomime by the Cambridge Footlights, a production of *Ali Baba and the Forty Thieves*. He played a swindler named Honest Achmed, who lures Ali into buying overrated junk.

Cambridge is a great cycling city, where students tend to get around on bikes. Akbar got around in a BMW. Even in this bastion of privilege, the BMW represented such an obvious marker of affluence that he would occasionally dissemble, telling people that it was somebody else's car he was borrowing. He joined a band. Their name was Muthafunk. He played the bongos. They mostly did local gigs at Cambridge colleges, but at one point Abdul let them perform in the lobby of the Mermaid Theatre. According to Muthafunk's saxophonist, Sanjiv Bhattacharya, Akbar rarely came to rehearsals, preferring to just show up for the gigs.

Having lived his whole life, apart from that tumultuous first year, on British soil, Akbar was blessed with a comfort in his own skin that is normally the prerogative of the native-born, and might have eluded his older siblings, who were more readily marked as immigrants. Whereas Ryaz and Alim both came off in person as cautious and staid, Akbar had a magnetic insouciance. The older brothers seemed 'monochrome', Bhattacharya recalled, whereas 'Akbar was full Technicolour'. He had the easygoing manner of a young man who knew that he was clever, wealthy and attractive and assumed that life was going to be kind to him. In a 1993 article about how he now stood poised, having only just finished classes at Cambridge, to take control of a celebrated London theatre, *The Times* observed that 'Akbar Shamji enters this unknown territory in the manner of a man whistling as he strides through the jungle.'

Within the Shamji family, the fifteen-month period that the patriarch had spent locked up, between 1989 and 1990, was regarded as a dire injustice. Abdul had given everything to his adopted country, and the country had repaid his gifts with grotesque indignity. In Abdul's telling, he may simply have flown too close to the sun. When Johnson Matthey Bank went under, a compromised British establishment had been looking for a fall guy. 'Let me remind you that *Gomba* did not go bust,' Abdul would fume. 'It was Johnson Matthey Bankers who went bust!' Through no fault of his own, he contended, he had become 'a convenient excuse' for the bank's downfall. Abdul was not wrong to bristle, as he often did, at the casual racism that was a regular feature of British life, and it was painful for him to have been rejected so unsentimentally by the very aristocratic elites he had laboured to cultivate. But in the self-absolving alternative history that the Shamjis concocted, the undeniable reality – of clubby gatekeeping and British bigotry – was whipped up into an operatic conspiracy in which Abdul was a blameless martyr who had been cruelly punished for the simple crime of ascending beyond his station.

One lesson the father seemed to have drawn from this whole ordeal was that his own high profile may have been partially to blame for his downfall. He would never again grant the sort of fulsome press interviews that he had accommodated with enthusiasm in the past. Akbar would intimate that his father might have given up on business in England altogether, saying that he had taken 'his Monopoly board' back to East Africa. Idi Amin, after a murderous and anarchic seven years in power, had finally fled into exile in 1979, and Abdul was now in the process of trying to reclaim all the holdings that Uganda had expropriated from him back in 1972.

To pay his Johnson Matthey debts, Abdul had been forced to sell his interest in the Duchess and Garrick theatres. But he was able to hold on to the Mermaid. After Akbar was installed as general manager, in early 1993, a man named Marc Sinden was summoned there to meet with him. Like the theatre's founder, Bernard Miles, Sinden was an actor who had worked in film and on the stage. Now he wanted to try something different, and the Mermaid happened to be looking for an artistic director. Sinden was impressed by Akbar when they met: he was very young but poised and self-assured. He dressed smartly and commuted between the Gomba offices on Park Lane and the theatre at Puddle Dock in the family's Rolls-Royce Corniche. With exquisite manners, Akbar had the aspect 'of an English gentleman', Sinden thought. He spoke in breezy, somewhat grandiloquent terms about his desire to infuse 'into the psychology of the world of commerce some of the humanity of the world of arts'.

After that preliminary interview, Sinden was invited, along with his wife, to dinner at the Shamji manse in Kingston upon Thames. He was struck immediately by the grandeur of the property. The house had been constructed with beams and bricks transported from a much older dwelling in Bury St Edmunds and rebuilt piece by piece by the Earl of Suffolk in 1901. One of the first things Sinden beheld upon entering the home was a giant model, in carved ivory, of the Taj Mahal. At dinner, Abdul completely dominated the conversation. His manner was punchy and defensive. 'I'm a Ugandan Asian,' he told Sinden, watching him closely for a reaction. 'Do you have a problem with that?' Everyone else in the family seemed cowed, Sinden thought. Akbar's mother, Zarina, was polite but hardly spoke. And Akbar, who had seemed so cocksure in their earlier meeting, now appeared to shrink at his father's table. 'I can't express how in awe he was,' Sinden said.

It is easy to charm a person who talks too much: all you have to do is listen. Sinden spent most of that evening politely nodding and agreeing with his voluble host, and not long afterwards he was appointed artistic director of the Mermaid. The theatre had just launched the Muhammad Ali show. Bringing the production to London had been Akbar's idea. He had no special affinity for boxing, but he seemed drawn to the star power of Ali. Akbar proved to have a knack for publicity and an instinct for how to orchestrate a glamorous occasion. In the interests of promoting the show and getting press coverage, the Shamjis had arranged for the champ himself to fly to London for the premiere.

The champ wanted £10,000 for his trouble, which the Shamjis agreed to pay. With all the expenses associated with launching and promoting the show, the family decided to raise outside money and approached a former boxer turned businessman named Tony Breen. A self-professed 'Ali freak', Breen was happy to contribute, seeing this as an opportunity to meet his hero. He had one stipulation, however. The theatre business is fraught with risk. Most productions lose money, but on the rare occasion when a show really hits, it can generate outsized returns for investors. So underwriting a play is a bit like buying a lottery ticket. For *Ali*, the Shamjis agreed with Breen, in writing, that his investment would be secured. What this meant was that if the show turned into a hit, his upside would be limited, and they would take the lion's share. But if the show *lost* money, Breen would still get his investment back. On these terms, he agreed to contribute £35,000. Breen liked Akbar and found him persuasive. 'We really hit it off,' he said, noting that, had things turned out differently, 'we might have been friends for life'.

Ali arrived at Heathrow Airport, and Breen went to pick him up and ferry him to Park Lane, where the Shamjis had worked some connection to arrange for comped rooms at the Grosvenor House Hotel, where Abdul had once allegedly tried to bribe a Member of Parliament. 'That was the way they worked,' Breen said. 'They would use the influence and the publicity power of whatever they were doing to get favours.' Akbar, with his to-the-manner-born nonchalance, wasn't starstruck or grovelling or tongue-tied in the presence of his celebrity guest. On the contrary, Breen thought, he seemed 'pretty cool with Ali'.

On the night of the premiere, Ali pulled up outside the Mermaid in a white Rolls-Royce and was immediately mobbed by fans. The event had been conceived as a fundraising gala, with proceeds from the £125-ticket sales going to support a show business charity, the Grand Order of Water Rats. Akbar was beaming, dressed in black tie and – in a Michael Jackson flourish – white socks. The producers arranged for Ali to sign a pair of boxing gloves, which they planned to display in a glass case in the Mermaid's foyer. After the show, Akbar installed all around the theatre pictures of himself posing with the champ, just as his father had done with his photos of Margaret Thatcher. As Sinden recalled, 'There were photographs *everywhere* of Akbar with Ali.'

But the play flopped. One article suggested that British audiences would not be interested in 'a show which seems American to its core' and pointed out that the sheer size of the Mermaid, with its six hundred seats, made the theatre 'feel cavernously empty when there are few people in it'. The play 'did nothing at the box office', Tony Breen acknowledged. It quickly closed. As if to compound the humiliation, after the gala, thieves broke into the Mermaid through a window and stole the £15,000 that had been raised for charity – along with the boxing gloves signed by Ali. Later, Breen would wonder if there wasn't something suspicious about the theft that night, but at the time he just felt sympathetic with the Shamjis over the failure of the play. 'Fucking hell,' he told Akbar. 'That's a shame.'

Nevertheless, Breen did want his money back. All of it, as they had agreed. At first Akbar told him that the family would 'sort it out', that his father was just 'organizing' the funds. But the Shamjis didn't come through with the money. Breen had a printing business that was doing well, but not so well that a shortfall of £35,000 would not cause him some anxiety. As Akbar and his brother Alim continued to prevaricate, Breen considered legal action. But he had learned that the Gomba Group was merely a holding company, so even if he could prevail in a lawsuit, it might be difficult to actually force anyone to pay him.

It was for this reason that Breen decided, in his words, to 'get a little bit heavy with them'. He was a boxer himself and could be intimidating when circumstances required it. As the bonhomie he had enjoyed with Akbar gave way to impatience, and then anger, Breen began showing up at the Gomba offices on Park Lane unannounced. At one point he suggested that if they didn't have the cash, the family should just give him their Rolls-Royce in lieu of payment. But they couldn't do that, Akbar and Alim protested: their father would never allow it. If the Shamjis were so rich, Breen wondered, why couldn't they pay him what they owed? They did have an enormous family fortune, Akbar conceded. The problem was that it had been illegally expropriated by Idi Amin back in 1972. 'That was the main excuse for everything,' Breen recalled. ' "My dad's owed £30 million from the Ugandan government." ' Increasingly desperate, Breen walked into the office one day and discovered Alim sitting at a desk that was covered in a big collection of jewellery. There were diamonds, gold rings, watches. The style was a bit garish and outdated, but there was obvious value there.

'I'll take this,' Breen said, scooping everything into a bag.

'You can't do that!' Alim objected. 'It belongs to my dad.' But his dad wasn't there, and Alim was meek-tempered and not the kind of person who was going to physically restrain Tony Breen.

'I walked out with a bag of jewels,' Breen said, 'and that's all I ever got.'

He sold many of the items to jewellery stores, piecemeal, feeling self-conscious about it, 'like a burglar'. There was one piece in particular, a platinum watch, that seemed like the sort of thing that would have been presented as a gift to favoured clients. It was emblazoned with a name: Johnson Matthey Bank.

As all of this was happening, Marc Sinden was learning that when it came to the Shamji family, unpaid debts were not so much an anomaly as the rule. He had not been in his role as the Mermaid's artistic director for long when he realized that 'something was very wrong' at the theatre. The Mermaid did not produce shows in-house but tended instead to enter partnerships with outside theatre companies. After collecting the ticket sales for a show, however, the Shamjis often failed to pay the companies their share. Frequently, they did not pay the theatre's own staff. Or they did pay, but with cheques that bounced. On payday, some Mermaid employees would actually run to the bank, hoping to be the first to deposit their cheques before the account ran dry. Vendors went unpaid so frequently that many quit doing business with the theatre altogether. The Mermaid's chief electrician, Lorraine Richards, couldn't purchase the light bulbs she needed, because suppliers who had been stiffed would no longer sell to her. During one performance, by a Shakespeare troupe, several lamps started randomly strobing. 'It was a very psychedelic effect... for *The Merchant of Venice*,' the director of the show recalled.

Things got absurd. The Mermaid ran out of toilet paper, and staffers cut up rolls of paper towels and offered them to theatre patrons, apologetically. The phones didn't work, because the bills were unpaid. In the dead of winter, the heating system quit functioning, because the Shamjis had neglected the gas bill, and it grew so cold in the auditorium that patrons could see their own breath. When a leak developed in the roof, nobody fixed it, and rain drenched the seats. Bailiffs began showing up with 'nauseating regularity', Sinden remembered. As the bills piled up, he would make pilgrimages, just as Tony Breen had, to Park Lane.

'You walked in and there was the father, with his back to the window, behind this vast desk, looking like a short, fat Hollywood mogul,' Sinden recalled. It seemed faintly ridiculous to visit one of the most opulent addresses in London and beg for funds to pay for light bulbs and toilet paper. As the Gomba executive Michael Hendry observed, Abdul was simply 'unable to come to terms with the fact that if you had something, you had to pay for it'. In these meetings, Sinden sometimes fixated on one glaring incongruity in Abdul's presentation: there was a giant hole in the ceiling of his office. This was not some minor dent. It was a great void, perhaps six feet across. Nobody ever acknowledged it in Sinden's presence or offered any explanation for how it had come to be there. Or fixed it. Over time, Sinden came to see, in that hole, a metaphor for the entire Shamji operation.

It increasingly seemed that there was something fishy going on at the Mermaid. The Shamjis had clearly invested money in the place, yet they didn't seem particularly interested in putting on plays. 'There was a fully equipped restaurant and kitchen, all stainless steel and gleaming, that had never been used. There were piles of monogrammed cutlery with the Mermaid logo, and china plates all still in their boxes,' Sinden said. 'It was as though I'd walked into a hospital that was fully equipped but they'd forgotten to put the patients in it.'

Tony Breen agreed. 'You had this enormous building that was kind of a white elephant sitting in the middle of London, with lots of money being spent in it,' he said. 'But it didn't seem to do anything commercial – and they didn't seem to care.' Breen was starting to wonder whether the whole enterprise might be some sort of money-laundering operation. (A lawyer for Akbar Shamji denied this claim, calling it 'absurd'.)

Sinden developed a different theory. The Mermaid sat on land that had become much more valuable than the theatre itself. He discovered that a clause existed in the original contract between the Mermaid and the City of London Corporation, which owned the land, stipulating that if the theatre remained 'dark' for twelve months out of any two-year period, then the leaseholder – in this case the Shamjis – could apply for a change of use for the site. The Mermaid occupied such a unique physical position, Sinden observed: 'This island in the middle of the City of London – that would be worth a lot of money to the right person.'

One evening, he was working late at Puddle Dock, contending

with a mountain of unpaid invoices, when he realized that the air-conditioning wasn't working. Alone in the theatre, Sinden went looking for the room that contained the A/C unit. It was housed in a utility cupboard he had never had occasion to visit, and when he got inside he encountered an unusual sight: five metal filing cabinets.

'Weird place to keep filing cabinets,' Sinden thought.

Four hours later, he had not left the utility cupboard and was sitting cross-legged on the floor, surrounded by piles of paper. None of the accounting for the theatre added up, and there were multiple corporate entities and bank accounts in different names. Sinden was no accountant, but he was beginning to believe that he might have stumbled onto 'a gigantic fraud'.

When the Shamjis originally took over the theatre a decade earlier, they had created the Mermaid Theatre Company to manage it. This new subsidiary of Gomba Holdings proceeded to rack up a lot of debts – because the Shamjis refused to pay their bills. Soon the theatre company owed more than a quarter of a million pounds. In addition, the family had deducted more than £100,000 from the pay cheques of employees who worked at the theatre, for the ostensible purpose of making National Insurance contributions. But the family didn't actually pay the money to the government; they just took it out of the cheques and used it to bankroll the business. When creditors tried to force the Mermaid Theatre Company to pay up, they were unsuccessful – because the Mermaid Theatre Company had no assets. The company was just a subsidiary of Gomba Holdings, and Gomba Holdings didn't have any assets, either, apart from the lease on the theatre. After accumulating this huge number of debts, the Shamjis simply dissolved the Mermaid Theatre Company, firing the staff without redundancy pay. As Tony Breen put it, 'When things go tits up, they'd just liquidate the company.'

After the demise of the Mermaid Theatre Company, for an interval the theatre had gone dark. But then it reopened, under the management of a new company, this one called Comfortcall. Except that Comfortcall was also a subsidiary of Gomba Holdings and was also run by the Shamjis. Comfortcall followed the same pattern:

running up huge debts, refusing to pay them, then going out of business, only to be succeeded by a *third* company, Quorumcrest, and starting the game all over again. 'Phone calls weren't answered, faxes weren't paid attention to, registered recorded delivery letters were returned,' recalled Bettina Jonic, who ran a theatre company that launched a production at the Mermaid but never received the box office proceeds. After she pursued legal action against Quorumcrest, bailiffs raided Gomba's offices. But they couldn't find anything to seize – because Quorumcrest had no assets.

Abdul Shamji had built his empire on debt, and it now appeared that he had enlisted his sons in following the family modus operandi. Akbar 'was his father manqué', Sinden concluded. 'He wanted to be like his father. But the father was a crook, simple as that. If you shook hands with him, you'd count your fingers afterwards.' It saddened Sinden to think of poor Bernard Miles, who, after giving everything he had to the theatre, ended up dying basically penniless while the Shamjis repurposed the place for this scam. One evening, a few weeks after his discovery of the filing cabinets, Sinden was at a dinner party when he was randomly introduced to a detective superintendent at the City of London's fraud squad. When Sinden happened to mention that he had become suspicious about his employers, the detective confided, 'We've been after those bastards for years.'

Cautiously and very quietly, Sinden began to cooperate with authorities, making copies of bank statements and other bits of paperwork that he found stashed in the filing cabinets at the theatre. But he must have raised suspicions, because one day he was summoned to Park Lane, where a furious Abdul accused him of being a whistleblower. In June 1994, just over a year after he had arrived at the Mermaid, he was fired by the Shamjis, who cited 'conduct prejudicial to the interests of Gomba'. By that time, Quorumcrest had followed its predecessors and gone out of business – with debts of £180,000 and no assets. As for Akbar, he had resigned his position as general manager and disappeared from London altogether.

Chapter 9

SUSPICION OF MURDER

AKBAR SHAMJI WAS SUMMONED for a second round of questioning with police about the death of Zac Brettler on 4 March 2020, the day London reported its first death related to Covid-19. The city felt suspended in that eerie moment when a tsunami is visible on the horizon but has not yet hit. Thirty-two new cases of the virus were reported in England that day, bringing the number of confirmed cases in the UK to eighty-five. Supermarkets were overrun with panicked shoppers stockpiling groceries. The government of Prime Minister Boris Johnson had hinted at the prospect of a lockdown. But at the same time, Johnson himself was reassuring, urging citizens to 'go about our normal daily lives' and gamely advising that 'the best thing you can do is to wash your hands with soap and water while singing Happy Birthday twice'. The previous week, a Singaporean student had been attacked on Oxford Street by a group of Londoners who punched and kicked him, shouting, 'I don't want your coronavirus in my country!'

When he was first interrogated, in December, Akbar had lied to the police, and they had made it clear that they knew he was lying. In his account of the evening of 28 November, he had completely left out the detail about how, after leaving Riverwalk, he had driven back to the building, gone up to Verinder Sharma's flat, come back down, walked around to the Thames, and peered into the river at the very spot where Zac had plunged into it. When the detectives confronted Akbar with the fact that they had CCTV footage showing him doing all of this, he had stammered, by way of explanation, 'It's a nice bit of the river.' This was just a random smoke break he had decided to take at three in the morning, he contended, adding, ridiculously, 'I spend a lot of time outside.'

The detectives made little effort to hide their scepticism. Instead they had focused on another inconsistency in his story. Akbar maintained that the reason he had returned to the apartment was to 'say goodnight'.

'Who did you speak to when you went back up?' one of the detectives asked.

'Verinder and Zac,' Akbar said.

'And what were they doing?'

'Chatting.'

'About what?'

'Life. Parents. Business. Getting off drugs,' he said.

Was he completely sure they were *both* there? the detective asked. Akbar went silent.

'This is very important.'

'No, I understand,' he said quickly. 'I'm almost certain that I spoke to both of them, and we hugged, and said goodnight.' He had a specific memory of Verinder and Zac getting ready for bed before he left. 'There was use of the bathroom... I think there was teeth brushing.'

'So how did you say goodbye to each person?'

'Well, there was a hug for sure.'

'For each person?'

'Yeah,' Akbar said. 'It was almost, like, a collective hug.'

Like his father, Akbar could occasionally exhibit a somewhat casual relationship to the truth. Even so, it is intriguing to wonder what he figured might happen when he related this story to the police in that first December interview, because again he was lying – and again they knew it. Akbar couldn't have hugged Zac goodnight, because the CCTV feeds to which the police now had access made it clear that by the time Akbar arrived back at apartment 504, Zac had already gone off the balcony.

It was a cold, wet, miserable late-winter day on 4 March. The interrogation began at lunchtime, at Charing Cross Police Station. The detectives offered no explanation as to why it had taken them three months to invite Akbar back for further questioning. He had been free to enjoy the holidays with his family. But the officers pointed out in no uncertain terms that Akbar had been arrested 'on suspicion of murder'. They made it clear that they were not at all convinced that Zac's death was 'a cut-and-dried suicidal jump', and assured him that he wouldn't be sitting there if he weren't a suspect.

Akbar was accompanied by his lawyer. One of the detectives, Alex Mallen, commenced his line of questioning by saying, 'There are some inconsistencies in what you've said which don't necessarily tie into what we have seen in the investigation.' This was a rather cordial way of letting a suspect know that the police were aware that they'd been lied to. Perhaps Akbar had been flustered in his earlier interview, Mallen volunteered generously. 'I suspect being arrested for murder is quite something. You may have been nervous.' If indeed this was simply a matter of a heroin-addicted suicidal fabulist who chose to end his life, Mallen pointed out, there was no reason for Akbar to be anything but forthcoming. 'Now is the opportunity for you to be truthful,' he said.

'I really don't think I've got anything,' Akbar said. He was worried that he might inadvertently say too much, he explained, and he indicated that Daniela was concerned about such a possibility as well. 'Because I tend to talk too much.'

'It seems like you do want to talk,' Mallen suggested.

'I really have said everything,' Akbar insisted. 'I poured my heart out the first time.'

But the discrepancies between Akbar's account and the known facts posed 'a little bit of an issue for us', Mallen interjected. 'Bearing in mind what you have been arrested for.'

'I understand it's serious, yeah, obviously,' Akbar said. But in truth he had just been a 'bit player' in this story, he suggested, and he had 'really tried to be super helpful'.

One of the investigators, Natalie Wallen, pulled up the video of Akbar coming around the side of Riverwalk and looking into the Thames.

'That's me, I guess,' he murmured glumly.

'So you agree that's you?'

'Yeah,' Akbar said.

'You *don't* know that's you,' his lawyer interrupted. 'Because we can't *see* that's you.'

'I can't see that's me,' Akbar repeated obediently.

'My client doesn't know that it is him,' the lawyer said.

'This is the river wall,' Mallen said, 'and you have looked over just *here*.' He indicated the location where Zac had just plunged into the water. 'It's a great coincidence, is it not?' He looked at Akbar. 'It seems a great coincidence to me, and I don't believe in coincidences.'

Akbar said that he normally didn't believe in coincidences, either, but that this really *was* a coincidence. In any case, he hadn't seen Zac in the river, or known that he was in the river.

The interrogators did not seem convinced. 'Let me remind you that intentionally misleading the police could be considered an offence in itself,' Wallen said. Even if Akbar was not ultimately charged with murder, the detectives cautioned him, he could still be charged with perverting the course of justice.

At this point, Akbar seemed to try a different tack, summoning a bit of huffy indignation. He was *extremely* troubled to hear such *scurrilous* insinuations that he might in *any* way try to mislead the authorities or be *remotely* dishonest or uncooperative, he said. He had simply been very tired on the night in question and may have confused a few details in his retelling of events.

'If I'd had a night like this,' Wallen said dryly, 'I would remember it.'

In addition to Akbar's visit to the river, the impossibility of the timeline he presented and his farcical dissembling, the police had another ground for suspicion. When they initially interviewed Akbar, they had asked to see his telephone, and he had surrendered it to them. Now they informed him that they had downloaded its contents. 'It must have been fascinating reading,' Akbar said awkwardly. 'Slightly embarrassing that you know me this well.'

If this was a joke, the cops didn't laugh. What concerned them, they said, was that Akbar appeared to have deleted some of his messages before turning over the device. 'Was there anyone you called that made you think you needed to delete those messages?' Wallen asked.

'No,' Akbar said, before adding, 'Unless I was hiding something from my wife. But I doubt it.'

Wallen pulled up a spreadsheet displaying the phone's contents, and pointed out that Akbar appeared to have deleted some of the data starting on 21 October and ending on 29 November. 'That's just over a month before this happened up until the day after Zac has come off the balcony,' Wallen said. 'Why would you have deleted call data from that period?'

'I've no idea,' Akbar said. 'I don't recall.' He did delete messages from time to time, he mentioned, but this was just good housekeeping or a way to get rid of anything embarrassing, such as 'naked photos'. He purged the phone periodically, he said, and may have randomly done so 'on that day'.

Hours after Zac died?

To Akbar, that was just another coincidence.

He appeared to have deleted all his messages with Verinder Sharma in the month leading up to Zac's death but not his messages with Zac. And Verinder, who also surrendered his phone, had taken no such precautions, so police were able to access Akbar's messages with him anyway. What emerged from these exchanges between the three men was a picture of a gathering crisis. When Akbar made his trip to Turkey, Zac really had been calling and texting him frantically; about that, he appeared to be telling the truth. Zac had said that he needed to see Akbar. These clues appeared to buttress Akbar and Verinder's claim that Zac was a depressed kid who had simply killed himself in the early hours of 29 November.

But there were also messages indicating that Verinder had grown unhappy with the boy he knew as Zac Ismailov. As evidence, text messages can be fiendishly difficult to parse. It's a distinctive medium, different from spoken language and also from other modes of writing, such as letters or emails. Texts can be intimate and informal, like pillow talk, and often cursory – full of shorthand, abbreviations, typos, emojis and indecipherable allusions. But to anyone reading the texts between Akbar and Zac, it was clear that something had gone badly wrong between Zac and Verinder.

On the second-to-last day of Zac's life, 27 November, Akbar sent him a message:

> Zac, you have all the information you need already but you have not thought it through and you really should think it through for yourself but to give you some pointers: V has risked his life and freedom to have the authority he has, people should show him reciprocal kindness to the kindness he has shown. You have intimate knowledge of the life he lives and the roads he's taking now versus the ones he has taken to get where he is, you have ignored all of this against the background of offering support for his children and making promises and commitments and not coming through on them even after he was able to house you.

Verinder was entitled to something from Zac, Akbar seemed to be suggesting, some sort of 'reciprocal kindness', after everything he had done for the boy. In fact, Zac appears to have made 'commitments', not just to repay Verinder but to take care of his children somehow. Akbar concluded by saying that he would set a meeting with Verinder the following day: Thursday, 28 November.

In the interrogation room, Wallen cited this message and asked, 'What's that about?'

'I've got no comment about any of that,' Akbar said. 'No comment about the thing between the two of them. Yeah. It's dragging me into all this trouble.'

Clearly Verinder was upset with Zac, Wallen pointed out. 'And then suddenly this boy has gone flying over a balcony.'

'Please don't forget the web of lies Zac had built,' Akbar interjected. 'He got himself in a mess.'

'What had he lied about to Verinder?'

'What *hadn't* he lied about?' Akbar blurted. 'The fact that his dad had died, to start there. The fact that his mum was in Dubai.'

'Why was Verinder upset with Zac?'

'I'd be more focused on why Zac was upset with himself,' Akbar suggested.

Wallen pulled up a different text exchange, in which Zac told Akbar that he wanted to call Verinder. 'No, bro,' Akbar replied. 'That would not be a good idea.'

Why wouldn't it be a good idea? she wondered.

'I can see where you're going with this,' Akbar said. He could see how it might look from the outside. 'Verinder's angry with Zac—'

'If it's not as bad as it looks,' Wallen interrupted, 'then why not tell us?'

※

Akbar's wife, Daniela Karnuts, was listed in his contacts as 'Mama i-Phone'. He had not deleted his text messages with her. On the morning after the long night at Riverwalk, she had sent a message to a family group chat they maintained with their two children: 'Dad had a function at his gangster friend's and decided to sleep in the car.'

'Are you scared of Dave?' Wallen asked.

'Am I scared of him? I'd be fucking mad not to be, frankly, 'cause he is a scary guy,' Akbar said. 'But did he do this?' He did not, Akbar insisted. Zac had been 'like a kid' to Verinder, he claimed. 'So I am not trying to cover up some shit for him.'

The trove of digital evidence investigators had gathered might prove that Akbar was lying, but it also absolved him of any direct participation in Zac's death. After the building's cameras captured Verinder's daughter Dominique leaving Akbar at 1:46 a.m., he and his dog got into the Mercedes and drove away. Something must have prompted Akbar to turn around, though, because less than half an hour later he returned to Riverwalk, and the CCTV captured him arriving out front at 2:23 – the very minute that, on the Thames side of the building, Zac stepped out onto the balcony.

The tape didn't lie. Akbar could not have caused Zac's death, because he was not in the apartment until moments after it happened. He might have been arrested on suspicion of murder, but Riverwalk's security cameras had provided him with an unbeatable alibi. So why lie? Why change his story? Why keep repeating 'no comment'? Mallen asked if perhaps he was 'worried about some sort of reprisal'. If that was a concern, he said, then Akbar should tell them, so they could 'put you at ease and look after you so you feel more comfortable'. But whether he was terrified of retribution or scared of exposing himself in some manner or just constitutionally incapable of telling the whole truth, Akbar wouldn't tell the police what they wanted to know.

This was intensely frustrating for the detectives, in part because Akbar's cooperation, however limited and dishonest it might be, was better than what they were getting from Verinder, who was stonewalling them completely. But Akbar's reticence was also a problem, because they had discovered a different set of messages on his phone, which he would not explain – messages that cast Zac's death in a new and more ominous light. Over the course of that final evening at Riverwalk, while Akbar was with Zac and Verinder, he had been texting with a third man who was not in the building. Of all the evidence the police had uncovered, Akbar's exchanges with this man may have been the most alarming.

'Who is Mervin?' Wallen asked.

'He's an old friend of mine,' Akbar said. 'From the music business.'

Chapter 10

THE GREAT SHAM

THE SAXOPHONIST OF MUTHAFUNK, Sanjiv Bhattacharya, had been raised, like Akbar, in an immigrant family; his parents had moved to England from India before he was born. Sanjiv did well in school and ended up at Cambridge, but he often experienced a mild discomfort when it came to his cultural identity. Though he felt very English, it sometimes seemed as if he might never be regarded as truly English by his English peers. Yet he didn't feel particularly Indian, either. The first- and second-generation South Asian immigrants he knew were hardworking, industrious and – at least it seemed to Sanjiv – often repressed and less than fully happy. As a teenager, he found himself yearning 'for a different way to be Indian', he recalled. 'The Indians I knew were all a bit square and boring. There were no Indians on TV. We just weren't *cool*.'

Muthafunk was 'one of those jazz-funk kind of bands', in Sanjiv's description. When they advertised for a percussionist and Akbar Shamji showed up with his bongos, he seemed completely different from any Indian person Sanjiv had ever met. Akbar was 'rich and sexy and connected and confident', he recalled. 'We'd go off in his lovely BMW, smoking spliffs and listening to tunes, and he'd drop me off and I'd always wonder, *Where does he go next?*' Sanjiv had grown up in Wimbledon, not far from the Shamji property in Kingston upon Thames, but in very different circumstances. When Akbar mentioned that his family home had a life-sized train set upon which kids could take rides around the garden, Sanjiv was agog. 'The grandeur and the folly of it,' he said. It sounded 'a bit Vegas'. He found it thrilling to hang around with Akbar, because when you were with him, nothing seemed impossible. 'He's a confidence man,'

Sanjiv reflected later – so confident that he inspired confidence in others.

After Cambridge, Muthafunk broke up and Akbar went off to run the Mermaid, but the two stayed in touch. Sanjiv moved to London and became a journalist. He knew nothing of Akbar's failures at the Mermaid; in fact, from a distance, his impression was that his former bandmate was busy conquering the theatre world. One day in 2000, Sanjiv had just been laid off by *GQ* magazine when Akbar got in touch. He was living in Los Angeles now, he said, adding casually, 'Why don't you join me at this record label?'

Akbar was such a personable fellow that he had a tendency to pick up unlikely friends. At some point during those post-Cambridge years, he had developed a friendship with an actor and bon vivant named Peter Land. Land was quite a bit older than Akbar. Born in New Zealand in 1953, he had immigrated to England in 1977 and was now close to fifty. He was also terrifically wealthy. Land had married the English dancer and choreographer Gillian Lynne, who was famous for choreographing the show *Cats*. When she designed the dance numbers for the original Andrew Lloyd Webber production, she had negotiated, as part of her compensation, to receive a small percentage of all future revenue from any performances of the show. *Cats* went on to become one of the most successful musicals of all time, running for two decades in the West End and eighteen years on Broadway and ultimately playing to more than fifty million people in twenty-six countries. Thanks to this inexhaustible gusher of revenue, the couple enjoyed a conspicuously glamorous life, with homes in London, Gloucestershire, the South of France, New York and New Zealand. But in the late 1990s, Land had left his wife, amid speculation in the press that he was gay. 'He was just a man who married an older woman and hadn't quite found himself yet,' Lynne told *The Guardian* in 1999. 'He had a wonderful marriage and then the not-finding-himself came out and he had a journey to make.'

It was during this period of personal exploration that Peter Land moved to Los Angeles, where he and Akbar set out to become movie producers. Land had connections in Hollywood, so the two of them would drive around town and take meetings, hoping to get a movie off the ground. 'Peter's whole thing was that he was in theatre and knew all these showbiz people,' Sanjiv recalled. 'He was going to take his young Indian prince with oodles of money around LA and get him set up. That was their mission when they first came.'

Akbar moved into a rental home with a pool in Benedict Canyon, an exclusive enclave up above Beverly Hills, where Hollywood luminaries such as Jack Warner and Cary Grant had built their estates and where, in August 1969, the Sharon Tate murders took place. Akbar's rental, on Benedict Canyon Drive, seemed to have been built with its back to the street: when you drove up to the house, all you could see was an anonymous-looking stucco wall and a garage door. It was 'a very Akbar house', Sanjiv thought, because what was actually going on inside was 'sort of hidden'.

Akbar told Sanjiv that if he moved to LA, he could crash at the house until he found a place of his own. The plan to become a movie producer had not panned out, but Akbar and Land had pivoted to the record business, and it was in a new music venture that Akbar wanted Sanjiv to join him. Sanjiv was at a 'low ebb' in his life, he would say later, without a job or any real prospect of one. And Akbar possessed the kind of magnetism that could inspire a person to buy a one-way plane ticket to the other side of the world. 'He was the first person I'd ever met who was unapologetically proud when it came to being Indian,' Sanjiv said.

'Look at us,' Akbar would say to Sanjiv. 'We triumph. There's Indian immigrants everywhere, and everywhere we go, we kill it.' This sense that Indian identity might be a superpower rather than a handicap was intoxicating for Sanjiv. *Fuck it*, he decided. He would relocate to LA. He wouldn't pursue the sort of reliable but dull existence that his mother wanted for him. He would be 'Indian like Akbar', taking big risks to achieve big ambitions. Alongside Akbar, he decided, he would 'kick those doors open'.

The name of Akbar's record label was Soulife. Peter Land would later assert that he had 'co-founded' Soulife, but, as Sanjiv discovered, the truth was more complicated. The company had actually been established by a pair of experienced record producers named Mark

Sparks and Chris Dawley. Sparks hailed from Wadesboro, North Carolina, and had worked with the rappers Salt-N-Pepa, getting a producing credit on one of their biggest hits, 'Shoop' (1993). Dawley had managed a moderately successful rap duo, Nice & Smooth. Together they assembled a loose consortium of Black artists, many of them with connections to North Carolina. After abandoning an earlier company, Sparks and Dawley relocated to Los Angeles, and their whole entourage of musicians and friends – some forty people, all told – eventually moved with them. 'We want Soulife to be a brand name that says "community",' Dawley told *Billboard* in 2000, and he meant it literally: Soulife became a big commune of friends who preferred to work, live and travel in a pack.

How a pair of English transplants like Akbar Shamji and Peter Land might have become members of this little collective of Black musicians from North Carolina remained slightly unclear, but by the time Sanjiv arrived in California, Akbar had already insinuated himself into the centre of the Soulife crowd. Sanjiv's hunch was that he had probably succeeded in earning the affection of his new business partners through some combination of his own charm and his own money. Or, rather, his father's money. Anyway, safe to assume he had not won them over with his skills on the bongos. If Akbar was an odd fit for Soulife, Peter Land was even more incongruous. 'He wears scarves. In the summertime,' Sanjiv pointed out. The denizens of Soulife seemed to get along with Akbar, but they were openly quizzical about Land, and some were outright homophobic. 'Why's Akbar running around with this fag?' they would say.

As far as Sanjiv was aware, there was nothing romantic or sexual about Akbar's relationship with Land; it was just a close friendship with an older man. In fact, Akbar was living in the house on Benedict Canyon Drive with a girlfriend from his Cambridge days. After crashing with them for a while, Sanjiv moved into a shared house that was paid for by Soulife. He wasn't sure what he had expected, exactly, but when he got to California there didn't seem to be much for him to do, because nobody appeared to be working all that hard. Soulife had offices in Studio City, but people seemed primarily to be hanging out and partying. As a principal in the company, Akbar was supposedly overseeing an ambitious slate of projects, including a rap imprint called Soulife Raw and a nascent film division. He mentioned to Sanjiv that he intended to 'run a studio' someday, and Sanjiv marvelled once again at his friend's moxy: that he would move to Los Angeles, in his twenties, and his stated ambition would be not just to get a job and build from there – but to run the whole town.

'There was talk of scripts, a lot of big talk,' Sanjiv recalled. 'There was a book by some Crip that they were trying to option.' But what Akbar seemed mostly to be doing was cocaine. Sanjiv – still very much in Akbar's thrall – joined him. 'We were kind of the only ones doing any coke,' he noticed. 'These cultural differences were so stark. There was Peter, who was fine wines and penny loafers. Then there's Akbar, with his daddy's money, gaudiness and cocaine. And then all the Black guys, who wouldn't touch cocaine.'

In England, Akbar had struck Sanjiv as supremely comfortable in his own skin as a rich Londoner of Ugandan Asian extraction. But away from that familiar context, under the bright sun of Southern California, Akbar seemed to be going through an identity crisis. He loved hip-hop culture, and when he spoke with his Black business partners, it was in an idiom that made Sanjiv uncomfortable. Akbar used the N-word, for instance. 'There was something sort of thrilling and abhorrent about it – which is Akbar in a nutshell, really,' Sanjiv said. 'I thought, "You can't *do* that." We both loved hip-hop, and here we are with a bunch of Black musicians and the N-word flying around... but it's not for *us*.'

'My family is from Africa,' Akbar would say when Sanjiv challenged him. 'We're sand niggers.'

For Sanjiv, this change in the friend he so admired was dismaying. Akbar was 'trying to show his swagger', he thought. 'But it didn't look right on him.' Some of the other people at the label assumed that Sanjiv, being Indian, must be Akbar's cousin.

Soulife ended up releasing one hit, a 2001 track by the artist Sunshine Anderson called 'Heard It All Before'. It peaked at No. 18 on the charts. But Mark Sparks and Chris Dawley tended not to credit Akbar with playing any role in this success, much less Peter Land.

'Chris and I are like Batman and Robin,' Sparks told an interviewer in 2001. 'Or Starsky and Hutch.'

'It was an enterprise in which Akbar was so full of himself and so full of cocaine that he was spending a tonne of money, and kind of getting bullied out of his money by some of the tough guys from North Carolina,' Sanjiv would say later. New people kept showing up in town, announcing that they were the manager of this or that group. According to Sanjiv, 'The feeding frenzy for the Akbar dollars was getting a little bit crazy towards the end.'

Jack Ponti, a music industry veteran who met Akbar during this period, shared Sanjiv's impression of what was going on. 'He didn't know anything about the business, and people were like, "Eh, new guy in town with money",' Ponti said. 'I was astonished. It's like, "Why do you have so many employees? You have one fucking artist!"' Akbar had a decent heart, Ponti thought. He just wasn't a good businessman. And rather than educate himself about the industry and focus on the unglamorous work of incremental progress, 'everything had to be a bases-loaded home run'. In Ponti's view, 'Akbar was haunted by a demon of "When am I going to be as good as my father?"'

Then one day his father showed up in LA. The sudden arrival of Abdul Shamji felt almost like a royal visit. 'You know at the start of *Downton Abbey*, when they've got a dignitary arriving and everyone's running around polishing the crockery? It was that sort of feeling,' Sanjiv said. It was jarring for him to watch Akbar transform in Abdul's presence. 'He's so much taller and more physically imposing than his father, but he was always making himself small, sort of bowing and scraping,' he recalled. One night, the three of them went out to dinner – at Benihana – and Akbar seemed eager to show his father that he was making a success of himself. But Abdul was not impressed. He had been 'looking at the numbers', Sanjiv said, and he didn't seem particularly happy. At one point Abdul pulled Sanjiv aside and asked, quizzically, 'Is it working, this label?'

Not long after that visit, Soulife imploded. Sanjiv never gathered precisely what had gone down. He suspected that Abdul may have decided he was done subsidizing his son's California ambitions, and that without the money being pumped into the company by his father, the whole basis for Akbar's involvement just evaporated. There were other tensions between people at the label. Peter Land returned to London, where he ended up getting back together with his wife. One day, Sanjiv came home to the company apartment where he'd been staying to find that the locks had been changed. He tried to reach Akbar, but he had disappeared, sequestering himself, Sanjiv would later hear, in a rehab programme for cocaine addiction.

'It was a very Akbar story,' Sanjiv concluded. Despite getting locked out of the apartment, Sanjiv decided to stay in Los Angeles and lives there to this day. But he never spoke to Akbar again. In Hindi, the suffix *-ji* at the end of a word is an honorific. In later years, Sanjiv would ponder the little coincidences that sometimes imbue life with bitter poetry. The clue was right there all along, in his friend's name: Akbar Sham-*ji*. Akbar, the great sham.

When London detectives investigating the death of Zac Brettler examined Akbar's telephone, they discovered a string of messages from Zac's final hours at Riverwalk between Akbar and a person who was identified in the phone as 'Mervin'. The detectives did not know who Mervin was at first, but his full name was Mervin Sealy, and he was an American businessman, originally from North Carolina, who was an old friend of Akbar's from his Soulife days.

Mervin had come onto the scene in Los Angeles towards the end, according to Sanjiv Bhattacharya. As was typical with Soulife, it was never entirely clear what role he played in the company. But he and Akbar had remained friends. These days, Mervin spent a lot of time in China, where he ran some kind of building materials concern in Guangzhou. On LinkedIn he described himself as a 'serial entrepreneur'. He often travelled, and his Instagram account was full of photos of an amiable, slightly sleepy-looking guy posing in exotic locales. The week Zac died, Mervin happened to be in London on business. He was staying at Le Méridien in Piccadilly – which is the reason Akbar had access to the club lounge where he met Matthew and Rachelle.

When Akbar brought Zac to Riverwalk on Thursday the twenty-eighth, he did not intend to stay, because he had plans to get together with Mervin later that evening. It appeared, from their text messages, that Akbar had enlisted Mervin to get him some under-the-counter prescription drugs, specifically the amphetamine Adderall. (Mervin, Akbar explained to the cops, was 'a bit of an expert on tablets'.) The two men had some back-and-forth over text that evening about when they might be able to meet. At 7:58 p.m., shortly before Akbar and Zac arrived at Riverwalk, Mervin sent a message saying, 'Please let me know when you're heading back to Mount Street.' But Akbar didn't reply, and soon it became clear that something was happening at Riverwalk, something dire, which meant that Akbar would not be able to meet up with Mervin after all.

'Do you have something for me?' Akbar asked at 10:35. He couldn't leave Riverwalk but wanted Mervin to bring the drugs to him. He didn't say exactly what was happening inside the apartment at that moment, but it was clearly a crisis, and he seemed extremely agitated. 'I am not fucking playing,' Akbar wrote. 'I have just been heating up knives and clearing up blood.'

Mervin responded: 'Are you playing?'

'I'm not fucking around, nigger,' Akbar told him. 'Shit's about to go wrong. Wrong!'

Chapter 11

A JIGSAW IN THE DARK

THE RABBI HUGO GRYN was a great teller of jokes and stories, an endless font of playful banter and allegories of moral instruction. As he got on in years, Hugo would joke that he was entering his 'anecdotage', but the truth was that he had been a storyteller all his life. Around the dinner table in Marylebone, he would recount whimsical tales of the almost mythically utopian childhood he had enjoyed in the foothills of the Carpathian Mountains, in a little town called Berehovo. The identity of the place seemed up for grabs, as war and conquest kept rewriting Europe's map. In one of Hugo's folksy parables, a man is asked where he is from and he replies, 'I was born in the Austro-Hungarian Empire, educated in Czechoslovakia, started working in Hungary, did a stint in Nazi Germany, and then lived, worked and raised my family in the Soviet Union.' His interlocutor remarks, 'My, you must have travelled a great deal,' to which the man says, 'Not at all. I never left Berehovo!'

Because the national flag flying over the town in any given year could feel almost arbitrary, Hugo's childhood was simultaneously provincial – his father, Géza, was a prosperous forest developer – and cosmopolitan. At home, the family spoke mostly Hungarian, but when visitors came they would switch to Yiddish, Czech, German, or Hebrew, depending on who was over. Géza owned a fleet of handsome yellow forestry trucks, with the family name emblazoned prominently on the side. He liked to tell his children, proudly, that one day they would inherit those trucks. Géza had a passion for growing things and maintained orchards full of fruit trees: cherry and apricot trees, apples and peaches and pears. As a child, Hugo had the job of culling the plums that collected on the orchard floor and packing them into barrels, which local men would haul away to be distilled into the fiery plum brandy known as slivovitz.

In his adult home in London, Hugo still liked to partake of a glass of slivovitz after dinner, along with his ever-present cigarette. But his wife, Jacqueline, knew never to prepare boiled cabbage in the home, because the aroma it gave off reminded Hugo of the smell of burning flesh. The arcadian tales the rabbi related to Rachelle and her siblings about his childhood in Berehovo often didn't have an ending, and the children learned not to ask. As they got older they came to understand that all those stories ended the same way: when Berehovo's Jews were annihilated.

On the day Hugo arrived in Auschwitz, in 1944, and stepped off the train with his family, a gaunt man in a striped prison uniform approached him on the platform. He was muttering under his breath, like a madman, and as he passed Hugo he hissed in Yiddish, 'You're eighteen and you have a trade.' The family joined a long column of new arrivals waiting to be processed, and when Hugo reached the front of the queue, he told the Nazi administrators that he was nineteen and a carpenter. In fact, he was only thirteen. But that lie saved his life. Hugo was shunted into one queue, along with his father, for people who could work; his little brother, Gabriel, who was just ten but looked even younger, was sent to a different queue, and their mother, Bella, tried to follow him. Nearly the whole family was killed: grandparents, aunts, uncles. But by some miracle, Hugo and Géza survived Auschwitz and were transferred to a slave labour camp in Upper Silesia. They lived by their wits, and when the rations consisted of only a cup of watery soup and a little hunk of bread, Géza would forfeit part of his portion for his son. 'I suppose I got to know him in a way that is very different from the way in which sons generally perceive their fathers,' Hugo would later remark.

That winter, they ended up on a forced march from Silesia to Berlin. People were dying of starvation and illness, and when they did, the Nazis would leave them where they fell. At one point, the prisoners were permitted to rest for a few minutes, and Géza and Hugo sat down on the slushy roadside. Looking up, Hugo saw a truck approaching. A yellow truck. It was one of Géza's forestry trucks, which had been confiscated by the Nazis. As it passed, they saw their family name still painted on the side. It was a surreal moment, and it felt so pathetic to Hugo that he needed to break the silence.

'Just you wait,' he said. 'One day you'll have it back again.'

No, not that one, Géza told his son. That one is for you.

Géza died of typhoid and malnourishment just a few days after he and Hugo were liberated by the Allies, in May 1945. He had lost one child to the camps – Gabriel was gassed at Auschwitz – but he had managed to protect the other. It was only later that Hugo would fully comprehend the magnitude of Géza's parental sacrifice: he died because he had given up his own food to keep his son alive.

In 1946, Hugo arrived at Prestwick Airport, in Scotland, with a group of two dozen other teenagers. When the war ended, he had returned to Berehovo and was overjoyed to discover that his mother, Bella, had somehow survived. But Bella wanted to stay there, and Hugo saw no future for himself in that part of the world. So he left. (Bella later died of cancer.) At fifteen, Hugo found himself milking cows at a Scottish farm school and learning English as quickly as possible. He would eventually adopt the middle name Gabriel, in tribute to his departed brother. 'Before long, I managed to get a place at a university,' he later wrote. The two years at Cambridge would become an important aspect of Hugo's life story, one that undergirded his status not just as a Holocaust survivor and religious leader but as a man of letters and a public intellectual. He didn't boast about it in any sort of ostentatious manner – Hugo was too subtle for that – but he did hold on to that purple-and-white Cambridge scarf, a little visual reminder.

After Hugo's death, one of his closest friends, the historian Martin Gilbert, wrote his obituary in *The Times*. Gilbert had studied history at Magdalen College, Oxford, and written a biography of Winston Churchill and histories of the Second World War and the Holocaust. He described the extraordinary tragedy of Hugo's early years and related the inspiring story of how he had been 'awarded a scholarship to study mathematics and biochemistry at King's College,

Cambridge', noting that he had received both a bachelor's and a master's degree. Gilbert remarked on the widespread impact of the rabbi's life, mentioning that he had been named a Commander of the British Empire in 1992 for his work on interfaith relations.

After the obituary was published, Gilbert telephoned Rachelle's sister Naomi. 'I've just had this odd call from the *The Times*,' he said. Someone from Cambridge University had got in touch with the paper to say that they had been unable to locate any record of Hugo Gryn ever being a student there. As Naomi began to sort through the huge volume of papers that her father had left behind, she discovered some exercise books from the period between 1946 and 1948. But they weren't from Cambridge. They were from Sir John Cass Technical Institute, a vocational school in London's East End.

Rachelle did not know what to make of the idea that her father might have fabricated this element of his biography. It was not as though his life would be anything less than distinguished without that detail. Perhaps it was a youthful fib that Hugo had told in those early days, before he had actually become the illustrious Rabbi Hugo Gryn – one that he was subsequently obliged to live with. In 1994, two years before his death, Hugo appeared on the popular BBC radio programme *Desert Island Discs*. When the interviewer asked about his time at Cambridge, you could hear him deflecting, clearly not wanting to talk about it, as doing so would leave him with no choice but to countenance the misinformation. But when he didn't answer, she asked again:

'What did you read at Cambridge?'

'Mathematics,' Hugo said.

It was a lie. Almost certainly, it had started as a small lie. A juvenile lie. At the time he first uttered it, it may have seemed a necessary lie, like the lie he told at Auschwitz, the lie that had saved his life. Nor were those the only lies. In fact, the way that Hugo had managed to secure passage to the UK in the first place was by telling another lie, claiming that both of his parents were dead in order to qualify for a relocation scheme that was reserved for orphaned children. His mother was still very much alive at the time. Indeed, according to Naomi, it was his mother who had encouraged him to tell the lie.

But the truth is, everybody lies. We all do it, in ways large and small, more often than we might care to admit. Scholars known as 'deception scientists' have studied the psychology of lying and concluded that as a human behaviour, it is incredibly common. Most studies on the subject have found that the average person lies at least once or twice a day. But this may be an underestimate, because the methodology of these studies usually depends on self-reporting by subjects, and when people answer questions about how often they lie, they might very well be lying.

It is also important to remember that Hugo's whole life was, on some level, an invention. He arrived in Scotland alone, 'middle-aged' as a teenager, he would later say, having witnessed humanity at its most depraved. He would later go off to Hebrew Union College, in Cincinnati, to study to be a rabbi, and become a genuinely learned man, a friend and peer to some of the great intellectuals of his day. He eventually became the very thing, in other words, that he'd been pretending to be. But there must have been some moment, early on, when he decided that it might be necessary to build a bridge between the life he had and the life he wanted, and that bridge was a lie about studying mathematics and biochemistry at Cambridge.

Zac inherited his rich, gravelly baritone from Hugo, and there are photos of Hugo as a young man in his twenties, before his face filled out, in which grandfather and grandson bear a resemblance. But they never met each other: Hugo died four years before Zac was born. In June 1996, he was diagnosed with brain cancer, and two months later, he was dead. Rachelle was quick to dispel any notion that the legacy of her famous father might have cast some great shadow over Zac's life. If anything, she felt, Zac and Joe were surprisingly indifferent when it came to that aspect of their family history. In London's close-knit Jewish community, there could be certain advantages to 'playing the Gryn card', as Rachelle put it. But her sons never did. Nevertheless, Hugo was such a protean figure that he continued to loom large in the family, and in London more broadly, long after his death. At the West London Synagogue, where Zac had his bar mitzvah, a big photo of his grandfather hung just inside the entrance.

Only after Zac died did his parents learn that he had been telling lies for longer, and to a far greater extent, than they had realized. The tendency may have originated in his childhood gift for repartee. In the same way that a stand-up comedian is forever tweaking reality and rearranging it into jokes for the entertainment of others, Zac appears to have developed, in that early penchant for gags and stories, a sense that the truth can be a malleable thing. It may be that he came to understand something about the essential gullibility of human nature. Most of us have a default setting to believe other people. We take one another at face value to a degree that is shocking when you stop to think about it, not because we don't recognize that deception exists but because, really, who has time to fact-check everything they hear? Zac told stories as a child that may have been designed as jokes – *I can read, I just don't have my glasses* – only to find that people sometimes took them seriously.

When he first arrived at Mill Hill, Zac told some of his new classmates that his mother was dead. At the time, he was just thirteen. One friend from this period thought that he may have invented this new persona – a sad boy grieving his dead mother – in order to accelerate friendships, particularly with girls. Compassion can be a shortcut to intimacy. Empathetic people will make themselves emotionally available to a stranger who seems to be suffering.

'He'd always had a slightly preternatural ability to tell stories,' Matthew acknowledged. When Zac started to board at Mill Hill, at fifteen, it was 'a little like when you first go to college. Living away from parents for the first time. It dawns on you that you're meeting people who know absolutely nothing about you,' Matthew continued. 'We've all had that experience of being at school where you get a reputation for something you did when you were twelve years old, and then when you go to college it actually dawns on you that you've got a tabula rasa. It's a reset point. You feel like you've got a little bit of editorial control in a way that you didn't previously.' This is what Matthew believes must have happened to Zac at Mill Hill. 'In that boarding school environment, with people who had this mind-boggling access to money, Zac all of a sudden had a space in which he could create another version of himself.'

Zac had claimed to classmates that he was extremely rich. 'He told me his family had a house on Hamilton Terrace, in St John's Wood,' Dimitris recalled. Andrei Lejonvarn remembered Zac saying that his family lived at One Hyde Park. The Candy brothers' development clearly played an outsized role in his imagination. Zac told Andrei that his father was an arms dealer, like the guys in *War Dogs*. The family drove a pair of Range Rovers, he claimed. Andrei played tennis with Zac; they were doubles partners, and on one occasion Matthew had to drive them to a tournament. Before Matthew picked them up, Zac mentioned to Andrei that *both* of the Range Rovers happened to be in the shop for repairs, so his father had been supplied with some paltry courtesy car. He was not happy about it, Zac added, so Andrei shouldn't under any circumstances ask about the Range Rovers. 'He will freak out,' Zac warned.

When Matthew arrived, in his Mazda, Andrei said nothing about the Range Rovers. But as they drove to the tournament, he experienced some confusion. On the basis of what Zac had said about his father, Andrei had been expecting someone a bit scary, or at least tough: a hardcore international gun smuggler. But instead, here was bespectacled, considerate Matthew, full of gently inquisitive questions about tennis and school. 'He's, you know, a nice guy,' Andrei said later, adding, 'You could smell the bullshit.'

Over time, other Mill Hill friends started smelling it, too. According to Dimitris, it became almost a joke. People were initially intrigued by Zac's outlandish stories. 'He would go, "I'm doing oil deals with some Russians",' Dimitris recalled. ' "I've got a lot of connections with people in Nigeria. I know the prince. I sold electric cars to the Romanian government." ' Zac claimed to Dimitris that he had a net worth of 'twenty million', and at one point he even showed him a printed bank statement, much like the suspicious bank statement he showed Matthew. But Dimitris knew him too well to take anything he said especially seriously. Whatever he might claim about his family's finances, Zac had the trappings of an average middle-class seventeen-year-old. At a restaurant, he always wanted to split the bill. When Dimitris suggested they go visit the house in St John's Wood, Zac told him, 'Oh, we're renting it out.'

On some level, this was all part of Zac's shtick, Dimitris said, noting that 'some people just wanted to hang with him because he was quite funny'. Once, Zac claimed to his dorm-mates that he was so good at cricket, he was now sponsored by New Balance.

'No, you're not. You're full of shit,' someone said.

'You're a compulsive liar,' Andrei chimed in. 'You need to stop.'

For a moment, Zac seemed thrown by this accusation. But then, after some thought, he appeared to take the criticism seriously. 'I know,' he said reflectively. 'I'm a compulsive liar.' This had been a problem for him, he said, going all the way back to a terrible accident he had when he was a kid and—

'Zac! No! Stop!' Andrei said, cutting him off. 'You're doing it again!'

Privately, Dimitris warned him: 'Be careful what you say sometimes. Because people may not trust you again, and trust is, like, the biggest thing.' Over time, he noticed that Zac could forge friendships quickly but had trouble sustaining them, in part, Dimitris thought, because everyone eventually came to doubt what he said. As another close friend from Zac's final years put it, 'If you're lying to your friends, it's a bit of a lonely place to be, isn't it?'

When he left Mill Hill and started as a day student at Ashbourne College, Zac was offered another opportunity for a reset. Rather than settle into his own skin, he instead continued to try on different personas. One friend from Ashbourne recalled him referencing a Russian model, Daria Radionova, who sprang to notoriety in 2019 after she purchased a Lamborghini and bedazzled it in two million Swarovski crystals. Zac mentioned that Radionova was 'like a sister to him', the friend said, though she suspected that they did not know each other.

Another Ashbourne friend, who played football with Zac in a local league, recalled him showing up to practice one week with some new tattoos peeking out from underneath his T-shirt. They were reminiscent of the tattoos decorating the torso of the actor Viggo Mortensen in the 2007 film *Eastern Promises*, about a Russian gangster in London. Zac had a pair of ten-pointed stars, a picture of the Kremlin and – in Cyrillic – the words FOR HOLY RUSSIA. Questioned by his teammates, Zac intimated that they were gang tattoos, of the kind the mafia bestowed upon new inductees. His teammates just rolled their eyes. The following week when Zac came to practice, the tattoos were gone. After Zac's death, Rachelle discovered among his possessions a receipt for temporary tattoos that had been purchased on the internet. The 'Russian Prison Set', the website that sold them suggested, was a good option for people who had 'watched "Eastern Promises" one too many times'.

The Brettlers could occasionally discern a kind of magpie technique in their son's deceptions. He would often pluck genuine details he had encountered in one part of his life and repurpose them, as fiction, in another. 'My brother was very clever, but very good at adding snippets of the truth,' Joe said. Zac had once heard his parents mention an Indian man of their acquaintance who was in the rubber business, and he borrowed this detail and applied it to Verinder Sharma. So when he told Matthew and Rachelle about his new landlord, Verinder wasn't a gangster but a rubber tycoon.

One day not long after Zac's death, Rachelle was out walking in Maida Vale when she spotted Zamira, the woman from across the street with whom she thought Zac might have had a romantic dalliance. When they had crossed paths previously, Zamira had always behaved as though she didn't know Rachelle, walking right past, and she was about to do the same again when Rachelle summoned the nerve to introduce herself. Zamira had no idea who she was, which startled Rachelle. But she was more shocked to learn the woman's full name: Zamira Ismailova. In creating his Ismailov alter ego, Zac had borrowed her last name.

In a local café, Zamira and Rachelle sat down to talk. As it turned out, Zamira had known Zac by another name altogether: Thaimas. They had met several years earlier, when he approached her on the street and said that he had just spotted thieves casing out her Bentley. 'By the way, I'm your neighbour,' he volunteered. 'I know you're from Russia.' Then he added, 'I'm from Kazakhstan.' His father was an oligarch, he explained. When Rachelle informed Zamira that she was Zac's mother, the woman was shocked. She had thought that his mother was killed in a car accident.

'He said he was twenty-three,' Zamira continued, and that he lived alone in the apartment on Lauderdale Road. Because the building had a communal front door that opened onto the street, if Zamira saw Rachelle or Matthew or Joe going in and out, she had just assumed they were unrelated residents from some other apartment. Even though she was a native of the region herself, Zamira had completely believed Zac's claim of being from Kazakhstan. They spoke in English, but he occasionally sprinkled in a word of rudimentary Russian. London is full of children whose families and fortunes come from abroad but who are raised to be thoroughly British. 'I believed him,' Zamira said. 'I never doubted what he said.'

When Rachelle mentioned that she thought the relationship might have been physical, Zamira exclaimed, 'No!' She seemed mortified. 'He was a little boy. We were friends.' She mentioned that, in addition to her small son, she had a daughter who was roughly Zac's age. So she did not see him in that light. If she cooked something, she would make him a plate, she said. 'We do that when we cook in Russia: we give to neighbours. In England, they do not do that. But I knew he was from USSR and he was a boy, alone.'

After their meeting, Zamira agreed to show Rachelle the texts she'd exchanged with Zac. 'Chef made sushi do you want any?' he wrote one evening, suggesting that he had a personal chef. 'Spaisibo, Thaimas,' she responded, thanking him in Russian. 'I am on a diet.'

On New Year's Eve in 2017, Zamira invited Zac to join her family's celebration. When he got home, after midnight, he wrote to her, 'Thank you for having me this evening. I am so happy to have made friends with you. You are an amazing person. I wish you a happy new year full of health and inshaalah success. X.'

'Thank u Thaimas. Happy to have u as Friend,' she responded. At times, Zac seemed to be flirting with Zamira, or making it sound as though he had an exciting nightlife. 'I am very stressed so I need to party hard,' he wrote one night. 'Going to club. Will talk with you when back.' At one point he announced that he had met a girl on holiday.

'Good,' Zamira replied. 'Where from. How old.'

'Kazakhstan. And 20,' Zac texted, attaching a photo, which he had presumably found somewhere on the internet, of an attractive brunette posing in a red dress and a top hat.

'She looks older,' Zamira wrote. 'She is not 20.'

One evening, Zamira was out with friends at Annabel's, the Mayfair nightclub, when she looked up and saw Zac walking towards her. 'How did you get in here?' she asked.

'Oh, I'm a member,' Zac said casually. They chatted briefly, then Zac walked back to his table, where Akbar was waiting for him, and mentioned to Akbar that the beautiful woman he had just been speaking with was his ex-girlfriend.

Sometimes Zac would try to shake Zamira down for business contacts. 'Do you know anyone who works with oil in UAE,' he once asked. But what came through most strongly in their text exchanges was Zac's loneliness.

> Zac
> Can I speak with you quickly I need to talk to someone.

> Zamira
> Now? What happened.

> Zac
> I can't really deal with anything I just feel really shit.

> Zamira
> Why u feel shit. What is bothering u.

> Zac
> I am just scared. And it is very weird feeling. I just feel really isolated.

When Zac announced to Zamira that his father had died, she told him, 'Only u can be strong. Allah takes the best first,' adding, 'With time u will make ur own family.'

'It's just weird,' Zac replied. 'Usually I have my dad phoning me everyday asking how is everything. Talking to me. And it just really hurts me now.'

'Of course it does,' Zamira wrote back. 'But weird you didn't go to funeral.' Like so many of Zac's peers, she was starting to become sceptical about his stories. His father had died, but there was no mention of a funeral. In fact, his life didn't seem to be in any way disrupted. 'Many questions I have,' she texted. Perhaps he would find it helpful to see a therapist, she suggested.

> Zamira
> I only want u tell me the truth.

> Zac
> I am so confused.

> Zamira
> U don't need to pretend or lie to me about anything. Be real. I am like older sister for u.

Zac promised Zamira that he would never lie, assuring her in broken English, 'If one thing it is that I am honest.'

'There is no such thing as reproduction,' Andrew Solomon writes in his book *Far from the Tree*. There may be some narcissistic sense in which, as parents, we strive to mould our offspring in our own image, tweaking them here and there to make a better version of ourselves. But the truth is that often it doesn't work out that way, whatever the parents do. You can raise two children in more or less the same manner and end up with two wildly different adults. Our children are not us, Solomon points out: 'They carry throwback genes and recessive traits and are subject right from the start to environmental stimuli beyond our control.' The truth about parenthood, he concludes, is that it 'abruptly catapults us into a permanent relationship with a stranger'.

After Zac's death, the Brettlers began to understand him in a deeper and more complete way than they ever had when he was alive. Others might have seen through his inventions, but he was selective about which lies he told and who he told them to, so Rachelle and Matthew had not been exposed to many of his most outlandish fabrications. It was confusing: on the one hand, he seemed to have been so contemptuous of them, to reject everything his parents were and hoped to be. On the other hand, he had clearly wanted to impress them, and told many pointless little lies to make himself look a bit bigger and more assured in their eyes. Why else would he show them that fake bank statement indicating that he had £850,000? After a young couple named Charlie and Sophie moved into one of the apartments upstairs, Zac mentioned to his mother that he'd been out at Annabel's one night and seen them there. They'd been impressed, he said, that there was 'so much champagne on our table'. After he died, Rachelle asked Sophie about the encounter. But it hadn't happened.

'We never go to nightclubs,' Sophie said.

At one point after his death, Rachelle called a clinical psychologist, Giray Cordan, who had met with Zac for a few inconclusive sessions. 'There is so much we are discovering about Zac – in his death – that was not true,' Rachelle told the doctor. It felt like trying to 'piece together a jigsaw in the dark'. In his final years, Zac had become a 'heat-seeking missile', she continued, and ultimately he found himself in 'a very dangerous place'. Really, 'inside his *head* was a dangerous place', she was forced to admit. 'But he didn't know that he could say, "Mum, I need some help."'

'These situations often leave families with questions they can't answer,' Cordan told her. But the Brettlers wanted answers, and not just about who their son had really been in life. They wanted to know how and why exactly he had died.

Chapter 12

LIGHTS OUT

WHEN SCOTLAND YARD DETECTIVES recovered the messages in which Akbar Shamji told Mervin Sealy, his friend from the music business, that he'd been 'heating up knives and clearing up blood', they did not immediately share these findings with the Brettlers. Rachelle and Matthew were aware that an investigation into Zac's death was underway, but initially they had little sense of what that might entail. After the authorities finally realized that the corpse discovered by Vauxhall Bridge might be the missing teenager Zac Brettler, his parents were summoned to the mortuary near Canary Wharf. Because they knew that this would be a difficult excursion, they asked an old friend of Rachelle's, Jeannie Lorenz, to join them. Jeannie worked as an end-of-life doula, helping people with terminal illnesses, as well as their families, to cope with the reality of death. She had started her career working as a traditional doula, assisting women with pregnancy and childbirth, but eventually she transitioned into a new role, helping guide people through the shattering experience of bereavement.

Many marriages do not survive the death of a child, but Jeannie's impression was that Rachelle and Matthew were managing. They seemed to understand and accept that they would grieve in different ways. Matthew appeared to be developing a prosecutorial determination to understand the mechanics of his son's plunge from Riverwalk and to figure out who precisely was responsible, as if Zac's death were a maths problem to be solved. Rachelle found less comfort in logical inquiry and instead kept coming back to what her son might have been thinking and feeling in the final moments of his life. Was he in pain? Did he know that he was going to die? When Zac was alive, Rachelle had often spoken to Jeannie about how worried she was for him, and the dilemmas she faced about how to parent such a child. Now Jeannie sought to reassure Rachelle that Zac's death was a freak outcome: an unpredictable event that was totally outside her control rather than the product of any parental neglect.

The mortuary was housed in a cold, drab brick building. Matthew did not think that he could handle the sight of his lifeless son, so he chose to remain in an outer room. But Rachelle had spent so much time wondering about Zac in recent days that now she wanted to see him. With Jeannie by her side, she entered a small room with an interior window that was covered by a curtain. Then the curtain was pulled aside, and through the glass she saw her son. Zac lay on a slab, face up, his body mostly covered by a sheet. His skin was pale, all the colour drained from it. He was positioned in such a way that they could see only one side of his face and were spared the sight of his other cheek, which had been damaged. Even so, his nose looked different to Rachelle, misshapen somehow. She wanted desperately to kiss her child, to take him in her arms, at least to put a hand on his body. But the mortuary staff said that she could not touch him. The corpse had yet to be subjected to a complete autopsy; in the event that Zac's death involved foul play, it was important that she not contaminate the body.

As Rachelle and Jeannie rejoined Matthew and left the mortuary, everyone was quiet. It was a strange part of the city, Jeannie reflected. One moment you were surrounded by the forlorn working-class homes of the old East End, then suddenly you crossed into the ultramodern landscape of Canary Wharf. It felt like time travel. Rachelle suggested they stop at Ole & Steen, an upscale Danish bakery. It was late morning, before the lunch rush, and as they sat there eating, Jeannie thought that this is when it starts to feel surreal: you walk back into the world after identifying your dead teenager, and all the gears of daily life are still whirring, obliviously, as if no tragedy has transpired. People go to work, exchange pleasantries, play games on their phones.

Matthew said he wanted to visit Riverwalk, to look at the spot where Zac's body had been found. Rachelle had no interest in going, so Jeannie volunteered to accompany him. They took the Tube to

Vauxhall, rode the escalator aboveground, and walked past MI6 and onto the bridge. But as they traversed the river and Matthew looked up at the building, he was greeted by an eerie tableau: there was activity on the fifth-floor balcony, a group of people clad in ghostly white hazmat suits, going in and out of Verinder's flat. Matthew had seen enough cop shows to recognize what was happening. They were combing the place for forensics.

A week later, Matthew and Rachelle visited Belgravia Police Station, where they were met by a middle-aged detective inspector named Rory Wilkinson, who would be running the investigation. Wilkinson had the avuncular countenance of a local vicar. When a death like this happens, he assured the Brettlers, 'we have the whole office helping'. With some thirty-three thousand officers, the Met is one of the biggest police forces in the world. The investigation would draw on 'vast' resources, Wilkinson promised. Forensic data, such as fingerprints and DNA, would not be much help, because Zac and Akbar had been in and out of Verinder's apartment for months. But by Wilkinson's estimate there were as many as eighty CCTV cameras in the surrounding area. The police had collected Zac's phone and iPad. They had also downloaded the contents of Akbar's phone, as well as Verinder's. The average mobile phone contains 'the equivalent of thirty times the entire works of Shakespeare', Wilkinson cautioned the Brettlers. So this would be a slow process, but a thorough one. His team would interview witnesses, checking for discrepancies in their accounts. By the end, Wilkinson said, there should be 'no unanswered questions'.

In preparation for the meeting, Matthew had drawn up a detailed chronology of events in the days surrounding Zac's death. It was six pages, single-spaced, and Matthew had devised an abbreviation system to refer to the central players: ZJB for Zac, AS for Akbar and so forth. The document was a helpful building block for the detectives, but also a poignant illustration of Matthew's tendency to sublimate his own anguish into the clarity of meticulous busywork.

Matthew had also begun to conduct a few informal inquiries of his own. From the moment the Brettlers first heard the name

Verinder Sharma, when Zac moved into Riverwalk for the summer, they had searched for some trace of the man online. As Indian names go, Verinder Sharma is not especially distinctive. There was a psychiatrist in Ontario who had the name, and a *Virendra* Sharma who served as a Member of Parliament for South Ealing. But the Brettlers had been able to find virtually nothing on their son's new friend and landlord. After Zac went missing, however, Matthew ran the name through Companies House, an online database that lists registration details for businesses incorporated in the UK, and finally he got a hit: a single entry for a Verinder Kumar Sharma. Matthew happened to remember that when he and Rachelle had spoken over the phone to Verinder, during their visit with Akbar at the Méridien hotel, the name on Akbar's iPhone read 'VKS1'.

What if the *K* stood for Kumar? The Companies House listing for Verinder Kumar Sharma said that his birth year was 1964 — which seemed about right. He was registered as a director of Axx Solutions Limited, a business that had been incorporated a year earlier, in 2018. It wasn't clear what the company did, precisely. Under 'Nature of business', the listing offered some enigmatic boilerplate about 'consultancy activities'. There was only one other corporate officer identified: a second director of the company, named Barry Paul Lavers. But by extraordinary coincidence, that happened to be a name that Matthew knew.

From his father, Benny Brettler, Matthew had inherited a truly formidable memory. He had a good friend, a man named Adrian, who lived nearby in Maida Vale. Adrian was an avid golfer who played at a club called the Buckinghamshire, just outside London. Sometimes, in conversations with Matthew, Adrian would mention the regulars at the club, and Matthew, for no good reason apart from being Matthew and having a brain that happened to function that way, would file those names away. One of them, he was certain, was Barry Lavers. What were the chances it was the same person? On the day he learned that Zac was dead, Matthew telephoned Adrian. Was the Barry Lavers he played golf with by any chance Barry *Paul* Lavers?

He was. Adrian called later to report that he had spoken to Barry, and that the Verinder Kumar Sharma whom Matthew had found on Companies House was indeed Barry's partner – and lived at Riverwalk. When Adrian mentioned that he was a family friend of this teenager who had recently died, Barry had known exactly who he was talking about.

'The oligarch's son,' he said.

In fact, Barry had *met* Zac: Verinder had introduced the boy as his protégé. Zac had been homeless and sleeping on a park bench when Verinder found him, Barry told Adrian. As for Zac's death, he was under the impression that it was a suicide. 'What a tragedy,' Barry said.

According to Barry, Verinder was 'a lovely guy', and if Zac had been staying with him, then he would have been well taken care of. Barry didn't say what exactly Axx Solutions did, but he shared one other detail that Adrian relayed, which Matthew found particularly intriguing: Verinder Sharma had been living at Riverwalk rent-free.

'Nick Gold pays for that apartment,' Barry told Adrian.

This was another name that was familiar to Matthew. A flamboyant investor who divided his time between Miami and London, Gold was in his forties and very fit, with the kind of tan that would be improbable for London at any time of year. He was something of a tabloid fixture, owing to his brief marriage to a minor reality TV star, Laura Zilli, an ill-fated union inaugurated with two elaborate wedding receptions, one of which featured a performance by Boy George. Zac had mentioned Nick Gold to his parents from time to time, going so far as to suggest that he was friends with him. But Matthew and Rachelle never took the notion very seriously: Gold was just another name in Zac's menagerie of flash London businessmen, more of a 'fantasy friend' than an actual friend, Rachelle thought. This new information from Barry Lavers complicated that picture, however. Why would an ostensibly legitimate London businessman like Nick Gold be providing a free luxury apartment to an unsavoury figure like Verinder?

The police had not been able to identify any individuals – apart from Verinder – who might have witnessed Zac's plunge into the Thames. It had happened in the dead of night, in winter, at a building that on a good day could seem conspicuously underpopulated. And despite the profusion of surveillance cameras in and around Riverwalk, it appeared that only a single camera had captured Zac's fall – the one at MI6. The secrecy enshrouding that agency meant that the police were somewhat awkward in their handling of this footage. At first they didn't even tell the Brettlers about it. Then they were coy about where precisely it had come from. They wouldn't permit the Brettlers to watch the video themselves, so instead Rory Wilkinson described it to them. It was dark and grainy, he said, and captured from a great distance away. On the video, Zac exited the apartment and moved to one end of the tapered balcony. Then he crossed to the other end. In total, he was on the balcony for only about a minute. And he appeared to be *alone*. In other words, nobody pushed him. He jumped.

When it came to describing the actual details of Zac's death, Wilkinson expressed some trepidation. 'I don't want to upset anybody,' he said.

But it was precisely such specifics that Rachelle had been yearning to know. 'You're not gonna upset me,' she assured him. 'I'm hardy.'

Zac jumped from the balcony, Wilkinson explained, and he nearly made it clean into the river. But on the way down, before he landed in the water, his hip clipped the embankment wall. Rachelle flinched at the thought.

From an investigative point of view, the existence of this video seemed to offer proof that Verinder had not pushed Zac off the balcony. But that didn't mean he was off the hook, Wilkinson suggested. 'If someone is so *scared* that they jump – even if it's of their own volition – that still is obviously a criminal offence,' he said. 'A serious one. Possibly murder.'

The Brettlers were also alarmed by something that they had learned from the coroner's office. During the initial autopsy, the pathologist examining Zac's body had studied his broken jaw and concluded that, unlike most of his other injuries, it could not be readily explained by the fall. The doctor was sufficiently concerned that he suspended the examination, recommending that the case be turned over to a special pathologist who conducts a more extensive inquiry when there are signs of foul play. Verinder Sharma was a tough guy and appeared to have a temper. He trained as a boxer, and there was now some indication that by the time Zac jumped off the balcony, he may have already had a broken jaw.

There was one final clue that seemed to seriously undermine Verinder's assertion that Zac had simply committed suicide. Verinder had claimed to detectives that he was asleep by the time Zac left the apartment: he had said goodnight, taken a sleeping pill and discovered that his guest was missing only when he woke up the next morning.

The MI6 camera told a different story, however. After Zac went off the balcony, the camera registered movement in the apartment – passing shadows in the brightly lit windows, too far away to ascribe to anything concrete but coinciding with Akbar Shamji's return to the apartment moments after Zac's jump. As Riverwalk's own cameras had confirmed, Akbar came back to the building and entered Verinder's apartment. But then he left, and at 2:46 the flat was plunged into darkness. Zac was in the apartment, and then he wasn't. And afterwards, while Akbar went down to stare at the spot where Zac had gone into the river, Verinder turned out the lights in the apartment and went to bed.

Chapter 13

THE LITTLE FELLA

WHEN MICKY MCAVOY, the mastermind of the Brink's-Mat robbery, walked out of prison in 2000, he looked different than he had when he went in. He was nearing fifty now, and during the sixteen years he'd spent behind bars, middle age had come for him, and his physique, once lean and strong, had softened. Early on, McAvoy had been determined to break out of prison, going so far as to plan a daring escape in which a helicopter would land in the yard long enough to pick him up. But authorities caught on to the plot, and eventually he resigned himself to life inside. He got married to his devoted girlfriend, Kathy Meacock, in a ceremony held in the gymnasium of Leicester Prison. Kathy spent the long years of Micky's confinement living in a comfortable farmhouse in Kent that had been purchased in the aftermath of the gold heist using funds channelled through a shell corporation based in the Isle of Jersey. In Micky's absence, she enjoyed the company of a pair of rottweilers. Their names were Brinks and Mat.

McAvoy always maintained that he had been cheated out of the Brink's-Mat gold and had never received his rightful share of the £26 million, though many suspected otherwise. Upon his release, Micky and Kathy moved into a suburban home southeast of London, in Locksbottom. Even as a free man he would live under intensive surveillance, because the Metropolitan Police were still hoping he might lead them to the missing gold. But if he did have loot squirrelled away, Micky was too savvy to show his hand. And when he and Kathy wanted a respite from the surveillance, they could always escape to the privacy of their second home, in Spain.

London might offer an attractive base for the criminally inclined, but it does have one conspicuous disadvantage: the weather. So when it is time to retire or to go on the run, the discerning British crook often finds himself in Spain. In *Sexy Beast*, a movie released the year McAvoy got out of prison, Ray Winstone plays an English gangster who retires (unsuccessfully) to the south of Spain. In the opening scene he reclines under a broiling sun, his belly distending over a pair of tiny yellow Speedos, and murmurs, 'Bloody hell... You could fry an egg on my stomach.'

In 1978, following a diplomatic dispute, Spain's government elected not to renew its extradition treaty with Britain, which meant that suddenly there was a place just a short flight from soggy London that had terrific food and immunity from investigation or prosecution. Plus, it hardly ever rained. The Costa del Sol came by its name honestly: full-on sunshine 320 days a year. By the 1980s, as many as a hundred major British criminals were living openly in Spain. Murderers, drug runners, sex offenders, thieves. The London papers rechristened the area the 'Costa del Crime'.

Even after a new extradition treaty was established, in 1985, Spain held on to this reputation as a balmy refuge for wanted men. The Spanish police were famously complacent, and Scotland Yard was often obliged to route any requests for law enforcement assistance through Europol or Interpol. The process was 'a real rigamarole', as one former London cop put it. In other parts of the world, detectives often cultivate relationships with their counterparts in neighbouring countries, because one predictable thing that criminals do is skip town. If the place they flee to is just a short distance away, you might suppose the cops in country A would want to enlist the cops in country B to help locate such fugitives. And there *have* periodically been initiatives in which British police touted their cooperation with Spanish law enforcement. But in practice, if you were an English crook and you could get as far as Spain, you might as well be on the moon. Nobody was coming for you.

McAvoy would later claim that during his years in Spain it had just been him and Kathy enjoying the quiet life of retirees, 'cut off' from the old associates of his criminal days. But this was not quite true. In fact, Micky was still actively engaged, in the years after his release, with a loose fraternity of hardcore London hoods. To a younger generation of thieves and racketeers, McAvoy was royalty:

the unrepentant architect of one of the greatest heists in British history. 'Micky McAvoy is a very well-respected man,' one English murderer who knew him in Spain declared. He was held in such high regard, in fact, that in 2003 he was enlisted to resolve a violent dispute that had broken out among a cohort of London gangsters and was threatening to spiral into an all-out war. One of the chief antagonists in this clash was a diminutive young drug runner. To his criminal associates he was known by various nicknames. They called him 'the Little Fella', or 'Indian Dave', or often just 'I.D.' But his legal name was Verinder Kumar Sharma.

While London's formal economy was remaking itself into a service sector for global plutocrats after the closure of the docks and the slow decline of British manufacturing, the city's criminal economy was undergoing a transformation of its own. The entire criminal ecosystem was reinvented during the late 1980s and early 1990s, and the roots of this transformation traced back to, of all places, Texas. The chemical known as MDMA was originally synthesized in 1912, by the German pharmaceutical company Merck, which had been searching for a drug that would cause blood to clot. MDMA didn't end up performing very well as a blood-clotting remedy, but by the mid-1980s another use had been discovered: as a party drug. At the Starck Club in Dallas, revellers started taking the drug recreationally, on a night out, and found that it induced an intense experience of euphoria. Soon MDMA was rebranded, becoming known as Ecstasy, and use of it spread. The phenomenon jumped from Dallas to New York, and then to London, where nightspots like the Hug Club and Taboo began hosting 'Ecstasy Parties'. Rave culture was born on the margins of social life in Britain, with unlicensed parties in underground clubs and abandoned warehouses, where young people danced all night, fuelled by acid house music and MDMA.

But by the early 1990s, club music and Ecstasy were becoming more mainstream – and commercialized – as dance promoters started opening their own fully licensed nightclubs. The clubs needed security, the ravers wanted drugs, and these two factors, in tandem, fundamentally reshaped what it meant to be a criminal in

London. For older crooks of Micky McAvoy's generation, being a professional criminal had often meant doing stickups, and from the Great Train Robbery, in 1963, to Brink's-Mat, two decades later, McAvoy lived through what the veteran British crime reporter Duncan Campbell once described as the 'golden age for armed robbery'. By the early 1990s, banks were still getting robbed virtually every day in London – there were nearly three hundred bank robberies in 1992 – but there were signs that the party was coming to an end. London was an early and enthusiastic adopter of surveillance cameras, and ubiquitous CCTV made it more difficult to stick up a bank and get away with it. Also: there were fewer banks. With the rise of ATMs, and eventually of online banking, thousands of bank branches closed. The decline of the bank-theft industry meant that the next generation of up-and-coming London criminals would be forced to seek their fortunes elsewhere, and many turned their attention to the rave scene.

'I first met Dave in approximately 1994,' Andy Baker recalled. Their first encounter was at a club called Embargo on the King's Road in Chelsea. Baker was heavyset, with an air of jovial menace. He had grown up in South London and trained to be a surveyor but ended up drifting into nightclub work during the late 1980s. Many of the new clubs opening in that period were operated by posh boys from good schools who had started out as rave promoters. Baker, who had a fondness for nicknames, referred to them as 'the Plums'. The Plums tended to hire tough bouncers with cockney accents. The owners might have been aristocrats, but they liked to 'flirt with a little bit of criminality', Baker explained, describing them, with a dismissive chuckle, as 'Saturday night gangsters'. Baker ran security for Embargo, and when he first met the man he would come to know as Indian Dave, it was because Verinder had turned up as a customer at the club, accompanied by a few friends.

Verinder had grown up in Loughborough, a market town in Leicestershire. His parents were immigrants from northern India. Loughborough had long been a hub of Britain's textile industry, known for its hosiery factories, which churned out socks and stockings. Just as Matthew's father, Benny Brettler, had found employment in the textile business in Manchester, Verinder's father, Hans

Raj Sharma, got a job in the hosiery factories of Loughborough. By the standards of the day, Loughborough offered immigrant families a real opportunity for upward mobility. When the factories began hiring people of colour, in the early 1960s, white employees had protested. But the surge of immigrants injected fresh energy into a tired industry, and Loughborough prospered in the 1970s, even as factories in other parts of Britain were closing. A simple terraced house could be purchased for as little as a few thousand pounds, there was a good university and a technical college, and the local schools were racially integrated. To be sure, there was bigotry. When Verinder was eight years old, in 1972, hundreds of Indian workers at Mansfield Hosiery Mills, a red-brick factory, organized a strike, protesting a system of race-based discrimination in which immigrant workers were excluded from the more lucrative jobs held by whites. But there were also opportunities for a first-generation immigrant family like the Sharmas to find a toehold in the middle class.

Little is known of Verinder's early years. In Baker's description, he came from a 'traditional Indian family that played cricket on Sunday'. He had two older brothers, Vinod and Vijay, who were more straitlaced and ended up following their father into the textile trade. But by the 1980s Verinder had already become involved in crime. The month he turned twenty-three, in 1987, he was convicted at Wood Green Crown Court, in London, on charges of forgery and using a false instrument, and received a three-year prison sentence. Short, wiry and handsome, Verinder was a sharp dresser with a commanding voice and a big personality. Not long after his release from prison he became a fixture on the club scene and began to make his presence known. Initially, he earned money from cigarette vending machines, which were ubiquitous in nightclubs of that era. He was uninhibited and had no trouble sparking up a conversation with a stranger, particularly if he thought there might be some advantage in doing so.

Verinder and Andy Baker eventually went into business together, running security firms. In theory, their job was to manage who got through the door at a club and to resolve altercations as they arose. In practice, the portfolio was more expansive. 'If people have headaches, I've got aspirins,' Baker recalled. 'People ring me up if they have problems. Indian Dave is a skinny little Indian, I'm just a fat fella.' Yet together they could offer muscle to people who needed it, he explained, by drawing on a loose fraternity of London bouncers. Baker insisted that he and Verinder regarded themselves as *consultants*, enunciating the word in a wolfish manner that indicated it was a euphemism. They worked for dance clubs and strip clubs and bars, and the line between conventional paid security and something more akin to protection money could sometimes blur.

The clubs were full of easy marks: naive civilians, many of them well-to-do, looking to spend money on a night out. Indian Dave possessed a predatory eye for the partygoer with deep pockets and soft hands. Having identified his target, he would advance, shark-like, across the dance floor. Sometimes it was as simple as sticking an unsuspecting stranger with his drink tab. On other occasions, Indian Dave would follow a patron out of the club and demand that he turn over his wristwatch. But Verinder also learned to play a longer game, making no immediate ask but finding ways to insinuate himself into the lives of people who had money, cultivating a queasy friendship, before turning on them, ferociously, with demands. His behaviour was such a problem that some clubs tried to ban him. But in practice he always managed to sneak back in, because he was becoming the sort of feared individual whom people hesitated to cross. And anyway, he was friends with all the doormen.

'He was super aggressive when we first met, quite forceful,' recalled one wealthy Londoner Verinder extorted in this manner. He had telephoned the man out of the blue one day, demanding a big cash payment. When the man refused to meet with him, Verinder simply rattled off a London street address. It was the home of the man's mother. The threat was unmistakable, and not the sort of thing the receiver could take lightly – because both Verinder and Andy Baker were linked to real incidents of extreme violence.

Howard Spooner was a young club owner in the late 1990s who had attended Gordonstoun, a posh boarding school in the north of Scotland. Spooner had forgone university to get in on the nightclub boom, and he took over Embargo, quickly turning it into a great success. He hired Andy Baker to run security, and one day Baker asked him to open the club during the afternoon so that he could 'interview' someone. At the appointed hour, Baker arrived along with Verinder Sharma and several other men, one of whom looked quite beaten up and appeared to be there under duress. This was the first time that Spooner had ever met Indian Dave, and he quickly realized that Verinder and Andy were not interviewing the man in any conventional sense. As Spooner waited in the entrance to the club, he heard terrible screams emanating from inside. 'I was twenty-four. This was my first business,' he recalled. It was a frightening situation, and he did not know what to do. After a while, Indian Dave appeared. He was shaking, his eyes pinned, his nostrils flared, coked off his head. His hands were covered in blood. Verinder held a plastic bag, and Spooner could see that it contained a pair of pliers and a hacksaw. 'I don't know what happened,' Spooner said later. 'But the folklore is that they castrated the guy.'

Baker would occasionally invoke the name of a nightlife impresario, Stuart Cadwell, who ran Spearmint Rhino, a famous strip club on Tottenham Court Road. 'He called Dave Sharma a "Paki", even though he's Indian, not Pakistani, and he called me a fat cunt,' Baker said, before adding, in a studiously neutral tone, 'He ended up getting attacked by a machete.' One night in 2002, as Cadwell was leaving his club, a pair of men accosted him with a machete. Bleeding heavily, Cadwell managed to crawl back into the club and was rushed to a hospital, but nobody was ever charged in the attack. Baker spoke of this incident as if the machete had somehow assaulted Cadwell all by itself, and when pressed, he denied any personal involvement. But it must have been helpful for the sort of reputation that he and Verinder were cultivating that there were vivid rumours to the contrary.

This is an odd paradox of a career in the underworld: the more widely you are known for horrific violence, the less you will be obliged to resort to it. If your chief racket is extortion, a credible threat is the most efficient method of doing business. Dating back to the early days of Indian Dave's collaboration with Baker, during the 1990s, the Metropolitan Police suspected both men of having links to gangland murders. They just couldn't prove it.

Over time, Sharma and Baker's crew came to include some exceedingly dangerous individuals. One good friend of both men was a young maniac named Gary Nelson, who was known as 'Tyson', because he bore a resemblance to the fighter Mike Tyson and had a hair-trigger temperament to match. Tyson came from a Jamaican family in South London. By the time he was twenty-one, he had done stretches in thirty-three different prisons. Rather than rehabilitate him, he said at the time, all prison did was 'teach me... what I could endure'. At twenty-four, Tyson murdered a police constable named Patrick Dunne. On that particular evening, he had actually just finished murdering somebody else – a bouncer who had disrespected him at a nightclub – when Dunne, who happened to be on duty in the neighbourhood and had heard the gunshots, approached. Tyson shot him without hesitating. Witnesses heard him laughing as he climbed into a waiting car and fled the scene.

Few events spur police into action like the killing of one of their own, and after a massive investigation, Tyson was arrested and charged with conspiracy to murder. But a year later he was back on the street, after prosecutors dropped all charges against him, citing a 'lack of evidence'. The challenge, one detective on the case explained, was that nobody would testify. People were terrified, because Tyson 'had a hold over the community'. After one witness in an unrelated case supplied evidence about Tyson to police, he was found hanging in his prison cell the next day. 'Looks to have been suicide,' the judge in the case declared. But other witnesses trying to decide whether *they* should give evidence against Tyson might not have been so sure.

In 1993, still at large, Tyson was driving a lime-green BMW through South London when another motorist, in a moment of casual road rage, made the mistake of flipping him the middle finger. Tyson pulled over, produced a semiautomatic pistol and fired a volley of bullets into the man's vehicle. The driver was not hit, but Tyson faced trial for this broad-daylight shooting and sauntered into the dock at the Old Bailey festooned in bling. The authorities might not be able to get him for the murders, but at least they could keep him off the streets. He got eight years. After starting his sentence at Belmarsh, a high-security prison, Tyson ran out of his cell one day, naked and oiled from head to toe so that his body would be slippery, and assaulted his guards with a snooker cue. He was transferred to a different maximum-security facility, where he extorted drugs and money from other prisoners, beat up fellow inmates and attacked staff. At Scotland Yard, Tyson became known as 'the UK's most dangerous man'. 'I would describe him,' one detective said, 'as a killing machine.' Yet in 1999, when Tyson had served only half of his time, he was released. (Under British criminal justice rules, even the most violent offenders often serve only half their sentences.)

To Verinder and Andy Baker, this was a cause for celebration. They saw Tyson rather differently than the cops did. 'Lovely boy,' Baker said. 'Slightly misunderstood.' Their little entourage had taken to congregating at a new table-dancing club in Park Royal called For Your Eyes Only. The club was popular with young traders of the post-Big Bang generation who worked long hours at City banks and brokerages, then went out for champagne and lap dances. Baker and Verinder had a contract to do security for the club, and it became their de facto base of operations. 'That was our little spot,' Baker recalled fondly. It was a three-hundred-seat venue, neon-lit, with chrome stripper poles and TVs tuned to Sky Sports. Waitresses in red minidresses prowled the tables, emptying ashtrays and serving drinks.

Verinder spent so much time at For Your Eyes Only that when criminal associates needed to speak to him, they would just telephone the club. He had a girlfriend named Tara Spencer-Clarke, who lived in Battersea, and together they had two daughters: Dominique, who was born in 1996, and Matisse, born in 2000. In a photo taken when Dominique was a little girl, she gazes pensively at the camera, with dark hair and big, dark eyes, flanked by Tara on one side and Verinder on the other. He's got close-cropped hair and a preoccupied smile. As it happened, Verinder had another girlfriend who was a dancer at For Your Eyes Only. Confusingly, she was also named Tara. He referred to them as Tara One and Tara Two. With this Tara he had a son, who was born in 2002, named Chanze.

'My dad basically was not a very active parental role in my and my siblings' lives,' Dominique would later say. The children's early years coincided with a busy phase in Indian Dave's career.

A massive volume of drugs was entering London's nightclubs and, perhaps inevitably, Verinder wasn't just minding doors and shaking down club kids but importing narcotics himself. He did this in partnership with another ex-doorman and friend, a burly Glaswegian named Dave King. Known as 'Muscles', on account of his statuesque physique and his fondness for anabolic steroids, King was a formidable brawler who had spent time in prison. Once, during a nightclub altercation, he produced a ten-inch knife and slashed a man in front of a dance floor full of people. Muscles was flamboyant. He had done occasional work as a bodyguard for celebrities, such as the singer Robbie Williams, and he owned a number of legitimate businesses, including a tanning salon. In the recollection of one gangland associate, 'This geezer came swaggering through, pushing people about, dripping in gold, giving it the big "I am".'

Muscles and Indian Dave became close friends, though they were quite different. Verinder liked to keep a low profile and remain somewhat elusive. Despite having two families, he had no fixed abode. Instead he rented places on a short-term basis, and occasionally he would store some of his belongings at Muscles's home. They liked to party together, and both men had a taste for cocaine. One former law enforcement official who listened to intercepted phone calls among members of the group recalled conversations 'about their nostrils being burned out' after a big debauch with Russian prostitutes. There's a photo of Muscles and Verinder, taken on a night out. Muscles towers over his friend, dressed in a black leather jacket, his hair frosted blond, his arm around Verinder, who smiles at the camera with a beer in his hand.

In 2002, the two of them arranged to import a shipment of fourteen kilos of heroin from Turkey. But British customs intercepted the load and arrested both Muscles and Indian Dave, along with three other men. During the weeks they spent waiting to make bail, Muscles and Verinder shared a cell. The experience of cohabiting in tight quarters and sharing a toilet in the corner can put a strain on any relationship. Verinder had a sentimental streak, and before bed every night he would kiss a photo of his children. Muscles teased him about this, which Verinder resented. Then, in one early court hearing, the government announced that it would be dropping all charges against Muscles – but not the other defendants. They cited a lack of evidence, but it seemed immediately suspicious that this would apply to only one member of the conspiracy. Verinder exclaimed, in open court, 'He's a grass!'

This was a grave charge. To accuse someone of being an informant amounts to the ultimate slander in criminal circles. Micky McAvoy spoke of informants as 'Judases who should have been drowned at birth'. In the end, the prosecution would collapse altogether ('insufficient evidence'); the defendants were released, and all charges were dropped. But an unsettling question hung in the air. Could Verinder's close confidant and business partner, a man he trusted implicitly, have been willing to secure his freedom by selling out his friends?

When Gary 'Tyson' Nelson got his early release from prison after the road rage case, the detectives assigned to the murder of Constable Patrick Dunne were outraged. They had continued to investigate the case, trying to gather enough evidence to finally charge Tyson in Dunne's killing. One challenge was that they had initially been unable to recover the murder weapon. There had actually been two guns used in the shootings that night: a Browning semiautomatic and a more exotic number, an Italian-made self-loading pistol. The detectives believed that the guns had come from one of their own – a retired Met Police officer named Sidney Wink, who, after leaving the force, had gone into business as a black-market supplier of untraceable firearms. Wink was suspected of having supplied the guns used by Micky McAvoy and the Brink's-Mat robbers as well. But when officers visited Wink at home to try to interview him in connection with the Constable Dunne killing, he fled and was later found dead in an alley by his house, where he had used one of his own guns to shoot himself.

By early 2003, Tyson was living in southeast London, in a plush apartment by the Thames. Police were still watching him closely, and had managed to plant a listening device inside his residence. When the bug picked up something that sounded like a weapon being loaded, the detectives finally had grounds to move in. On 12

February, they burst into the flat and arrested Tyson for weapons possession.

According to one of the lead investigators, a detective named Keith Butler, the surveillance in the Tyson case had yielded an unrelated but pressing fragment of intelligence. Under British law, when authorities learn that there is a credible threat to a person's life, they have an affirmative duty to inform that person of this danger, a procedure known as an Osman warning. In January 2003, just before Tyson's arrest, Detective Butler had made contact with Verinder Sharma. 'We have reason to believe your life may be in danger,' he said. 'It's up to you to take reasonable steps to look after yourself. But do so within the law.' Butler's advice to Indian Dave was 'Get out of London.'

The detective did not specify how he had come by this information or who might harbour such ill will towards Verinder. But he didn't need to. A week before Tyson's arrest, while authorities were still monitoring his home, they recorded a phone call in which Indian Dave told his friend about the warning.

'I'd take that very serious, man,' Tyson told him. 'If it's that fucking Muscles.'

Tyson, being the sort of person who resorts to gunfire during a minor traffic altercation, was not overly cautious by temperament. But now he seemed genuinely concerned.

'Have you got a bodyguard?' he asked.

Verinder didn't.

'Get a bodyguard,' Tyson advised. 'Now.'

One day the previous year, in the spring of 2002, before the intercepted heroin shipment and the fallout between Muscles and Verinder, a man named Graeme Hammond had received a visit from Indian Dave. Hammond had started his career as a printer, running off promotional flyers for nightclubs. But eventually he went into the nightclub business himself, becoming the owner of a string of establishments from Romford to Ipswich to Manchester, which all shared the kind of unimaginative Orientalist names that are a staple of British nightlife: Buddha Bar, Opium Lounge, etc.

The clubs had been badly in debt, so Hammond purchased them for only two pounds but agreed to take on the £1.6 million that they owed to creditors. According to one of Hammond's former employees, he was not really the owner at all, but 'a bit of a patsy' for some gangsters. Hammond held formal title to the clubs because the real owners needed a 'clean' name – someone without a criminal record – on the licence.

For security, Hammond enlisted the services of Andy Baker. But according to subsequent court testimony, Baker had designs on the clubs. One evening, Hammond was in his printing office, in Clapham, when Baker and Verinder Sharma knocked on the door, accompanied by a couple of henchmen. 'I'll tell you what's going to happen,' Verinder told Hammond, coming in hot, as was his custom. 'We're taking everything you've got. Your cars, your motorbike. And I want £150,000 from you.' As Hammond later recalled, 'Indian Dave then grabbed hold of me, and dragged me into the main office where all the computers were.' Verinder punched Hammond, sat him in a chair, produced a knife with a six-inch blade, and pressed it into Hammond's throat. Hammond could feel the knife breaking the skin and the blood starting to run down his neck. 'Who do you think you are to tell us what we can and can't have?' Verinder growled. Then he jammed one of his fingers directly into the open wound on Hammond's throat.

It wasn't clear how Hammond had wronged these men, if he had at all. The point was that he had things they wanted. They bundled him into a car, where Verinder sat next to him in the back and continued to beat him, until one of the others told him to settle down. Hammond had grown so bloody that they worried some other driver might see him and alert the police. One of the men passed Hammond a black bomber jacket to cover his head with. An abiding personality trait of Indian Dave's was that he could find a way to feel sorry for himself in almost any situation. Now, even as he kept pummelling Hammond in the back seat, he lamented that he was not able to spend more time with his children, blaming Hammond for keeping him from them. As if in recompense, he unstrapped the expensive watch on Hammond's wrist.

When they arrived at their destination, Hammond found himself at the strip club For Your Eyes Only. Verinder felt so comfortable at the venue that he had no problem bringing a bloody hostage there during business hours. As they bundled Hammond through the club, frightened dancers and intimidated customers steered clear. The gang eventually brought Hammond back to his apartment, where they held him captive. They took him to a bank on Clapham High Street and forced him to empty his bank account. They made him turn over the keys to several cars. 'If you try to contact the police, you're a dead man,' Verinder told him. 'If any of us are arrested, you're a dead man.' The crooks wanted Hammond to sign over ownership of the nightclubs, and they appeared to be settling in for a long siege; at one point, one of the captors went out to purchase saline solution for his contact lenses. As Hammond said later, 'I thought I was going to be killed.' But unbeknownst to Hammond's kidnappers, his fiancée had alerted the police, who swooped in and made arrests. Andy Baker and Verinder Sharma were both charged with false imprisonment, along with their two accomplices, David Davenport and Delaney Smart.

When Verinder appeared in court and his full legal name was read out, his codefendants burst into laughter. They'd only ever known him as Indian Dave. To put up the surety for his bail, Verinder enlisted his older brothers, Vinod and Vijay. They were both civilians, not criminals, and the experience could only have been scary and humiliating; to Andy Baker, who saw them in court, they looked ashen.

It appeared that after years of prolific criminal activity, Indian Dave might finally be forced to answer for his actions. But on the opening day of the trial, in June 2003, when Baker and the other defendants filed into Inner London Crown Court, Verinder was nowhere to be found. Instead, a delegation of homicide detectives arrived, looking agitated. One of them approached Andy Baker and said, 'What can you tell me about the murder of Verinder Sharma?'

Indian Dave had disappeared. After he went missing, his burned-out BMW had been discovered. Somebody had torched it. But the authorities had no idea what might have happened to him. No human remains were found in the vehicle, and no corpse turned up elsewhere. Andy Baker hadn't killed him. But when he made a few phone calls to find out if anybody had seen Verinder, nobody had. When detectives searched a property that Verinder had been using, they found his British passport, which made it seem unlikely that he could have fled the country. So where was he? With the mystery of this disappearance hanging over the proceedings, the trial of Baker and his two remaining codefendants moved forwards.

Baker had retained a prominent barrister named Anthony Arlidge. This was their first time working together, but Arlidge turned out to be a formidable litigator. During the two-week trial, at which Graeme Hammond testified for the prosecution, Arlidge was able to raise so many questions about Hammond's credibility that the jury ended up voting to acquit all three defendants. (Some close observers of the case believed that there may have been jury tampering, but no solid proof was ever offered.) Asked about the case now, Baker denies any responsibility for the violence visited upon Hammond and invokes his exoneration by the jury, before murmuring slowly, 'Hammond was very slow on returning consultancies,' and then, even more slowly, '*Someone*... may... have attacked him.'

In future years, Arlidge would represent Andy Baker in many other cases, defending him against charges of murder, shootings, blackmail, false imprisonment and GBH. Baker once beat the charges in a case alleging that he tried to force the director of a professional football team, Queens Park Rangers FC, to resign – at gunpoint. Sometimes, after an acquittal, Baker would thank Arlidge profusely for his expert lawyering, then say, 'I might be needing your services again in six to eight months' time.' In total, Arlidge secured no fewer than fourteen acquittals for Andy Baker over the years, leaving him free to focus on his many criminal enterprises. After celebrating his victory in the Hammond case, Baker received a phone call.

'Hello, mate,' a voice said. It was Verinder.

'Dave, where the fuck *are* you?' Baker asked.

'I'm in Monaco.'

Long before Zac Brettler invented a fictitious alter ego, Verinder Sharma had one too: Justin Patel. And unlike Zac Ismailov, Justin Patel had a passport. Verinder would have known that the crude effort to stage his own death with a torched BMW was unlikely to fool the police for long. But what it would do is provide a temporary distraction to occupy the authorities until he was safely out of Britain. At some point, without any forewarning to his codefendants, Verinder decided that it would be better to hide out on the Côte d'Azur than to risk a hefty prison sentence by going to trial. Andy Baker and Verinder would work together again and remain friends for many years, but Baker never trusted him in quite the same way after he abandoned the trial and allowed the authorities to think, however briefly, that Baker might have murdered him.

By that point, Verinder was contending with more pressing concerns. He had intuited, correctly, that if he could just get out of England, the South of France was as good a place to hide as Spain. 'He might as well have been on a desert island,' one of his criminal associates declared. 'When you're gone... you're *gone*.' The problem was that Dave 'Muscles' King still appeared to want Verinder dead. The initial warning from police had come in January 2003, after Verinder beat Graeme Hammond and held him hostage but before the trial in that case. Matters of pride and macho peacocking can be so paramount for young criminals that a simple beef spirals out of control. It seemed that Muscles wanted vengeance on Verinder for having accused him of being a police informant, so it was probably prudent for him to continue lying low. Fortunately, he had a place in Cannes, an apartment on a fashionable shopping street, rue d'Antibes.

The problem was that Verinder was not suited to a life of exile. He still had lots of business interests in London, all those 'consultancies'. And he was also just lonely. He was 'over there on his own', an associate pointed out. 'And he's a people person.' Verinder was full of contradictions. He was conspicuously diminutive (thus his other gangland nickname, 'the Little Fella'), yet he carried himself like a bigger man. He projected confidence and swagger but could often be emotionally needy. He would be the soul of the party one evening, then mired in self-pity the next. 'He'd moan and groan,'

Andy Baker recalled. Another friend remembered joining him for a party on a yacht. Everybody was drinking and having fun, but Verinder seemed morose. 'I went, "Dave, what's up?" And he said, "I miss my kids."'

All the charges in the heroin case had been dropped by now, and after the acquittals in the Graeme Hammond case, Verinder was desperate to come home. But shortly before he fled London, he had received a *second* Osman warning from the Metropolitan Police. Once again, they refused to mention any names about who specifically might be posing the threat, but they advised Indian Dave that his life was still very much in danger. Verinder's friends would come and visit him in Cannes to try to cheer him up. One of them was an ex-plumber turned armed enforcer who had striking blue eyes and was named Roger Vincent. On 1 September 2003, Vincent was visiting Verinder in France when together they placed a call to Tyson, who by this point was back in prison on weapons charges after police raided his home.

'The Little Fella's with me,' Vincent told Tyson. (The authorities were recording the call.) 'He's gonna go and face the music, bless him.'

He passed the phone to Verinder, who said, 'I've just gotta go back now, innit?'

There was a risk that police would throw Verinder in jail upon his return for absconding during the Graeme Hammond trial. But Tyson pointed out that he could always say he had left only because the police themselves had told him his life was in jeopardy. 'They can't do nothing, mate,' Tyson assured him. 'So far as they're concerned, you're too fucking scared.'

'That's it. Exactly,' Verinder said, warming to this plan. 'I still don't know whether my safety is... Do you know what I mean?'

That was the problem: he *didn't* know about his safety. The authorities he could handle; he'd get a slap on the wrist, maybe serve a few months at most. But the conflict with Muscles was a different matter. He couldn't return to England until he knew for sure that it was safe to do so. As a court document would later put it, Verinder Sharma could not come home 'until the coast had been made clear'.

For a guy who was an avid user of cocaine and steroids and made his living in the clandestine economy, Muscles was something of a homebody, with a predictable routine. He lived in a semi-detached house on a quiet residential street in Stevenage, Hertfordshire, an hour north of London, with his partner and their young children. Five days a week, often accompanied by his best friend, Ian Crocker, Muscles went to the Physical Limits Gym, in Hoddesdon, to lift weights.

One day in September 2003, an armed robber from Manchester named Dean Spencer approached the house in Stevenage, along with an accomplice, armed with a .38 pistol. But when Muscles came to the door, flanked by Crocker, the sheer size of the bodybuilders – and the fact that Muscles happened to be wearing a bulletproof vest – was enough to make these would-be assassins reconsider, and both of them turned and fled. 'They were twice as big as me,' Spencer told his girlfriend afterwards, complaining that the individual who had hired him to do the killing simply wasn't paying enough. 'This is a hundred-grand thing.'

In the aftermath of this botched hit, Verinder's friend Roger Vincent, the blue-eyed ex-plumber, had another phone call with Tyson. 'No one has one-tenth of the arsehole you and me have got,' Vincent said angrily, adding, 'If you want something doing, you've gotta do it your fucking self.'

At 7:15 the following morning, Ian Crocker picked up Muscles in his Peugeot and they drove from Stevenage into Hoddesdon, arriving at Physical Limits by 8 a.m. The gym was a modest two-storey building with a few plastic chairs clustered around the entrance. After lifting for an hour and twenty minutes, Crocker and King exited the gym. They were getting into the Peugeot when a white van pulled up and a masked man aimed an assault rifle at them and opened fire. Muscles went down, killed almost instantly. Crocker sought cover in the footwell of his Peugeot and was hit by shrapnel but survived.

It was a busy weekday morning in a bustling market town, a brazen time and place for a drive-by shooting. There were two members of the execution team: a driver and the shooter. They peeled off in the white van. Witnesses later observed the men dumping the van and setting it ablaze, then climbing into a waiting Mercedes, holding a red bag. One onlooker recalled that one of the men had piercing blue eyes. The next day, a couple were out walking on the Norfolk Broads when they spotted a man in the distance. He hurled a red bag into the water, then ran off. When he was gone, they made their way to the water's edge and retrieved the bag. Opening it, they discovered an assault rifle.

The gun was an AK-47 variant with two handles, a folding stock and a curved high-capacity magazine. It had originated in Hungary, passed through the hands of a notorious Belgian gunrunner, and been smuggled into England, in contravention of the country's strict gun laws. This reportedly marked the first time in history that a fully automatic weapon had been used to murder someone in Britain. The rifle had discharged twenty-six armour-piercing bullets in three seconds.

Roughly three weeks after the murder of Dave 'Muscles' King, Verinder Sharma finally returned to England. He presented himself to authorities and apologized for having fled the country rather than face trial in the Graeme Hammond case, and he was given a perfunctory sentence of three months in Brixton prison. After doing his time, Verinder was released, with no remaining charges against him.

While Indian Dave was doing his stint in Brixton, the Hertfordshire Police were investigating the murder at Physical Limits Gym. It took them nearly a year, but in August 2004, detectives arrested Roger Vincent, along with a second man, David Smith. Ample forensic evidence, such as fibres and DNA, linked both men to the killing. But there were indications that Vincent and Smith had not acted alone, and that this was a contract murder. When the survivor, Ian Crocker, was questioned about who might have wanted to kill his friend, he said that Muscles 'had fallen out with an Indian man in the group, and that there had been threats between them'. In fact, police would learn that before the 3 October shooting, Vincent had travelled to the South of France – where he met with Verinder Sharma. Then, he had flown to Marbella, on the Costa del Sol, for an audience with Micky McAvoy. The men in this little circle regarded McAvoy with such reverence that they referred to him as 'Dad'.

'What about Dad? Did you see Dad over there?' Tyson asked during his phone call with Vincent on the day before the killing.

They had, Vincent said. And Dad 'wanted this done'.

One late summer day in 2005, at a squat modern courthouse in the town of Luton, the trial of Roger Vincent and David Smith began. Security was extremely tight. Armed officers lined the courthouse hallways, and a police helicopter hung in the sky above. The jury would be bused to and from the courthouse each day so that nobody could tail them home. 'Roger Vincent was lethal, utterly ruthless,' one official who was involved in the trial recalled. 'But he was also cocky, quite charming and determined to get away with what he'd done.'

If Vincent had reason to be optimistic, it was because he had beaten a murder charge before. In 1994, a man named Robert Magill was ambushed and shot to death while walking his dog in a wooded area in Hertfordshire. It was a contract killing, and Vincent was tried for the murder. He denied involvement in the killing, and one witness who came forward in support of his claim of innocence was none other than Barry Lavers, the golfer who would go on to become business partners with Verinder Sharma. Lavers made a submission to the court in which he related a complicated story about going on a spontaneous holiday with Vincent to Tenerife several weeks before the killing. The lead detective in this earlier murder prosecution was a crooked cop named Christopher Spackman, who, as it happened, had long-standing ties to Roger Vincent. Vincent ended up getting acquitted in the case, and another man – a former boxer and bouncer named Kevin Lane – was convicted instead and spent twenty years in prison. Lane always fiercely protested his innocence, arguing that Roger Vincent had got away with murder.

Accused of this new killing, of Dave 'Muscles' King, Vincent took the stand, in a pinstriped suit, and once again proclaimed his innocence. As a witness for his own defence, he was affable and slightly cheeky. 'All of my adult life I've been around crooks,

I suppose,' Vincent acknowledged. 'Going to boxing venues all the time, nightclubs, security companies.' It's not like you wake up one day and think, 'I want to be a professional criminal,' he explained. 'It just sort of happens.'

But Vincent could not have murdered Dave King in Hoddesdon that morning in 2003, he insisted, because he was at home in Hazlemere. This time he had two corroborating witnesses. One was his girlfriend, Julie Taylor, who testified that she had been with him all morning. The other was Barry Lavers. Having served as a witness when Vincent stood accused of one killing, Lavers now appeared in court to back up his alibi in another. 'I saw him in the morning,' Vincent said of his friend. Barry had come over to the house to pick up a golf putter, he explained, adding, 'We're both mad on golf.'

The problem with Vincent's alibi was that police had been able to track the movements of his mobile phone that morning, and it was in Hoddesdon at the time of the shooting. So he could not have been at home with Julie and Barry Lavers. But perhaps the most tantalizing shard of evidence in the whole seven-week trial was a call that had been made from Vincent's mobile phone just three minutes after the shooting. It was a brief call, to a phone in the South of France, and the prosecution asked who the number belonged to.

'An Indian fella,' Vincent said. 'Justin Patel.'

Both police and prosecutors knew by now that Justin Patel was Verinder Sharma. In fact, they had developed quite a clear picture of what had transpired in the case. 'This is a tit-for-tat killing,' one of the detectives said during the trial. Muscles 'took a contract out on Sharma', then Sharma, after learning from police that he was in danger, took out a contract on Muscles.

One of the prosecutors, Andrew Bright, pressed Vincent about his phone call after the killing. 'You were ringing up to say, "Dave, good news. Job done. He's dead."'

'What sort of callous person would I be to kill a friend?' Vincent protested.

'The sort of person who, within two seconds, pulled out a machine gun and emptied twenty-six bullets straight into his body.'

Vincent and Smith were both convicted and sentenced to decades in prison. It was a triumphant moment for justice, in theory. But an awkward question lingered during the proceedings. 'One thing puzzles me,' Vincent said on the stand. 'Where's Dave Sharma? Why isn't *he* in the dock?'

'I expect you know precisely where he is,' Bright said.

'Well, he was in prison,' Vincent said. 'He was in from November.' Police were already investigating the murder by the time Verinder returned to England and served his three months in Brixton, getting released only in February. Had nobody spoken to him?

'He is your friend,' Bright redirected. 'Do you know where he is?'

'Haven't got a clue,' Vincent said. 'I know he's been in the country up until recently.'

'Well, when you get his address,' Bright said, 'perhaps you would be kind enough to let us know.'

Indian Dave was not on trial because he had vanished once again. Or not vanished, exactly, because his whereabouts were not a mystery: he'd simply returned to his sanctuary in the South of France. The whole theory of the prosecution's case was that Verinder, with the mentorship of Micky McAvoy, had resolved this gangland dustup by having Muscles killed. Police went so far as to announce that Indian Dave was wanted for questioning. But then they took no steps to track him down. They knew the pseudonym he was living under in France, but they do not appear to have worked very diligently to find him. During the trial, the front page of a local paper featured a photograph of Verinder under a banner that read WANTED and noted that 'a key figure in this incredible saga is still at large'. In a press briefing after the verdict, police acknowledged that they were still looking for Verinder Sharma.

But then nothing happened. Though it now seemed clear that Indian Dave had authorized a broad-daylight contract killing with a fully automatic assault weapon, the authorities made no effort to secure his extradition. It was as if, having convicted the shooters, they felt satisfied that their work was done.

'Every time Sharma got arrested, he seemed to get away,' one former law enforcement official who investigated him recalled. 'He was particularly slippery and quite sinister. But he never got his own hands dirty: he employed contract killers.' At one point, the official recalled, the Metropolitan Police had a list of the ten most wanted criminals in the UK, and 'Sharma was on the list'. After the verdict in the killing of Muscles, Verinder stayed out of England for a while. But he appears to have been less concerned about British authorities than he was about reprisals from his fellow gangsters. He was 'petrified about coming back', according to the testimony of Roger Vincent, because there were people in London who thought 'he might've been responsible' for the Dave King murder. If any allies of Muscles sought revenge, the result could be an all-out war. Eventually, Micky McAvoy, in his capacity as godfather to all these reprobates, was enlisted to engineer what prosecutors would describe as an 'underworld truce'.

Finally it seemed safe for Verinder to come home, so he quietly slipped back into England. Though police were fully aware that the man they had been looking for was now back in the country, they made no effort to arrest him. As Keith Butler, the detective who had initially given him the Osman warning, explained, 'If you've got two convicted of the murder, why would you want to make the effort of trying to convict someone of conspiracy to murder?' Indian Dave was 'clearly the one that organized' the killing, Butler said. 'I have no doubt about that whatsoever. But proving it is a whole different thing.'

The former law enforcement official who'd investigated Verinder, upon learning that he had reappeared in London, expressed surprise that he could have crossed back into the country without being arrested. The warrant for Sharma had 'been withdrawn', a police officer explained. 'We've spoken to him,' the officer told the official. 'But nobody wants to charge him. The case is now closed.'

'Hang on,' the official objected. 'He was involved in a *murder*.'

By 2019, when Sharma was arrested on suspicion of murder in the death of Zac Brettler, he had been living openly in London for years. Many of his closest associates had ended up in prison for long stretches. After years of gathering evidence on the murder of

Constable Patrick Dunne, authorities succeeded at last in securing a conviction against Tyson. Detectives had found the murder weapons buried in a London graveyard, after an anonymous tip instructed them to follow a trail of crosses that had been scrawled in lipstick on various graves and would direct them to where to dig. Tyson received two 'life' sentences, with a minimum term of thirty-five years. Andy Baker, after his improbably long string of acquittals, was finally sent away as well. In 2018 he was convicted in two major cases in Bristol involving cocaine, blackmail and illegal debt collection, and sentenced to eleven years. As he walked out of the courtroom, he sang the chorus of an old Clash song: 'I Fought the Law and the Law Won'.

One of the detectives who investigated Baker described the 'bully-boy tactics' he employed to collect debts or extract money from people. It was a modus operandi that he shared with Indian Dave. Yet over all those years, Verinder somehow managed to spend no real time in prison. He claimed to be reformed and to have moved on from his gangster past. But the truth was that he continued to extort wealthy Londoners, using violence, or just the threat of it.

The more Matthew and Rachelle Brettler learned about Verinder's murderous past and thuggish present, the more horrified they were to think that their son could have become so deeply involved with him, could have *lived* with him, and been stuck in the flat with him on that final night. It made them shudder. What made Akbar Shamji think it was a good idea to introduce a naive eighteen-year-old boy like Zac to such a monster? What was it Akbar had told them at the Méridien? London can be 'dangerous if you're a kid with lots of money'. How could he have thrust Zac into the clutches of Indian Dave?

A terrible scenario was starting to come into focus: Verinder was a carnivore in London's criminal ecosystem who had spent more than two decades identifying people with money, then separating them from it. As he said to Graeme Hammond: 'We're taking everything you've got.' When Akbar introduced Zac Ismailov, this gormless, abandoned billionaire's boy, it must have seemed to Indian Dave like the ultimate prize. *Take the kid in. Mentor him.* Verinder would have known just what to do. *Play the long game. No demands up front.* In fact, he could make Zac feel as if *he* might be the one getting the better end of the bargain: a place to stay, a powerful friend. As the police harvested the communications between Akbar and Verinder from those final days before Zac's death, it became clear that after nearly six months of this long game, the oligarch's son had never produced any money, and Indian Dave was growing impatient. 'I want 5% of that 205 million,' Verinder told Akbar in one message. 'I'm thinking fuck this little kid,' he said in another. At 4:30 p.m. on Zac's final day, Verinder texted Akbar, 'He's not allowed to run away now.'

One friend of Zac's, who had seen him a few days before his death, told the Brettlers that he had seemed nervous. They had driven around West London together, but he was constantly looking over his shoulder. Zac had mentioned to the friend that he was worried his family might be in some sort of danger, and he spoke about possibly going to the police for help. When detectives gained access to Zac's iPad, they found that two days before he died, he did an internet search for 'witness protection uk'.

'Prove that this isn't actually a murder,' one of the detectives had said to Verinder during his interrogation. While the MI6 video might establish that he hadn't physically pushed Zac from the balcony, it seemed undeniable that something nefarious had happened in that Riverwalk flat during those final hours, and that Indian Dave was responsible. Rory Wilkinson, the lead detective, had assured Rachelle and Matthew that the Metropolitan Police would move heaven and earth to find out what had happened to their son and make sure that whoever was to blame would be prosecuted. Perhaps, after decades of getting away with it, Indian Dave might finally be held to account. But then, one day in December 2020, just over a year after Zac's death, Matthew was at home when he received a phone call from Wilkinson. 'There's some information I felt I needed to share with you,' Wilkinson said. 'Sharma has been found dead.'

PART III
THE BALANCE OF PROBABILITIES

Chapter 14

THE CIPRIANI FIVE

LONDON IS SUCH A beautiful place that it can be easy, as you stroll around the city, to forget that much of it was built on imperial plunder. London is the capital of pristine facades, often painted in wedding-cake shades of cream or ivory; the city's dominant aesthetic is a literal whitewash. To launder something – whether it is cash or a reputation – is to mingle the dirty with the clean, and one consequence of London's new identity as a twenty-four-hour laundromat for dirty money is that the city is full of crooks with pretensions to legitimacy and businessmen who seem a little crooked.

When Russia's oligarchs first arrived in the English capital at the turn of the millennium, they required a lot of local help: they needed lawyers and bankers, tax advisers and security consultants, real estate agents and spin doctors. A generation of smart, eager, morally elastic young British professionals enthusiastically signed on to serve as fixers of every stripe. Among them was Scot Young, a charismatic hustler with carefully trimmed stubble, who had grown up in tenement housing in Dundee, Scotland. Young sometimes described himself as a graduate of the exclusive English boarding school Stowe, but, much like Hugo Gryn's stories about his tenure at Cambridge, this was a fib. In truth, Young was a high-school dropout who had started his career as a drug dealer in Scottish nightclubs. He ended up moving to London, where he went into the real estate business and eventually became a trusty facilitator for the exiled Russian billionaire Boris Berezovsky. On the oligarch's behalf, Young would purchase lavish properties, sometimes serving as front man and using shell companies. He assisted Berezovsky in the paperwork jujitsu of moving funds out of Russia, then hiding or laundering the cash as necessary.

This was lucrative work: Young bought grand homes for his own family, showered his wife, Michelle, with extravagant gifts (a Range Rover, a million pounds' worth of jewellery from Graff), and sent his daughters, Scarlet and Sasha, to the very sorts of expensive schools that he claimed to have attended himself. When a friend of his, an English lawyer named Stephen Curtis, who worked with the Russian tycoon Mikhail Khodorkovsky, purchased an Agusta helicopter to commute to a Gothic castle he had bought on an island off the Dorset coast, Young put in an order for an Agusta helicopter of his own. At Cipriani, a pricey restaurant just off Berkeley Square, Young would dine with Berezovsky and a number of other friends, including a couple of English property developers, Paul Castle and Robbie Curtis, and an ex-rock manager named Johnny Elichaoff. This little circle of friends would become known as the Cipriani Five. They shared a certain hard-driving camaraderie, fuelled in some cases by a great deal of cocaine, and approached conspicuous consumption as though it were a competitive sport.

Eventually Scot Young dumped Michelle, igniting a ferocious divorce proceeding in which he claimed to be bankrupt, having lost all his money, and Michelle countered that in fact he was hiding a fortune that might amount to billions. After a judge held him in contempt for refusing to provide financial information, Young was jailed for six months. But he kept fighting his ex-wife. He had taken up with a former model, Noelle Reno. In 2014, Reno landed a lead role in a reality TV series, *Ladies of London*, which chronicled the triumphs and travails of a loose coterie of craven social climbers. Young made fleeting appearances in a number of episodes, looking hungover and nervous, with a sweater knotted around his neck. According to an onscreen caption, he was 'rumoured to be worth millions'. Reno and her friends alluded, vaguely, to Young's 'offshore' business dealings, and there was a suggestion that he had undergone the brief stint in lockup not out of any unwillingness to pay child support but because he felt obliged to protect his 'business partners'.

For a certain kind of adrenaline junkie, working for the Russians in London could be intoxicating. But there was also, unmistakably, a whiff of danger. Berezovsky was waging a very public battle against his former protégé Vladimir Putin, from the apparent safe harbour of Britain, where he managed to obtain political asylum. But there were a number of attempts on his life, including a foiled 2003 plot involving an assassin who was planning to stab Berezovsky during a court appearance in London using a fountain pen that had been loaded with poison. That same year, one of Berezovsky's lawyers, Stephen Moss – an associate of Stephen Curtis, the attorney with the helicopter – was found dead of a sudden heart attack, at forty-six. To be sure, sometimes a heart attack is just a heart attack. But the Kremlin had a reputation for employing the dark arts of targeted assassination, so at a moment when the Russian state seemed intent on killing Berezovsky, the abrupt death of one of his legal advisers occasioned a tremor of discomfort among the other front men and friends in his circle.

One evening in early 2004, Stephen Curtis was flying to his Dorset castle in his Agusta helicopter when the pilot lost control and the aircraft plummeted out of the sky, crashing in a field and exploding in a massive fireball. Both Curtis and the pilot were killed. Before his death, Curtis had grown fearful about his own safety, hiring a team of bodyguards, installing a panic room in the castle, and telling one relative, 'If anything happens to me in the next few weeks, it will not be an accident.' Nevertheless, local police chose to treat the crash as in no way suspicious, and an inquest the following year ruled the death an accident. Scot Young decided that, on reflection, maybe he didn't need a helicopter, after all, and hastily cancelled his order.

In October 2006, a forty-one-year-old Russian diplomat in London, Igor Ponomarev, had a heart attack after a night at the opera. There were some indications that he might have been poisoned, but it was impossible to say, because his body was whisked out of Britain and flown to Russia on a diplomatic plane. The next month, an ex-Russian spy named Alexander Litvinenko was poisoned in the bar of a Mayfair hotel, by drinking a cup of tea that had been laced with radioactive polonium. The doctor who examined Litvinenko's body, measuring the precise quantity of polonium he had ingested, was a leading English expert in radiation absorption named Matthew Puncher. He, too, would later end up dead, in his Oxfordshire home, having been stabbed repeatedly, his body riddled with wounds from two different knives. (A police investigation concluded that it was suicide.)

A pattern was emerging. One by one, people who had consorted with or crossed powerful Russian interests were dying under mysterious circumstances on English soil. 'Britain asks few questions about the provenance of new Russian wealth,' Robert Service, a professor of Russian history at Oxford, said in 2007. 'Hence the hit men who keep arriving on our shores.' The Litvinenko case was so obviously and indisputably a targeted murder – the Kremlin assassins who carried out the hit left a radioactive trail behind them, carelessly exposing random hotel employees – that the British government had little choice but to acknowledge Moscow's responsibility. But even in that extreme case, all Britain could muster by way of reprisal was the polite expulsion of a few Russian diplomats. And in every other instance in which there was any possibility of doing so, British authorities simply categorized suspicious deaths as accidents or suicides and declined to investigate further.

One afternoon in 2010, one of Scot Young's Cipriani friends, the real estate man Paul Castle, walked out of his office on Brook Street, descended into the Tube station at Bond Street and threw himself into the path of an oncoming train. Two years later, a second member of the Cipriani circle died, in exactly the same manner, when Robbie Curtis was killed by a Tube train at Kingsbury station. The following year, it was Berezovsky's turn. He had been extremely careful. After Litvinenko's poisoning, Berezovsky's security detail had begun to carry a Geiger counter so that they could sweep any room or vehicle for radiation. Increasingly, the oligarch had been sequestering himself at his vast estate in rural Ascot. It was there that he was discovered one day in 2013, dead in a locked bathroom, hanged from a shower rail with his favourite cashmere scarf. He had a fractured rib and a fresh wound on the back of his head. But police declared the death non-suspicious and quickly closed the case.

By the following year, Johnny Elichaoff was dead, too. He had once been in the music business, managing Tears for Fears, but he had become addicted to painkillers and money ('His God was money,' a close friend said), and he had got into business with unscrupulous people. Elichaoff plunged to his death from the roof of Whiteleys, in Bayswater, one of Britain's oldest luxury department stores.

A vicious killer appeared to be stalking London: gravity. In each of these cases, there were circumstances – debt, drugs, divorce, depression – that made suicide plausible. But the fact of so many sudden deaths over a short period involving high-flying London businessmen with Russian connections seemed dubious on the face of it. Scot Young was now the only member of the Cipriani Five who was not dead. This sort of thing can make a person paranoid.

And Young had been paranoid to begin with. For a long time he had feared that he might die violently. One night in 2009, he phoned the police at 3 a.m. and begged for protection, saying he was 'going to be assassinated by gangsters and the Russian mafia'. About a month after Elichaoff's death, Young was at home one evening at his Marylebone apartment. He telephoned his daughters, Scarlet and Sasha, but neither of them picked up, so he left upbeat voicemails, telling Sasha that he would try her again in the morning. Five minutes after leaving that message, Young plummeted from the window of his fifth-floor apartment and his body was impaled on the spikes of a wrought iron fence below. He was fifty-two.

Arriving at the scene, police made a quick determination that the death must have been a suicide and announced that there was nothing to investigate. They didn't even bother to dust the apartment for fingerprints. Young's daughters, along with his ex-wife, Michelle, were certain that his death had been not a suicide but murder. Later, when Scarlet and Sasha let themselves into the apartment, they noticed that the window their father had come out of was quite small. He was not a small man; it was difficult to imagine him launching himself out of such a tight opening. When a family friend inquired whether the Metropolitan Police had gone through all the available CCTV footage to see if anyone else might have entered or exited the building, a detective told them, 'I would suspect probably not.' Peering out the fifth-floor window, Scarlet and Sasha made a chilling discovery: on the facade on either side of the window, the sisters spotted lateral scratches on the brick. It looked like scrape marks left by fingers, as if their father had been clawing desperately at the wall to stop himself from being thrown out.

In 2017, *BuzzFeed* published a groundbreaking investigation identifying fourteen men 'who all died suspiciously on British soil after making powerful enemies in Russia'. According to the report, US intelligence agencies possessed evidence suggesting that numerous deaths that had been characterized by the London police as suicides were actually murders. Why would British authorities be so complacent in the face of a brazen targeted assassination campaign? One answer was an institutional culture of timidity in English police departments, which, after decades of budget cuts, greeted any hint of international intrigue by simply declaring themselves outmatched. Though it still enjoyed a reputation for competence, owing to its long history as one of the most famous police forces in the world, the truth was that Scotland Yard was severely underfunded. Half of the police stations in England had been shut down since 2010, and some twenty thousand officers had been let go. A recent assessment by the police inspectorate found that the Met was failing in almost all work areas and that one category in which it was particularly ineffective was 'investigating crime'. The force wasn't equipped to solve basic, unsophisticated crimes such as burglary, never mind homicides carried out by foreign intelligence services and dressed up to resemble suicides or accidental deaths.

But if the plodding ineptitude of Scotland Yard offered one explanation for the strange reluctance of British authorities to investigate suspicious Russia-linked fatalities, there was another, much darker possibility: Britain had become so reliant on the largesse of Russia's oligarchs that decisions had been made at a high level not to persecute London's new mafia class, and to instead extend to them the courtesy of being able to kill their enemies in England with impunity. By the time Litvinenko was assassinated, Britain had become the biggest investor in Russia's energy sector. One national security adviser to the British government told *BuzzFeed* that ministers were desperate not 'to antagonize the Russians'. A report by the think tank Chatham House concluded that the tepid response by British officials to Litvinenko's murder had sent a signal to the Kremlin extending carte blanche, for all intents and purposes, to kill again. And, sure enough, the killing continued: in 2018, another former Russian spy, Sergei Skripal, was poisoned, along with his daughter, by a nerve agent in the English city of Salisbury. Both were sickened but survived the attack. Others were not so lucky. The assassins, a pair of Russian hit men, had stored the nerve agent inside a bottle of perfume. After the operation, they discarded the bottle – which still contained enough of the deadly chemical to kill thousands of people. A Wiltshire man named Charlie Rowley later happened upon it. The perfume 'looked expensive', he said. So he presented it to his partner, Dawn Sturgess, as a gift. She was forty-four and had three kids. She sprayed the contents of the bottle on her wrists and rubbed them together. It killed her. That same year, another Berezovsky ally, a Russian businessman and Kremlin critic named Nikolai Glushkov, was found dead at his home on the outskirts of London. He had been strangled with a dog leash. His daughter said that his killer had tried to 'stage' the death as a suicide. (The case remains unsolved.)

Zac Brettler had been fascinated by the 2014 death of Scot Young. Occasionally he would intimate to Rachelle that he had learned the truth about how Young had ended up impaled on that iron fence in Marylebone. Matthew and Rachelle had not followed the story of the Cipriani Five or the other deaths in London all that closely. But when Zac died, in 2019, his own fall seemed to share a few uncanny similarities with these other cases. Considering that Zac had posed as a Russian, and that he had been introduced to Akbar Shamji by Mark Foley, who worked for Roman Abramovich, it raised an obvious question: could malevolent Russian forces have somehow been involved in his death? This had been Rachelle's fear from the moment Akbar told her about Zac's alter ego – that he might have crossed the Russians, with fatal consequences.

Verinder Sharma's death, a year after Zac's, only compounded this aura of intrigue. Detective Rory Wilkinson informed the Brettlers that Verinder had died in his Riverwalk apartment, apparently from a 'drug overdose', possibly a 'suicidal drug overdose', and that police were treating the death as 'non-suspicious'. But when Matthew pressed for more details, Wilkinson said something strange.

He couldn't tell them more, because he didn't *know* much more, he said; he and his colleagues were being 'kept sterile' from the investigation into Verinder's death.

What did *that* mean? the Brettlers wondered. Was it some kind of conflict of interest for the lead detective investigating Zac's death to know the circumstances in which his own prime suspect wound up dead? And if police could not determine whether Verinder had died by suicide or accidental overdose, didn't it stand to reason that there might be a third possibility, namely murder? But Wilkinson would tell them no more. Verinder was the only person who 'knew for sure' what had happened to Zac, he pointed out. And now he was dead.

In her 2019 book *From Russia with Blood*, the lead reporter in the *BuzzFeed* investigation, Heidi Blake, describes how citizens in Putin-era Russia became acculturated to a certain 'dissonance' in day-to-day life. They could no longer trust that a suicide or an overdose or a heart attack or a fall was really what it appeared to be. Occasionally fellow citizens just died suddenly, and while there may have been rumours suggesting foul play, the official story foreclosed any hope of achieving real answers, and so nobody could ever say for sure. This erosion of accountability and erasure of the clean line separating fact from conspiracy created a 'fog of ambiguity', Blake writes, that could hang over a whole society, as thick and impenetrable as the smog that once hung over the Thames. When Rachelle and Matthew considered the death of their son, and the death of the last person to see him alive, they experienced that same eerie dissonance, a sensation they had always associated with corrupt societies in other places, like Russia, rather than with the city they called home.

The Brettlers had two sons, then they had one, and the feeling of dislocation they experienced after Zac's death was only exacerbated, and made more strange, by the onset of the Covid pandemic. When lockdowns began, Joe stayed with his parents at home, and their new family dynamic felt particularly stark in the isolation of pandemic life: suddenly they were a household of three. Matthew and Rachelle had been assured by Scotland Yard that police were working diligently, but for months at a stretch there were no updates, and the Brettlers were unsure whether this was a quirk of the pandemic or the way a murder investigation normally operates. With no word from the cops, and with so much of ordinary life suspended, they found themselves turning the facts of Zac's death over in their minds and wondering how it could possibly have happened. The more Rachelle and Matthew thought about Akbar Shamji and Verinder Sharma, the more angry it made them. In the days between Zac's disappearance and the identification of his body, these older men had both maintained that he was still alive and had merely run off to score drugs. Both had promised to help find Zac and bring him home, though they must have known full well at the time that he was already dead. And to think that Matthew and Rachelle had been so *thankful* to these men and expressed such appreciation for their kindness and generosity. Sitting with Akbar at the Méridien – 'Akbar the family man, with two children and a well-known wife,' Matthew sputtered – while he lied to them so brazenly and they, in their desperation, were so ready to believe him.

Grief can function like a time machine. Life goes on: you return to work and celebrate the holidays and keep getting out of bed each day. Winter gives way to spring, one month leads to the next. But in your mind you keep getting jerked back to these specific painful moments in the past. This was the uncanny existence in which the Brettlers found themselves. They bought groceries. They made dinner. They looked after their surviving child. But at the same time, on some bone-deep level, they could not assimilate this new reality in which their nineteen-year-old son was dead. 'I literally had a stomachache for months after he died,' Rachelle recalled. 'Because you're having to digest grief.' In endless conversations and in their private thoughts, they returned incessantly to different moments on the timeline, trying to identify off-ramps: *If he hadn't gone to Riverwalk that night. If Akbar had never introduced him to Verinder. If there'd been a more aggressive psychiatric intervention. If he'd never attended Mill Hill...* As they reconsidered Rachelle's brief conversation with the driver, Carlton, on the morning after Zac's death ('That can't be his mum. His mum's in Dubai'), Matthew started to wonder if that whole encounter had not itself been a charade.

'There was no chance of Zac being at the apartment,' he pointed out – because Verinder almost certainly knew by that point that Zac was dead. So why send the driver to knock on the door? Could these men have been so cynical and devious that, hours after Zac's death, they were already preparing a sort of alibi, a ruse to suggest that they had been trying to find Zac because he was just off looking for drugs, even though in truth they knew exactly what had become of him?

For at least a year after Zac's death, Rachelle felt as though she were living on that balcony with him, shivering in the cold night air, locked out of the normal existence she once knew, trapped in a kind of limbo between life on solid ground and the abyss. The awful conundrum of her son's final moments – the inconclusiveness – felt like a 'madness', she thought. She found a measure of comfort and healing after Zac's death by speaking to her therapist. Joe also started seeing a therapist after Zac died.

Family friends suggested that it might be a good idea for Matthew to have a professional he could talk to. But Matthew had never gone in for therapy and didn't feel the need to do so now. He had a supportive community of close friends, people he had known for many years, and he claimed to feel no real inhibition about opening up to them. He was so analytical by temperament, he pointed out, that he was quite capable of analyzing himself.

What he did do, in 2020, was enroll in a master's degree programme at King's College London. The subject was conflict resolution. In his professional life, he often intermediated between different financial institutions, so he liked the idea of studying the process of finding the point at which two parties can come together and make a deal. The courses were all virtual, because of the pandemic, but Matthew relished being back in school again after so many years, the rigour and community of it. Besides, he liked the idea of trying to immerse his restless mind in something 'that isn't Zac's death'. Matthew was the oldest student in the course, by some margin. But he got along with his young classmates and found them stimulating and impressive. They did not know that Matthew had recently lost a child, and he did not tell them. 'It's quite a lot to put on people,' he explained. He often struggled with this dilemma of how much to reveal about the tragedy that had engulfed him. When he reconnected with old friends he hadn't spoken to in a while, they would ask, 'And how are the children?' Matthew would hesitate, thinking, 'I'm not going to lay this story on them.' At first he wondered if he might be disrespecting Zac's memory somehow by opting not to tell people. But it's also not fair when people innocently ask and then feel awful for having done so, he thought. So often he would dissolve the awkwardness with humour, saying, with a gentle smile, 'You're going to really regret asking that question…'

At night, Rachelle would sometimes find herself scrolling, with a touch of masochism, through social media posts, looking at pictures of the Sharma and Shamji families: Verinder's daughters, Dominique and Matisse, appeared poised and confident, posing at a birthday party; Akbar's children, Safiya and Akbar Jr, seemed so elegant and happy and alive. On 29 November 2020, the one-year anniversary of Zac's death, Safiya posted a picture of her father, grinning, next to the regal Weimaraner, Alpha Nero, on a sofa upholstered in blue velvet. Akbar's wife, Daniela Karnuts, was often interviewed in the media, talking up her brand, Safiyaa, as if her husband had not recently been arrested on suspicion of murder. Daniela was the kind of creative entrepreneur who, under different circumstances, Rachelle might have featured in a *How to Spend It* article for the *Financial Times*. When Meghan Markle made one of her final public appearances as a member of the royal family, she wore a red caped dress by Safiyaa. 'It was a moment that will go down in history,' Daniela proclaimed, optimistically, to *People* magazine. She enthused about the ways in which her business was adjusting to the changing market conditions of the pandemic, pivoting to 'luxurious cashmere sweaters' and 'languid tunics'.

Matthew had always enjoyed taking long bike rides to clear his head. When Zac was alive, it was an activity they sometimes did together. From time to time during the pandemic, Rachelle and Joe would join Matthew and the three of them would cruise around London on their bikes, zipping straight down the middle of the wide, deserted streets. Rachelle would go for solo rides as well, and sometimes she'd find herself in Mayfair. On one of these jaunts, she passed 52 Berkeley Square, Akbar's business address, where she had once met Zac to take Alpha Nero on a walk. By the entrance, Rachelle saw something she hadn't noticed before: a panel featuring no fewer than twenty-five buzzers, each bearing the name of a different business. Either the accommodations were very crowded inside or this was all sleight of hand – an illustrious street address that in reality was just a mail drop.

One day she was cycling along Mount Street when she spotted Akbar. It was the first time she had seen him since their meeting at the Méridien months earlier. He was talking on his phone outside the Connaught hotel, a sumptuous heirloom of the British aristocracy now owned by the ruling family of Qatar. To Rachelle it looked as though he didn't have a care in the world.

Later she would acknowledge that it might not have been a total coincidence to find herself cycling down the very street where Akbar Shamji lived. The truth was that she had been haunting that corner of Mayfair. Yet when she spotted him outside the hotel that day, lean and courtly, with his sharp jawline and his elegantly shaggy hair, she couldn't summon the nerve to get off her bike and confront him. Anyway, what could she say?

She wondered sometimes if she might pass Daniela. The two of them had never met or spoken, but Rachelle knew what she looked like, having studied the glamorous photos of her on the internet. If she did ever run into Daniela, she knew what she would say: 'I'm Zac's mum. As a mother, is there anything you can tell me about what happened that night?'

Britain was finally coming out of the pandemic in November 2021 when Detective Rory Wilkinson paid a visit to the Brettlers in their flat on Lauderdale Road. Two years had passed since Zac's death, and Matthew and Rachelle had felt a growing sense of impatience for some kind of deliberate police action. Verinder Sharma might be dead, but Akbar Shamji was still very much alive, and he had not been charged with a thing. This meeting would represent their first real update on the status of the investigation, and they weren't sure how disgruntled they should feel. Rachelle and Matthew shared a strong instinct to always be polite and cordial, to never sound arrogant or entitled. It went against their every impulse to assert themselves in a demanding fashion. But after two years of waiting, they were starting to wonder if that had really been the best approach. As they all took seats in the front room, the Brettlers asked for permission to record the meeting. They knew this would be an important conversation, and afterwards they would want to study every bit of evidence that was about to be revealed.

Wilkinson began by pulling out a detailed summary of the case. 'I can't give you a copy of this,' he said apologetically, as it contained sensitive information. But he would read aloud to the Brettlers from it. Detectives had assembled a great deal of digital evidence, from phone records to CCTV, and there were important elements of the timeline that Wilkinson would now be able to fill in. Both Akbar and Verinder had claimed to police that on Zac's final night, after Akbar left the Riverwalk apartment and drove away, Verinder had simply gone to sleep. But this was a lie, because police had discovered that at 2:12 a.m. Verinder telephoned Akbar and they had a call that lasted nine minutes.

'Two minutes after the conversation finishes... Zac falls,' Wilkinson said.

'Do you think Zac was listening?' Rachelle asked. Perhaps something Verinder told Akbar on that phone call had prompted Zac to flee to the balcony.

'It could be all sorts of things,' Wilkinson said noncommittally, before returning to the call data. 'Zac falls from the balcony at 2:24 a.m.,' he continued. 'At 2:26 a.m. – so two minutes after Zac has fallen – Sharma makes another call.' This time he telephoned his daughter Dominique, Wilkinson said, and the call lasted for three minutes and twenty-eight seconds.

'Who calls people at two thirty in the morning?' Matthew interjected. How had Dominique explained the call in her police interview?

Dominique had not been formally interviewed for the investigation, Wilkinson said awkwardly. But she did provide a statement in which she described coming to the apartment that evening after receiving a call from her father saying that 'Zac had betrayed them'.

Both Brettlers were taken aback to learn that police might not have questioned such a crucial witness in the case. But Matthew was startled, also, by this small revelation about Dominique's conversation with her father. 'She's the first one to talk in those terms, isn't she?' he asked Wilkinson.

'"Betrayal"?'

'That's a very strong word,' Matthew pointed out.

The Brettlers were eager to talk with Wilkinson about their theory that Verinder had sent the chauffeur, Carlton, to their apartment that Friday morning to 'lay an alternative trail', making it seem as though he and Akbar did not yet know that Zac was dead. But Wilkinson seemed dubious about this idea, intimating that these men didn't strike him as clever enough to concoct such a ruse.

'They might not be smart, but they're not totally stupid,' Matthew said. And 'if a nineteen-year-old falls from your balcony, that focuses the mind'. Anyway, what did Carlton say when the police asked him about it?

They hadn't spoken to Carlton. In fact, the police did not even appear to have worked out what Carlton's last name might be. One challenge in any investigation is sorting out which witnesses have something valuable to offer and which are merely tertiary to the matter at hand. In the various text messages they had obtained, the police had uncovered evidence of numerous business deals involving Zac, Akbar and Verinder. There was talk of a 'football agent', of some kind of standoff with 'debt collectors', and of a man named Oliver Harris. But Wilkinson told the Brettlers that he didn't know what sort of business arrangement there might have been between the men, and he did not appear especially eager to find out, as if all that talk was somehow beside the point. He seemed to discount out of hand the hypothesis that Zac's death could have resulted from a business deal gone wrong, and that it might therefore be important to figure out the precise nature of Zac's business arrangements. Police had not bothered to look into who the football agent might be, or who the debt collectors were. Nor did they make any effort to speak to Oliver Harris. The only thing that mattered, Wilkinson stressed, was that for a period of time there had been a bond of trust between Akbar and Verinder and Zac – and in Zac's final days, that trust appeared to have broken down. Zac seemed increasingly desperate, and while it might be tempting to dismiss claims by Akbar and Verinder that he was suicidal, evidence existed from *before* Zac's death that he might have been. On the afternoon of Zac's final day, Wilkinson informed the Brettlers, Akbar had sent a message to Verinder saying that Zac was 'basically on suicide watch with us right now'.

This was an upsetting thing for the Brettlers to hear – but they didn't buy it. Clearly Zac had found himself in some kind of serious trouble in those final days, and Matthew and Rachelle were prepared to believe that their son might have told people he was suicidal – in the same way that he had told people he was addicted to heroin – as a cry for help, or for absolution. But they simply could not accept the idea that Zac might actually have had any genuine intention of killing himself. There was nothing in Zac's psychiatric background to indicate a penchant for suicide: no history of depression, no previous attempts, no suicidal ideation that they were aware of. And he'd been planning for the future. Zac didn't want to end his life; on the contrary, he seemed so ravenously impatient for his adult life to *begin*. One of his last messages to Rachelle, hours before his plunge into the Thames, was about paying for a driver's education programme so that he could obtain his licence. After Akbar returned the weekend bag that Zac had brought to Riverwalk, Rachelle had gone through it, gently handling her son's prosaic belongings, which now seemed like precious artefacts. Zac had always possessed a punctilious streak, and Rachelle found all the essentials he would need for a long weekend: toiletries, stacks of underwear and T-shirts, everything neatly folded. She repacked the bag and stored it in Zac's old bedroom, as if he might come home one day and need it. And anytime the notion of Zac deliberately taking his own life was entertained, her mind would flash, instinctively, to that bag. 'This is not the bag of someone who is planning to commit suicide,' Rachelle said.

But then, sometimes suicide isn't planned; it's often quite spontaneous. Perhaps Zac felt cornered by his own deceptions, Wilkinson ventured. After all, he had misled these men for months into believing that he had great wealth, and now they appeared to be figuring out that he'd been lying. He had 'betrayed' them – that was the word Verinder had invoked to Dominique – and now he would be forced to answer for what he had done. Besides, there was another reason Zac might have been feeling desperate and fearful that his falsehoods were about to catch up with him: he was completely out of money.

Before Zac's nineteenth birthday, in September 2019, Matthew and Rachelle had given him access to approximately £18,000. The money was rightfully his; it was the accumulation of many smaller cheques that his grandparents had given him throughout his life, along with gifts from his bar mitzvah. But the funds had remained untouched, gathering interest in a Santander account for which Matthew served as custodian. After Zac turned eighteen, he had started to ask his parents for access to the money. He badgered them for months before Matthew finally consented. But, as Matthew saw it, Zac was no longer a minor, and it *was* his money; Joe had been given access to all of his bar mitzvah money when he turned eighteen. Legally speaking, the parents had no justification for withholding the funds, and perhaps this could be an opportunity for Zac, who now appeared to be getting his own fledgling businesses off the ground, to learn financial responsibility. So Matthew transferred the money to Zac's HSBC account. It was only in retrospect that the Brettlers determined that Zac had never had £850,000 at his disposal and that he'd falsified the record he showed Matthew on his iPad. The £18,000 he did have apparently came in handy for maintaining the illusion that he was an oligarch's son, paying for Ubers and picking up the tab just often enough to seem credible. But London is an expensive city, so Zac appears to have burned through the funds quite quickly. When Matthew consulted the HSBC statements, he found that by the day Zac died, he was down to just £4 in the account.

At the very moment when Zac's funds were dwindling to nothing, Wilkinson told the Brettlers, Verinder Sharma had been growing more aggressive in his assertions that he should be entitled to some share of Zac's imaginary fortune. It was clear from the messages that 'things have gone wrong', Wilkinson said. 'They are working out that Zac doesn't have £7 billion,' he continued. 'They obviously had their eyes on the prize, as it were.'

'I'm highly sceptical about this 205 million,' Akbar told Verinder in one voice memo. 'Is anything fucking real?'

'Ask him how much he has been given to live on,' Verinder wrote to Akbar, suggesting that they 'go to a cash machine with his card'.

Judging by the messages, it appeared that Zac might have made promises to Verinder to provide him with some money. But Verinder was growing impatient – and angry – to the point where, in one message, Akbar advised Zac to 'not speak to him at all' and instead to rely on Akbar as a go-between. At one point Verinder sent an audio message to Akbar in which he spoke about how the two of them should be entitled to 'fifty per cent of everything he owns'.

'Wow,' Rachelle murmured sardonically. 'Fifty per cent of four pounds.'

On that final night at Riverwalk, twenty minutes before he went off the balcony, Zac had emailed his mother for the last time: 'All good x.' He was using his iPad, and Wilkinson now informed the Brettlers that a minute after Zac hit send on that email, he had done an internet search for 'what to do with skin burns'.

Matthew was immediately reminded of the text exchange between Akbar and his friend from the music business, Mervin, about how Akbar was 'heating up knives and clearing up blood'. Surely these two clues must be connected?

'So, first of all, there was no sign of any burns on Zac,' Wilkinson said, in a tone that suggested he was gently steering Matthew away from a tempting rabbit hole. 'There were no signs of any stab wounds or knife wounds...'

Even so, Matthew thought, it couldn't be a coincidence that Akbar was talking about heating up knives and a few hours later Zac was googling about skin burns. Had they asked Mervin what *he* thought Akbar was referring to?

'We haven't,' Wilkinson said, adding, with a hint of impatience, 'I think he's just a friend of Shamji. He has nothing to do with this.'

Wilkinson seemed like a kind man, and Matthew did not want to offend him by telling him how to do his job, but he couldn't restrain himself. 'I don't have all the sort of knowledge that you guys have,' he said carefully. 'But if I were in your shoes, and I came across something like that, I would *want* to go down that rabbit hole and find out what *was* that? Why was he sending a message like that?'

Maybe it was a threat, Rachelle suggested. What if Verinder had told Zac, 'I'm going to burn you', even if he didn't follow through with it?

She kept coming back to the image of Zac's supposed friend Akbar Shamji craning over the river wall to peer into the Thames. Zac was shirtless when he was found the next morning, she pointed out, and his 'skin was luminous white'. The tide was high when he jumped. Could Akbar have seen him there, in the water, drowning?

Not necessarily, Wilkinson said. Sometimes a body will plunge deep beneath the surface and stay there for a while before popping back up. In Zac's case, it seemed likely that the reason he did not end up getting carried further downstream, and instead was found on the muddy bank in front of Riverwalk when the tide receded, was that the stone foundation of Vauxhall Bridge would have blocked the current, creating a little cul-de-sac on that edge of the river.

The thought that Zac may have been alive after he hit the water was what Rachelle kept returning to – those 'few minutes of brain activity'. It was tempting to wonder if, in those final seconds of consciousness, he might have glimpsed Akbar, looking down at him from above and doing nothing.

But Zac's hip had hit the wall on the way down, Wilkinson noted. That's a big impact. He was probably unconscious as soon as he hit the water.

Was there any chance, Rachelle asked, that if Zac had just managed to land directly in the river, he might still be alive today?

'Without the wall?' Wilkinson thought for a moment. 'I can't say.'

Rachelle's mother, Jacqueline, had been known, in her youth, as a great beauty. Jacqueline had a younger sister, Sonia, who was less glamorous and always a bit in her shadow. As a young woman, Sonia decided to move to California, and Rachelle always believed that she had left England in part because to stay might mean feeling somewhat 'eclipsed' by her older sibling. In Los Angeles, Sonia got married and found a job as a personal assistant to Charles Bronson, the moustached film star of such B movies as *Death Wish* (1974) and its sequels. Bronson often played a vigilante forced by the corruption or incompetence of the authorities to take matters into his own hands. Sonia worked for him on the 1984 thriller *The Evil That Men Do*, which concerns an assassin who comes out of retirement to avenge the death of his friend. ('When the system of justice doesn't work... *Bronson* does,' a dramatic voice growls in the movie's trailer. 'When the courts can't do what they must... *Bronson* will.') But Sonia was eventually diagnosed with a rare neurological disorder, Fahr syndrome. The condition is incurable and can lead to the gradual deterioration of motor function, seizures and dementia. She grew depressed, and one year, on her birthday, she tried to kill herself by running into traffic on the freeway in LA. Then, in May 1997, ten days before her sixty-fourth birthday, Aunt Sonia tidied up her apartment, did a load of laundry, wrote a note to her husband, Ron, lay down on her bed, and shot herself.

When she learned about the circumstances of Sonia's death, Rachelle was full of respect for her aunt's decision. 'She did it, really, as sweetly as one could,' she reflected. Sonia's prognosis was dreadful, and she wanted to end her life on her own terms and at a time of her choosing, with some dignity. 'I think of her as a very brave woman,' Rachelle concluded. When the Metropolitan Police began to suggest that perhaps Zac had committed suicide, Rachelle found herself thinking about Aunt Sonia. There was no stigma in her family associated with the taking of one's own life. On the contrary, it was a choice that, at least in the case of Aunt Sonia, Rachelle was able not only to accept but to admire. Sitting in her front room talking to Rory Wilkinson, she just did not believe that her son had been suicidal, and she felt clear-eyed enough about the issue to be certain that she was not simply suffering from the selective blindness of parental denial.

After two years of what the police maintained was intensive investigation, Wilkinson seemed unable to deliver any definitive conclusions. Instead he spoke about Zac's death in the detached tones of a philosophy professor ruminating on the fundamental unknowability of human existence. 'Something I found in this investigation is it goes both ways,' Wilkinson mused. When he first read Akbar's texts to Mervin about heating up knives, 'I'm thinking, "Crikey!"' But then, reading the messages in which 'Zac's saying he's suicidal... there's a certain amount of that that rings true.' Wilkinson stopped short of any firm pronouncement that Zac had killed himself, but he returned again and again to the possibility. Zac had been 'spinning stories', he noted. He'd told a lot of lies. Perhaps in the end what he wanted was 'to walk away'.

Before Scot Young, the Berezovsky front man, went out the window of his apartment in Marylebone, he had been admitted to a hospital on one occasion after taking a bunch of tranquilizers and superficially cutting his wrists. In the aftermath of his death, this incident was cited as an indication that Young probably *had* jumped out the window of his own volition. But the doctors who saw Young at the hospital had concluded that the wrist-cutting incident was not a bona fide suicide attempt at all; rather, he had 'wanted people to think he was suicidal', because he owed millions of pounds to angry creditors and was looking to buy time. If Zac Brettler told the men to whom he'd promised money that he was suicidal, then such utterances should be understood in a similar light, his parents thought. After all, Zac lied about *everything*. He lied about being the son of an oligarch, and living in One Hyde Park, and being addicted to heroin. It seemed a bit opportunistic for the police (to say nothing of Akbar Shamji) to decide that on this one matter of being suicidal, Zac might suddenly start telling the truth. Wasn't it more likely that the reason Zac told the older men he wanted to die was because he was terrified of them?

Wilkinson had a gentle face and seemed earnest and sympathetic as he listened to Rachelle and Matthew. But when it came time to respond to all their anxious questions and theories, he would not offer much beyond an existential shrug. In the grand scheme of things, it ultimately didn't matter if Verinder Sharma had caused Zac's death. 'Whether it's true or not, we can't prove it now anyway, with Sharma gone,' he said. But what about Akbar? the Brettlers wondered. He had delivered their son to this gangland brute with a long history of violence. By Wilkinson's own account, Akbar had lied promiscuously to the police. Couldn't he be charged with obstructing justice somehow?

The trouble, Wilkinson explained, was that in the United Kingdom, lying to the police, by itself, is not a crime. So the fact that Akbar had lied, and lied so brazenly, was of little consequence. And while there *is* a crime for perverting the course of justice, the authorities had determined that because the MI6 video appeared to show Zac jumping from the balcony, and nobody pushing him, it would be impossible to make the case that he was murdered. So they couldn't prove that Akbar had been an accessory to a crime – because they couldn't prove that any crime had been committed in the first place.

Chapter 15

PRIVATE INVESTIGATIONS

THERE WAS NO SINGLE eureka moment when it dawned on the Brettlers that the Metropolitan Police had given up on solving the mystery of their son's death. It was more of a gradual awakening. Throughout his adult life, Matthew had possessed a kind of default expectation that as a citizen of a big, prosperous city like London, he could place a lot of faith in the authorities. This unexamined confidence was surely at least in part a symptom of his own advantages: he was a white man in a nice neighbourhood, well-off, highly educated, reasonably well-connected. But Matthew was also just upbeat by disposition and tended to take a generally benign view of other people, so he had always maintained some baseline trust in the system. After two years of waiting, however, with no firm answers to show for it, and in the face of Rory Wilkinson's repeated suggestion that perhaps Zac's death was just a run-of-the-mill teen suicide, Matthew was forced, in a way that he never had been previously, to fundamentally question that trust.

When Rachelle was in labour the first time, with Joe, Matthew had been by her side in the hospital during the hours before the birth. As a midwife looked after Rachelle and nurses came in and out, Matthew took a good-natured interest, as was his habit, in what everybody was doing, asking questions and listening carefully to their answers. He examined all the devices, including the monitor that measured the baby's heartbeat in the womb. At one point, when no doctor or nurse was about, Matthew noticed that Joe's heart rate was somewhat elevated. Figuring that this was probably normal, Matthew kept a casual eye on it. But now, suddenly, the heartbeats started accelerating. The midwife, who was in the room, did not appear to have noticed, so Matthew sounded the alarm. First-time parents are often overly anxious. Confused by the science of childbirth, they are prone to undue panic. But in this instance, Matthew's warning proved to be spot-on: Joe had become stuck in the birth canal – 'sunny-side up', as Rachelle put it – and the position was putting stress on his heart. All at once, Rachelle was being wheeled into an operating theatre, flanked by doctors and nurses, and Joe was delivered, safely, by emergency C-section.

If you happened to mention to Matthew that you were taking a night flight to Mumbai, he was the sort of person who, for no reason beyond his own curiosity, might consult a website that tracks flights, deduce the one you were likely on, check the make and model of the aircraft, and take a peek at the prevailing conditions on the route. He liked to know things, and to find things out. Professionally, he might have been a finance guy who spent his career structuring complex deals, but temperamentally, he was a natural investigator. In the early phases of the police investigation into Zac's death, Matthew had been impressed by everything Rory Wilkinson was saying about leveraging the formidable resources of Scotland Yard to answer all the relevant questions. Wilkinson had seemed determined, systematic and oriented to detail. 'It was exactly along the lines of if I had done it,' Matthew reflected with approval. But when the MI6 video of Zac jumping emerged, taking the possibility of a standard murder prosecution off the table, and then the principal suspect in the case turned up dead, it was as if Wilkinson and his colleagues had 'completely lost interest', Matthew said. The detectives continued to make noises about pursuing various leads, and they assured the Brettlers that the case was still open, but Matthew would ultimately conclude that at some point in the spring of 2020, just months after Zac's death, the police had quietly stopped trying.

This left him, like the protagonist in a Charles Bronson movie, with no choice but to continue the investigation himself. One chilly Sunday morning in February 2022, not long after the visit from Rory Wilkinson, Matthew entered Café Society, the brightly lit eatery on the ground level of Riverwalk, and sat down with the proprietor, Pino D'Amore. Matthew had received an email out of the blue a few months earlier from a veteran London journalist named John Sweeney. During the pandemic, Sweeney had often taken long walks along the Thames, stopping at Café Society on the way. He befriended Pino D'Amore, and one day Pino related to Sweeney the story of the dead body he'd seen on the riverbank in 2019. Pino even shared with Sweeney a photograph he had taken of Zac's corpse. Sweeney had worked for the BBC for many years, producing investigative documentaries on North Korea and the Church of Scientology. 'I'm planning to write an article about the death,' he emailed Matthew. He had been in touch with a source at the Metropolitan Police, he said, who told him that the 'prime suspect' in the case had died but that 'they are investigating a third man for perverting the course of justice'.

The Brettlers were not sure that they were ready for such an article. And when they spoke to Sweeney, he suggested that if he was unable to get an assignment from some prominent news outlet, perhaps they could instead just pay him directly to investigate the story. One figure he mentioned was £20,000; he could make a podcast, maybe, perhaps even write a book. The notion of paying a journalist in this fashion made the Brettlers leery, however. So they stalled for time, and eventually Sweeney moved on to other things. But he did introduce Matthew to Pino D'Amore.

A dapper Lombardian with neatly trimmed white hair, Pino spoke with a thick Italian accent. He remembered Verinder Sharma well, he told Matthew, because he used to come into the café from time to time. Pino knew nothing about the circumstances of Verinder's death. But he had a vivid recollection of the morning Zac's body was found. The police had come and gone surprisingly quickly, Pino thought, whisking the corpse away on a boat. He told Matthew that he had spoken with a local man who also knew Verinder and had suggested to Pino that Zac's death might be linked to 'the Russians'.

The café was a convivial space, with views across the river to MI6 and shelves lined with boxes of Cipriani pasta. The place was empty as they sat and talked, but Pino explained that some of his regular customers were doormen who worked at Riverwalk. Matthew wanted to know more about these people. Detectives had taken the statement of a woman named Ana Nunes, who was head concierge of the building. On the morning Zac was discovered, Nunes had just arrived for her 8 a.m. shift when she was informed by colleagues that 'a body had been found in the river'. One of the doormen, a man named Bogdan, told her that just prior to her arrival, the tenant in 504 – Mr Sharma – had placed a call from his apartment to the front desk. What he said, Bogdan told Nunes, was 'Has someone jumped from the balcony?'

In her statement to police, Nunes did not mention what Bogdan had said in reply to this inquiry from Verinder. But at 8:10 a.m. Verinder had called down to reception again. This time, Nunes took the call herself.

'Can you please tell me,' Verinder asked, 'if someone jumped from the balcony?'

'Don't worry, Mr Sharma,' Nunes told him reassuringly. 'No one jumped from the balcony. It's nothing to worry about.'

One unadvertised amenity of London's finer luxury apartment complexes is a policy of absolute discretion. Nunes had only just arrived at work. The lobby in which she took up station featured an impressive wall of glass offering a panoramic view of the police investigation that was unfolding just outside. She knew that police boats were at that very moment attending to a body that had been found on the riverbank. Why would Mr Sharma, in 504, be inquiring – not once, but twice – about whether the body had come from inside the building? She might have wondered.

But the truth is that London is full of people like Ana Nunes: hardworking service professionals, often immigrants, who earn a modest living by catering to the rich. And one unspoken law of any such vocation is that it is not your job to wonder. 'I didn't ask him for any more information or ask why he thought this may be the case,' Nunes told the police. And she did not tell them this on the day Zac was found, because she didn't even *talk* to investigators until 2 March 2020, three months later. On the morning Zac was discovered, the police do not appear to have entered Riverwalk at all or questioned any of the building's staff, because they were certain that the body must have floated in from somewhere else along the Thames. And Nunes and her colleagues didn't bother to flag down any of the officers to inform them about the Riverwalk resident who kept asking if someone had jumped from one of the balconies.

Pino agreed to help Matthew track down some of the Riverwalk concierges. But unsurprisingly, perhaps, they still felt bound by the doorman's omertà. 'I would like not to get involved in that no more,' Bogdan texted Matthew, refusing to speak with him. 'I am sorry.'

There was another doorman named Tibor, Pino said, who had recently left Riverwalk to take another job. Perhaps *he* might talk. A week or so later, Matthew returned to Café Society, this time accompanied by Rachelle. Tibor, from Hungary, was a slender man in his forties, dressed in a black leather jacket. He was visibly uncomfortable, as if just sitting with the Brettlers for a coffee might violate some professional oath. But, grudgingly, he started to talk.

Tibor had been off work on the Friday when Zac's body was found, and had not returned to Riverwalk until after the weekend. When he got back to the building, he told the Brettlers, he had spoken with another concierge, a man named Panos, who *had* been at work that morning. After hearing about the body, Panos told Tibor, he had gone out to the river so that he could see it for himself. Akbar Shamji, in one of his police interviews, had mentioned to the detectives that there was a doorman named Panos who had seen the body and had specifically reassured Verinder, 'It's not Zac.' This was the reason, in Akbar's telling, that he and Verinder had been convinced, even after the discovery of a body right in front of Riverwalk, that Zac must still be alive. Zac's name had been on a short list of people who could freely access apartment 504 without a concierge having to call up for permission to let him in, Akbar pointed out. The doormen 'all knew him', knew what he looked like. And Panos had said it wasn't Zac.

The Brettlers already had grounds to be sceptical of this story, because if Akbar and Verinder were so sure that the body in the Thames was not the missing teenager – that it was a total red herring, another coincidence – it seemed bizarre that neither of them would have made any mention of it whatsoever to Rachelle and Matthew that day at the Méridien. But at Café Society, Tibor gave them a more immediate reason to doubt the story: the whole premise of it was untrue. Panos *had* recognized the body, Tibor said. He had told Tibor, definitively, that it was Zac. Panos had not reported this to the police that morning or at any point after that. Nor had Tibor or anyone else in the building. Matthew tried to get Panos to speak to him, but without success. Tibor told the Brettlers that after Panos had quietly disclosed this detail about recognizing Zac's corpse, he had made a gesture, pinching his forefinger and thumb together, then running them across his lips: *Keep your mouth zipped.* Matthew was beginning to suspect that the silence of Riverwalk's staff might signify more than a general instinct for discretion. 'It feels like somebody somewhere has told the concierges not to co-operate,' he said.

Though the police were on notice, from Akbar, that Panos had seen the body – and that he had spoken to Verinder about it that morning – detectives never interviewed Panos. They didn't talk to Tibor, either. In her statement (which the Brettlers eventually received from the police), Ana Nunes reported that on 30 November, the day after Zac's body was discovered but several days before it had been identified, Verinder had telephoned the front desk and spoken to her again. This time he asked her to remove Zac's name from the list of approved visitors to the building. 'He did not give me any reason,' Nunes said, nor did she ask for one. 'I accepted this and removed Zac from the database.'

Tibor shared another intriguing clue: at some point before Zac's death, he had been on duty one day when he saw a visitor to Verinder's apartment, a Black man he thought looked like a chauffeur. After going up to the flat, the man had exited the lift carrying a duffel bag that was open – and full of cash. Matthew wondered if this chauffeur might have been Carlton, the driver Verinder had sent to Lauderdale Road. He had developed a theory that Carlton might work for the London businessman who'd supposedly been paying Verinder's rent: Nick Gold. Zac had often spoken to his parents about Nick Gold, even claiming that they were friends. Officially, Gold was an entrepreneur and investor, but he also had a reputation as a professional gambler who gravitated to the corners of London's economy in which outsized risks could yield outsized rewards. Some years earlier, Gold had been banned by the British Horseracing Authority after an inquiry into race fixing found that he had engaged in a 'corrupt or fraudulent practice'. (No criminal charges were ever brought.) Nick's father, Peter Gold, had got in trouble for conning the Swedish state in a scheme in which cheap road salt was fraudulently marketed, at a gargantuan markup, as sophisticated 'ice-melting chemicals'. Nick was part owner of the Box, an infamous erotic cabaret with a posh clientele that was located down a dingy alley in Soho and known for its 'fetish burlesque'. He was famously partial to cocaine.

As it happens, Nick Gold had been friends with Scot Young and Johnny Elichaoff and several other prominent London businessmen who died in mysterious circumstances. 'Nick was probably the most connected man in London that I'd ever met,' a private investigator who once worked for him remarked. 'He knew absolutely everybody.' He lived such a risky life, making big bets, going into debt, then making bigger bets in hopes of covering his losses, that one longtime friend of Gold's said, 'I'm just completely surprised and relieved that Nick is still alive.' The only reason he hadn't wound up dead himself, the friend continued, was that 'he is so good at making people believe that he's about to make a billion'.

At the Méridien hotel, Akbar had told the Brettlers, 'Nick Gold and Verinder are sort of best friends.' But Gold also occupied a milieu that felt more proximate to Matthew and Rachelle's than the underworld of Indian Dave. Gold was Jewish, and the Jewish community in London was small enough that there wasn't too much distance between any one person and any other. His ex-wife lived with his children in a large house half a mile from their apartment, on Hamilton Terrace in St John's Wood, the same swank boulevard where Zac, in his oligarch guise, had pretended to be purchasing a home. The Brettlers knew people who were friends with the Golds. At their urging, one of these friends asked Nick whether he had known Zac.

'The Russian kid?' Gold said.

'He isn't Russian,' the friend corrected. 'He's Rabbi Hugo's grandson!'

Gold acknowledged that he had been friends with Verinder, but he denied knowing anything about Zac or his death. How would he have been connected to Verinder in the first place? the Brettlers wondered. One possible answer was that Verinder had become not just a debt collector but a lender of last resort for a certain kind of Londoner who needed cash but might not be able to obtain it from a bank. Nick Gold was a notoriously feast-or-famine kind of guy; there were tabloid stories about his bankruptcies and debts of as much as £22 million. When police questioned Verinder in March 2020, they mentioned that a large sum of cash – roughly £20,000 – had been found hidden in his apartment. According to the private detective who worked for Gold, 'Nick owed money to Indian Dave.' The two of them had known each other for many years, and 'Indian Dave had lent him just shy of a million pounds on one occasion.' In that instance, Gold had used the money to short a stock – successfully – and paid Verinder back, the investigator said.

But in his own inquiries around London, Matthew heard a different rumour about a property deal that Gold had allegedly entered into with Verinder, in the South of France. Like Indian Dave, Gold enjoyed spending time on the Côte d'Azur. Their real estate deal had apparently generated a substantial profit, but Verinder was not able to collect his portion, because at the time he had been hiding out from the authorities. According to the rumour, when Verinder later reappeared in London and came to collect, Gold did not have enough liquidity to pay him. So, as a kind of down payment, he offered to supply him with a luxury apartment on the Thames.

The other London businessman Matthew had started to fixate on was Oliver Harris, who had come up in text messages between Akbar and Verinder during the days leading up to Zac's death, and who *also* happened to live on Hamilton Terrace. Zac's phone records indicated that he had been speaking with Harris in the last week of his life. From the texts, it appeared that some sort of discord had broken out between Harris and Verinder. 'Oliver is a pussy, believe me,' Verinder wrote to Akbar on Zac's final day.

Akbar wrote to Verinder, 'I didn't know he' – meaning Zac – 'asked you to put it on a football agent,' adding, 'I also didn't like the fact you were so fucking worried about some cunt called Oliver who you spooked.'

When police questioned Akbar about this exchange, he denied

knowing Oliver Harris himself but said, 'Zac was very worried about some guy called Oliver that Verinder's had some conversation with, and I got drawn into the middle of it.' Pressed for more detail, he mentioned that 'Zac had some guy who was a football agent. He wanted Verinder to do something with him.' What had Akbar meant, the cops wondered, when he spoke of Zac asking Verinder to 'put it on' the football agent?

'"Put it on" would typically mean…put some force on him,' Akbar replied.

Oliver Harris was the son of a well-to-do family, a 'bit of a flash boy', in Matthew's opinion, whose lifestyle was not necessarily commensurate with his identifiable professional achievements. When he was contacted by Clive Strong, the private detective the Brettlers had hired, to ask why he had been communicating with Zac, Harris had started the conversation by revealing that he had recently been robbed in his own home at gunpoint. Beyond that, he wouldn't tell Strong much, apart from acknowledging that he had known Zac. So now, through an intermediary – a local Orthodox rabbi – Matthew requested a meeting with Harris, and the three of them convened one day at Harris's apartment. It was a spacious, elegantly furnished ground-floor unit, with a garden. Harris looked to be in his early forties, with an olive complexion and dark hair. Before they could talk, he asked Matthew to wait while he stepped out into the garden, donned a pair of ceremonial leather straps known as tefillin, wrapping them around his wrists with the assistance of the rabbi, and then proceeded to recite a prayer. To Matthew, this interlude felt oddly timed and a bit theatrical, as if Harris wanted to preface their conversation with a demonstration of his own piety.

When Harris returned, he seemed awkward and on edge. He told Matthew that he wanted to help, but he insisted that he had not known Zac well or had any business dealings with him whatsoever and that he had no information to contribute about his son's death. Matthew thought that Harris was obfuscating. Asked about Indian Dave, Harris claimed that he hadn't really known him, either, but he acknowledged knowing that Sharma was a dangerous person. 'He's got a reputation for intimidating people,' Harris said, 'by holding them over the edge of a balcony.' He referenced Robbie Curtis, the property developer and member of the Cipriani Five who had been killed by a Tube train in 2012. At some point before Curtis's death, Harris said, Indian Dave had apparently threatened him. But beyond that, he didn't have anything to offer, apart from his sympathies.

'What did you think?' the rabbi asked as he and Matthew left the apartment.

'I don't think he's being completely honest,' Matthew replied.

'It's difficult to know what's true and what's not,' the rabbi murmured with a shrug.

Matthew was annoyed. Did the rabbi not adhere to some deeper moral code? How could he not share Matthew's indignation at the apparent evasions of his congregant, this supposedly prayerful man to whom he had just ministered, so showily, in the garden? The mention of a connection between Indian Dave and the death of Robbie Curtis was unnerving. 'It's like watching a crime thriller on TV, except it's your own life,' Matthew told Rachelle afterwards. 'If Zac *is* somehow connected to these shady figures, there's part of you that doesn't want to look too hard,' he said, adding, 'You don't want to become another victim.'

Both Matthew and Rachelle had started to feel alienated in their own city, to see the whole metropolis in a more sinister light. It was a strange sensation to move around St John's Wood, picking up groceries or stopping for a cup of tea in a café, and knowing that there might be people around them, people from their own community, who had connections to Verinder Sharma or to other elements of London's criminal subculture and who perhaps knew more than they did about their son's death. 'It's been eye-opening,' Rachelle remarked. 'This whole world we did not know about, this underworld that exists on our doorstep.'

'Sometimes it really makes me hate London,' Matthew said. 'It makes me want to leave.'

In one of the text messages detectives shared with the Brettlers, Verinder had instructed Oliver Harris to go to the apartment on Lauderdale Road and see if Zac was there. Harris responded that he had done so but that Zac did not appear to be home. As part of his own investigation, Matthew obtained the footage from the building's CCTV system. He went through the tape painstakingly, hour by hour in the days around Zac's death, but he couldn't find any trace of Harris ever coming to the apartment. What he did discover was the moment on Zac's final night when Akbar had pulled up outside in his Mercedes and Zac had climbed into the car. Once Zac got in, the Mercedes disappeared from the frame, headed to Riverwalk.

Scrolling through the tape, Matthew witnessed another moment he had not known about, before Akbar's arrival, when Zac was waiting for him on the street. Suddenly a familiar figure appeared in the video. It was Joe, coming home for the evening. Relations between the brothers had been strained, and as Matthew silently watched this tape of the final encounter between his two sons, he saw Joe walk right into the building without saying hello.

'Zac's standing twenty yards away, but he doesn't say anything,' Matthew said, in a voice that was heavy with sorrow. 'He doesn't acknowledge him in any way.' After a long pause, he said haltingly, 'It's a very tender area for me ... because I think Joe was probably a little harsh on Zac.' Of course, Zac was harsh on Joe as well. Matthew had always hoped that his boys might grow up to be as close as they had once been as children. Instead they had only grown further apart, and it was painful for Matthew to consider that Zac's death had robbed them of any chance to knit back together over time. He hated to consider that Joe's last interaction with his brother would forever be marked by that dreadful sense of irresolution. Matthew had never spoken to Joe about the footage. He opted not to tell Rachelle about it, either.

'I've known Matthew for forty years,' a close friend of his, Andrew Fingret, remarked. 'He is very analytical, but that doesn't mean that he doesn't feel pain. He might be able to hide it better than others, because he focuses on the facts.' When Fingret thought about the agony that both Rachelle and Matthew were experiencing, he was awed by the sheer power of it. 'You know when you go to the doctor and you haven't got *words* for the pain? It's a pain I couldn't ever know,' he said. 'Because I haven't got children.'

'You might want to talk with my uncle,' a childhood friend of Zac's named Jesse told Matthew at one point.* The uncle's name was Alex, Jesse said, and he had a certain acquaintance with London's underworld. If Matthew and Rachelle were curious about Zac's possible entanglements with criminal types, Uncle Alex could offer a few insights. After a childhood in North London, he had moved to Russia, where he became a cage fighter, then worked as a money launderer for the Russian mob. He'd got to know a lot of people over the years, Jesse suggested, and might be able to help them.

Matthew arranged a meeting at an outdoor café in Regent's Park. Uncle Alex turned out to be a great bear of a man, packed with the kind of dense muscle that one tends to associate with prison. (In Russia he had spent time behind bars.) But he appeared to be an approachable fellow, with a ready smile and small, mirthful eyes, and he seemed genuinely eager to help. Alex had known Zac a little bit, he told Matthew. He could sense the boy's attraction to London's underbelly and had tried to 'warn him off'. When Jesse introduced them, Alex had quickly surmised that Zac was a poseur. Zac had told him that he had 'half a million pounds cash' and that he needed 'someone to clean it'. He claimed to have made the money dealing drugs.

This was a shock for Matthew. He and Rachelle had at times suspected that Zac was dealing, but they'd never heard it suggested so concretely. Alex didn't believe it, in any case, he told Matthew. Zac claimed to have been in possession of a 'line' – a phone used for drug sales, which meant access to a lucrative customer base – and said that he had sold the line to some Albanians, which was how he had come into all that money. But Albanians wouldn't pay for a line, Uncle Alex scoffed. And they certainly wouldn't pay half a million.

Even so, Alex liked the boy. Zac had a Walter Mitty quality, he thought. Sure, his modus operandi might have been to 'fake it till you make it', but Zac would hardly be the first entrepreneur of whom that could be said, and he seemed to be faking it reasonably well. At a certain point, Alex had come into possession of some bales of fibre-optic cable. He did not elaborate on precisely how he had

---

* Both Jesse and Uncle Alex are pseudonyms.

acquired this rather specific commodity, and Matthew opted not to ask. But suffice to say that he'd been on the lookout for a buyer, and it turns out that when you're looking to unload a bunch of fibre-optic cable, lining up a buyer is not necessarily easy. Hearing about this predicament, Zac had informed Alex that he had a business partner who might be able to help: Akbar Shamji. So the three of them arranged to meet at the Dorchester hotel, a gaudy palace of overconsumption that is favoured by wealthy foreigners.

Uncle Alex was not impressed by Akbar. At all. They had scarcely sat down before Akbar pulled up a picture on his phone of the Indian prime minister Narendra Modi presenting him with some award. This gesture may have been intended to buttress his claims about knowing the sorts of people in India who might be looking to purchase fibre-optic cable, but it seemed effortful and slippery. Akbar also appeared to be on a first-name basis with the bartenders at the Dorchester, which in Uncle Alex's view might be disqualifying all by itself.

'I've known too many Akbars,' he said ruefully.

Nothing ever came of the deal. Akbar had made assurances about producing a buyer, but he never followed through. Since Zac's death, however, Uncle Alex had developed an interesting theory. He didn't believe that Zac had fooled Akbar with his pretence of being the son of an oligarch. Or rather, maybe he *had* fooled Akbar at the beginning, but the ruse hadn't lasted. Akbar had told Matthew that Zac always spoke with a faint Russian accent. But when Alex met Zac and Akbar together at the Dorchester, Zac had spoken like the English kid he was. 'Akbar is giving you shit,' Uncle Alex told Matthew. 'He knew *exactly* who Zac was.'

If this was the case, Alex went on, then it meant that Akbar must have been in league with Zac on some kind of con. And if *that* was true, then the person they were tricking had to be Verinder Sharma. It could be tempting to construe Zac as a kind of Tom Ripley, the sociopathic con man of the Patricia Highsmith novels who seeks to upgrade his lifestyle by preying, brilliantly, on the gullibility of others. But what precisely was the con here? What was Zac hoping to achieve? Perhaps Akbar had been fooled by Zac initially and had introduced him to Indian Dave – only to realize that he'd made a dangerous mistake. 'You can do a cover story for a month or two,' Uncle Alex said. But if the people you're trying to con happen to be con men themselves, eventually they are going to see through it. ('Not that there's anything wrong with that,' he added hastily, of the choice to be a con man. 'That's their lifestyle.')

Uncle Alex told Matthew that he had been acquainted with Verinder and, while Akbar might have been a joke, Indian Dave was a serious customer. Verinder's death was unlikely to have been a suicide *or* an overdose, Alex declared with conviction, noting, 'It's very similar to how Russians would kill someone.'

With Verinder dead, there was only one person who could tell the Brettlers what had happened to their son, Uncle Alex said. That was Akbar, and he wasn't going to tell the police anything – of that much they could be certain. So Alex had a suggestion. 'You need to take him off the street,' he said. 'Put him somewhere and ask him questions.'

'You mean,' Matthew said jokingly, 'if I got some nasty people to take him into a dark room?'

'Go to his house,' Uncle Alex said. He wasn't joking.

Matthew blanched, too flabbergasted to speak. 'He likes women,' Uncle Alex continued, warming to this stratagem. 'Get two women to come up to him and say, "Let's go to a hotel."' Scarcely believing his good fortune and anticipating a night of rollicking hedonism, Akbar would surely accompany these beautiful strangers to a hotel room – only to find Uncle Alex there waiting for him.

'It's not hard,' Alex said amiably. 'Akbar will give you all the answers.'

Matthew, who had suddenly developed a stammer, blurted something about how perhaps under the circumstances it might be most prudent to allow the official investigation to run its course.

Uncle Alex seemed genuinely disappointed.

In February 2022, Russia invaded Ukraine. This unprovoked incursion into another nation's sovereign territory was quickly condemned by the international community, including Great Britain. It was a dramatic moment, and it occasioned fresh scrutiny of the role that the post-Soviet oligarchs and their money had played in London in recent decades. Many of London's Russian plutocrats continued to maintain close links to the regime of Vladimir Putin, which raised uncomfortable questions about the indirect complicity of English individuals and institutions that had come to rely on the largesse of Putin's cronies. *The Times* ran a report on how sanctioned oligarchs 'convicted of embezzling hundreds of millions of pounds are sending their children to Britain's private schools'. A new round of international sanctions was initiated, forcing the mega-yachts of the oligarchs to chart a course for the Maldives, lest they be seized by authorities. The UK government issued its own sanctions against more than twelve hundred individuals. 'The halcyon days of the oligarchs in Britain have come to an end,' *The Daily Telegraph* declared. Even Roman Abramovich was sanctioned, leaving him with little choice but to sell his interest in Chelsea Football Club. (Chelsea fans, less concerned about the niceties of Westphalian geopolitics than they were about the money Abramovich had spent to improve their team, chose to interrupt a tribute to the people of Ukraine at the beginning of a match by filling the stadium with a rowdy chant of 'Roman Abramovich! Roman Abramovich!')

It was during the month of the invasion that the Brettlers met with Detective Rory Wilkinson again, this time at Hammersmith Police Station. The Crown Prosecution Service had decided not to prosecute Akbar Shamji for perverting the course of justice – or for anything else. In a sequence of letters, the Brettlers had sought a formal appeal of this decision, called a Victims' Right to Review, but were denied on the grounds that they were not victims. After requesting a meeting with prosecutors to discuss this denial, they received a letter that read, 'Sadly, a meeting cannot be offered to you as these are only provided to families who have been bereaved through homicide.' The bureaucratic obfuscation and semantic games had reached the point where Rachelle and Matthew were starting to feel as if they were trapped in a Kafka novel.

Wilkinson expressed his sincere condolences once again, attesting that police had gone to inordinate lengths to determine what precisely had happened to Zac. Detectives hadn't merely been 'going through the motions', he insisted. 'This is something we've put everything we can into.'

This time, after months of doing their own investigating, the Brettlers were feeling less inclined to take his word for it. Had detectives ever interviewed the 'famous Mark Foley', the Chelsea Football executive? Rachelle wondered. He was the first person they knew of who appeared to have fallen for Zac's Ismailov con, and it was his vouch that allegedly persuaded Akbar that Zac really was an oligarch's son.

'I don't think so,' Wilkinson said. 'No.'

How about Daniela Karnuts? Rachelle asked. On the night Zac died, Akbar had got home very late and Daniela had refused to let him sleep in their flat. Did they discuss what had happened that evening? Did Akbar tell her Zac had gone missing? How did he explain the death?

'She was interviewed,' Wilkinson said, before catching himself and saying that, no, hang on, actually – she wasn't interviewed. But they did get a statement. Then, catching himself again, he said sheepishly, 'We haven't interviewed her and... we don't have a statement.'

Apologizing for his confusion, Wilkinson explained that he'd been thinking of Dominique, Verinder Sharma's daughter. They definitely got a statement from her. Dominique had received a phone call from her dad moments after Zac went off the balcony. Had she ever explained to the police what *she* thought was going on that night?

'So... you are asking me quite detailed questions,' Wilkinson said uneasily. 'And I'm feeling a little bit... I'm not quite sure where you're going.'

Matthew and Rachelle were recording the meeting, with Wilkinson's consent, and they pressed on with their inquiries. The police hadn't spoken to Nick Gold, even though he was the one who'd provided the Riverwalk apartment to Verinder. They hadn't spoken to Oliver Harris, though he appeared to have possibly been engaged in some sort of deal with Verinder and Zac and had been calling and texting with them in the days preceding Zac's death. And what about Akbar's music-business friend Mervin Sealy? Matthew had suggested in their last meeting that detectives should seek out Mervin. Had he ever explained what he thought Akbar was getting at in that text about knives and blood?

'So, we've not interviewed Mervin,' Wilkinson said. Then he added, more firmly, 'But Mervin wasn't there.'

'I really have to say, I find that astonishing, if I'm being really honest with you,' Matthew said, struggling to suppress his indignation. 'I'm not trying to tell you how to do your job, but simply that to try and build a picture of what's going on in that apartment...'

'Yes, but the trouble is, he doesn't know what's going on,' Wilkinson said.

'We don't *know* that,' Matthew replied. 'We haven't asked him!'

Confronted by the righteous anger and rigorous preparation of these two grieving parents, Wilkinson made a good show of emphasizing his own professionalism and compassion. But as Matthew and Rachelle subjected him to their litany of questions, he sounded increasingly like a teenager who had thought he might not need to study for the test. A note of petulance crept into his voice. It was beginning to feel, he grumbled, as if Matthew was the detective 'interviewing *me*'. The Brettlers had 'obviously done good, detailed work', Wilkinson said uncomfortably.

'Are you going to offer me a job?' Matthew joked, to cut the tension.

'Ha,' Wilkinson said. 'No.'

Anytime the Brettlers made the case that Akbar should be charged with *some* sort of crime, Wilkinson would object that it could be difficult to prove anything beyond a reasonable doubt. Police and prosecutors could not simply base their decisions on the 'balance of probabilities', he stressed. They needed proof. And there was just no getting around it: Zac's death looked like a suicide. 'I think he jumped,' Wilkinson said. 'He has been living a lie with these people. He obviously and clearly is not happy... There are *issues*.'

'But this is a suspicious death, Rory!' Matthew objected, his voice hot. It is a well-established maxim of law enforcement that the first twenty-four hours of any homicide investigation are the most important. Cops sometimes refer to this period as the 'golden hour', and after even a single day elapses, the likelihood of solving a murder starts to diminish. In Zac's case, four full days had gone by between the moment he left the apartment from the balcony and the moment police finally entered the place to search it. In the interim, Verinder had arranged for a maid service to come and clean the flat. That delay was squarely attributable to the fact that Akbar Shamji had kept quiet for four days about his knowledge that Zac was dead. 'There's no jury in the land that would not convict this guy!' Matthew declared.

'I totally get your frustration,' Wilkinson said. He did not dispute that Akbar had lied to investigators. The trouble, he pointed out, somewhat pathetically, was that 'we can't force anyone to tell us what happened'.

At this point, Rachelle cut in gently. 'I'm not a lawyer,' she said in a soft voice. 'I'm not a policeman,' she continued. 'But are there any other ways of looking at Akbar's involvement?' She was pleading with him now. A *'cover-up* has gone on', she said.

'I am satisfied we've done everything we can,' Wilkinson concluded flatly. The job of the police, he seemed to be suggesting, is not to be Sherlock Holmes; it's not to *solve mysteries*, but to build cases that can translate into criminal charges. The unfortunate bureaucratic reality was that with no obvious charges to bring, the triage of policework meant that detectives simply had to move on to other things. There would still be a formal inquest, a procedure that might provide one further opportunity to explore the circumstances of Zac's death, but that was not a forum for assigning criminal blame, and the police investigation was now effectively over. The Brettlers might not like it, he started to say.

'It's not that we don't like it,' Matthew interrupted. 'It's that we find it incomprehensible.'

'You don't like it *because* it's incomprehensible,' Wilkinson said.

But in truth, Zac's death was not entirely incomprehensible to his parents. In fact, the more they thought about the many details of the case, the more they were coming to feel that they did have a rough sense of what had happened. The authorities couldn't prove that Zac had been murdered because he *hadn't* been murdered in any straightforward sense. But just because Verinder Sharma had not physically hurled him from the balcony, that didn't necessarily mean, by default, that Zac had chosen suicide. Since visiting Riverwalk himself, Matthew had been thinking a lot about physics. If Zac had wanted to end his own life, the most obvious way to do so would have been to drop from the balcony straight down to the pavement five storeys below. Instead he had crossed from one end of the balcony to the other, before deliberately choosing to launch from the specific part of the half-moon structure that projected out closest to the river.

Because the building is set back from the Thames, Zac had to cover a horizontal distance of roughly ten feet to reach the water. So he lunged forwards, clearly hoping for a wet landing. This was no small jump. Matthew had walked the pedestrian path below, looking up at the balcony and then over at the river, pondering angles and trajectories. If you jump outwards from such a height, Matthew told Wilkinson, 'you'll continue to travel horizontally, although your real speed will be downwards'. When police examined Verinder's apartment, they took photographs pointing down from the balcony at the walkway and the river below. Through an optical illusion, when you gaze down from above, it appears that the distance to the water is much shorter. It looks like you could reach it if you jumped.

Matthew kept returning to something that a friend of his, an American guy who had attended West Point, had once told him. 'You know, the Marines is full of nineteen-year-old kids who think that bullets bounce off their chest,' the man had said. There's a sense of impregnability: they don't appreciate danger in the way that a more mature mind does.

Zac didn't jump off the balcony to die, his parents concluded – but to live. Verinder may very well have broken his jaw before he jumped; the special pathologist who examined Zac's body ended up attributing the injury to a hard impact, perhaps with the water or perhaps with a fist. It was impossible to say. But one thing was perfectly clear: whatever lay in store for Zac in that Riverwalk apartment, he thought that he had a greater prospect of survival if he took his chances on a swan dive. It was a desperate gesture but also a bravura one, the sort of escape you might see in a *Mission: Impossible* film. Zac was an athletic kid who had often lived his life as if he were a character in a movie. He must have thought he had a decent chance of making it. And he might even have succeeded in this Hollywood getaway, dropping clean into the black water of the Thames and surviving, crawling out somewhere downriver, and walking through the darkened streets of London all the way home, had his hip not clipped the embankment on the way down.

Chapter 16

POCKET DIAL

ONE DAY IN DECEMBER 2022, Rachelle and Matthew found themselves face-to-face – through the portal of a video screen – with Verinder's daughter Dominique Sharma Clarke. She had been summoned to testify at the inquest into Zac's death. Anytime there is a death in the United Kingdom in which the cause is unknown or apparently unnatural, authorities are obliged to hold a public inquest. Zac's inquest was allotted three days. That morning, Rachelle and Matthew had made their way to Poplar Coroner's Court, an antiquated brick building near Canary Wharf. Filing into the court's grim interior, they passed an ancient sign that read DO NOT SPIT, announcing in smaller type a penalty of forty shillings. They were accompanied by Rachelle's brother, David Gryn, and by three friends who had volunteered to join them for moral support. They also had a barrister with them, an intense young woman named Alexandra Tampakopoulos, who would have the opportunity to cross-examine witnesses. The proceedings would be presided over by a stern-looking senior coroner named Mary Hassell.

'We're here simply to try and find the answers to four questions,' Hassell murmured at the outset, in a deep, commanding voice that sounded faintly reminiscent of Margaret Thatcher. 'Who the deceased was, where he died, when he died, and how he came by his death.'

A number of statements were read into the record, from police officers and a paramedic who had responded to the scene on the morning of Zac's death, and from Bogdan, the Riverwalk doorman. (Bogdan made no reference in his statement to the repeated questions he had received from Verinder Sharma on the morning after Zac's death about whether anyone had fallen from one of the balconies.)

When it was Rachelle's turn to take the stand, she found herself overcome by emotion. 'My name is Rachelle Gryn Brettler,' she said, her voice already starting to quaver. 'I'm Zac's mum.' For the first seventeen years of his life, Zac had been 'bright, witty, quirky, lively', she said. 'You know, he was a pleasure. He was a pleasure to have as my youngest child.' But eventually he had started 'acting out, perhaps as other seventeen-year-old boys do'.

When Zac became entangled with Akbar and Verinder, Rachelle told the coroner, he'd been 'chancing', trying on a different identity. But 'I don't think he realized... the dangerous people he was playing with.'

Zac had not been suicidal, she declared. 'He was not depressed. I know what depression can look like.' Nor was he using heroin, she said, and she knew what that looked like, too.

'I'm not a woman in denial,' Rachelle insisted.

Hassell asked if Rachelle thought that Zac had lost his 'grip on reality'.

'No,' she replied. In a way, it would have been easier to understand if he had been seized by delusions, actually believing that he was Zac Ismailov. But he hadn't been. 'He was a canny boy,' Rachelle said.

'Do you think there was an endgame here?'

'I think there was,' she began. But what that endgame might have been, she did not know. 'I spent the last three years trying to understand the journey that got my son to be found dead on the foreshore of the Thames,' Rachelle went on. 'He wanted money and power. Fast.' The first time he pretended to be a Russian, it must have 'opened doors for him'. Zac had always been a bit of a gambler and an opportunist, tiptoeing right up to the line and sometimes over it, seeing what he could get away with. When he tried this gambit – masquerading as an oligarch's son – he'd probably been surprised by how easily it succeeded. 'Whoever Mark Foley is... introducing him... something has *worked*,' Rachelle said. 'He's not just our son from Maida Vale. He's now somebody else, and people are treating him different. They *want* him. They want his attention. But ultimately, it's all transactional,' she concluded. 'They want his money. This money that supposedly he had.'

What seemed indisputable, Rachelle said, was that when he entered Verinder's flat that Thursday evening, Zac had been walking into grave danger. All the talk of heroin and suicide that Akbar and Verinder had attributed to Zac was a 'charade', she told the coroner. What Zac had really been saying was '"Feel sorry for me." "Don't hurt me."' As a student, he would always come up with colourful excuses. 'He should have been an actor. He should have been a writer. He should be *something*,' she said. 'He shouldn't be a dead boy of nineteen.'

After Rachelle finished speaking, everyone was silent for a moment in the face of her despair. Then the coroner thanked her for her testimony. When it came to the role Verinder Sharma might have played in Zac's death, Hassell noted, she 'would have preferred Mr Sharma to give oral evidence'. Instead they would hear from his daughter.

Dominique's face filled a large video screen that had been set up in the courtroom. She was pretty, polished, in her twenties, with dramatic eyebrows, long black hair, and her father's sharp nose. She might have been a gangster's daughter, but she'd been raised primarily by her mother, Tara, and both parents had clearly intended for Dominique and her sister, Matisse, to live a different sort of life than Verinder had. In her childhood, Dominique played the harp and did equestrian lessons. 'He wanted her to have an educated life,' one friend of Verinder's observed, adding, 'He's still Indian. Indians love education. They're big on it.' In fact, Dominique had attended the same private school for girls where Rachelle and her sisters had once been students, Queens College, on Harley Street in Marylebone. She'd gone on to the University of Exeter. In her cyber-sleuthing after Zac's death, Rachelle had discovered a LinkedIn profile for Dominique, which listed entry-level jobs in real estate and a spell as an 'independent fine art broker'. It was written in an aspirational vernacular that Zac would have found familiar: 'I have worked extensively alongside prestigious art galleries and renowned individuals,' Dominique asserted, claiming 'a vast array of experience in all areas of business'. In recent years, Dominique had been able to spend more time with her father. She and Matisse would often join him for a family meal on Sundays. But Dominique appeared to be a young person caught between two worlds, like Meadow, the mobster's daughter from *The Sopranos*, who goes to a good university and cultivates a normal civilian life but can never quite outrun the fact that her father is in the Mafia.

After swearing to tell the truth, Dominique informed the coroner that she had been introduced to Zac 'by my father'. Zac had been 'homeless' when Verinder met him, she continued, and 'just kind of needed a mentor'. She added, 'My dad didn't usually introduce many people to the family. So Zac was obviously important to him.'

'Did you gain a sense,' the coroner wondered, 'of *why* he was mentoring Zac?'

It had been a difficult year for Verinder, his daughter noted. His two closest friends were a gangster and club owner named Trevor Floyd Smith and a convicted cocaine trafficker named Peter Aboro. In March 2019, Smith had died suddenly, in an accident on an all-terrain vehicle in New Zealand, and six months later Aboro had died of cancer. As a consequence, 'When Zac came into my dad's life, I think it was just kind of like they both needed help,' Dominique reflected. She added that for her father, being a mentor to Zac represented 'an opportunity to rectify in some ways the wrongs he had done in his parenting with us'.

Matthew and Rachelle were repulsed by this contention that Verinder might have served as some kind of surrogate parent to their child. But the story about the death of Peter Aboro rang a bell. Zac had attended Aboro's funeral, as Verinder's guest. He had mentioned this to his parents, though they hadn't known the identity of the man who'd died.

Over time, Dominique said, she had grown to like Zac. 'He was really sweet and made jokes,' she recalled. He told her that he came from 'a very wealthy Russian family' but that he had grown estranged from his mother and siblings after the death of his father.

Asked by the coroner about Zac's final night, Dominique said that late that evening she had received a phone call from her father, who sounded 'very upset'. By this point, she explained, Zac had become 'quite ingrained in the family'. Verinder told her that Zac wanted to 'admit something', and she should come to Riverwalk. In apartment 504, Dominique found her father with Zac and Akbar. Akbar's dog was there, too. There were glasses of bourbon on the table. Dominique told the coroner that she had the impression her father might be drunk. She asked Zac what it was that he wanted to confess. 'And he said, "I'm so upset, I've been lying to you. I'm a junkie."'

Dominique was shocked, she testified – and concerned, not least because her father also had a history of drug abuse. Zac was distraught, she maintained. 'Like, you could see him crying.' He told her that he didn't '"want to be here anymore".'

'Can you just explain that?' Hassell broke in. 'It's a slightly ambiguous statement.'

'My understanding,' Dominique said, 'is that he did not wish to be alive.'

Hassell seemed quite interested in Dominique's assessment of Zac's psychological state. She inquired whether he had appeared to be 'mentally unwell'.

'Um, I would say he was depressed,' Dominique opined. 'But I wouldn't say he was psychotic.'

Watching this testimony, the Brettlers were quietly seething. They couldn't understand why the coroner might be soliciting Dominique's clinical appraisal of Zac's psychiatric condition. It wasn't just that she had no expertise in the matter: she had an obvious incentive to make it look as if Zac had been suicidal.

Things eventually calmed down in the flat, Dominique said. A decision was made among the four of them to enroll Zac in a rehab programme the next morning. Verinder was neither angry nor upset, Dominique maintained. In fact, he had taken a sleeping pill and started 'dozing off'. By the time she was ready to leave, her father had climbed into bed and 'looked passed out'.

'And you then left?'

She went downstairs with Akbar, she said. Then they chatted in her car for a while.

'What did you talk about?'

She claimed that she could not recall all the specifics.

When they left the flat, had everything seemed all right between Verinder and Zac?

'Absolutely fine,' Dominique testified. 'There was no anger. No fear.'

And when she and Akbar finished their conversation and drove off in different directions, was she under the impression that Akbar had any plans to return to Riverwalk that night?

'No,' she replied. Dominique had driven home, she said, and did not speak to her father again until the next morning, when he telephoned to say that Zac was missing.

But that didn't seem right, because Verinder had placed that phone call to Dominique in the moments after Zac died – a call that lasted three and a half minutes.

'I got a call from... my dad's *phone*,' Dominique said carefully. 'But I couldn't hear anything... It was muffled.' It must have been a 'pocket dial', she ventured, insisting that she and her father had not exchanged any words. So, after that, she 'went straight back to bed'.

Remarkably, the coroner appeared satisfied with this explanation and did not press Dominique further. But she did inquire about whether Verinder had subsequently said anything to his daughter about what had gone down in the apartment after she left.

'When I spoke to my dad in the morning, he couldn't remember anything,' Dominique testified. 'So, no.'

Alexandra Tampakopoulos, the barrister representing the Brettlers, rose to address the witness, beginning her cross-examination by asking about the moment Dominique had first been summoned to Riverwalk. At 10:48 that evening, Verinder had texted her, 'Call me, it's important.' Two minutes later, they had a phone call.

'What was said in that conversation?'

'It was very late, and I had work the next day', Dominique said. 'So it was definitely a conversation of me understanding, like, "Is this something I need to come over for now?"'

Why did Verinder want you to get involved at all, Tampakopoulos asked, given that by your own testimony, you didn't know Zac very well?

'I mean, he's my dad,' Dominique said. 'I was very close with him.' People frequently 'assume my dad to be an angry man', she mentioned. But the truth was that Verinder just got upset. 'Like, he wasn't angry, he was *hurt*,' she said.

Jumping forwards to the supposed pocket dial she had received at 2:26 a.m., Tampakopoulos asked, 'What did you hear on the phone?'

'I couldn't hear much,' Dominique replied. 'I could hear noises, and I think there were definitely... there was definitely a voice... but it was not coherent.'

'Whose voice...?' Tampakopoulos pressed. 'Was it your *father's* voice?'

'No,' Dominique said. 'I definitely don't, like I say that I don't, I don't think the phone, it's not like, I don't think someone had the phone in their hand, I don't know, but it was not, like, a clear, like anything was clear on it.'

'You said to the coroner that when you left, your father was asleep,' Tampakopoulos noted. 'But that suggests that he *wasn't* asleep at 2:26, given that there was a call to you, and you could hear voices.'

'Um, I don't know,' Dominique said. 'When I left, he was asleep.'

Rachelle thought that Dominique had an air of credibility about her, even if half of what she was saying didn't make any logical sense. To Matthew it seemed that 'she started off being quite a plausible witness and then rapidly degenerated into clear lying'. The friends who had joined the Brettlers that day were similarly shocked by what they regarded as the obvious inconsistency of her answers. After all, she was under oath. But Rachelle's brother, David, was more philosophical. 'She's Sharma's daughter,' he pointed out. 'If I had a criminal dad, would I defend him? Probably.' (Dominique subsequently maintained that she only told the truth; her lawyer said that it would be defamatory to suggest that she told any lies whatsoever during this proceeding and insisted that her testimony was entirely truthful.)

There was another detail that cast doubt on Dominique's account. At 2:59 a.m., half an hour after the supposed pocket dial, Dominique had placed a call to Verinder. If everything was fine with Zac and her father and she had to wake up early for work, then why call again? Tampakopoulos asked.

'Probably just because I was, I don't know, a bit worried,' Dominique said.

'So there's something about what you hear in that call at 2:26 that worries you?'

'No.'

'You just said that's why you called.'

'I suffer from anxiety,' Dominique exclaimed.

'Was it because you were concerned about what was going on?'

'No.'

'Well, you can't have it both ways, Ms Sharma Clarke,' Tampakopoulos said impatiently. 'You're anxious or you're not anxious.' Then, switching gears, she said, 'Your father... was he prone to violent outbursts?'

'No,' Dominique said.

'Did your father have a violent temper?'

He didn't, she maintained.

Early on Friday morning, roughly half an hour before Baxter Willis spotted Zac's body on the shore outside Riverwalk, Verinder had sent Dominique a text message, at 6:41 a.m.: 'Dom, let them know they all better tread carefully around me... I will take no prisoners to protect my family.'

What did *that* mean? Tampakopoulos asked.

'I don't even remember that,' Dominique said.

'That message suggests, doesn't it, that there's been some *issue*, and someone – Zac in this case – he's not going to be taken prisoner. He's died. I mean, that's what that's a reference to, isn't it?'

'No,' Dominique said, although, given that she claimed not to remember the message at all, it was not clear what basis she would have for saying so.

Tampakopoulos had one final question. 'When did you find out that Zac had died?'

'Um,' Dominique said. 'I don't remember.' She paused. 'Uh. I don't remember. I can't even...'

'Thank you very much,' Tampakopoulos said.

When the Brettlers thought about their son's death and the subsequent conduct of the authorities, they were torn between two very different theories. The first and most obvious explanation was simple institutional incompetence: Rory Wilkinson, the lead detective, seemed like a sober, reasonably intelligent, notionally capable professional. Yet he also appeared to be maddeningly incurious when it came to their case – all the leads not pursued, all the witnesses not interviewed. Perhaps this was merely an example of official bungling by a big, ailing police bureaucracy that turned out to be not very good at investigating cases.

It might also have been true that the Brettlers had not helped matters, by choosing not to go public about Zac's death. This instinct for discretion could in part have been a function of Rachelle's background as the daughter of a famous rabbi; her reflex was to keep her family's private business out of the papers. But she and Matthew were also just naturally private people who wanted to mourn their son in peace rather than in the harsh glare of a media inquisition. Had they chosen otherwise and given press interviews, the London tabloids, which are famously insatiable when it comes to the mysterious deaths of young white people, might have put more pressure on Scotland Yard. Instead, there had not been a single mention of Zac's death in the papers, which made it easier for the police to handle the case with such lassitude, then abandon it in the manner that they had.

But lately Matthew had taken to wondering if perhaps there might be some other, more exotic explanation, some deeper intrigue playing out behind the scenes. Verinder Sharma had enjoyed a long career of prodigious criminality. Yet he had never spent any meaningful time behind bars. His cronies and contemporaries – Micky McAvoy, Gary 'Tyson' Nelson, Roger Vincent, Andy Baker – all ended up receiving long sentences. But Verinder always managed to skate. He had been arrested on suspicion of murder in Zac's case but never charged, and when Verinder died, Rory Wilkinson had claimed that for some reason he was prevented from knowing or reporting to the Brettlers the precise circumstances of his demise.

What if there was a missing piece of the puzzle? Matthew wondered. What if Indian Dave had secretly been a police informant?

Matthew didn't have any concrete evidence to prove that this had definitely been the case, but he found that once he allowed himself to entertain the possibility, it accounted for a number of anomalies that had bedevilled him. It would explain how Verinder had managed to stay at large for so long. It would be a reason that he could have lived as openly as he did in London, even as he continued to engage in violent debt collection and extortion. And it might explain the peculiar reticence of the police to pursue him while he was alive – or to be more transparent about the particulars of his death.

The problem with this kind of thinking, Matthew found, was that once you opened your mind to the possibility of such conspiracies, it was hard to stop from going further. It is sometimes difficult for police to draw a clear line between a source relationship – in which the cops offer some inducement to an informant in exchange for information – and something that looks more like official corruption. Often, an asset becomes a liability, as police handlers end up working for their crook informants rather than the other way round. Through much of its history, the Metropolitan Police has been sullied by endemic corruption, taking payoffs from bank robbers and drug dealers. One former Met official joked, in the late 1960s, that his lofty ambition for the force was to 'arrest more criminals than we employ'. In 2002, an internal investigation known as Operation Tiberius identified thirty-four serving officers and twenty-two former officers who were involved in 'corrupt networks'. The inquiry also found that organized crime had succeeded in infiltrating the City of London Police, Britain's National Crime Squad, the National Criminal Intelligence Service, Her Majesty's Customs and Excise, the Crown Prosecution Service, the jury system and the prison system.

Matthew happened to listen to a podcast one day that mentioned a notorious murder case from 1987 in which a private investigator named Daniel Morgan was found in the parking lot of a South London pub with an axe in his head. Despite five separate police investigations into Morgan's death, spanning three decades, nobody was ever convicted in the killing. His family believed that he was murdered because he had been on the verge of uncovering a network of crooked cops, and for years they continued to push for answers. In 2007, the Met acknowledged that a likely motive for Morgan's murder was that he had been 'about to expose a south London drugs network possibly involving corrupt police officers'. In 2021, the findings of an independent review were published, establishing that 'institutional corruption' had helped to conceal police failings in the case. This was not a matter of mere incompetence, in other words, but of a sustained, decades-long cover-up. The circumstances were obviously very different, Matthew told Rachelle after doing his own research into the case. An axe in the head is unambiguously a murder in a way that Zac's plunge from the balcony was not. And even today, Daniel Morgan's killing remains officially unsolved: no suspect has been charged. But the story made clear that Met detectives were not above burying a case when it suited them to do so. And Matthew was moved by the way the Morgan family had continued, over all those years, to seek answers.

When they met with Rory Wilkinson, Matthew decided to broach his theory directly. 'Do you think that – unbeknownst to any of us in this room – Sharma could have been a police informer?' he asked. 'And that because of his status as an informer, somebody somewhere has protected him?'

'I have no idea,' Wilkinson said. 'I think there are a lot of people who have the potential to be. But I have absolutely no idea.' When criminals do that work, their status is very carefully concealed, he pointed out. So Verinder certainly could have been an informant, Wilkinson said. But if he was, 'I wouldn't know.' And even if he *did* know, he couldn't tell Matthew.

'Could you find out?' Matthew asked. 'Is there somebody that you go and ask?'

There isn't, Wilkinson said. 'It is separated, that world, for obvious reasons.' He didn't seem particularly sure one way or the other. 'I mean, who knows?' he said, with his customary agnosticism. Wilkinson gave no indication, however, that he or his colleagues had met with any interference in their investigation.

Just entertaining the idea that this kind of conspiracy might be plausible can create an oceanic feeling in which the whole world seems unstable. In the same way that Zac's death, being unnatural, necessitated a public inquest, it stood to reason that Verinder's death must have triggered such a proceeding as well. But when Matthew asked the police whether an inquest had been scheduled, they claimed not to know. When he wrote to the coroner's office, they would not respond with any information about whether Verinder's inquest had already taken place or whether one might be expected in the future. All births and deaths in Great Britain are a matter of public record, so Matthew next consulted the General Register Office for England and Wales. But he could not find any record of the death of anybody anywhere in England in recent years named Verinder Kumar Sharma. Nor was there any kind of obituary or notice of a burial at a funeral home or evidence of a grave of any kind. Matthew had never been the sort of person who sees shapes in the shadows. He was too logical to be prone to paranoia. But now he found that it was impossible not to wonder: was Indian Dave really dead?

Chapter 17

A DIFFERENT LIGHT

WHEN DOMINIQUE SHARMA TESTIFIED at the inquest of Zac Brettler, she mentioned one thing, in an offhand manner, that neither the coroner nor the Brettlers' lawyer chose to interrogate but which seemed potentially noteworthy. When she left Riverwalk that night, Dominique said, her father had been lying in his bed in the master bedroom, having taken a sleeping pill. Zac, meanwhile, had been sitting up with his back against the headboard, in the same bed. It was a minor detail, but a curious one: they were going to share the bed that night.

There was a reason for this, as Verinder had explained to Clive Strong, the private investigator hired by the Brettlers, and then subsequently reiterated in his statement to police. There had been flooding recently in another bedroom where Zac would normally have slept. Apparently, Zac and Verinder were close enough that they intended to deal with this inconvenience by sleeping side by side.

As the Brettlers sifted through the facts of the case, many questions remained. But would it render some elements of this confounding narrative more explicable if some of the characters turned out to be gay? Akbar was in his mid-forties when he started spending time with Zac. Verinder was in his mid-fifties. Both men had children who were close to Zac's age, yet they very quickly developed their own quite intimate relationships with Zac. The older men were ostensibly heterosexual. But when detectives inspected Akbar's telephone, they encountered some material that made them wonder.

Akbar remained close with his old friend Peter Land, the actor whose late wife, Gillian Lynne, had made an enormous fortune choreographing *Cats*. In the days before Zac's death, Akbar had spent time with Land, and he informed the police that after waking up in his car on the morning after Zac's plunge into the Thames, he had ended up going to Land's home for a long lunch. It might have seemed like a logical move for the investigators to call Land into the police station and ask what Akbar said about the events of the previous evening. They didn't bother. But they did inspect text messages between Land and Akbar, which turned out to be conspicuously frisky.

On 20 November a week before Zac's death, Akbar texted Land, 'Sending you lots of love for your doctor's appointment and whatever is going on, will apply lots of love.'

'Oh boy,' Land replied.

'Physical, psychiatric, emotional, sexual, we've got all the tools you need,' Akbar wrote. 'We can also reach certain parts the average bear wouldn't find.'

During Akbar's second interrogation, in March 2020, the police had asked him about this exchange. 'We're not here to judge,' one of the detectives assured him.

'I wouldn't read anything into that,' Akbar said dismissively. 'It's just playful.'

On the twenty-ninth, as Rachelle Brettler was beginning to panic about her missing son and placed her initial call to the police, Akbar reflected, in a text to Land, on the midday lunch meeting that the two of them had just enjoyed. 'Today was another epic for you and I, and there will always be more,' he wrote. 'Because an abused child will always love his predator.' He added, 'But you are a predator and must be tamed by many, not one.'

Asked about this text, Akbar told the detectives, 'Peter, if and when you ever meet him, is an incredibly camp actor in his early seventies whose wife died, age ninety-four, twelve months ago. It's just a very strange round of dialogue with him. It obviously sounds strange,' he allowed. 'But there is nothing sexual with anything to do with Zac. And Peter and Zac don't know each other.'

On the evening of 1 December, the night before Akbar met the Brettlers at the Méridien and told them that their son was alive and probably off scoring drugs, he texted Land, 'I'm gonna watch "The Irishman" and go to sleep,' referring to the Netflix film about a mob assassin.

'Keep some love alive, won't you,' Land replied.

'For the record, I never change my dial when it comes to love and will not and cannot,' Akbar wrote. 'As for your condition, as it became clear, I'm no cure.' He added, 'I have to protect myself a little in that regard and try to unwind my recent blind foray into LGTCDRQ.'

When the police read this aloud to him, Akbar would say only, 'None of that is anything to do with Zac.'

One of the detectives, Natalie Wallen, said, 'We're not gonna tell your wife.' Then she read another text, in which Akbar and Land made plans to meet at Annabel's, the nightclub on Berkeley Square where Akbar and Zac had encountered Zamira Ismailova. Land wrote to Akbar: 'I will be there to ask you questions about young men and their fascination for you.'

'What did he mean by that?' Wallen asked.

'You've seen from my phone that Zac was always calling me,' Akbar said. 'My family all noticed it. "Why is this kid always calling you?"' Land had noticed, too, he said. 'He was just asking me why the kid was fascinated. There is zero to that,' Akbar insisted. 'Like, nothing. There is just no connection between Peter and Zac at all.'

'Were you in any kind of sexual relationship with Zac?' Wallen asked.

'No,' Akbar said emphatically. 'No, no, no, no, no, no. Not at all.'

The police had posed the same question to Verinder. But he had responded, as he did to every other question, with a 'No comment.' When they asked Akbar if he was aware of any such relationship between Zac and Verinder, he said, 'To me, there is zero chance of that.' Acknowledging that nothing in Zac's story was what it seemed at first, he said, 'It's been a strange...whole...event. But yeah, no way.'

When he met with the Brettlers, Rory Wilkinson had explained that one hypothesis the police had entertained was that Zac might have been 'raped and a victim of sexual assault before jumping'. This was a horrific thought, and not one that had occurred to Matthew or Rachelle. But Rachelle's brother, David, when he attended the inquest, had found himself wondering about the age gap between Akbar and Verinder and his nephew. 'He is a nineteen-year-old boy,' he said. 'Is someone coercing him to be in bed?' And there was another, more immediate reason to wonder whether there might have been some kind of sexual relationship between Zac and one or both of the older men. A forensic one.

A routine element of an autopsy is the anal swab, to test for the presence of any foreign genetic material. When the sample taken from inside Zac's body was examined under a microscope using a contrast dye, a single sperm was identified, which had been lodged inside his rectum. Had the medical examiners been able to recover a larger sample, police might have subjected it to DNA tests, to try and ascertain whom the sperm belonged to. But there was not enough of the material to work with. At a glance, this seemed to represent a seismic development in the case – an indication that Zac might have had sex with either Verinder or Akbar at some point in his final hours. It was also deeply jarring for the Brettlers to learn, because they had never seen any indications that their son might be gay or even bisexual.

'Was it like "Daddy looking after you"?' Rachelle asked Wilkinson, wondering about the nature of Verinder's relationship with Zac.

'It could have been,' Wilkinson said. But, considering this one fragment of evidence against the backdrop of everything investigators had learned, he continued, it was probably best not to read too much into it. To begin with, there was no definitive indication that the sperm had come from either Akbar or Verinder. It could have come from some third person who was not a suspect in the case. It might also have belonged to Zac, for all they knew; human sexuality is a mysterious thing, to say nothing of human hygiene. It could have been one of Zac's own sperm that somehow migrated there. There was also a chance – very slim, but impossible to rule out – that the sperm was just contamination from the river. 'It could have come from anywhere,' Wilkinson said. 'We just don't know.' He reminded the Brettlers that he and his detectives had access to all the communications between Akbar and Verinder, and to many of Zac's communications as well. They had found no indication whatsoever, in any of these messages, that Zac was engaged in a sexual relationship with either man.

As for Zac's sexual inclinations, Wilkinson noted gingerly that police also had access to 'Zac's internet search history, taken from his iPad'. He paused. 'I don't really want to go through it with you,' he said awkwardly. 'People are in private when they're searching the internet. They can search all sorts of things, and it doesn't really mean an awful lot.'

'As a mum,' Rachelle said, 'I'm interested to know what the heck he was searching for.' She could handle whatever uncomfortable revelations might be lurking in that search archive. 'I know he's probably gone to a very dark side,' she said.

The Brettlers might not have found Wilkinson particularly capable as a detective, but he clearly felt great sympathy for them, and now he seemed reluctant to show them Zac's search history, not just out of some sense of embarrassment or discretion but because he knew that grieving parents, desperate for clues about their dead son, might be inclined to read too much into a series of casual Google searches. Because Zac was gone, and his parents were seeking to solve not just the mystery of his death but also the mystery of who he had really been in life, there might be a tendency to treat those search terms as if they offered a precise snapshot of his state of mind. But in truth, anybody's internet searches are more ephemeral and random than that, more inconsequential.

'It's teenage boy research,' Rachelle said. 'I know there's a lot of pornography. I know there's probably...'

'Yeah, I mean it is what it is,' Wilkinson said uncomfortably. 'He was in private. And in a way... it maybe should stay private.'

'My problem is, as his mum, I want to know,' Rachelle insisted.

'Fair enough,' Wilkinson said finally. 'Fair enough.'

The police investigators had produced a document titled 'Appendix 83: Zac Brettler iPad Summary'. Rachelle and Matthew were nervous to examine this secret window into the psyche of their dead son. Sure enough, there was the Google search for 'what to do with skin burns', at 2:04 a.m. on 29 November, roughly twenty minutes before Zac's death. And there was the email he received from Rachelle, the one she had sent at 10:49 that evening, saying, 'I am a wee bit worried about you – are you seriously ok?' There was his response, 'All good x.'

There were indications that Zac had been engaged in low-level drug dealing – prescription drugs such as Xanax and Valium – using an Instagram account he had set up called Royal Borough Memes. There were quite a number of messages and searches related to various feigned injuries: Zac had pretended to have a herniated disc in his back, which required a back brace, so there were searches related to that, and for 'bruising on lower back', 'foot injury cast', 'get a black eye no pain', 'cover for face scars'. There were also searches related to heroin abuse and treatment programmes, which coincided with the time Zac spent with Akbar and Verinder on his final day, discussing rehab options for his supposed addiction. (In the search history, which stretched back to 3 November, more than three weeks before Zac's death, there was not a single mention of heroin until his final day.)

As Rachelle had predicted, there were plenty of searches of a sexual nature. Zac appears to have been interested in call girls: 'glamour models london escorts', 'pornstar escorts london', 'thai escorts london', 'arab escorts london', 'mature escorts london'. There were also searches for 'trans escorts'; for a number of dominatrixes with names like 'Herrin Bestrafung', 'Mistress German Conan', and 'Lady Velvet Steel'; and for 'london dominatrix walking man like dog'. There were searches for 'free sex' and 'no strings attached sex'. There was also a single search, on 12 November, for 'gay sugar daddy'. But Zac's searches did not seem to tell any one coherent story about his sexuality. Instead they had the eclectic, open-minded quality of a kid who was trying to figure out who he was and what he wanted.

It would be a queasy sensation to catch such an intimate glimpse of the private id of *any* other person, to say nothing of one's own child. Some of Zac's searches betrayed his reckless fixations: 'London gangsters', 'counterfeit notes dark web', 'ganja smuggling', 'Kosovo gang london', 'russian girl london drug'. He also searched for Nick Gold, the friend of Verinder's who was paying for the Riverwalk apartment. But many of the searches were painfully mundane, and indicative of a boy at a crossroads, trying to figure out what he should do with his life:

> 'do you have to pay university fees if you drop out'
> 'night club jobs london'
> 'football manager jobs'
> 'formula one jobs'
> 'tottenham hotspur careers'
> 'sports jobs london'
> 'betting companies jobs uk intern'
> 'academy football teams looking for players'
> 'sports tryouts london'
> 'easiest sport to become pro'
> 'how to become a pro dart player'

The police ultimately concluded that the sperm recovered from Zac's body, and the texts between Akbar and Peter Land, were red herrings. 'With the sort of depth we've gone into,' Wilkinson told the Brettlers, if there had been something sexual happening between Zac and Akbar or Verinder, 'we would have probably found fairly strong evidence to suggest it'.

There was a strange paradox in the digital surveillance they had accomplished: on the one hand, it was incredibly intrusive and appeared to offer a portal directly into Zac's most private thoughts. On the other hand, those random, impulsive, undigested thoughts were ultimately just a jumble. They did not yield any sort of coherent psychological picture – quite the contrary. In the end, the Brettlers were inclined to agree with police that if there had been a sexual relationship between Zac and one of the older men, it would have manifested in some more concrete form of digital evidence. Instead they were left with those searches, and the image of their son flailing around, at nineteen, in search of direction.

One day Matthew was listening to a podcast (he listened to a lot of podcasts) and heard a story about the early years of Bob Dylan. When Dylan was barely out of his teens and just starting his career, he used to tell fantastical stories about how he had been raised in Gallup, New Mexico, and run off as a child to join the carnival. He claimed that he was a descendent of the Sioux Nation and that when he first got to New York, he made ends meet by turning tricks in Times Square. None of this was true. In fact, even his name was an invention: Dylan was born Robert Allen Zimmerman, and he had a conventional suburban upbringing in Hibbing, Minnesota. In 1963, when he was twenty-two years old, he told an interviewer in New York, 'I don't know my parents. They don't know me. I've lost contact with them,' though his parents were at that very moment staying in a hotel around the corner, because he had invited them to watch him perform at Carnegie Hall.

'For Dylan, it became a game,' Matthew said to Rachelle. 'He created all sorts of elaborate tales about himself.' He was a trickster who confected a mysterious persona that may have been ridiculous but ultimately served him well. If you mentioned those adolescent fibs to Dylan today, he would probably 'laugh about it', Matthew ventured. 'But there are lots of people out there who have created a fantasy existence for themselves. And it hasn't prevented them from operating in the real world when their feet finally hit the ground.'

Chapter 18

HORNET'S NEST

'I NOW CALL AKBAR SHAMJI,' Mary Hassell said.

On the video screen, Akbar's hair was long and tousled. He appeared to be in a hotel room. After swearing to tell the truth, he testified that he had first connected with Zac through Mark Foley, 'who was very senior in the Chelsea Football Club hierarchy'. Zac had been introduced as the son of a 'wealthy Eastern European oligarch'. Akbar had never thought to second-guess this story, he told the coroner, because he trusted Foley.

Akbar no longer lived in London. Not long after Zac's death, he had been appointed chairman and 'chief vision officer' of a company called Bitzero Blockchain, which, in his description, was 'focused on delivering disruptive energy solutions to power the high growth demand in the data processing industry'. In the summer of 2022, Akbar had unveiled an audacious plan to convert a complex of Cold War-era missile silos in Nekoma, North Dakota, into a crypto-mining facility. Bitzero's North American headquarters would be located in the state, Akbar promised at a press conference, saying, 'We're torn between Fargo and Bismarck.' Bitzero had raised nearly $100 million in investment capital and was planning an initial public offering. One investor in the company was Kevin O'Leary, a celebrity businessman and one of the stars of *Shark Tank*, a successful reality television franchise built around entrepreneurship, which was overseen by Mark Burnett, the producer who had cast Donald Trump in *The Apprentice*. O'Leary was bullish on Akbar and his company. 'Data is the new oil,' he proclaimed.

The years since Zac's death had been good to Akbar's family. His son, Akbar Jr, had been admitted to Brown University, in Rhode Island, and was also finding success as a male model. Akbar Jr had matured into a beautiful young man, with sharp cheekbones and a brooding stare. He began making appearances in runway shows in Milan and Paris and in ad campaigns for Versace and Dolce & Gabbana. In a photo posted on Instagram, Akbar Sr, wearing a leather jacket and a big grin, posed in the fragrance aisle of a shop, pointing proudly at a huge picture of his son's face on an advertisement for Tom Ford *parfum*. Daniela continued to design gowns for glamorous and notable women and announced her intention to open new showrooms in Hong Kong and Singapore. Safiya, who wanted to become an actress, had been training at the Lee Strasberg Institute, in New York.

The coroner mentioned Verinder Sharma and asked Akbar, 'Were you friends or business associates?'

'Um,' Akbar stuttered. 'A little bit of both.' They had 'looked at a few projects together', he said. In Akbar's telling, he was only a bystander to this tragedy. 'I wasn't a chief protagonist,' he told the coroner. Really, this was a story about Zac and Verinder. 'It wasn't my apartment,' he stressed. 'Nor my drug addiction.'

Asked to recite the events of that fateful evening, Akbar claimed that he could not remember the details: 'It was a very foggy night in my mind. We had some alcohol. It was late.' But what he did know was that Zac loved being at Riverwalk and had wanted to go there that night. It did not feel, Akbar testified, as if Zac had been walking into danger.

'Did you think that he was suicidal?'

'What was clear was that he could not live with himself,' Akbar said. Zac was addicted to heroin and 'profoundly depressed'. Akbar had worried that he might take his own life. But over the course of that evening, Zac seemed to settle down, and they had made a plan to get him into rehab the next day, which was why Akbar felt comfortable leaving.

Then why come back, after driving away?

'I don't remember.'

Anything else about that night that might be helpful for us to know?

'Not really,' Akbar said. He wished he had grasped the full extent of the 'pain and torment' Zac had been struggling with.

And with that, Mary Hassell was done with her direct examination. But now Alexandra Tampakopoulos rose to her feet. 'Zac's parents really want to understand what happened,' she told Akbar. 'That's something you can understand, isn't it?'

'Yes, of course,' he said.

'If your son died in these circumstances, you would want to understand as much as possible about what happened.'

'Without a doubt.'

When Akbar was interrogated by police, Indian Dave was still alive, Tampakopoulos pointed out. This might have left Akbar feeling fearful and inhibited. But now, she said gently, 'you don't need to be worried about Mr Sharma'.

'I'm very happy to answer all your questions,' Akbar said. He was appearing at this inquest 'against advice of lawyers', he continued. He had no obligation to be there or to tell them a thing. But 'I feel for the parents,' he said. 'So I'm very happy to share, as a parent, everything I know.'

It seemed clear from the text messages on Zac's final day, Tampakopoulos said, that there had been 'a falling-out between Zac and Mr Sharma'.

'I wasn't directly involved in a lot of the business that they were doing,' Akbar said, before acknowledging that there may have been an issue with 'some debt collectors in Spain'. Zac was owed some money, he said, before correcting himself: 'Zac was *aware* of somebody who was owed money.' And he had asked Verinder to help collect it. Tampakopoulos quoted from the message Akbar sent to Zac in which he said that Verinder had 'risked his life and freedom to have the authority he has' and that Zac had offered 'support for his children' and had been 'making promises and commitments and not coming through on them'.

Verinder's debt-collecting business had 'sounded pretty intense', Akbar allowed. But unfortunately, he had no memory of the specifics of that particular message.

It doesn't help that you deleted your WhatsApp messages, Tampakopoulos pointed out.

But that's just 'something that I do', Akbar explained, very unruffled, elaborating that he deleted messages his kids shouldn't see. 'Just fun stuff. Naughty stuff. Boys' stuff.'

'So it's just a coincidence,' Tampakopoulos said, that the deletions happened to cover precisely the month leading up to the day 'Zac falls off the balcony'?

The coroner interjected, saying that she understood why Tampakopoulos was asking about Akbar's messages but that it was 'clearly not going to be a fruitful line'.

But Tampakopoulos kept pushing. What about the message from Verinder saying, 'Fuck this little kid'?

That was Verinder's 'style', Akbar said. Totally harmless. Just the way he talked.

To Rachelle's brother, David Gryn, it felt clear, watching the testimony, that on that final night, a vice had been tightening around Zac. Hearing the text messages read out loud 'felt like the buildup to when you come in front of the gang boss', David reflected. 'In the film, this is when you get beaten up or killed.' He was surprised, he added, that the coroner did not appear to regard the back-and-forth between Akbar and Verinder as more 'sinister'. Instead, she sought once again to cut off the questioning, telling Tampakopoulos, 'I don't think you're going to get any different answer than you have already.'

But Akbar is the only person who can help us understand these messages, Tampakopoulos protested.

'He's said he doesn't remember,' Hassell said, more firmly. Throughout the proceeding she had been calm and genteel, almost to a fault. Now she was becoming more aggressive, and not with the forgetful witness but with the Brettlers' lawyer.

'Madam, I am entitled to ask these questions,' Tampakopoulos said sternly. 'I would be very grateful if you'll allow me to do that.' Then she turned back to Akbar and asked what Verinder was talking about when he wrote, 'I want 5% of that 205 million.'

'Zac was always promising huge sums of money,' Akbar said. 'And I pretty clearly told Sharma... "I don't think there's any golden pot at the end of that rainbow."'

But what would be the *basis* for such a promise? she wondered.

'Presumably Zac didn't say, "I'll give you ten million pounds just 'cause."'

'Remember the context of the oligarch's son with the billion-dollar fortune,' Akbar said.

'So you're accepting, aren't you, that there was an understanding on Mr Sharma's part that he would be getting ten million pounds?'

'Ms Tampakopoulos,' the coroner broke in again. 'The purpose of this inquest is to understand how Zac died.' She appreciated that Rachelle and Matthew might have 'unanswered questions', but the witness had said repeatedly that his recollections were not vivid enough to answer them. 'This isn't *assisting* me,' Hassell said impatiently. 'All I'm getting is a discussion about money that Mr Shamji has said he can't interpret.' Her tone was final and severe. 'I won't allow you to continue in this vein.'

The Brettlers witnessed this exchange with a shimmering fury. At last, in this inquest, they had an opportunity to confront Akbar about his lies and cajole him into revealing the truth. In an inquest, unlike a criminal trial, the official standard of proof is not 'beyond a reasonable doubt', which had represented such an insurmountable hurdle for Rory Wilkinson and his detectives. The proper standard now was 'the balance of probabilities', meaning that it is the coroner's job to consider the evidence and arrive at the explanation that seems, on balance, to be most likely. Here, finally, was a forum in which they might be able to establish what actually happened at Riverwalk that night. Yet every time Tampakopoulos tried to put a little pressure on Akbar, Hassell would jump in and call her off. Part of the problem is that an inquest is designed to establish the basic facts of a death, not who should be held liable for it. Clearly Hassell had decided to take the narrowest possible view of what the proceeding would accomplish, and, as the coroner, she got to decide what evidence could be heard.

'Madam, this is absolutely relevant,' Tampakopoulos protested. These texts were from the very day Zac arrived at Riverwalk through the front door and then 'left from the balcony'.

But Hassell had made up her mind. Only two people knew the truth about how Zac died, she declared. 'And neither of them is here today.'

Unable to restrain himself, Matthew asked to be heard. 'Mr Shamji was present until forty-five minutes before Zac left the balcony,' he told the coroner. 'He was also present in the apartment ten minutes or so *after* Zac had left that balcony.' He looked at her intensely. 'So if anybody on this planet who is still alive has any capacity to share with Rachelle and me what happened... that person is Mr Shamji.' The reason that their lawyer was so adamant about posing these questions, Matthew explained, was that they needed to understand what would prompt Verinder 'to be so angry with Zac, and to cause this climate of fear that clearly was present in the apartment'. The 'discussion about money', as Hassell had called it, was anything but irrelevant: it might be the one thing that could *explain* Zac's death. Matthew was really pleading with her now. 'This is our only chance to get any sort of understanding as to why our nineteen-year-old son is not here,' he said.

Akbar testified for hours, his voice sonorous, his tone vaguely patrician. Sometimes he laid it on quite thick with the purported sympathy for Zac's family. At other times he exhibited a mild impatience with the whole proceeding. His evasions were many and proffered without apology or shame. He turned out to have a rather impressive ability to say farcical things with a straight face. When Tampakopoulos asked about the 10:35 p.m. text to Mervin in which Akbar had said that he was 'heating up knives and clearing up blood', Akbar responded that he had been 'tired and obviously a little bit drunk' and that he had wanted Mervin to come and pick him up, 'because I didn't want to drive'.

But that didn't exactly demystify the business about knives and blood. 'I just need a straight answer,' Tampakopoulos pressed. 'What did you *mean?*'

'I could've meant a hundred things whilst we were drinking,' Akbar said breezily. The one thing he definitely *hadn't* meant was that he was actually, literally clearing up blood. In fact, he hadn't meant blood as in 'out of your vein' at all, he said, seeming to have fastened, belatedly, on an explanation. '"Blood" is a more earthy, streety way of saying "bro",' Akbar continued. *That* was the spirit in which he'd used the word. He hadn't been 'clearing up blood'. He'd been 'clearing up, *blood*.'

This struck Rachelle and Matthew as such a ludicrous thing to say that it was almost hard to keep from laughing. After leaving Riverwalk that night, Akbar had spoken to Verinder on the telephone at 2:12 a.m. They talked for nine minutes, Tampakopoulos pointed out, right up until 2:21 a.m., just three minutes before Zac went into the river. 'What was that call about?'

'I just don't remember,' Akbar said.

'Your memory seems rather selective,' she said. Was Verinder 'extremely angry with Zac, and you were worried about what would happen'?

'Everything was fine,' Akbar insisted. He claimed to be unable to explain why he had gone around the building and peered into the river at exactly the point where Zac had just entered it, because he no longer had any memory of having done so.

The coroner had one more question for Akbar: had he ever spoken with Verinder afterwards about what had gone on in that final hour with Zac?

'I never pushed too hard,' Akbar said. Verinder had been 'close-lipped' about what happened that night, he said, adding, 'I'm not sure what kind of hornet's nest I would have been kicking.'

On some level, Matthew and Rachelle had known in advance that they were unlikely to emerge from the inquest with rock-solid conclusions. Grieving families frequently end up feeling let down by the inquest process, which in theory holds the promise of clarity but in practice often feels cursory and limited in scope. Even so, after the slipshod investigation by the police, the Brettlers had hoped to use the adversarial nature of the inquest to force some kind of reckoning. In that arena, they had thought, with lawyers and sworn testimony and cross-examination and a coroner functioning as a sort of judge, they would at least be able to underline in some official way the lies and complicity of Akbar and the contradictions in Dominique's claims. They also hoped that the coroner might lay to rest once and for all the theory that Rory Wilkinson seemed so partial to – that Zac had simply committed suicide. Perhaps their hopes had been too high going in, but the whole inquest felt anticlimactic. Though it had been scheduled to take three days, the hearing ended up lasting only two. Gallingly, at one point during the testimony, Mary Hassell appeared to be dozing off to sleep. (Both Rachelle's brother, David Gryn, and one of the friends who attended with the Brettlers confirmed seeing Hassell nod off; David wrote, in his contemporaneous notes, 'Coroner falling asleep.') Rather than any sort of rigorous interrogation of the evidence, the inquest felt like an obligatory formality. A fait accompli.

This was a pity, because the testimony did produce a number of intriguing clues. At one point, as Tampakopoulos was questioning a police officer, it emerged that when detectives had finally got around to searching the Riverwalk apartment, nearly a week after Zac's death, and had inspected the glass safety partition on the balcony, they discovered that one part of the glass appeared to have been recently wiped clean. It wasn't the whole partition that had been polished, just one area – the same rough area from which Zac had jumped. Was the glass wiped in the sort of manner one might use to remove fingerprints? Tampakopoulos asked.

'Potentially,' the officer responded.

Or blood?

'Potentially,' he said again.

It also came out in testimony that in the bathroom of Verinder's apartment and on one of the bedroom walls, investigators had noticed dark spatters that looked very much like blood. They took photographs of these brownish-crimson spots and smears. But remarkably, they never collected any samples of this substance to see if it really was blood, and whose blood it might be.

The most surreal moment of the whole inquest came as Tampakopoulos was interviewing one of the cops and abruptly broke off her questioning, in a state of embarrassment and alarm. The big video screen in the courtroom, upon which Akbar and Dominique had testified, was still live. Akbar had indicated a desire, after his testimony concluded, to continue watching the proceedings, with his camera off. But now, suddenly, the camera had been enabled, revealing to everyone in the courtroom a live image of a bathroom in which Akbar was taking a shower.

'It's just absurd!' Tampakopoulos exclaimed.

'MR SHAMJI!' the coroner practically shouted. 'I'M SURE YOU CAN HEAR ME!' A startled, naked Akbar hurriedly switched off his camera. 'I don't see any reason why it would be anything other than an accident,' the coroner said, regaining her composure. 'But if that happens again...I will terminate the call.' Then, pointedly, 'Because that was extremely off-putting.'

'Multitasking,' Matthew deadpanned. But there did seem to be a metaphor in the notion that, even as the Brettlers attended their son's inquest, roiled by emotion and listening anxiously to each piece of evidence, Akbar felt so unimplicated in the whole spectacle that he carried his device into the bathroom so that he could let the hearing run while he bathed.

At the end of the second day, Hassell delivered her ruling. She began by raising doubts about the credibility of Shamji's testimony. He seemed to remember some things very well and others not at all, she pointed out. When Akbar stared into the river, she said, it was clear to her that he was 'looking for Zac...because Mr Sharma gave him to understand that Zac had left the balcony'. Having said that, she continued, 'I still don't know what happened in those minutes before.' Could it have been suicide? That was, in some ways, the obvious explanation, she ventured. 'When a person appears to jump from a fifth-floor balcony, then what else are they expecting?' Hassell accepted Dominique's contention that 'she thought Zac was suicidal'. And yet, the 'whole background' didn't 'indicate a person who was suicidal'. So she opted for a so-called open verdict: neither murder nor suicide, a deliberately ambiguous ruling. 'I can't fill in the gaps; I can't speculate,' she said. 'I don't know what happened.'

Feeling slightly shell-shocked, Matthew and Rachelle left the Coroner's Court and walked to a nearby bar with their friends. Matthew was talking a lot, very quickly, processing in real time. Rachelle was more quiet. But everyone in the group seemed to share an acute sense of grievance. 'The whole idea of what it was somehow got lost in translation,' David Gryn said. 'Something really dubious has gone on. What world had Zac entered? And why, when he's dead, does nobody really investigate? It feels so *casual*.' He felt a deep sense of pity for his sister and her husband. 'You're isolated in these moments,' he reflected. To comfort them, or perhaps just to have something to say, he told Rachelle and Matthew, 'We're all witnesses. Something very wrong happened here.'

PART IV
SURVIVORS

Chapter 19

A CHANCE ENCOUNTER

I SPENT THE SUMMER of 2023 living in London, working on a television project. More than two decades earlier, in my twenties, I had lived in England for a couple of years as a graduate student, and though I had often gone back for visits, I was excited by the prospect of returning for a longer stay. London is especially glorious in summertime, and it was a thrill to introduce my children – two boys, who were ten and thirteen – to the many pleasures of the city. We took long walks, crisscrossing the bridges spanning the Thames, and spent lazy afternoons ambling around Hyde Park.

One stormy day that July, the television production had commandeered an office building on Chancery Lane, which for the purposes of the series had been redecorated to look like Scotland Yard. During a break in the filming, I fell into conversation with a stranger who happened to be visiting the set that day. He was a guest of the director and introduced himself as Andrew Fingret. He was a lawyer of about sixty, dressed casually in black, and he said that he had worked in the film business. He had a conspiratorial smile and a nimble sense of humour. We were talking about life in London versus New York when Andrew, who is Jewish, remarked on the relative smallness – and closeness – of London's Jewish community. I mentioned that an old friend of my parents happened to be a London rabbi named Julia Neuberger. It was a casual aside, not even name-dropping, really, just the serve-and-return of idle dialogue. But it completely changed the course of our conversation.

At Leeds University in the early 1980s, Andrew became friends with a fellow student named David, who came from Manchester, and David introduced Andrew to his best friend, Matthew Brettler. Andrew ended up attending Matthew and Rachelle's wedding, in

1998. During the years when the Brettlers were busy raising small children, they fell out of touch with Andrew. But eventually they reconnected at a party in London and ultimately grew closer in middle age than they'd ever been when they were younger. Andrew liked to play a conversational game he called 'Jewish Geography', a six-degrees-of-separation exercise in which Jewish people, upon first meeting, can suss out common acquaintances or other points of connection. When I got to talking with Andrew on the set that day, I had never met or heard of the Brettler family. But without realizing it, I had stumbled into a game of Jewish Geography. Julia Neuberger, my family friend, was the former senior rabbi of the West London Synagogue, the same position that for many years had been held by Hugo Gryn. In that capacity, she was Zac Brettler's rabbi. She had officiated his bar mitzvah.

'I may have a story for you,' Andrew told me.

Andrew was one of the friends who had accompanied the Brettlers to the Coroner's Court the previous December for the inquest. 'Some very close friends of mine have lost a child,' he told me. 'Their son died, under quite mysterious circumstances, by going off the balcony of a building into the Thames. After his death, the parents learned he'd been pretending he was the son of a Russian oligarch.' Matthew and Rachelle had been 'living through a nightmare', he said, and were still 'trying to find answers'.

Nearly four years had passed since Zac's death, and throughout that time the Brettlers had placed their trust in the authorities. After going through official channels and exhausting their procedural appeals, all they had to show for it was an inconclusive police investigation and an inquest with an 'open' verdict. It wasn't clear what, if any, options they had remaining. Verinder Sharma was dead, and Akbar Shamji seemed unlikely to ever be held accountable for the lies he had told about the circumstances of Zac's demise.

About a month after the inquest, in January 2023, Daniela Karnuts celebrated her fortieth birthday with an opulent dinner party at Oswald's, a private club on Albemarle Street in Mayfair. Founded by Robin Birley, the son of the Annabel's founder, Mark Birley – in fact, the very same son who as a little boy had been mauled by a tiger at the private zoo of John Aspinall – Oswald's was a fashionable venue. The club attracted celebrities, from David and Victoria Beckham to the film director Guy Ritchie. Prince William occasionally dined there, as did the One Hyde Park developer Nick Candy. Birley's clubs were also favoured by Conservative politicians. Another place he operated nearby, 5 Hertford Street, was so popular with Nigel Farage and other Eurosceptics that it became known in the press as the 'Brexit sex dungeon'. Akbar was a member at 5 Hertford and occasionally took meetings there. Though they were frequently described as 'exclusive', Birley's clubs were not really *that* exclusive. If you had the money, you could generally wheedle in. But the message of throwing a party at Oswald's or arranging lunch with a business prospect at 5 Hertford Street was unmistakable: come meet me in my native element, the bosom of the establishment. Several dozens of Daniela's friends came to Oswald's for the celebration under a big crystal chandelier in one of the club's private rooms. The decor featured a mix of colourful prints and the place had the cosy ambience of a country house in the middle of the city. There were jeroboams of good champagne. Akbar was there, beaming and resplendent, in a black dinner jacket, a crisp bow tie and tinted glasses. Peter Land was holding forth at one of the long, elegantly laid tables. A number of the women wore gowns in jewel tones from the Safiyaa label. The brand's young namesake, Safiya Shamji, looked chic and vivacious in a green dress with an elaborate fringe. Daniela herself wore a royal-blue sleeveless number that was cinched with a silver belt.

Partway through the evening, a tall figure in a dark suit entered the room and walked slowly towards Daniela. She was absorbed in conversation, so at first she did not see him, but then she looked up and her eyes went wide. It was Akbar Jr, who had flown in from Milan, where he had been modelling, to surprise her. Daniela stood, her face aglow with delight, and enveloped him in an enormous hug as the revellers looked on and applauded. Safiya later posted a video of the reunion on Instagram, and Rachelle Brettler, who continued to keep tabs on the online lives of the Shamjis, watched it: this heartwarming tableau, a son coming home to his mother.

The Brettlers felt isolated – and angry. Even now, there was no indication in the press or anywhere on the internet that Zac had died, much less that his life had ended under such confounding circumstances. They had just been starting to wonder what more they could do when their friend Andrew visited the TV production on Chancery Lane and happened to bump into me. A few days after that preliminary conversation, Andrew introduced me to Rachelle and Matthew.

We met at a coffee shop in Bloomsbury. The morning was warm, and we sat at an outdoor table. After some initial pleasantries, Andrew sat back so that the Brettlers could tell their story, and apart from the occasional question or murmur of encouragement from me, they proceeded to talk for nearly two hours. The whole tragic saga came tumbling out, raw and undigested, in fragments: Zac's childhood, his strange turn at Mill Hill, his friendship with Akbar, the shock of his death, the revelations about Verinder Sharma, the bizarre passivity of Scotland Yard, the fury the Brettlers felt at the inquest. We had agreed to talk with a prior understanding that Matthew and Rachelle were still uncertain about whether they were prepared to go on the record. Both felt a strong instinct to preserve their family's privacy. But they also felt tormented by a gnawing sense of irresolution and of resentment. 'We were too *obedient*,' Rachelle said.

A week later we met again, this time at the bar of a Soho hotel, and the Brettlers decided that they were ready to tell their story in a more public way. Rachelle continued to harbour a few misgivings. As a journalist herself, she understood that after crossing this threshold, there would be no turning back: any article I might publish seemed likely to contain details about Zac that would be difficult for his family to read. The tabloids – which up to now had been silent, because they knew nothing of the story – would swarm, feasting on the lurid details. Rachelle fretted about her mother, Jacqueline, who was now in her nineties, reading an unvarnished account of her late grandson. Matthew seemed more animated by a sense of indignation, particularly when it came to what he regarded as the desultory conduct of the authorities. 'Somebody needs to point a finger,' he said. 'Is this the kind of police force we want?'

Over the coming months, I would spend a great deal of time talking with the Brettlers and poring over documents related to the case. The more I delved into the details, the clearer it became that they were not wrong to feel the investigation had been mishandled. I often marvelled at the way in which the family had continued to function in the aftermath of Zac's death. 'It is extraordinary that they are still married,' Rachelle's sister Gaby remarked, pointing out that couples who lose a child often find it difficult to stay together, but that Matthew and Rachelle had found ways to support each other. Their approaches were different. Matthew tended to talk more in our conversations about the case, reciting endless specific details from memory. When I inquired about more emotional subjects, he could sometimes seem hamstrung. Then, on rare occasions, his emotions would come surging up, out of nowhere, taking us both by surprise. Once, when the two of us met for lunch during one of Matthew's visits to New York, I asked a casual question about his love of cycling and whether that was an interest that Zac had shared. Matthew, just as casually, was starting to respond that, yes, biking had been a thing he and Zac would sometimes do together when suddenly he was convulsed by a terrible sob. It was gone almost as soon as it started, and Matthew apologized – clearly embarrassed, and worried that *I* might be embarrassed. But in that instant, it was as if all the pain he normally kept locked away behind his controlled, cerebral facade had erupted in a spasm of anguish.

Rachelle was less self-conscious about surrendering to her feelings, and more prone to interrogate the psychological dimensions of her own grief. But she, too, had become quite conversant in the complicated details of the case, and she seemed happy to play buddy cop and fierce ally to her husband as he reinvestigated the mystery of Zac's death. She spent more time than Matthew did surveying the history of Zac's life and conjuring up counterfactual scenarios in which he might have survived: what if she'd never allowed him to board at Mill Hill and had just continued driving him to school each day? What if she'd moved with him, gone somewhere abroad, got him out of London before it swallowed him?

One surreal feature of sudden loss is the manner in which moments of incredible pain can end up stitched into the more quotidian fabric of daily life. During one of our conversations, Matthew reached for his phone to show me the photograph that Pino D'Amore had taken of Zac's corpse on the foreshore of the Thames. With his index finger, he opened his photo application, then flicked back in time, trying to locate the specific date when Pino had shared the picture. But the digital carousel was soon spinning so quickly that he overshot the mark. So he stopped it with his fingertip, then scrolled in the other direction, forwards in time, past happy pictures of Joe and Rachelle and himself, and Zac when he was alive. Throwaway domestic moments, sun-dappled holiday snaps – they all flew by at dizzying speed, until finally Matthew settled on a bleak picture, under a colourless sky, of Zac's body facedown in the mud.

The Brettlers might have been ready, finally, to speak publicly about what had happened to Zac, but what I discovered as I began my own investigation was that many others were not. I was able to track down quite quickly certain witnesses whom the police had never fully identified. I worked out the full name of Akbar's music-business friend, Mervin Sealy, by searching the nearly two hundred Instagram users who followed @mr_alpha_nero, the account dedicated to Akbar's dog. There was only one Mervin. But Mervin didn't want to talk. Neither did Carlton, the chauffeur Sharma had sent to knock on the Brettlers' door the morning after Zac died. Again and again, when people declined to speak with me, they would invoke some version of the phrase 'I don't want to get involved'. While some of Zac's friends from Mill Hill were happy to talk, others refused to get on the phone, evincing discomfort at the thought of being associated with him. His *teachers* at Mill Hill refused to talk. Classmates from Ashbourne College did not want to talk. The doormen at Riverwalk, who had got to know him over that summer when he was living there, did not want to talk. It was as if, in death, he had become an untouchable.

Zac had fooled so many people that some may simply have felt jilted and embittered, disinclined to dwell on how readily they had been duped by a fabulist, eager to erase him from their memories altogether. But there was something else that I often detected in these brief, unconsummated exchanges with people who refused to speak of him: fear. Because there was never any official declaration of how Zac had died, people seemed to believe that his death had involved foul play – that he was associated with a darker side of London, one they wanted to keep their distance from.

'I thank you in advance for your understanding, but Zac's death is an event which I do not wish to talk about,' Akbar wrote to me, after I emailed him proposing a conversation. 'I prefer to allow Zac and his legacy to rest in peace.' He did not seem defensive so much as aloof, as if I'd inquired about some bygone bit of business from which he'd long since moved on. And he *did* appear to have moved on. Akbar had been busy running his crypto-mining startup, Bitzero. The previous April, he had taken part in the Bitcoin 2022 conference in Miami, a raucous convocation of crypto bros featuring a keynote address in which the billionaire tech entrepreneur Peter Thiel demonstrated his distrust of paper currency by ripping up hundred-dollar bills. While he was in Miami, Akbar granted an interview to Kitco News, an online service that tracks cryptocurrencies and precious metals. The host, David Lin, introduced him as 'the new kid on the block' and noted that he was doing 'very important work'. Akbar wore a grey shirt under a dark jacket, with the sleeves unbuttoned at the wrist to reveal a collection of bracelets, which gave him the effortlessly louche aspect of a man who might feel slightly anxious about turning fifty. Jutting his chin and waving his hands around theatrically like a cartoon intellectual, he held forth on the history of the financial system and the wonders of the blockchain and the possibility that 'pegging to the Bitcoin will sort of be the future of how countries trade with one another'.

'Deep thoughts, Akbar,' Lin said.

But in the end, the grand plans to build a data centre for crypto mining in an abandoned nuclear missile installation never came to fruition. Akbar flew on a lot of planes and had a lot of meetings and raised a great deal of money from investors, but, practically from the start, Bitzero was missing progress benchmarks on the path to establishing the site. Marc Sinden, the former artistic director of the Mermaid Theatre, said that, dating as far back as the 1990s, Akbar's modus operandi had been 'big announcement, and then fuck all'. In

September 2023, Bitzero's board asked Akbar to resign and commissioned a due diligence report.

'Shamji has a history of unpaid debts, disputes with his partners and counterparties, and unsuccessful business,' the report began, noting that it was 'unclear whether Shamji has substantial personal wealth or if he is primarily financing his lifestyle and commercial activities with debt and/or money from investors'. The report unearthed a trail of defaulted mortgages, adverse judgments, court liens, and pissed-off business partners that stretched back decades. 'I've never seen anything like this in my life,' one executive associated with Bitzero marvelled. 'He deserves the Oscar for grifting.' Just two weeks after the report was submitted, a press release announced Akbar's appointment as chief executive of yet another company, this one called DarkByte, which billed itself – in language so laden with jargon that it was difficult to explicate – as having something to do with artificial intelligence.

As I began to dig into Akbar's personal and professional history, I found that nothing was quite as it seemed. When Daniela Karnuts spoke about her fashion label, Safiyaa, she liked to point out that it was named 'after my daughter'. Daniela appears to have been a nurturing presence in the lives of Safiya and Akbar Jr. But she is not their biological mother. Akbar, during his years in the United States, had met and married a woman named Megan McLaughlin, who grew up in Wyoming and worked briefly as a model. 'It was a pretty wild ride between those two,' one former business partner of Akbar's recalled. 'They were a lethal combination.' Abdul Shamji did not approve of his son's wife, the business partner said: 'She was white. She was American. She had no educational pedigree.'

Akbar's business interests during those years were no less tumultuous. He ended up getting sued in California by two musicians who asserted that they had written a bunch of songs for Soulife but had never been properly credited or granted appropriate intellectual property rights. Rather than simply pay the musicians or challenge their lawsuit in court, Akbar skipped town, taking his children with him and moving back to London. Megan was left behind in America. According to Jack Ponti, the record producer who worked with him during this period, Akbar somehow managed to win sole custody of their children.

Today Megan lives in Wyoming and still goes by Megan Shamji. She did not respond to my requests for an interview. But in 2018, she posted a snapshot on her Facebook page of Safiya and Akbar Jr, both in their teens at the time, looking happy. 'Good lookin kids ya got there!' one friend commented. 'Your daughter is a mini Megan,' said another.

After Akbar fled the States, a court in Los Angeles entered a default judgment against him – and ordered him to pay the two musicians $700,000 for 'breach of contract and fraud'. But in a situation that was reminiscent of the disgruntled creditors who had pursued the Gomba Group decades earlier, the musicians and their attorneys could not identify any assets in the United States that might be repossessed to satisfy the judgment. Rather than give up, the musicians retained legal counsel in the UK to see if they could enforce their debt in London. But Akbar responded that the figure they were demanding was simply not reasonable, and in any case he could not pay it, because he was 'broke'. Perhaps they might settle for some kind of instalment plan? In an email to one of their lawyers, he claimed, 'I don't have a great income or savings or property.'

'Shamji's position was that he was the spoiled child of a rich family and had little in the way of assets of his own,' Adrian Davies, a London barrister who worked on the case, recalled. 'He's been living this way for decades. He'd spent his whole life going round the world leaving bad debts behind him – in England, Los Angeles, wherever he goes, really.' His family would make funds available to him, but, in keeping with the old Gomba playbook, all the Shamji assets tended to be held by trusts. At one point, the lawyers were able to establish that Akbar was living in a nice flat in Chelsea, but they could not seize it, because it turned out to be owned by a family trust. After finally working out an instalment plan and making a few payments, Akbar defaulted. In February 2019, still under pressure from his American creditors, he formally declared bankruptcy in London. True, he might have been living in a £10 million apartment on Mount Street at the time, but it wasn't his. As he was careful to point out during one of his police interrogations, 'That's my wife's address.' It was right around the time of Akbar's bankruptcy that he was first introduced to a young Russian billionaire named Zac Ismailov.

༄

After receiving Akbar's casual brush-off, I wrote back a bit more pointedly, and this time he responded at greater length:

> Zac had built an extraordinary web of lies around his life and identity and he was clearly deeply tormented. I would imagine that his parents and sibling have already been through a great deal of suffering, understanding that he had built an entire identity ... based on his claims that his father had been murdered and a deep hatred for his mother. Such a level of hatred for his parents is not a pleasant area for anyone to contemplate ... As a father myself I really don't feel comfortable taking his parents deeper into these wounds, as this must all be deeply painful for them already.

As rhetorical gymnastics go, this was pretty impressive. Akbar was explaining his refusal to speak about Zac's death as a function of the tremendous empathy he felt for the Brettler family. In fact, he seemed to be suggesting that it would be indecent of *me* to subject them, in their bereavement, to any further investigation. 'These really are not subjects that I think it is fair to publish as they will strike publicly into the heart of that family which must already be in a great deal of anguish,' Akbar wrote.

Yet even as he invoked his own compassion, Akbar seemed to undercut it, suggesting that Zac had committed suicide because he hated Matthew and Rachelle. 'The fact is that Zac was somehow so tormented by them and his life that he would do anything to escape and finally found a way,' he wrote.

Akbar rebuffed my requests for a phone call or a Zoom chat, and an in-person meeting seemed unlikely. He wouldn't even give me a straight answer about where he currently lived. 'Work keeps me travelling a lot in the US, Canada and Scandinavia,' he wrote, adding, 'I spend time in London also.' But he now appeared more willing to entertain questions over email. So, after assuring him that the Brettlers were well aware that I was writing about the case, I inquired how he had come to believe that Zac could be the son of a Russian oligarch. 'Did you Google Zac or his supposed oligarch father to ascertain if any of the details of what he was saying were true?' I asked. There are only so many Russian or Kazakh oligarchs, I pointed out. 'A lot of people, upon hearing about a friend's enormously wealthy oligarch father, would look him up online. Did you not?'

'Zac was very clear that as a family they worked diligently to stay off the internet,' Akbar replied. 'I know several very wealthy families from that part of the world who have a presence in London who do that very efficiently.' Besides, he added, 'I was introduced to Zac by a well-respected English businessman,' who had met Zac at 'what he believed to be Zac's apartment at One Hyde Park.'

This was a reference to Mark Foley, the mysterious Chelsea Football Club executive who supposedly worked closely with Roman Abramovich and had introduced Akbar and his friend John Connies-Laing to Zac, with an eye to Zac's family investing in their Lisbon property deal. 'Personal introductions in London are far more trusted than social media,' Akbar wrote, 'particularly with Eastern Europeans who have to keep a lower profile here.'

At this point in our correspondence, Akbar made a surprising move, cc'ing Connies-Laing on his reply to me and inviting him to 'chime in'. Connies-Laing, who worked in the London property market, had been friends with Akbar for years. I knew from some of the police files that Akbar had sent him a message in the days after Zac's death, expressing a fear about Verinder Sharma: 'Last thing I need is for Dave and all his mates to be blaming me for bringing this fraud into his life.' He seemed to be a confidant.

When I emailed Connies-Laing to ask for more details about the circumstances of Foley's introduction, he wrote back confirming Akbar's account and added, 'Mark was well connected in the Oligarch world and I had absolutely no reason to think that Zac was not credible.' But who *was* Mark Foley? He appeared to have an extremely limited profile on the internet, lower than I would have anticipated for a senior executive at Chelsea. As far as I could gather, he ran his own company, Rawley & Co., which was based in Somerset. But I couldn't glean much about what the company did. Some online records identified him as a 'surveyor'. Another listing named him as a director of something called Chelsea Management Services. I found a photo online of a generic-looking middle-aged guy with soft features and grey hair. But Foley remained frustratingly enigmatic, and my efforts to contact him by phone, text and email met with no reply.

'Sounds like I should talk to Mark Foley,' I suggested brightly to Connies-Laing, as if I hadn't been trying to do just that for months. I asked him to put us in touch. But when I received Connies-Laing's reply, it was comically evasive. 'I spoke with Mark Foley and he asked me to inform you that he concurs completely with what I have told you,' he wrote, adding that Foley did not wish to speak with me himself.

Foley seemed to be a critically important figure in this drama. Both Akbar and Connies-Laing claimed that their faith in his endorsement was so absolute that they had never bothered to so much as google the name Ismailov. In fact, Connies-Laing claimed that he couldn't recall knowing Zac's family name at all, insisting, 'I just called him Zac.' This struck me as a curiously trusting basis for any adult, in any industry at all, to be doing business with a potential investor. But if there was any way to understand it, I figured it must hinge on Foley and his interactions with Zac. So I kept badgering Connies-Laing until, finally, he introduced me to Mark Foley.

In the Victorian era, the borough of Chelsea was a centre of artistic life in London. In 1890, a group of artists who lived or had studios in the area established the Chelsea Arts Club. Today the club still occupies the same ramshackle building on Old Church Street that has housed it since 1902. Though it is a members-only establishment, the Arts Club does not share the same gaudy millennial vibe as Annabel's or 5 Hertford Street. It is a creaky old place, with a membership that, while generally well-off, retains at least the pretence of bohemianism. The club holds monthly art shows, often displaying works by its members, and its biggest showcase is the annual charity auction, which takes place every spring and features some two hundred original works for sale. This is always a boisterous occasion, with multiple bars serving drinks and artworks crowding the walls from floor to ceiling.

The 2019 charity auction took place on a March evening, and one of the guests was Mark Foley. He was not a member but had been invited through some Chelsea connection, in the expectation that he might be interested in purchasing something. Foley arrived on his own, and began to make his way slowly through the rooms of the club. As he perused the art on the walls, he fell into conversation with another guest who appeared to have come by himself, a slim, casually dressed young man who introduced himself as Zac.

When I finally managed to speak to Foley, he turned out to be disarmingly open and affable, given how hesitant he had been to talk – and not quite the highflier that Akbar had made him out to be. What he actually did for a living, he explained, was 'manage a lot of properties' that belonged to Chelsea Football Club, but not in a direct capacity. He wasn't a club executive but a contractor. Nor did it sound, in Foley's telling, like he was a close personal adviser to the oligarch owner, Roman Abramovich. More like a 'conduit', he explained. 'If people wanted to get a deal in front of someone like Abramovich, I was one of the avenues,' he said. He generally did not bring these opportunities directly to the boss but instead would present them 'to one of Mr Abramovich's advisers'. Afterwards, he would often have no idea whether a given proposal had generated any interest. 'I wouldn't necessarily hear anything about it again,' Foley said. Given Akbar's proclivity for puffery, it should have occurred to me that the man he described in the inquest as 'very senior in the Chelsea Football Club hierarchy' might turn out to be a mid-level contractor who didn't even work for the team directly.

That evening at the Arts Club, Foley told me, he and Zac had struck up a conversation. 'He said his father was an investor living in London, but Russian,' Foley recalled. Zac was dressed in the 'below the radar' manner of a rich kid out on the town. He seemed very 'plausible' and was conversant in the world of real estate, dropping a few names. Zac mentioned that he was his father's 'right-hand man' and that his family was looking to make investments. To Foley, all of this tracked with his experience of a certain kind of wealthy Russian in London. 'I took him very much on face value,' he said. Zac proposed that they meet for coffee, and some days later they did, at a Starbucks in St John's Wood.

Interestingly, Foley was adamant with me that Zac had spoken to him without a trace of a Russian accent. He had also told Foley that his full name was Zac Brettler – not Ismailov. The more I pondered that initial encounter at the Chelsea Arts Club, the more it began to appear that Mark Foley might be patient zero in the story of Zac's career as an impostor, when his new identity was still only half formed. Matthew and Rachelle had no idea how Zac might have parlayed his way onto the guest list at the Chelsea Arts Club, nor did any of his friends. But once inside, he found himself in conversation with this man who was connected to Chelsea Football Club – and to its famous oligarch owner, with whom Zac had long harboured a fascination. Throughout his life, when Zac told lies, they often started as a riff, a joke, a line he was trying out to see if it worked. In this case, yearning to escape the staid bourgeois comforts of the life his parents had given him and to ascend into the glamorous echelon that Mark Foley must have seemed to inhabit, he told a lie. It was a particularly audacious lie, when you consider the person he was telling it to. Yet somehow, miraculously, it worked.

England has a colourful history of impostors who used to turn up in one part of the country or another and pose as titled aristocrats. In earlier epochs, such fraudsters would sometimes bear with them a letter of introduction from some noble personage and produce it as a way to ratify their bona fides. By fooling Mark Foley, Zac had managed to secure the contemporary equivalent of a letter of introduction from an unimpeachable source. Foley told me that he never had any intention of doing business with Zac, and that if he had, he absolutely would have conducted further due diligence. Instead, having done nothing whatsoever to fact-check Zac's story, he made an introduction to John Connies-Laing, who, with Akbar, was looking for investors to underwrite their plan for a pair of residential towers in Lisbon.

'From my knowledge of Russian investors, they are a fairly

secretive bunch,' Foley told me. 'You didn't always get the full story.' Zac had seemed like a familiar type. 'Young whiz-kid with lots of money,' he said. 'There are a lot of them around.'

But hadn't Akbar said that Foley visited Zac at an apartment inside One Hyde Park? Akbar must have been mistaken, Foley said, because that never happened. Zac *had* claimed that he lived in the building – and Foley had no basis for doubting it. 'It's not something you can look up and say, "Who owns that?"' he pointed out, because so many of the units are 'owned in company names'. But Foley never went to One Hyde Park with Zac. In fact, the only time he ever saw Zac inside an apartment was in another part of town, he said. He'd been in Regent's Park one day when Zac called and said that he was nearby, at an investment property his family owned. In Maida Vale.

'It was an ordinary three-bedroom apartment,' Foley said. 'Sparsely furnished.'

'Did that happen to be on the ground floor and basement level?' I asked.

'Yeah,' Foley said, wondering how I knew.

Rachelle had told me that on a couple of occasions during Zac's final years she had come home to find all the framed family photos in the apartment facedown. When she asked Zac why he had done that, he explained vaguely that he'd been using the front room for a business meeting. The 'investment property' Foley visited that day was Zac's family home.

One question that had come up at the inquest was whether Zac might have lost his grip on reality and succumbed to delusions. But the strongest indication that this was never the case was the care he took to tell different lies to different people, always with an eye to what they seemed likely to believe. Before finishing my call with Foley, I mentioned the story Zac had told his parents about how he'd helped Marina Granovskaia, the Chelsea Football Club director and Abramovich lieutenant, to purchase an apartment at One Hyde Park.

'I've never heard that,' Foley said. Then, sounding confused, 'Why would she need *him*?' After reflecting for a moment, he said it made sense that Zac would not have tried to peddle this particular fabrication to him, for a simple reason: 'I would be able to check.'

Chapter 20

THE BLACK BOX

WHEN MATTHEW'S FATHER, Benny Brettler, left Germany for England in 1939, he did so alone. Though he was only thirteen at the time, the decision to leave had been his, a staggeringly courageous choice for a child – and one that saved his life. After arriving in England, where he stayed at a Jewish youth camp in Devon before moving to a hostel in Ladbroke Grove, Benny could obtain no solid information about the fate of his family. As soon as the war ended, he wrote to his aunt and sister in Germany, but the letter was returned with a stamp that read HOUSE DESTROYED. Only later would Benny be able to confirm that with the exception of a single cousin, his whole family had been murdered by the Nazis. He was entirely bereft, solo in the world as a teenager, with no choice but to build a whole new life from nothing.

Benny was clever and unfailingly affable; his greatest skill, Matthew thought, was 'adapting and surviving'. So that was what he did. Mostly he looked ahead, focusing on the next step in front of him. Learn English. Learn a trade. Find a wife. Create a new family.

People did not talk much about 'trauma' in the aftermath of the war. In fact, for the first couple of decades, they didn't talk much about the Holocaust, either. It could sometimes feel as if the only way to survive the horrors of the recent past was to turn your back on them and run like hell into the future. Benny's past was unspeakably awful, and he had no intention of letting himself be defined by it. But nor could he completely let it go. One of Matthew's memories from his own childhood was of Benny recounting how he had placed advertisements in newspapers abroad, seeking information about any family who might have survived, and particularly about his younger brother, Moritz. He was just twelve when Benny left

Germany. Of course, the overwhelming likelihood was that Moritz had perished. Yet Benny could not entirely give up hope. So he sent these little futile missives out into the world, like those scientists who beamed radio messages into the cosmos, hoping someday to get a reply.

Before his departure from Germany, Benny had been sent by his parents to live with his aunt and uncle, who ran a successful furniture business in the city of Breslau, near the Polish border. They had been prosperous; they owned three apartment buildings in a desirable part of the city, as well as a factory. After the war ended and the national borders were redrawn, Breslau became part of Poland and was renamed Wrocław. A new Communist government took possession of many properties that had previously belonged to Jews. In 1998, following the collapse of Communism in Eastern Europe, Benny Brettler made a journey back to the city he had left nearly sixty years earlier. He had been doing research into his family's history in Breslau and he wanted to assert a legal claim to those four properties they had owned, the apartment buildings and the factory. 'If there's a chance to get some compensation, after all it was our *property*,' he said at the time, adding, 'One should really pursue these things for moral reasons.'

But the city that he arrived in looked different from the one he had left. Breslau had been bombed by the Allies, and large stretches of Wrocław had been rebuilt in the drab concrete idiom of Communist Poland. Benny was accompanied on his journey by a radio producer from the BBC, who captured his reactions upon returning to the city. 'That's the synagogue there!' he exclaimed, his voice filling with excitement. But the more he explored Wrocław, the more confused he became. 'I'm just disoriented,' he muttered. 'Everything's been turned round.' In the end, he couldn't find his family's apartment buildings or their factory, because they had been torn down, and other, unfamiliar buildings had risen in their place. 'Obviously, I'm disappointed,' Benny said, sounding bewildered and terribly sad. 'It's all gone.' Benny Brettler died in October 2020, but there was a sense in which his spirit of quiet perseverance and moral clarity hung over the efforts of Matthew and Rachelle to come to terms with the life and death of their son.

In February 2024, I published an article about Zac's death in *The New Yorker*. In the final days before it came out, Akbar Shamji had hired a lawyer, who threatened to sue the magazine; Dominique Sharma had lawyered up as well. The Brettlers had been anxious about the level of exposure the story would engender, but they experienced a sense of vindication on seeing it in print. For years they had wondered how affronted they might reasonably be entitled to feel over the bungling of the investigation. Now that the story was finally out, they were immensely relieved to discover that most Londoners who were encountering it for the first time appeared to respond with an indignation that mirrored their own. The story made the front pages in the British press, and a spotlight fell on the shortcomings of the Met. 'Police Failed Us, Say Parents of Public Schoolboy After Mysterious Balcony Death', ran a typical headline, in *The Daily Telegraph*. 'Our sincere condolences remain with Zac Brettler's family, and we understand the uncertainty about how their son died must continue to be the cause of unimaginable pain,' the Met said in a statement. 'The team worked hard to explore every possible hypothesis... but ultimately we were not able to provide fuller answers.' They asserted, rather blithely, given the evidence to the contrary, that 'every line of enquiry had been exhausted'.

But quite a few loose ends remained. One involved the death of Verinder Sharma. As I was working on the article, I had lodged a formal request for information about the status of Sharma's inquest. Had there *been* an inquest? Or was one scheduled for the future? The coroner's office would not give me a straight answer. Nor would Scotland Yard. When the Brettlers made their own inquiries, they were informed that in fact there might have been an inquest, or the *beginning* of an inquest, but that the proceedings had been paused for some unspecified reason and it was not clear when or if they would resume.

Another question involved the Riverwalk apartment where Verinder was said to have died. According to public records, the unit belonged not to any individual but to a company called Riverwalk Exquisite Residence S.A., which was registered in the British

Virgin Islands and had purchased the property in 2016, for just under £5 million. Under a new UK law passed in 2022, the actual owner of a foreign shell company transacting in the British property market should in theory be listed in public records. But on 7 February 2024, roughly forty-eight hours after the *New Yorker* article was published, an accountant applied for so-called protected status, to conceal the identity of the ultimate owner of this particular flat. It is rare for such status to be granted – yet in this case it was.

Clearly someone was trying to shield themselves from any association with the flat. But the accountant's intervention had come too late: certain websites automatically scrape the internet for company information, and some of them had already recorded the owner of this particular offshore entity. It was a Saudi princess, Her Royal Highness Princess Abeer bint Sultan bin Abdulaziz Al Saud. She was the daughter of a crown prince who had at least ten wives and thirty-two children. The family also owned a giant mansion on The Bishops Avenue, the thoroughfare in Hampstead that is often referred to as 'Billionaires' Row'. Apparently the Riverwalk flat was just an investment property, one that Nick Gold happened to be paying the rent for.

'I was paying for it,' Gold confirmed when I reached him on the phone. He spoke rapidly, in a manic zigzag patter, sometimes changing his tone or changing the subject mid-sentence. 'Indian Dave terrorized the whole Jewish community,' Gold announced. Verinder had been known for identifying wealthy Jewish businessmen in London and then extorting money from them, he said. He was a 'powerful fucking guy', who 'came with an army' and would antagonize those he claimed owed him money for whatever reason until they paid up just to make him go away.

But that was not why Gold had been paying Verinder's rent, he insisted. 'He was my friend,' he said. 'He was a really great friend of mine.' It could be useful to have a friendship with a fellow like Indian Dave in a city that sometimes turned dangerous. The fear Verinder engendered without even having to do much of anything meant that if you were the type of person who occasionally wound up in risky situations, then Verinder was a good sort of person to have in your corner. But Gold also seemed to have genuinely liked and enjoyed the company of the old gangster. There had never been any real estate deal in the South of France that left him in debt to Sharma, he said; that rumour was entirely untrue. He was paying the rent not because he feared Verinder or owed him anything, he asserted, but because Indian Dave had run out of money. 'He became a drug addict and lost his mind,' Gold said.

When I inquired about Zac, Gold maintained that he 'knew nothing about this kid', apart from the fact that he was supposedly some billionaire's son Verinder had taken under his wing. Nor did he know anything about the circumstances of Zac's death, he maintained. But about Verinder's death, Gold was unambiguous: 'He committed suicide. He overdosed on drugs.'

When I reached Oliver Harris, the St John's Wood businessman whom Verinder had supposedly frightened before Zac's death, he reacted with alarm, denying that he had been engaged in any sort of business deal with Zac and Verinder, as the police had suggested, but declining to speak with me on the record and demanding to know how I had found his telephone number. It bothered the Brettlers to know that Harris, who had held himself out to Matthew, in their meeting with the rabbi, as a pious man of faith, might know important details about the unravelling of Verinder's relationship with Zac and not be prepared to share them. But Akbar had suggested in one of his texts that Harris was frightened of Verinder, and my distinct impression when I contacted Harris was that he remained frightened even after Verinder had left the stage.

As Rachelle and Matthew continued to ponder these nettlesome questions, they thought that they might find answers hidden inside the phone and the iPad that Zac had left behind. The police had provided them with a selection of Zac's internet searches but had never turned over all of the emails and text messages they had extracted from his devices. When the Brettlers asked if they could have the devices back, Met officials confessed, sheepishly, that they had actually been lost somewhere in storage. Apparently these items, which were so precious to the Brettlers, had been mis-tagged by some police bureaucrat who subsequently left the force and could not be enlisted to correct the error and retrieve them.

A week before Zac's inquest, in December 2022, the devices

suddenly resurfaced, having finally been located. The Brettlers had asked the investigators to return the phone and the iPad 'unlocked' so that they could gain access to the contents. But when they turned on the power, they found that everything was still password-protected. They ended up sending them to several leading experts on data extraction. But the experts reported that police had been so careless in their efforts to get into the devices that they had left them in a state in which nobody else could access them. The police had a 'custodial responsibility' to take care of Zac's phone and iPad, Rachelle felt, one that they had abused. She and Matthew asked if Met detectives could share a copy of everything they had managed to download. Nobody ever told them 'no' explicitly, but months and eventually years went by and they never got it.

It probably didn't help that the cops, having witnessed the degree to which the Brettlers were prepared to audit their police work and reinvestigate the case, now had an obvious incentive *not* to hand over a bunch of new leads for them to pursue. But Rachelle also worried that she and Matthew had antagonized the police by speaking out about their dissatisfaction with the case, squandering whatever goodwill might have remained at Scotland Yard.

'They hate us now,' she said. 'All of a sudden Rory realized we weren't gullible, passive, grieving parents. From that moment on, they've been slightly closing ranks.'

But even if the detectives refused to give the Brettlers all the data siphoned from Zac's devices, in their own bumbling way, they did inadvertently provide another critical batch of technical information.

During the inquest process, the Brettlers had asked the police to turn over whatever data they had collected from Akbar's phone. In response to this request, an officer shared an Excel file with them. But that evening, when Matthew opened the file, it didn't look like it had anything to do with Akbar's phone. Instead, it seemed that the cops had mistakenly turned over the wrong item. The Excel file consisted of seventy-seven columns and 4,700 rows, and contained a long string of GPS coordinates. These corresponded, as it turned out, to the exact minute-by-minute location, over the course of more than a week, of Akbar Shamji's Mercedes.

When he was being interrogated by the police, Akbar had explained that at the time of Zac's death, he'd been driving a rental Mercedes that had been provided to him by the dealership while his own car was being repaired. What he likely did not realize, because it was buried somewhere in the fine print, was that this vehicle came equipped with a small black box that enabled the company to track the precise location of the car at any given time, as well as other data, such as the speed at which it was moving.

Initially, Matthew and Rachelle did not know what to do with this unexpected gift. The entries in the Excel file looked forbiddingly technical. Maybe this data had meant something to the police, but the Brettlers had no idea how to decode it. After the *New Yorker* article was published, however, they were approached by a young investigative journalist named Gabriel Pogrund, who worked for *The Sunday Times*. By coincidence, Pogrund had known Zac slightly: his brother had been one of Zac's childhood friends. But he had not previously been aware of the peculiar nature of Zac's death. 'I will remember him as a beautiful, mischievous, happy soul,' he wrote to Rachelle and Matthew, before offering his services in case they felt there might be anything further to investigate. The Brettlers ended up sharing the Excel file with Pogrund. Perhaps he could make some sense of it. When he and his colleagues examined the data, consulting an expert on this type of GPS system and eventually assembling a detailed log of Akbar Shamji's movements in the days around Zac's death, they made a remarkable discovery.

On Tuesday, 26 November 2019, Akbar had flown to Turkey on business. But he had to cut the trip short, flying back Wednesday night because some kind of crisis was unfolding in London. 'No more messages please till you land,' Verinder told him, instructing Akbar to 'arrange a meeting' with Zac upon his return. On Thursday, Akbar spent the day driving around London with Zac, then dropped him off in Maida Vale for some downtime before they headed to Riverwalk.

'Ready when you are,' Zac texted him at 7:16 p.m.

An hour later, the Mercedes appeared on Lauderdale Road with

Akbar behind the wheel and Alpha Nero in the back seat. The camera on the Brettlers' building captured Zac climbing into the passenger seat. By 8:50 the Mercedes had pulled into the driveway at Riverwalk and Akbar, Zac and Alpha Nero had made their way upstairs. Eventually Dominique came, parking her car in the basement lot, and joined them in apartment 504. A couple of hours later, she and Akbar came out with the dog and spent roughly twenty minutes talking in her car. Finally, at 1:46 a.m., Dominique drove off in the direction of her own home and Akbar climbed back into his Mercedes. A few minutes later, according to phone records, he telephoned Verinder, who was upstairs in the apartment with Zac. Verinder didn't answer, so Akbar drove away.

But what the GPS log revealed was that he did not drive in the direction of his home on Mount Street. Instead he commenced a slow, meandering route, heading west along the river, then pivoting east back into Pimlico, getting onto Vauxhall Bridge Road, and seeming to head back in the direction of Riverwalk, only to take a sudden U-turn at 1:59 a.m. Plotted on a map, the route made no logical sense. Either Akbar couldn't decide where he was going and kept changing his mind, or he was deliberately driving in circles, to kill time. At 2:10, as he drove by Victoria Station, he tried calling again, but again Verinder did not answer. Then, two minutes later, Verinder called back, and just as he took the call, Akbar swung the Mercedes in a different direction, turning northeast towards Buckingham Palace. Still on the phone with Verinder, he started to accelerate until he was streaking down the Mall at fifty miles an hour – twice the speed limit – and racing into Trafalgar Square. The streets would have been deserted at that hour, and Akbar coursed down Whitehall, flying past Downing Street, then the Houses of Parliament. After nine minutes on the phone with Verinder, he ended the call at 2:21. Two minutes later, he pulled up in front of Riverwalk at 2:23, just seconds before Zac's feet left the balcony.

The police had asked Akbar about none of this, even when the story he told them was flatly contradicted by the very GPS coordinates that they had in their possession. Indeed, having gone to the trouble of soliciting the information from the rental car company, the investigators appear to have never consulted it at all. When detectives asked Akbar what was discussed during his nine-minute phone call with Verinder, he said, 'I just don't remember. I really don't.'

But the clear implication of the tracking data was that when Akbar drove away from Riverwalk the first time, he intended not to go home, but to loiter in the general area – as if he was aware that something dreadful might be about to happen. He telephoned Verinder repeatedly as he drove around, then, the moment Verinder called back, Akbar must have heard something that sent him into a panic. Did Verinder say something about doing harm to Zac? If Akbar had heard such a thing, it would explain his sudden sprint back to Riverwalk. And if Zac overheard the same conversation, it might also explain his motivation to jump – to escape whatever it was that Indian Dave had in store for him.

After the *New Yorker* article was published, I heard from an old associate of Akbar's, a Belgian American businessman named François Pham-Quang. After growing up in California, François had moved to London as a young man in the 1990s. This was in the aftermath of the Big Bang, when foreign bankers swept into the city. Still in his twenties, François became one of the youngest managing directors at Lehman Brothers. He was making a lot of money, but he found himself pining for a more dynamic social life. Through mutual friends, he was introduced to Akbar Shamji.

At the time, Akbar was still bouncing back and forth between London and LA. He seemed to be living precisely the kind of glamorous life that François aspired to. So far as François was aware, Akbar's record label, Soulife, had been a great success; he knew nothing of the manner in which the business had imploded. So he was enthusiastic when Akbar proposed that they launch a label of their own, with François supplying some of the capital. A 2003 press release announcing the formation of Bardic Records noted that François had a Lehman Brothers pedigree and described Akbar as a 'financial leader'.

It ended badly, as things so often did with Akbar. It wasn't just that François came to feel he'd been taken advantage of in the business. At one point, Akbar and his then wife Megan had wanted to spend some time in New York, so François arranged for a friend to rent them an apartment. They 'trashed the place', he said, and made so many expensive long-distance phone calls that they ran up enormous bills, then never paid them. It was only later that François was able to consider how naive he'd been. 'I was the perfect target,' he told me. London was saturated with money, and some people were just looking to 'mop up what was there'. To understand Akbar, François suggested, you had to grasp that he was always on the lookout for people who had access to capital. Invoking Zac's death, he said, 'That's why the story about this kid, you know, it resonates quite a bit.'

Akbar may not have been a violent person, but that didn't mean he wasn't predatory. In his disguise as an oligarch's son, Zac must have looked like another well-heeled sucker to be taken advantage of. A fatted calf. As much as Matthew had come to loathe Akbar, it seemed clear to him that the whole situation had ended up spinning out of Akbar's control. When the Brettlers spoke to Uncle Alex, he had pointed out that a real criminal would never have returned to the scene of the crime – much less gone over and stared into the Thames. Zac might have got in over his head with Verinder, in other words, but Akbar had, too.

So much of who Akbar was turned out to be illusory. Like his father, Abdul, who financed an empire on debt and showed off pictures of himself posing with Margaret Thatcher, Akbar was a confidence man. He often shared a picture of his own, the one of him shaking hands with the Indian prime minister Narendra Modi. In the photo, Akbar, dressed formally in a dark suit, shakes hands with Modi, who is resplendent in a white shirt and a cream vest with a Nehru collar. The prime minister appears to be handing Akbar some kind of certificate. This image was featured prominently on the website for one of Akbar's companies, with a caption that explained, 'In 2015, Akbar was one of only 8 recipients of the prestigious "Re-Invest Award" from PM Modi.'

But when I tried to learn more about this prestigious award and the basis upon which it is conferred, the only references I could locate online seemed to lead me back to Akbar's website. Confused, I wondered if it might be possible to find out more about the event at which the photo was taken. A fragment of text on a screen behind

Modi indicated that it was some kind of 'expo' held in Delhi in February 2015. Sure enough, Modi had inaugurated the Global Renewable Energy Investors Meet & Expo, or 'RE-Invest', that month, and it did appear that awards were presented that day. So perhaps Akbar calling it the 'Re-Invest Award' was just a bit of shorthand.

Then I found a video of the event. It was a large gathering, with Modi and other officials arrayed on a dais before a brightly lit gallery full of roughly two hundred people. And indeed, early in the event there was a ceremony during which a series of individuals approached the stage to shake hands with Modi and receive an award. But these certificates of commendation, as they were called, were going to Indian *states* – Gujarat, Rajasthan, Punjab – in recognition of their 'outstanding performance in the field of renewable energy'. The people accepting the awards were all government officials. So where did Akbar fit in?

When the Indian states had all been recognized, an announcer said that, next up, twenty-seven private companies would present Modi with 'commitments' pledging to promote green energy. Now the executives were coming up to shake hands with the prime minister, but they weren't *accepting* awards, as the state officials had done, but rather handing Modi their certificates of commitment. And there on the video was Akbar, striding up to the stage, holding his certificate. The photo on the website portraying Akbar as the 'recipient' of an award really does appear to capture a moment in which the prime minister is handing Akbar a piece of paper. But the video revealed that the opposite was true. Akbar shook hands with Modi and turned over his commitment certificate. Then he walked away empty-handed.

One reason that it is so difficult to know precisely what happened at Riverwalk is that Zac was by no means the only impostor in the apartment that night. Verinder Sharma was a leg-breaker posing as a benevolent mentor. Akbar Shamji was a dilettante posing as an accomplished entrepreneur. And Zac was just a London teenager, posing as the son of an oligarch. Each was pretending to be something he wasn't, and each was caught up in the glitzy, mercenary aspirational culture of modern London. 'It was three bullshit artists, selling air,' Rachelle said.

Chapter 21

UNDERTOW

HUGO GRYN DIED WITH more than one secret. In 1988, when he was fifty-eight years old and at the height of his fame, the *News of the World*, a London tabloid, published a scandalous report claiming that 'Britain's top TV rabbi' had a 'secret love child'. The article alleged that a little girl named Ester, who was a member of his congregation, had been seen calling him 'Daddy' at the synagogue. According to the account, Hugo had been carrying on an affair with Ester's mother, a woman named Angela Wood. But when the story came out, Hugo told his wife and children that it wasn't true. They knew Angela: she was a single mother who taught classes at the synagogue, and a close friend of Hugo's. He was Ester's godfather, in fact, but not her father, he insisted. In a sermon delivered to the whole congregation, he condemned the article as malicious 'gossip'.

Hugo's wife, Jacqueline, may have chosen to believe him. At least initially, Rachelle did, too. Her father was quoted in the *News of the World* saying, 'I have every confidence in my community and they have every confidence in me.' Angela told the paper, 'It's none of your business who Ester's father is.' But if you read the story carefully, neither of them explicitly denied the claim. A year earlier, in 1987, Hugo had featured prominently in an hour-long documentary, directed by his daughter Naomi, about the role of the Sabbath in Jewish life. It captured heartwarming scenes of Rachelle and her siblings gathered around the family table in Marylebone. At one point in the film, a little girl appears in a brief interview and says, with a giggle, that what she doesn't like about the Sabbath is that 'you can't watch television'. It is Ester, sitting on her mother's lap. She has a full face and a cheeky smile and bears a notable resemblance to Hugo Gryn.

One Saturday, some time after the *News of the World* article had come out, Rachelle and her brother, David, drove by Angela's house on a hunch and saw Hugo's car parked out front. That was the moment when she knew. Within the Gryn household (and, to some extent, their wider community) Hugo's second family became something of an open secret. The rabbi continued to deny to Rachelle and her siblings that he was Ester's father. They suspected otherwise but didn't speak openly about it, preferring to live in willed semi-denial. Angela and Ester continued to attend the synagogue. The Gryn children were deeply shaken by this revelation about their father, yet they found themselves unable to condemn him, perhaps out of a sense that as a Holocaust survivor he should be entitled to some margin of moral dispensation. Hugo had lost his whole world in adolescence, then married young. He was such a life force, and lived so abundantly, with such defiant joy; was it not possible to construe his impulse to fall in love a second time and to father a child out of wedlock as a by-product of that same defiance, as if he needed to live more lives than any one life had to offer? Rachelle thought that, having cheated death, Hugo sometimes lived as though the normal rules that governed other mortals might not apply to him. When he was dying of cancer, Naomi arranged a clandestine visit to the hospital by Angela. 'All of us colluded,' Naomi reflected, in protecting their father from the full consequences of his own actions. He had so often seemed larger than life, but in reality he was all too human.

After Hugo died, Rachelle and her sisters, recognizing that they had a half sister out there who had also lost a father, developed a relationship with Ester. At the time, she was just fourteen. The whole scenario remained quite fraught, but they developed a real affection for her, and it felt important to acknowledge, in some quiet way, this blood relative who had never been acknowledged in any public fashion by the father they shared. The sisters periodically kept in touch over the next several years, as Ester grew up, eventually going off to Cardiff University, where she studied psychology. She was creative, a good singer, a teller of jokes and a talented mimic. After spending a couple of summers in Ghana, she ended up finding a job working with refugees in London. She had a particular ambition to help young people who had become separated from their parents. But in

2006, when Ester was twenty-four, she went to Hampstead Heath station one day and jumped in front of a moving train.

Zac never knew Hugo, or Ester, but Joe told me that he and his brother both grew up knowing this troubling chapter of their family's history. It was Rachelle who first related the story to me, and eventually I spoke about it with each of her siblings. The Gryns felt that it would be a mistake to draw any facile parallels between Ester's death and Zac's. But what struck me was not that there might be some causality between the secret life of Hugo Gryn and that of his grandson, so much as the prevalence of secret lives in general. Rachelle was the daughter of one person who lived a double life and the mother of another. 'It happened with my father, and it happened with my son,' she reflected, wondering out loud whether there might be some continuity in her own behaviour when it came to loved ones who were less than honest with her. 'Perhaps there's a lack of questioning on my part?' We were speaking during Passover, and she mentioned that at the family seder the previous evening they had recited the parable of the Four Sons. 'There is the wise son, the wicked son, the simple son, and the son who doesn't know how to ask,' Rachelle said. 'Maybe that was me, with Zac. I didn't know how to ask.'

In the thirty years since Hugo's death, nobody had spoken publicly about his secret; apart from that *News of the World* article (which is not archived anywhere on the internet), there was no trace in the public record of any connection whatsoever between Hugo and Ester. I wondered whether the family instinct for privacy that had succeeded in keeping Zac's death out of the press for so long might have its roots in this earlier tragedy.

Rachelle had been correct to worry about the exposure that would stem from the decision to finally speak out about Zac's death. Suddenly the Brettlers' private calamity had become a public thing, a kind of commodity, a 'true crime' story. 'Did This Public Schoolboy and Grandson of a Celebrity Rabbi Jump to His Death to Escape Being Tortured with Hot Knives by a Gangster He Thought Was His Friend?' *The Daily Mail* blared, comprehensively. Hours after my

New Yorker article was published, John Sweeney, the London journalist who had introduced Matthew and Rachelle to the café owner Pino D'Amore and had briefly entertained the notion of publishing an article of his own, took to Twitter, where he had a substantial audience of a quarter of a million followers, and posted the photograph Pino had taken of Zac's corpse.

'Rachelle has just sent me your Tweet featuring a photo of my dead son,' Matthew texted Sweeney as soon as he saw it. 'I have not shared that distressing photo with close family, let alone a wider audience. It is highly insensitive of you to use it and I would really appreciate your taking it down.'

Initially, Sweeney refused. 'I believe that when a 19-year-old dies like this in the heart of London, it is in the public interest to understand what happened and why,' he wrote back to Matthew. 'Practically, the image is now in the public domain, so that ship has sailed.' This struck Matthew as a curious assertion, inasmuch as the photo was in the public domain only because Sweeney had just put it there. 'I can't imagine you, as a father, would wish to see your child's dead body on a Twitter feed,' Rachelle wrote in her own note to Sweeney. 'Please have some decency and humanity.' The next day, Sweeney took the image down and apologized.

One afternoon, Rachelle picked me up in her car and we drove north through the outskirts of London until we reached Mill Hill. We parked by the main entrance and walked around the perimeter until we found a footpath that took us into the grounds. It was March. The sky was pale and the trees still bare, but the grass was punctuated by little clusters of yellow daffodils. School had just let out for the day, and the fields were crowded with students playing sports. These were the same fields where Zac played rugby and cricket. It had seemed 'idyllic' when he first arrived there, Rachelle said. In the distance, some unseen coach kept blowing a whistle.

Rachelle mentioned that she had recently stumbled upon the Instagram account of a Turkish artist named Alper Yesiltas, who, for a fee, would take a photo of a dead loved one and use artificial intelligence to create a new, eerily realistic picture of what that person might have come to look like in later years. She commissioned Yesiltas, and he sent her back a photo of her son at forty, which she now showed me on her phone. The Zac in the picture had the same high forehead and curly red hair, the same long face and serious eyes, but his countenance seemed gentler, more benevolent, as if, free at last from the turbulence of adolescence, he had finally grown comfortable in his own skin. This version of a Zac who lived brought Rachelle some solace. He looked at peace. He looked like he might have turned out okay. He also looked a lot like Matthew.

After leaving Mill Hill, Rachelle and I drove to Hoop Lane Cemetery. When we arrived, it had just closed for the day, but Rachelle flagged down a caretaker and explained that she was Hugo Gryn's daughter, and he kindly opened the gate and let us in. Hugo's grave – a long slab of white marble – occupied a desirable plot, close to the entrance. Next to it was Zac's grave, made of sleek black stone, with clean edges. 'I spent my life trying to make life right for him,' Rachelle said, and just because your child is dead doesn't mean you stop. So she wanted 'the nicest stone, the nicest shape, the nicest typeface'. At the foot of Hugo's grave there was a small bucket full of smooth stones. We each picked one out and laid it on Zac's tomb.

A few years after Zac's death, Dame Margaret Hodge, a Member of Parliament who had served as an elected representative for half a century, published a report with King's College London called *Losing Our Moral Compass*, in which she argued that over the prior decade 'foul play has flourished' in Britain. The nation's global reputation for financial integrity was being squandered, Hodge suggested, as 'our corporate structures, our booming property market, and our army of enablers in the successful financial services sector serve to facilitate corruption'. In a surreal affirmation of the very message Hodge was seeking to deliver, after she published it, a wealthy Kenyan-born London businessman named Mohamed Amersi, whom she had mentioned briefly in the report, threatened to bring legal action against King's College, which proceeded to withdraw the publication.

After a flurry of sanctions and speechifying following Russia's invasion of Ukraine, the British political establishment seemed uncertain about how soon it might be safe to settle back into complacency.

The state might have tried to crack down, but many oligarchs used litigation to protect their interests, and the government was often forced to acknowledge that it simply did not have the resources for legal fights with billionaires. 'We are, bluntly, concerned about the impact on our budget,' the director of the National Crime Agency had told Parliament in 2019, 'because these are wealthy people with access to the best lawyers.'

Some oligarchs relocated to places such as Turkey or the United Arab Emirates. Nick Candy, who, along with his brother, Christian, had built Zac's supposed former home, One Hyde Park, gave an interview in 2023 in which he claimed that London was dead and Dubai was the future. 'Yes, of course, it's going to attract some money which may not be the cleanest money,' Candy said, but London had benefited from that sort of money as well, he pointed out. 'So let's not be naive.' For some buyers, the fact that a handful of Russians who were closely linked to the Putin regime were being forced to sell their London holdings represented an opportunity. 'The oligarchs today are from China,' Trevor Abrahmsohn, the London real estate agent who caters to the super-wealthy, observed with satisfaction, adding that there will always be new buyers arriving in London 'to feast themselves'.

Roman Abramovich was reported to be selling some of his London properties, in addition to unloading Chelsea Football Club. But he found other ways to protect his wealth. On the eve of Russia's invasion, he hastily restructured large parts of his fortune, placing assets into billion-dollar trusts in the names of his children. This was just the state-of-the-art version of the old shell game played by Abdul Shamji, who, on paper, did not own anything at all. London was still full of professional facilitators eager to help protect or conceal a dubious fortune. At times, the unwillingness of the political class to take on the corrosive power of foreign money could seem downright comical. Critics had long complained that rich Londoners were able to live virtually tax-free in the city by declaring 'non-dom' status. But in 2022, it emerged that Akshata Murty, the wife of then Prime Minister Rishi Sunak, was *herself* a non-dom. After this fact was publicized, she committed to pay UK tax on all her income, and in 2024, the government announced that it would begin the process of phasing out the non-dom system altogether. The notion that London's richest residents might have to pay taxes like everybody else caused something of a panic, with dire warnings of a 'wealth exodus'.

When public officials in post-Soviet Moscow developed a taste for graft, the Russian billionaire Sergei Pugachev once observed, they became 'like people who had drunk blood. They can't stop.' The same might be said of the English economy. Asked by *The Daily Telegraph* about the diminished presence of the oligarchs in London following the invasion, another Russian tycoon said, 'I would suggest you go to Annabel's pretending to be a wealthy Russian.' In no time, he predicted, you will find yourself surrounded by 'guys wanting to take your money'.

In 1967, Otto Frank gave a television interview in which he spoke about his daughter Anne Frank, who had been murdered by the Nazis. In the final years of Anne's life, the Frank family had hidden out in Amsterdam, living in close quarters, and throughout that period she had maintained a diary, which, after Otto published it in 1947, became a landmark work, read by millions of people around the world. For some time after Anne's death, Otto had been unable to bring himself to read the diary. But when he finally picked up this private document that his child had left behind, he was startled by the depth and nuance of her reflections. 'It was quite a different Anne than I had known as my daughter,' Frank said, in his careful, accented English. 'What really her feelings were, I could only see from the diary.' Otto had been very close to Anne, he pointed out, so it was interesting to consider how little he had understood about her. 'Most parents don't know, really, their children,' he said.

The feeling Frank describes, of not being able to fully understand one's own adolescent child, has surely been compounded for parents in the era of social media. Zac Brettler's teenage years coincided with a period of history during which the texture of human existence subtly changed. At night, he would lie in the darkness of his bedroom, his face aglow in the reflected light of his iPhone, and any momentary impulse he had, as expressed by his index finger on a touchscreen, could give rise to a kind of digital undertow, pulling him deeper into his own preoccupations. His interests – in supercars, rich people, luxury real estate – were compounded by the algorithm. Zac might not have been delusional in a clinical sense, but he did inhabit a world in which social media was beginning to blur the boundary between reality and fantasy. Increasingly, any sense of a shared conscious existence was starting to give way to a more individualized, algorithmically bespoke form of virtual reality, in which our most personal and idiosyncratic anxieties and aspirations are reflected back at us, and magnified, by our smartphones.

It's a peculiar sensation, but one most people who have spent any time on social media will be familiar with. Scroll with your thumb through your algorithmically generated feed and, if you linger for a millisecond on some diversion, the programme notices, filing away that information and tweaking what it shows you accordingly. When I started researching this book, I would often take a short break and open Instagram. Early in the process, I stumbled on a whole subgenre of accounts devoted to London real estate, in which upbeat, attractive brokers give guided tours of penthouses and sumptuous estates. I didn't follow any of these accounts on Instagram, but as they were randomly presented to me in different reels, the programme intuited that I was interested and kept serving me more. It gave me some insight into the manner in which Zac might have been pulled away from the world of his parents and sucked into a very different London.

As I continued work on the book, something unsettling started to happen. All those London real estate videos on Instagram began to get supplanted by another, very different sort of reel. I can't pinpoint how or when it started. I must have been randomly presented with a video showing somebody falling and then lingered on it for a moment too long. Soon I started seeing more videos of people falling: high-diving off a cliff, BASE-jumping from a skyscraper, leaping into a quarry with friends; parkour daredevils vaulting off rooftops, bungee jumpers vanishing into a bottomless gorge, skydivers stepping out of planes and into the void. Before long, I couldn't open Instagram without being confronted by the sight of someone plummeting to earth.

Chapter 22

THE KID'S HOME SAFE

IN THE SPRING OF 2025, when I'd been investigating this story for nearly two years, I connected with a longtime associate of Verinder Sharma's. He would speak only on the condition that I keep his identity secret, but he knew a great deal about Verinder's sordid enterprises. 'His main trade was debt collecting from other drug dealers and other criminals, because they couldn't go to the police,' the man said. In London, Verinder was 'the big bad boogeyman', he continued. In some circles, just invoking the name 'Indian Dave' was enough to make people pay.

When I posed a casual follow-up about Verinder's techniques, the man volunteered something that startled me: 'Dave's favourite thing was warming up the knife,' he said.

On occasions when it becomes necessary to inflict physical pain upon a person who owes you money, the man explained, if you heat up the blade of a knife, it will 'just melt into him'. This ritual is so effective, he pointed out, that most of the time you don't even need to cut anybody: just heating the knife in a theatrical fashion is all it takes. 'You put it on the stove,' he said. 'You toss it, you turn it. You make him *see*... Then you walk towards him with it.'

Sensing my alarm, the man chuckled. 'It scares you, doesn't it? When you hear it, even.' This was Indian Dave's 'go-to method', he said.

Neither the Metropolitan Police nor the coroner overseeing the inquest into Zac's death ever bothered to take very seriously the message Akbar sent to Mervin from Riverwalk, in which he said he'd been 'heating up knives'. No knife wounds or burn wounds were found on Zac's body, detectives pointed out, so this was not the kind of clue that might necessitate any further investigation. In their judgment, it was just a fragment of meaningless banter. Another red herring. But if Indian Dave had felt entitled to a share of Zac's supposed fortune, and if one method he used to extract money from people was 'warming up the knife', then Akbar's message takes on a more dire and consequential meaning. After all, one of the last things Zac did before he died, just minutes before he jumped, was to search on his iPad for 'what to do with skin burns'.

'Can you explain this?' I asked Akbar in an email, spelling out what I had learned. 'Were you guys actually heating up knives that night? Or just threatening to?'

He never wrote back.

Questions lingered about Verinder. How exactly had he died, if he had died at all? And had he been a police informer? I started tracking down retired Scotland Yard detectives, on the theory that some grizzled ex-cop out there must think of Indian Dave as the crook who got away. I ended up speaking with dozens of former law enforcement officials but never succeeded in locating anyone who nurtured the kind of Ahab-like obsession I had in mind. There were detectives who'd spent years pursuing Verinder's more high-profile associates, such as Gary 'Tyson' Nelson and Andy Baker. And there were plenty of people who had heard of Indian Dave. But nobody appeared to have spent much time focusing on him.

When I laid out the anomalies in Verinder's story – decades devoted to extortion and mayhem but hardly any time served, the withdrawn arrest warrant after the murder of Dave 'Muscles' King – numerous former law enforcement types allowed that it certainly *sounded* as if he could have been an informant. Clive Strong, the private investigator and retired Met detective who had been engaged by the Brettlers, suggested without prompting from me that one way to explain the oddity of Rory Wilkinson being 'kept sterile' from the investigation into Verinder's death would be if Verinder had been 'working for an intelligence service or something like that'. But Strong emphasized that he had no concrete evidence that this was true. A former law enforcement official who worked on the Dave King case said, 'I have previously wondered if Sharma was some sort of informant.' But even if he had been, the official told me, 'no one will ever confirm that for you'.

Verinder's own associates were adamant that he was no snitch. Andy Baker pointed out that it is easy to defame someone in the underworld by calling them a grass, and seemed sceptical of any suggestion that Indian Dave might have been secretly cooperating with police. The friend who told me about Verinder's fondness for heating up knives was similarly dubious. 'Dave wasn't a grass,' he declared. 'He just had good lawyers and was very clever.'

Several of the ex-cops I spoke to recommended I seek out a man named David McKelvey. A former detective chief inspector who retired in 2010 after twenty-eight years with the Met, many of them working on high-level organized crime, he was known to everyone as 'Mac'. Though he was an outspoken critic of police corruption, which he believed to be endemic at Scotland Yard, Mac was also something of a gadfly, who maintained warm relations with a wide variety of former officers. When I reached him and brought up the name Indian Dave, the first thing he said was 'I do remember from days gone by an Indian Dave. This was a man out east who was an informant.'

I hadn't even had a chance to preview the informant theory: he just volunteered the information on his own. 'He was quite a prolific informant for a detective on the 2-Area Drug Squad,' Mac said. 'If I remember rightly, the level of intelligence he was putting out was quite high. It was importations, guns, organized crime.' The name of the detective who had handled Indian Dave was Chris Cubitt, Mac told me. They were still in touch, and Mac volunteered to reach out to him on my behalf.

Cubitt was no longer with the police – and had retired under a cloud of suspicion. During a court proceeding involving an unrelated murder, he had been described as a 'corrupt police officer'. An official report in that case further characterized him as 'dissolute and wholly treacherous, an intimidator, bully and abuser of his position of trust'. No charges were ever brought against Cubitt, who left the force in 2007, after thirty years on the job. But Mac outlined for me the prevalence of a kind of symbiotic relationship that can develop between longtime crooks and the police. 'All these people, they all end up being an informant,' he said. 'Most of the really good villains worked out very early that's what you had to do.'

When I followed up after our initial conversation to see if Mac had spoken with Cubitt, he didn't get back to me. For several weeks I continued to send him messages, but he would never respond. Finally, after about a month of pestering, he agreed to talk again.

'I spoke to the chap,' Mac told me. 'He said it's not the same Indian Dave.'

Over months of asking around, I had never heard any suggestion whatsoever that there might be a *second* Indian Dave. 'This chap that he ran was not a wealthy person, by any stretch of the imagination,' Mac said. 'It definitely wasn't the same chap.'

'Could you tell me more about this other Indian Dave?' I asked.

'Not a lot,' Mac said flatly. 'I don't know who he is, I don't know anything about him.'

In our first conversation, Mac had seemed garrulous and gruffly charming, but now he was halting and awkward. I suppose there is some possibility that what he was saying was true, and there really was a second Indian Dave. But it seemed more plausible to me that Mac had spoken too freely the first time, and Cubitt was now trying to reel the truth back in. When I managed, later, to track Cubitt down myself and asked him if he had ever handled Sharma as an informant, he insisted that he had never known anyone by the name Verinder Sharma *or* Indian Dave.

One April morning in 2024, Matthew and Rachelle sat down in their front room with a laptop and signed in to a much postponed virtual proceeding: the inquest into the death of Verinder Sharma. There *had* been an earlier inquest, they now discovered. Or part of one. Verinder had died in December 2020, just as Rory Wilkinson had said, and an inquest had commenced shortly thereafter. But it was called off halfway through, over a dispute between Verinder's daughters and one of the witnesses. Their disagreement centered on an incident that neither of the Brettlers had been aware of.

On the one-year anniversary of Zac's death, 29 November 2020, paramedics were summoned to Riverwalk. It was a Sunday, the day

Dominique and Matisse often joined Verinder for a family lunch. The daughters met the paramedics at apartment 504 and said that their father had taken a substantial drug overdose. He'd been 'stressed and under pressure', they explained, because he was 'helping police with their inquiries surrounding a murder'.

Verinder had always had a depressive streak. His daughters described a man who was emotionally manipulative. Recently he had been drinking heavily and taking cocaine and crack, which made him volatile. 'He never used to get angry with me if he was sober,' Matisse said. The situation had grown so dire that at a certain point both sisters cut off contact with their father, vowing that until he sought treatment, they would not see him. Isolated and unhappy, Verinder tried to kill himself. Over the course of several days, he took a hundred tablets of the opioid painkiller tramadol, along with ninety sleeping pills, washing them all down with a litre of vodka and another of rum. 'He said he was sick of this world,' Dominique told the medics.

Verinder was groggy when they found him in apartment 504, but still alive. One of the medics noticed that the door to the balcony overlooking the Thames was open and expressed concern that this might reflect a 'potential hazard' for their suicidal patient. Verinder did not want to go to the hospital. He'd never liked doctors. Though he was close to sixty years old, he didn't have a general practitioner. But after a lot of persuading, he consented to ride in an ambulance to St Thomas' Hospital, two bridges away on the south bank, facing Big Ben.

At the hospital, Verinder told staff that he had wanted to kill himself because he recently lost several important people in his life and felt 'abandoned' by his family. He also mentioned the 'murder investigation'. But he ended up recovering from the overdose. According to the National Health Service clinicians who examined him, he appeared to be stable and expressed a desire to be discharged. But when a doctor explained this assessment during the first inquest into Verinder's death, in 2021, Dominique had interjected, 'I *begged* them to keep him!' According to Dominique, she had told hospital staff, 'I promise you now that he will do it again if you let him out.'

The difficulty, from the hospital's perspective, was that they could not legally hold a grown man of sound mind against his will, even if he was depressed. So they sent Verinder home. On Sunday, 13 December, his daughters joined him for another family meal, but in subsequent days he began to text them awful things. He told Matisse that he was going to kill himself, then blocked her messages, then unblocked her long enough to accuse her of not even being concerned that her own father was going to kill himself, then wrote, 'off to the pharmacy', and blocked her again. It was shocking to reflect on how abusive this behaviour was – a glimpse of the sadism for which Indian Dave had a reputation. In his final days, Verinder seemed almost to be taunting his daughters. He texted Dominique photographs of the pills he intended to take.

The following Sunday, Dominique and Matisse were counting on the usual family lunch, but their father was not answering his phone. They called the front desk to ask if one of the concierges could check on him. Riverwalk's unshakable commitment to tenant privacy meant that building staff was not authorized to enter any of the apartments unless invited by the occupant to do so, and when the concierge used the intercom to call up to the flat, Verinder did not answer. His daughters would have to come themselves.

Arriving at Riverwalk, they used Dominique's key to enter the flat. The place was quiet and still, no lights on, just pale white walls and that view of the river. Matisse headed for the master bedroom, and Dominique followed. There they found him, crouched over on his knees beside the bed. He was shirtless; Dominique saw a familiar tattoo on his rib cage, a picture of a set of hands holding prayer beads. There was something of the supplicant in Verinder's posture. A gesture of surrender. Dominique put a hand on her father. He was cold.

'Well,' Rachelle murmured tartly after the coroner ruled the death a suicide, 'we learned there was no conspiracy in which he was whisked away and is not dead.' Much of the inquest had ended up focusing on the appropriateness of the decision by the NHS to release Verinder over the objection of his daughters. This coroner had been surprisingly aggressive in her questioning of an NHS official about what kinds of institutional 'learnings' might be drawn from the experience. In fact, the coroner mentioned that the concerns expressed by Verinder's daughters during the initial inquest had prompted a whole internal investigation by the NHS into ways in which the handling of such situations could be improved in the future. 'We obviously can't bring our dad back,' Matisse said at the end of the proceeding. 'However, it's nice to hear that there are things in place now so that families can be heard more.'

'It's so weird,' Matthew remarked to Rachelle. 'The NHS as an institution has been forced to account in a way that with the police as an institution we never got remotely close to.'

It was tempting for Rachelle to conclude that Verinder must have been tortured by guilt over what had happened to Zac. Surely it could not be a coincidence that the first overdose took place on the anniversary of Zac's plunge. She thought about the posture of Verinder's body and found herself wanting to believe that it reflected some sort of contrition. Then again, she pointed out, he could've leaned over just to vomit on the floor. Rachelle was struck by the testimony about how 'aggressive' Verinder got when he'd been drinking, and noted that this sounded nothing like the benign description that Dominique had presented at Zac's inquest. 'I've only been to two inquests, one for our son and one for the man who was in the room when he died,' Rachelle reflected. 'I feel no compassion,' she said. 'He doesn't get to have my pity.'

One day I paid a visit to Indian Dave's old gangster associate Andy Baker, who had recently been released from prison after nearly a decade. Baker is a large man, with penetrating blue eyes, an intense handshake and a monitor on his ankle. He commenced our conversation by inquiring after my wife and children – by name. It was a chilling introduction, but a revealing one. Baker wasn't threatening my family per se. He was just letting me know, with a smile of exaggerated courtesy, that he knew who they were. It gave me an insight into Indian Dave and how he had operated, always hunting for the Achilles' heel. The one area where nearly all of us are vulnerable is our families.

Baker was not immune to this himself: he had children. 'I liked being a criminal,' he told me. 'I lived like a maharaja. I had so much fun.' But now that he was out of prison, he was determined to stay out, he said, because of his kids.

The only way to interpret the final encounter between Verinder and Zac, Baker said, was to conclude that Verinder had lost his edge. Perhaps it had become harder to make money. Perhaps his mind had been softened by drugs. 'Everyone around him was either dead or in prison,' Baker pointed out, so he had no support network. And as a parasitic operator who had devoted his entire adult life to sucking others dry, he was probably nervous about the financial precarity of retirement. There's no pension plan for an ageing gangster. Baker was amazed that Verinder had so easily fallen for Zac's ruse. Why not check up on him? Why not put him in front of a native Russian speaker and see if the two of them could converse? Indian Dave must have been really desperate to be fooled by Zac so thoroughly.

'He wouldn't have liked that,' Baker continued. 'He would have found that an affront.' If word got around that he'd been conned by a kid – had even taken the kid into his home – it could have become a real problem. 'He would've found that hugely, hugely embarrassing,' Baker said. Maybe he hit Zac, breaking his jaw, or maybe he just threatened to. Maybe he produced a knife and heated the blade over an open flame. But knowing Indian Dave, Baker told me, it would have been only logical for the boy to assume that he was not going to make it out of that flat alive.

Before we parted ways, I asked Baker if he thought he would succeed in staying away from crime and he assured me that, for his kids, it would be worth it. Then he told me a story about the last time he saw his own father, when he was ill at the end of his life and Baker went to his house for a final visit. As Andy was getting ready to go, his father said, 'Give me two rings.'

This was an old custom they had: Andy would call the house and let it ring twice, just to signal to his father that he'd arrived home all right. But Andy was a grown man now, a seasoned gangster (and perennial murder suspect) who could presumably look after himself.

'Dad, you're dying,' Andy said.

'I'm going to worry about you till the minute I die,' his father told him.

So Andy went home, called his father, let it ring twice, then hung up and went to bed. In the morning, his sister telephoned. The old man had died overnight. Before passing away, he'd said, 'Two rings, the kid's home safe.'

In emails to me, Akbar Shamji suggested that because the police investigation had run its course and never resulted in any charges, he had effectively been found innocent. 'There really is nothing else to say,' he told me, making clear that whatever drama the Brettlers might still be going through, he was ready to put this whole matter behind him.

That would be difficult to achieve, however. In the aftermath of the publicity about the case, Akbar had been asked to step down from his position at DarkByte. In 2024, he launched a new website, which described him as a 'visionary leader at the intersection of renewable energy, advanced technology, and sustainability' and announced that following 'the success of Bitzero' he now found himself at 'the forefront of the deep nanotechnology space'. Akbar Jr's modelling career was booming, and if you strolled through the swanky shopping district of any major city, you could see him staring down at you, dressed like a midcentury Sicilian pimp, in a black-and-white ad campaign for Dolce & Gabbana. At Wimbledon in the summer of 2024, the Princess of Wales, Kate Middleton, made a rare public appearance after her cancer diagnosis attired in a vibrant purple dress by Safiyaa. But when I spoke to Akbar's friend John Connies-Laing, he told me that the public revelation of the circumstances surrounding Zac's death had 'ruined Akbar's life'. Daniela had split up with him, Connies-Laing maintained, and his children hardly spoke to him. He had left London and was now rumoured to be residing somewhere in the Dominican Republic.

Matthew did not need a new police investigation to establish that Akbar was a bad man, he told me. 'I know that he's a bad man. And I think that he knows he's done bad things.' Sometimes, when the Brettlers described their feelings about Akbar, I was reminded of Raskolnikov, the protagonist of *Crime and Punishment*, who commits a terrible crime and appears to get away with it but is then tormented by his own shame and paranoia and ends up finding salvation only when he atones and faces exile in Siberia. 'He has not come out of this scot-free,' Matthew said. 'I think he is going to live in his own little prison.'

'People often say "time is a great healer", but I am not so sure,' Hugo Gryn used to say. I felt sometimes, when I spoke to Matthew and Rachelle, as if they were trapped in a little prison of their own, or rather a kind of purgatory, an endless loop in which Matthew would forever be trying to solve the mystery of how Zac had died, and Rachelle would forever be yearning to go back in time and intervene in some way to save his life. More than one friend of the family suggested to me that the fuel that kept their obsessions burning was guilt, that they were desperately trying to parent their child now in a way that they had been unable to do when he was alive.

When I asked about this one night, as the three of us were having dinner at a little Italian restaurant in Maida Vale, both Brettlers readily conceded that it was true. 'It's very hard as a parent to lose a child of that age and not to feel some sense of responsibility,' Matthew said, and his personal sense of guilt ran deeper still. 'As you know, all of my family was wiped out,' he said. 'And I feel, you know, what have I done to keep the family going? I was the father of two children and now I'm only the father of one. So I've halved the continuation story.'

At the same time, since going public the Brettlers had started to hear from other parents who connected in one way or another with what they had experienced with Zac: parents whose children suffered from a corrosive anxiety over not being richer than they were, or whose teenagers seemed to have been swallowed up by Instagram or TikTok and to have lost their bearings. Rachelle even heard from the mother of another London boy who'd been pretending that he came from an oligarch family. It felt strange to think of their loss as a cautionary tale, but Rachelle liked the thought that *something* good might come from Zac's death. And it was less lonely knowing that there were other parents out there contending with similar dilemmas.

'My concern is what do Matthew and Rachelle want?' one close friend of theirs told me. 'They're alive. Zac's not; but they are. And they need to find a way to live with that grief, rather than it constantly haunting them.'

In the spring of 1947, Hugo Gryn wrote a short story with two very different endings. He had only just arrived in Britain and had been feeling lonely and defeated. The story was about a young boy who has suffered a great deal, and in one ending he kills himself. In the other ending, he is very desperate and *wants* to end his life, but he holds out just long enough for things to start getting better. Interestingly, during the same period when Hugo wrote the story, in the late 1940s, Benny Brettler had what Matthew thinks was probably a 'nervous breakdown', though they would not have called it that at the time. When Benny came out of it, 'it wasn't that he completely jettisoned his experiences,' Matthew said. 'But I think he'd kind of removed himself from the equation and become an observer, as a coping mechanism. I think it's a real challenge to live, when you have that weight on you,' he continued. 'You've got to keep going.'

'I would say that's what both our dads have done,' Rachelle said. Gaby, Rachelle's sister, told me that when they were growing up as Hugo's daughters, 'you didn't look into his eyes and see the barbed wire, you just saw a very loving father', and Rachelle seemed determined to do at least that much for Joe. 'She has made herself get out of bed and have a full and active and interesting life,' Gaby said. Rachelle and Matthew might not have realized it, growing up, or might not have thought they would ever need it, but the greatest gift they had received was this astonishing example, on both sides of the family, of how to live joyously in the face of loss.

'It's choosing life,' Rachelle said.

Matthew had never felt particularly religious, but the biblical verse she was alluding to was one that had always resonated with him, from Deuteronomy: 'I have put before you life and death, blessing and curse. Choose life – so that you and your children after you will live.'

Grief might be a process, but it is not a problem that you solve. For five years, the Brettlers had spent an inordinate amount of time poring over the mystery of Zac's death, and their diligence had exposed, at least partially, a matrix of power and secrecy and corruption in contemporary London, a dimension of their own city that they had never recognized before now. The very fact that some of their inquiries remained inconclusive seemed itself to speak to the malign power of the metropolis – the empty mansions, the offshore accounts, the tainted riches, the anonymous shell companies, the amoral businessmen, the predatory thugs, the incompetent authorities, the grandeur of all those dazzling surfaces obscuring a netherworld of shadow.

But for all the unknowability still surrounding Zac's case, it was a bit like an impressionist painting: if you stood close to the canvas, it looked incomprehensible, a riot of wild brushstrokes and confusing details. Stare long enough and it could drive you mad. But if you just took a few steps back, the truth was not so complicated, and it all came into focus. Zac had pretended to be the son of a Russian oligarch, with access to a great fortune. He had fallen in with two men who were attracted to his money, one a charlatan who had just declared bankruptcy, the other a gangster who was worried about retirement and on the lookout for a final score. At a certain point, the men realized that they'd been tricked and Zac found himself trapped with the gangster. Well aware of the man's capacity for violence, he walked out to the balcony and leapt towards the safety of the Thames.

EPILOGUE

ONE CHILLY DAY IN January 2025, Rachelle and Matthew approached a building in the Houses of Parliament to meet with two senior police officials. The meeting had been arranged by Georgia Gould, a new Member of Parliament who represented their district. The Brettlers arrived a bit early and stopped in at a Caffè Nero. While they were waiting to order their coffee, Matthew spotted two grey-looking middle-aged men joining the line behind them.

'I'll bet those are the guys,' he told Rachelle.

He was right. When they reached the office where the meeting would take place, the policemen they'd seen in the coffee shop both gruffly introduced themselves as 'Dean', which the Brettlers found quietly amusing. Detective Superintendent Dean Lanfear and Detective Chief Inspector Dean Purvis were both quite senior at the Metropolitan Police, and they had agreed to speak with Matthew and Rachelle about the case. As an aide took notes, Matthew launched into a presentation about the Met's many failings. Initially, the Deans just listened, but when Matthew had said his piece and they started to engage in conversation, he was surprised by how knowledgeable they were about the details. When Matthew asked if he could record the meeting, they told him he couldn't. But the Deans allowed that mistakes may have been made in the wider investigation. They stopped short of offering any formal apology, but they did acknowledge, to a degree that no representative of the police ever had before, that there were aspects of the inquiry that could have been handled differently. They made it sound as though Rory Wilkinson had been running the investigation with a great deal of autonomy. One of the Deans said that the case still came up in his conversations with Rory, practically on a weekly basis, and that misgivings remained in some corners of the Met about the fact that Akbar Shamji had never been charged. The Brettlers still wanted some public acknowledgement of fault by the police. But it was interesting to know that Rory Wilkinson might be haunted by the case, just as they were.

Joe never did end up finishing university after Zac's death. But he was working now for a London brand and marketing consultancy, which he enjoyed. We met one evening at a pub in Shepherd Market, a corner of Mayfair that is known for bars and restaurants where English gangsters rub elbows with investment bankers. Joe arrived on his bike, despite the rain. He lived in Pimlico now, not far from Riverwalk, and as we sat down he explained that it's often impossible for him to chart a route through the neighbourhood that does not take him past the building. The sight of it can still occasionally startle him with a jolt of pain. 'It elicits different responses depending on my mood,' he said. But then again, the Thames itself felt like 'a constant reminder', he said. Joe still intermittently had dreams about Zac, he told me, but they were mostly happy dreams, and in them Zac was always young. Rachelle's brother, David, had said something similar. As time has passed, he remarked, the swaggering, tormented fabulist Zac who died in 2019 has been edged out in his memory by a younger, less troubled kid: the cheeky, giggling little ten-year-old boy.

Joe was twenty-six now and wore round wire-framed glasses and a small gold earring. When I ordered a beer, he asked for a pot of tea. He was feeling slightly under the weather, he explained, but he also tends to be careful about what he eats and drinks, and we spoke about sleep patterns and health and wellness. He likes his job. Lately, he said, his firm had been consulting for a company that does 'super high-end children's birthday parties'. He wanted to impress upon me how much he loved his brother, whatever tensions they may have sometimes felt in life. How much he loves him still. When I enquired about his parents, Joe spoke of them with warmth and affection. Zac's death had 'brought them closer together', he said, adding, 'I'm closer with them, too.'

Finishing our drinks, we stepped out into the blustery evening. We were in a narrow street, and before Joe headed off to retrieve his bike, he pointed out the building directly across from us. It was 5 Hertford Street, the private club founded by Mark Birley, where Akbar Shamji was a member and would sometimes meet business prospects. It was a handsome old townhouse with an unmarked door. The windows emanated a warm glow, and through them I could see uniformed staff members bustling about. It looked like they were setting up for a party.

In 1873, Mark Twain and Charles Dudley Warner published *The Gilded Age*, a novel that would bestow its title on an era of bounding progress and deep inequality in America. When the book was published in England, Twain and Warner felt the need to contextualize the curious phenomena reshaping their country for a British audience, so they included an explanatory preface to the British edition. 'In America nearly every man has his dream, his pet scheme, whereby he is to advance himself socially or pecuniarily,' they wrote. It was this 'all-pervading speculativeness' that was the subject of the novel. 'It is a characteristic which is both bad and good, for both the individual and the nation,' they continued. 'Good, because it allows neither to stand still, but drives both for ever on, toward some point or other which is ahead . . . Bad, because the chosen point is often badly chosen, and then the individual is wrecked.'

One day in the summer of 2019, Matthew's mother, Judith, was celebrating her eightieth birthday, so the family organized a small party at his sister-in-law's house, in Herne Hill, south of the river. It was a lovely lunch. Joe came, and Zac did as well. The cousins all hung out in an open kitchen, and Zac looked more relaxed and benign than he had in quite some time, joking and laughing the way he always had when he was younger. He ended up leaving the party early to return to Riverwalk, where he was staying that summer. But he knew that when his parents drove home to Maida Vale, they would head north across the river, and he told them to call him when they were approaching Vauxhall Bridge. When the party was over, Rachelle, Matthew and Joe piled into the family car. As they drove past the MI6 building and onto the bridge, Rachelle telephoned Zac, as instructed, and then they all looked up and saw him, there in the distance on the fifth-floor balcony, a tiny figure, waving.

ACKNOWLEDGEMENTS

My first and deepest thanks go to Zac's family. When we initially met, Rachelle and Matthew Brettler were uncertain about whether they were ready to go on the record. That they ended up trusting me enough to lay bare such a private and often painful history will always mean a great deal to me. I hope I've written a book that feels commensurate with the magnitude of that gesture. That is not to say that aspects of this account won't leave them feeling discomfort. But to their enormous credit, the Brettlers recognized that the only way to tell a story of compounding deceptions was with an honesty that was bracing, unblinking and complete. Joe Brettler was remarkably open, thoughtful and generous with his time. The wider Gryn clan was supportive, and the fact that they ultimately came to accept the idea of my including not just Zac's secret life but Hugo's – that willingness to let a family secret go – struck me as a profound act of clarity and acceptance.

If the director Anthony Byrne hadn't invited his friend Andrew Fingret to the set of *Say Nothing*, I might never have heard Zac's story; I believe I owe you both a nice dinner. At *The New Yorker*, David Remnick and my longtime editor Daniel Zalewski were enthusiastic about the idea of an article. Teresa Mathew, Hélène Werner and Yinuo Shi fact-checked the piece, and Teresa then fact-checked the book with rigour and wisdom and laughter and asides about the delicious things she was baking even as we talked through the many subtle frailties she had uncovered in my work. Linnea Feldman Emison also checked one chapter. Thanks, as ever, to low-key legal superhero Fabio Bertoni. Eleanor Martin copyedited the article. Giada De Agostinis worked on the photography for that piece, then helped source images for the book, commissioning the photograph of Riverwalk by Mattia Balsamini and the retouching of the portrait of Zac by Andela Preradovic.

Over twenty years at *The New Yorker* I've accumulated a cohort of colleagues and beloved friends whom I consult (or just procrastinate) with on a daily basis, a number of whom read the book in draft form and offered astute critiques. In particular I'm grateful to Rachel Aviv, Gideon Lewis-Kraus, Isaac Chotiner, Ed Caesar, Sam Knight, Heidi Blake, Ben Taub, Larissa MacFarquhar, Nick Trautwein, Rozina Ali and, once again, Daniel Zalewski. Diego Lasarte provided early research help, and a pair of excellent law students, Liz Brown and Clare Lonergan, worked as research assistants over the summer of 2024.

A big chunk of the manuscript was written during a nine-week residency at the Centre de Cultura Contemporània de Barcelona. Thanks to the CCCB for hosting me, and to Judit Carrera, Susana Arias, Marta Millet Agustí and Queralt Arumí Agramunt for extending such a warm welcome to my family. Thanks also to Barcelona pals Núria Alemany Pérez, Aniol Rafel, Jaume Bonfill and Ricard Gil.

The mighty Bill Thomas, my editor and publisher at Doubleday, knew this was a book before I did. Thanks to Dan Novack, Michael Goldsmith, Todd Doughty, Chris Howard-Woods, Anne Jaconette, Khari Dawkins, Oliver Munday (who designed the cover of the US edition), Will Palmer (who copyedited the book), Andrea Monagle, Vimi Santokhi and everyone else at Penguin Random House. I'm also very grateful to Ravi Mirchandani, who acquired the book for Picador, and to Mary Mount, who edited and published it, as well as Joanna Prior, Alpana Sajip, Lyndon Branfield, Kate Green, Siobhan Slattery and the whole Pan Mac team in London. Thanks to Mark Bateman, for the UK legal read. Thanks to Tina Bennett, who (as my dad would say) keeps the wolf from the door, with help from Phoebe Rhinehart and Molly Wright. Thanks to Karolina Sutton, Helen Manders and Peppa Mignone; to Anna DeRoy and Andy Galker; to India Tehranchi and Jon Phillips; and to Nancy Aaronson and her colleagues at the Lyceum Agency.

Thanks, for various reasons, to Henry Finder, Sai Sriskandarajah, Jonah Weiner, Julie Tate, Shanti Avirgan, Bob Kolker, Eliza Griswold, Paul Murphy, Gabriel Pogrund, Emanuele Midolo, Julia

Neuberger, Chloe Fordham, Tristan Redman, Sebastian Neave, Simon Watson, Diego De Giorgi, Richard Quinn, Kelefa Sanneh, the late, great Duncan Campbell, Kevin Macdonald, William Pike, Bradley Hope, Basia Cummings, Maya Jasanoff, Charlie Baker, Rowan Pelling, Jody Rosen, Brad Simpson, Nina Jacobson, John Arlidge, Jason Burns, Dave Park, Emily Maitlis, Issy Wood, Rebecca Weiner, Kavita Puri, Alex Godoy, Tristram Radden Keefe, Beatrice Radden Keefe, Michael Wahid Hanna and Michael Shtender-Auerbach. Thanks to Itamar Srulovich and Sarit Packer, for feeding me. Thanks to dear friends Liz Oestreich and David Fein: they know why.

It felt a bit weird to be working on a book about the corruption of London at a moment when the United States was jettisoning the Foreign Corrupt Practices Act, preparing its own 'golden visa' programme, and undergoing a precipitous slide into authoritarian rule. When I've felt tempted over recent months to succumb to the gravity of despair, what's kept me on my feet and moving forwards is small moments of kindness, friendship, courage and compassion. Above all I found hope in my family. Justyna tends to know what I'm going to say before I say it, and at this point words hardly suffice. But what a life we've made.

This is also a book about parental love, and while working on it I often thought about my own adolescent sons, Lucian and Felix: how fiercely I love them, how desperately I want to protect them from this world and prepare them for it. Parenting is not a science, boys. Bear with me.

To my own mum and dad, who I'm somehow still learning from even now, this one's dedicated to you.

A NOTE ON SOURCES

This book is based chiefly on countless hours of conversation with Rachelle and Matthew Brettler, stretching over more than two years. The three of us also texted a great deal, often daily. This unusual degree of reportorial access meant that much of the story could be related in an intimate fashion, hewing closely to the Brettlers' point of view. So if there are moments in the narrative when Matthew and Rachelle (and, by proxy, the reader) believe certain things that will later turn out to be untrue – that Akbar Shamji thought Zac was still alive and wanted to help find him, for instance, or that Verinder Sharma might have faked his own death – it is because the experience of reading the book should ideally evoke, as much as possible, the same sequence of confusion, misapprehension and revelation that Zac's family went through.

From the moment Zac went missing, his parents took the unusual step of documenting their search for him, often by recording their conversations. One phenomenon that bedevils any work of non-fiction is the way in which time can distort or elide certain memories, if not rewrite them altogether. But these recordings offered an unusually reliable, high-fidelity record of what was thought, said and done in the hours, weeks and months after Zac died.

In addition to the recordings, Matthew wrote contemporaneous memos and timelines that he shared with me, along with a host of other artefacts – texts, emails, letters, photos, videos, eulogies – that greatly enriched the narrative. Joe Brettler was also a crucial source, sharing his perspective on his brother and his parents in numerous conversations, as were Rachelle's siblings, David Gryn, Naomi Gryn and Gaby Massey, and Gaby's son Adam. Naomi kindly welcomed me into her home and shared a trove of archival material from Hugo

Gryn's life, from his sermons and writings to official records from his earliest days as a teenaged refugee. The two books Naomi co-authored with her father, *Chasing Shadows* and *Three Minutes of Hope*, were invaluable resources, as were her documentaries, *The Sabbath Bride* and *Chasing Shadows*. Hugo really deserves his own comprehensive biography; I hope somebody will write it. In reconstructing the life of Baruch 'Benny' Brettler, I relied on a terrific oral history interview that he gave to Professor Christian Goeschel of the University of Manchester in 2015. Also helpful was a segment from the *Today* programme on BBC Radio 4 in 1998 (I have the recording but not the airdate), which covered Benny's return to his hometown of Breslau (now Wrocław), and Matthew's eulogy for his father.

The Metropolitan Police declined to cooperate with either the *New Yorker* article or this book. My repeated requests to interview Rory Wilkinson or other members of the investigative team were rebuffed. Police did not respond at all to a detailed set of fact-checking queries related to the material in the book, but in an earlier statement to *The New Yorker*, a spokesperson extended 'sincere condolences' to Zac's family and claimed that investigators had explored 'every possible hypothesis' in the case.

Over the course of their investigation, however, detectives shared many significant files with the Brettlers, including the transcripts of interrogations and police interviews, crime scene photos and investigative reports containing text messages, phone records and some of Zac's internet activity. This material was turned over to the family without any stipulations about what they could do with it. They chose to share it with me.

While based primarily on my own original reporting, this project was deeply informed by the work of other authors. In particular, I should cite the books of Oliver Bullough (*Moneyland*, *Butler to the World*) and Tom Burgis (*Kleptopia*, *Cuckooland*), whose writing on Britain's role in facilitating a certain kind of corruption helped shape my perception of these issues. Books by Catherine Belton, David Hoffman and Mark Hollingsworth and Stewart Lansley helped me understand the post-Soviet oligarchs. I also found the plays *A Very Expensive Poison*, by Lucy Prebble, and *Patriots*, by Peter Morgan, instructive. The excellent book *From Russia with Blood*, by my friend (and now colleague) Heidi Blake, was an indispensable source not just on the Kremlin's campaign of murder in Britain but also on the ineffectual response of the Metropolitan Police. I was also grateful for decades of terrific crime coverage by Duncan Campbell (whom I befriended as I was writing this book, and who died in May 2025) and Michael Gillard (whose newsletter *The Upsetter* is one of the last remaining sources for regular hard-hitting crime reportage in the UK).

Gabriel Pogrund of *The Sunday Times*, along with his colleagues Emanuele Midolo and Venetia Menzies, uncovered important new details about Zac's final night. They also generously shared with me the underlying data analysis used to produce their article on the black box in Akbar Shamji's Mercedes. I could not have told the story of the rise and fall of Abdul Shamji without a remarkable two-part series from 1986 on ITV's *World in Action*, which was reported by Michael Gillard (who, in another familial coincidence, is the father of the crime reporter mentioned above). In relating Akbar's disastrous foray into the theatre business, I relied on a radio documentary, 'The Unpleasantness at the Mermaid', presented by John Waite and produced by Graham Ellis for the programme *Face the Facts*, which aired on BBC Radio 4 in 1994.

Arranging to speak with Andy Baker was not easy. He had recently got out of prison, and his release was governed by a set of conditions that did not permit speaking to a journalist. But he managed to obtain a dispensation from authorities to talk with me about certain matters. It was the first time he had ever engaged with a journalist, and our conversations illuminated many aspects of Indian Dave's criminal career and the wider demimonde of – to use Andy's favoured euphemism – 'colourful characters'. As I was finishing the book I got word that Andy had been recalled to prison. The reason was not, as I might have presumed, that he had returned to a criminal lifestyle. According to his lawyer, Andy got locked up again because he had taken his sons to watch their team, Crystal Palace, play in the third round of the FA Cup, in apparent contravention of the conditions of his release.

After exchanging many emails with me while I was writing the *New Yorker* article, Akbar cut off communication. He hired an attorney, who sent a letter threatening legal action. The lawyer's name was Andrew Brettler. 'No relation' to Zac Brettler, he hastened to point out. But Matthew, unable to resist a rigorous plunge into the genealogical record, discovered that Akbar's lawyer *was* in fact a distant relative; you just have to go back four generations.

Andrew Brettler asserted that any portrayal of Akbar as a 'disreputable businessman' was 'outrageous', 'reckless' and 'malicious'. As I was working with a fact-checker, Teresa Mathew, to finalize the manuscript for the book, we sent Akbar 237 fact-checking queries, so that he would have the opportunity to comment on all the material relating to him and his family. He never replied.

Nick Gold *did* respond to his fact-checking memo, saying that he disputes 'nearly all of the points outlined in your inquiry' and threatening a lawsuit of his own. Gold condemned 'numerous inaccuracies' in my reporting, without actually specifying any particular thing that might be inaccurate. I approached multiple members of Verinder Sharma's immediate and extended family, none of whom agreed to speak with me. Through a lawyer, Dominique Sharma disputed the suggestion that she was anything but truthful in her testimony at Zac's inquest.

Obtaining court documents in the UK is unreasonably difficult. Though transcripts of legal proceedings are often prepared, there is no tradition of preserving these records or making them readily available to the public. In fact, once a case is fully adjudicated, they are often destroyed. After months of trying to obtain transcripts of the 2005 murder trial of Roger Vincent, I was informed that, pursuant to UK document retention policies, they had . . . not been retained. Because newspapers in Britain (as in the United States) have drastically cut back on court reporting in recent decades, there was only scant press coverage of the trial, so that was not a solution. In this instance, I was able to obtain some partial transcripts from a friendly lawyer on a tangentially related case. But the same challenge arose when it came to the 2003 trial in the Graeme Hammond case: no records preserved by the court. Here again I was eventually able to secure helpful documents from someone who had access to them. But this is a real issue, for the news business, for the good health of government and the courts, and for future historians: if the media is not in a position to provide reliable contemporaneous accounts of court proceedings, then UK courts should start preserving these records and making them more accessible.

In the notes that follow, I have adopted a slightly different approach than in my previous books. I have opted not to include notes for facts that have been widely covered in the press; so when I assert that Roman Abramovich bought Chelsea Football Club in 2003, there is no note. Likewise, when it is self-evident from the context of a quote or detail that it comes from an interview with one of my central characters ('To Joe, it seemed...'), I have not included a note. Otherwise, the book is comprehensively endnoted, with the exception of quotes or details that come to me from sources who spoke on the condition that I not identify them by name. A number of these sources proved to be essential. They know who they are, and I'm grateful to them.

NOTES

ABBREVIATIONS

PEOPLE
MB: Matthew Brettler
RGB: Rachelle Gryn Brettler
ZJB: Zachary Josh Brettler
AS: Akbar Shamji
VS: Verinder Sharma
JCL: John Connies-Laing
PRK: Patrick Radden Keefe

RECORDS AND PROCEEDINGS
AS interrogation 1: Akbar Shamji Police Interrogation, 5 Dec. 2019
AS interrogation 2: Akbar Shamji Police Interrogation, 6 Dec. 2019
AS interrogation 3: Akbar Shamji Police Interrogation, 4 Mar. 2020
GS statement: statement of PC Gemma Scott (witness), 6 Dec. 2019
JM statement: statement of PC Judith McCabe (witness), 6 Dec. 2019
MB eulogy: Matthew Brettler eulogy for Zachary Brettler, 15 Dec. 2019
Méridien recording: recording of a conversation between MB, RGB, AS and VS, 2 Dec. 2019
NW statement: statement of DC Natalie Wallen (witness), 7 May, 2020
Police debrief 12 Dec. 2019: recording of a meeting between RGB, MB, Rory Wilkinson, Phil Lane and Lena Rentall, 12 Dec. 2019
Police debrief 25 Nov. 2020: recording of a conversation between RGB, MB and Rory Wilkinson, 25 Nov. 2020
Police debrief 9 Nov. 2021: recording of a meeting between RGB, MB, Rory Wilkinson and Phil Lane, 9 Nov. 2021
RV case summary: case summary prepared by the prosecution, *Regina v. Vincent*, Luton Crown Court, 8 Mar. 2005
RV summing up: judge's summing up, *Regina v. Vincent*, Luton Crown Court, 18 Aug. 2005
RV testimony: testimony of Roger Vincent, *Regina v. Vincent*, Luton Crown Court, 1–5 Aug. 2005
VS inquest: inquest touching on the death of Verinder Kumar Sharma, Inner West London Coroner's Court, 17 Apr. 2024
VS interrogation 1: Verinder 'Dave' Sharma Police Interrogation 1, 5 Dec. 2019
VS interrogation 2: Verinder 'Dave' Sharma Police Interrogation 2, 4 Mar. 2020
ZJB inquest: inquest touching on the death of Zachary Brettler, Poplar Coroner's Court, 13–14 Dec. 2022

PROLOGUE
1 under circumstances of such secrecy: Janina Gosseye, 'The Spectre at Vauxhall Cross: Architecture of the State, Between Community and Monarchy', *Journal of the Society of Architectural Historians, Australia and New Zealand* 32, no. 3 (2022), published in *Blueprint* 330 (Sept.–Oct. 2013); 'Hi-Tech Fortress Where Secrecy Reigns Supreme', *Independent*, 22 Sept. 2000.
1 a bottlenose whale: 'Lost Whale Dies After Rescue Bid', *BBC News*, 21 Jan. 2006.
1 its level plummeting by as much as twenty feet: 'The Cruel Thames', *Guardian*, 14 Feb. 2024.
1 artefacts of previous civilizations: 'Signposts to Prehistory: Thames Foreshore Intertidal Landscape', Prehistoric Society, Dec. 2014, https://www.prehistoricsociety

.org/sites/prehistoricsociety.org/files/resources/ps-signpost_river-thames.pdf;
'London's Top Secret', *London Archaeologist*, Winter 2010/2011.
1 a quarter of the globe: Sathnam Sanghera, *Empireland: How Imperialism Has Shaped Modern Britain* (London: Penguin, 2021), p. 31.
1 half of all exports: Eric Hobsbawm, *The Age of Empire 1875–1914* (Vintage, 1989), p. 51.
2 the black water could: Peter Ackroyd, *Thames: The Biography* (Anchor, 2007), p. 274.
2 Dickens saw in the river: Charles Dickens, 'Down with the Tide'. Originally published in *All the Year Round* 3, no. 62 (21 July 1860).
2 was meant to evoke: 'An Iconic Building', SIS (website), https://www.sis.gov.uk/our-history.
2 declined by 80 per cent: Simon Jenkins, *The City on the Thames* (Pegasus, 2020), p. 291.
2 an American trucking executive: Marc Levinson, *The Box: How the Shipping Container Made the World Smaller and the World Economy Bigger* (Princeton University Press, 2016), pp. 62, 70. Some point out that people had been shipping cargo in various types of containers before, but as Levinson observes, Malcom McLean's vision was grander, requiring 'not just a metal box but an entire new way of handling freight. Every part of the system – ports, ships, cranes, storage facilities, trucks, trains, and the operations of the shipper themselves – would have to change.'
2 The word 'smog': the term appears to have first been coined by Henry Antoine Des Voeux, in a letter to *The Times* on 27 Dec. 1904. See Karen Clay and Werner Troesken, 'Did Frederick Brodie Discover the World's First Environmental Kuznets Curve? Coal Smoke and the Rise and Fall of the London Fog', Working Paper No. 15669, National Bureau of Economic Research, Jan. 2010.
3 converted a derelict warehouse: 'How Britain's Shocking Art Movement Got Its Start', BBC, 25 Apr. 2016.
3 but curiously devoid of residents: Jenkins, *City on the Thames*, p. 323.
3 'You have people with': 'The London Skyscraper That Is a Stark Symbol of the Housing Crisis', *Guardian*, 24 May 2016.
3 'potentates, monarchs, chiefs, sultans': Trevor Abrahmsohn, interview by author.
4 A former deputy mayor: 'Londoners Miss Out as Homes Built as "Safe Deposit Boxes" for Foreign Buyers', *Guardian*, 30 Dec. 2014.
4 there is a statistical correlation: 'London's Surplus of Empty Luxury Apartments Revealed', *Delano*, 29 Nov. 2018.
4 ghost mansions: 'London Mayor Targets "Ghost Mansions" and "Zombie Flats",' *Washington Post*, 18 Sept. 2017.
4 charges of conspiracy, false accounting and theft: 'New Year Honours', *BBC News*, 31 Dec. 2011.
4 'Imagine the parties': 'Gerald Ronson: Property Patriarch Still Going Strong After Six Decades of Ups and Downs', *Evening Standard*, 11 Nov. 2016.
4 rumoured to include Tom Jones: recording of a conversation between MB, RGB, AS and VS, 2 Dec. 2019 (hereafter cited as 'Méridien recording').
4 In the early hours: the particulars related to Zac Brettler's fall are explored in much greater detail, with citations, later in the book.

CHAPTER 1: THE BIG I AM
9 a rainy evening: London weather report for 20 Sept. 2000, Weather Spark.
9 a soft tuft of red hair: unless otherwise noted, biographical details relating to members of the Brettler family are derived from multiple interviews with MB, RGB and Joe Brettler.
9 could remember anyone: they subsequently remembered that Rachelle's aunt Sonia in California had red colouring, and a maternal great-grandfather of Matthew's did as well. Rachelle had always assumed that her grandmother Sadie's red hair was 'from a bottle', but she realized after Zac's birth that perhaps it was not.
9 'He looks like he's been here before': MB eulogy for Zachary Brettler (hereafter cited as 'MB eulogy').
9 'The *zing* of that': ibid.
10 the rabbi was to overcome: Adam Massey, interview by author (relating the story of his own birth). Adam's mother, Gaby – the one who actually gave birth – quibbled with this story, pointing out that Hugo did not have to be restrained from entering. But I wanted to include it because Adam told it to me, and even if it has taken on the fable-like exaggerations of family legend, it illuminates something important about Hugo.

10 In 1939, he had left: unless otherwise indicated, information on the life of Baruch 'Benny' Brettler is derived from interviews with MB; the text of the eulogy MB delivered at Benny's funeral in 2020; a 1998 segment on the *Today* programme on BBC Radio about Benny's return to Breslau; a case file maintained by World Jewish Relief; and the video of an oral history interview Benny did with the University of Manchester in 2015.

10 Margaret Thatcher deregulated: 'London Reclaims a Heritage', *New York Times*, 22 Sept. 1986. Some argue that the importance of the Big Bang has been overstated and that it was a manifestation of deeper economic trends that had been unfolding over the course of the prior two decades. See David Kynaston, *The City of London*, vol. IV: *A Club No More, 1945–2000* (Pimlico, 2002), pp. 696–97.

10 something of an old boys' club: 'Big Bang Has Changed London in Myriad Ways', Associated Press, 17 Feb. 1987.

11 Foreign banks swept into: 'Nerves, Nerves, Nerves', *Forbes*, 11 Aug. 1986.

11 looked like meritocracy: yes, of course, this was not a *true* meritocracy. But you take my point.

11 'taking trains they never knew *existed*': 'London Reclaims a Heritage'.

11 drug became so pervasive: 'The Big Snort', *Sunday Times*, 26 Oct. 1986; Albert L. Kraus, 'Cocaine Arrives in the City', *Journal of Commerce*, 13 July, 1987.

11 greatest wave of new construction: 'Docklands: Will It Stay a Cut-Price Ghost Town?', *Financial Times*, 11 Jan. 1992.

11 visit to the Isle of Dogs: ibid.

11 The price of flats: Kynaston, *City of London*, p. 720; 'End of the Old Boy Network', *Times*, 15 Oct. 1986.

11 Thatcher acknowledged that: 'London Reclaims a Heritage'.

11 the German carmaker felt: 'A New Colony East of St Paul's', *Times*, 19 Oct. 1987.

12 one BBC report suggested: 'How the Big Bang Changed the City of London For Ever', *BBC News*, 27 Oct. 2016.

13 'chocolate stained with nicotine': Naomi Gryn, ed., *Three Minutes of Hope: Hugo Gryn on the God Slot* (Continuum, 2010), pp. 6–7.

14 'He was the funniest': Adam Massey, interview by author.

15 relatives would consult: Naomi Gryn, interview by author.

15 for his favourite sports car: David Gryn, interview by author.

18 'dangers both physical and moral': Norman G. B. James, *The History of Mill Hill School, 1807–1907* (Andrew Melrose, 1909), p. 17.

18 'Zac came into meeting' : Andrei Lejonvarn, interview by author.

19 Voltaire marvelled: Voltaire, 'Letters Concerning the English Nation (1733)', National Constitution Center, https://constitutioncenter.org/the-constitution/historic-document-library/detail/voltaire-letters-concerning-the-english-nation-1733.

19 Saudi royal family purchased: Mark Hollingsworth and Stewart Lansley, *Londongrad: From Russia with Cash, the Inside Story of the Oligarchs* (Fourth Estate, 2009), p. 131.

20 'They steal and steal and steal': Chrystia Freeland, *Plutocrats: The Rise of the New Global Rich and the Fall of Everyone Else* (Penguin, 2012), p. 188. The friend was Sergei Kovalev, who recounted the quote to the *Financial Times*. 'Moscow's Group of Seven', *Financial Times*, 1 Nov. 1996.

20 he and six other men controlled 50 per cent: Hollingsworth and Lansley, *Londongrad*, p. 31.

20 Others, like Roman Abramovich: Abramovich has long contested any suggestion that he acts on behalf of the Kremlin. But the fact that he maintains close ties to the leadership in Moscow has been widely documented over the past two decades. See, for instance, Catherine Belton, *Putin's People: How the KGB Took Back Russia and Then Took On the West* (Farrar, Straus and Giroux, 2020); 'Our Oligarch', *Jewish Currents*, 3 Mar. 2022; and 'Roman Abramovich's Abrupt Transformation from Shunned Oligarch to Wartime Envoy', *Wall Street Journal*, 1 Apr. 2022. When he was sanctioned by the UK in 2022, ministers cited 'clear connections' between the oligarch and Vladimir Putin and said that he was among a group of businessmen who had 'blood on their hands'. 'UK Imposes Sanctions on Roman Abramovich Over "Clear" Links to Putin', *Guardian*, 10 Mar. 2022. After appeals by Abramovich's lawyers, both the UK and the EU were forced to revise the language of their sanctions to eliminate any suggestion that he had a direct connection

to the war. A statement from Abramovich's legal team said that he 'does not have the ability to influence the decision-making of any government, including Russia, and has in no way benefited from the war.' 'EU Downgrades Sanctions Rationale Against Roman Abramovich', *Jerusalem Post*, 23 Feb. 2025.
21 'as the jungles of Sumatra': 'Boris Brags About London's Exotic Army of Billionaires', *Times*, 28 Nov. 2014.
21 number had jumped to 20: Hollingsworth and Stewart, *Londongrad*, p. 165.
21 Abramovich remarked in 2003: ibid., p. 163.
21 'We don't screen the mafia': 'Cash and Caviare', *Guardian*, 8 Sept. 1994.
22 former teachers described him: 'The Dizzying Social Rise of Russian Scion Evgeny Lebedev', *Town & Country*, 21 Feb. 2021.
22 'It was the children of oligarchs': Lejonvarn, interview.
23 'He said, "I remember you"': Unless otherwise noted, material relating to Zac's friend Dimitris comes from two long interviews with him; I have withheld his last name at his request.
25 He didn't drink alcohol: Lejonvarn, interview; Dimitris, interview.
25 by the Manchester artist L. S. Lowry: 'Revealed: Why LS Lowry Turned Down Honours', *Manchester Evening News*, 27 Jan. 2012.
25 'against social distinction': 'The People's Artist Comes in from the Cold', *Observer*, 8 June 2013.
26 'Argos catalogue for rich people': 'How to Spend It: The Shopping List for the 1%', *Guardian*, 19 July 2018.

CHAPTER 2: A FAST LIFE
30 after befriending a Catholic priest: Hugo Gryn, interview by Sue Lawley, *Desert Island Discs*, BBC Radio, 10 July 1994.
30 Hugo visited Cambridge with her: Naomi Gryn, interview by author.
31 Rachelle wondered if perhaps: RGB to Dr Giray Cordan, 1 Nov. 2018.
32 an administrator wrote to Rachelle: P. D. Hunter to RGB, 4 Nov. 2016.
33 'more in rage': statement of Dr Roger Howells, ZJB inquest; Roger Howells to Linda Bello, 2 Feb. 2018.
33 Zac complained that his parents were: Roger Howells to Linda Bello, 2 Feb. 2018.
33 Could he be bipolar?: this sequence of conditions Rachelle wondered if Zac could be suffering from is drawn from RGB to Roger Howells, 4 Jan. 2018; RGB to Howells, 24 Jan. 2018; RGB to Dr Giray Cordan, 1 Nov. 2018.
33 She explained to Howells: RGB to Roger Howells, 4 Jan. 2018.
33 'I really am at my wit's end': RGB to Roger Howells, 27 Jan. 2018.
34 'he is focused on being very wealthy': Roger Howells to Linda Bello, 2 Feb. 2018.
34 report from the physician: 'Report re. Zachary Brettler', Westminster Child and Adolescent Mental Health Service, 3 May 2018.
35 Bawany told Dimitris: Dimitris, interview by author.
35 incorporating it that September: Certificate of Incorporation, Omega Stratton Limited, 24 Sept. 2018.
36 In a fit of suspicion: RGB to Roger Howells, 29 Jan. 2018.
36 installed a hidden video camera: statement of Matthew Brettler (witness), ZJB inquest.
36 children in a £10 million apartment: I was able to confirm that Akbar and Daniela resided in an apartment on the second floor of 92 Mount Street. On a walk through the neighbourhood in late 2023, Rachelle and I noticed that the flat was empty of furniture and a crew was busy repainting the interior. Subsequently, I discovered a listing for this unit on the website of the realty group Knight Frank. The price was £9.5 million. To be certain this was the same property, I consulted with a source who had visited the family and taken photos inside the Mount Street apartment. One of the pictures features Akbar at the central island, and the kitchen around him – the window, the cabinetry, the light fixtures – is a precise match for a photo of the kitchen in the Knight Frank brochure.
36 an award from Narendra Modi: image of Akbar Shamji and Narendra Modi, CPEC (website), https://cpec.io/visionary (website no longer available).
37 In 1673, Lord Berkeley of Stratton: Arthur Irwin Dasent, *Piccadilly in Three Centuries* (Macmillan, 1920), pp. 45n1, 209.
37 'has gratified a lifelong ambition': 'Buys

'$25,000,000 Worth of London', *Detroit Free Press*, 29 June 1919.
37 Winston Churchill spent the first years: 'Residences of Winston and Clementine Churchill', International Churchill Society, www.winstonchurchill.org.
37 Lord Clive, the so-called: William Dalrymple, *The Anarchy: The Relentless Rise of the East India Company* (London: Bloomsbury, 2019), pp. 234–35.
38 a vivacious gambler: Brian Masters, *The Passion of John Aspinall* (Coronet Books, 1989), pp. 108–12.
38 'close the gulf between the species': 'John Aspinall, Gambler and Zoo Owner, Dies at 74', *New York Times*, 1 July 2000.
38 published a coffee table book: John Aspinall, *The Best of Friends* (Pan Macmillan, 1976).
38 once said of his own children: 'John Aspinall, Gambler and Zoo Owner'.
38 assistants were killed: ibid. See also 'Controversial Zoo Owner John Aspinall Dies at 74', *Guardian*, 29 June 2000.
38 Birley was an aristocrat: 'Mark Birley: Obituary', *Guardian*, 29 Aug. 2007.
38 resented every minute of it: 'Inside the World's Most Exclusive and Naughty Nightclub', *Daily Mail*, 5 Feb. 2016.
38 'smell of exclusivity and sex': 'Sex, Tipsy Tories & Elizabeth David', *Independent*, 8 Nov. 2014.
38 Lady Gaga once commenced: 'Inside the World's Most Exclusive and Naughty Nightclub'.
38 the animal lunged: Masters, *Passion of John Aspinall*, pp. 165–68.
38 He survived but was permanently disfigured: 'Hurly Birley', *Vanity Fair*, 1 Feb. 2008.
39 your father with his mistress: 'Annabel's: A Tale of Love, Snobbery, Revenge... and Some Jolly Good Cocktails', *Independent*, 15 Oct. 2006.
39 People started to joke: 'Hurly Birley'.
39 themed 'Russia' weeks: 'Inside the World's Most Exclusive and Naughty Nightclub'.
39 at which they dressed up: John Aspinall threw one such party as late as 1985, to celebrate the Feast of Torgamba and herald the addition, to his home zoo, of a Sumatran rhino. His place in Kent was redressed for the festivities as a 'Polynesian bazaar', and costumed extras were hired to mingle with the guests. 'Michael Howells on Creating a Legendary Party', *British Vogue*, 28 Dec. 2016.
39 Alpha Nero had his own dedicated account: after my article about this case was published in *The New Yorker* in early 2024, the @Mr_Alpha_Nero account was made private.
40 'in Akbar's orbit': statement of Rachelle Gryn Brettler (witness), ZJB inquest.
40 in front of One Hyde Park: AS to PRK.
40 Trumpeted by its own: 'A Tale of Two Londons', *Vanity Fair*, 13 Mar. 2013.
40 Liechtenstein, the Cayman Islands and Liberia: 'One Hyde Park: Anybody Home?', *Sunday Times*, 20 Nov. 2011.
40 a Ukrainian billionaire: 'War Has Tamed Ukraine's Oligarchs, Creating Space for Democratic Change', *Washington Post*, 8 Dec. 2022; 'Libel Warriors', *Kyiv Post*, 11 Feb. 2011; 'English Courts in the Dock on "Libel Tourism"', *Financial Times*, 1 Apr. 2008.
41 spent £16 million at the shop: 'Zamira Hajiyeva: Wife of Jailed Banker Is Told to Explain Fortune', *Times*, 21 Dec. 2020.
41 to acquire property sight unseen: Hollingsworth and Lansley, *Londongrad*, p. 123.
41 the brothers borrowed £6,000: 'Transcript: Candy Says Property Buyers Want Dubai Luxury, Not London Crime', *Bloomberg*, 27 Apr. 2023; 'Candy Brothers: "One Day They Were Likely Lads, Then They Were Everywhere"', *Guardian*, 20 Oct. 2014.
41 an apartment in Belgrave Square: Hollingsworth and Lansley, *Londongrad*, p. 107; 'A Tale of Two Londons'.
41 became multimillionaires: Hollingsworth and Lansley, *Londongrad*, p. 113.
42 Jacuzzi on a private jet: 'Candy Brothers: "One Day They Were Likely Lads"'; 'The Upstarts' Empire', *New York Times*, 29 June, 2012.
42 'a vulgar symbol': 'A Tale of Two Londons'.
42 The writer Peter York: ibid.
42 'the Brothers Bling': 'How the Bitter Row Between Billionaire Candy Brothers and Businessman Mark Holyoake Escalated', *iNews*, 6 Oct. 2017.

42 dating back to 1799: 'The Madness of King George III's Non Dom Tax System', *Financial Times*, 1 Mar. 2015.
42 money they made in the colonies: Arun Advani et al., 'The UK's "Non-Doms": Who Are They, What Do They Do, and Where Do They Live?', CAGE Policy Briefing No. 36, April 2022.
42 London as 'the best tax haven': 'A Tale of Two Londons'.
42 His daughter, Isabella Monaco: 'Nick and Christian Candy, Ultra-luxe Property Developers', *Financial Times*, 3 Mar. 2017.
43 Porsche Cayman: 'Candy Brothers: "One Day They Were Likely Lads"'.
43 'most powerful woman in football': 'Marina Granovskaia: Chelsea's Fixer and the Most Powerful Woman in World Football', *Daily Telegraph*, 15 May 2014.
44 'Investment into R&D': ZJB to Antony Buck.
44 seemed older than his years: Antony Buck, interview by author.
45 brandished a thick stack of fifties: police debrief 12 Dec. 2019.
45 a successful television producer: 'Malcolm Craddock: Obituary', *Guardian*, 25 Aug. 2015.
46 offered Zac a place to stay: Méridien recording; recording of a telephone call between MB, RGB and Clive Strong, 2 Dec. 2019.
47 It was £850,000: recording of a telephone call between MB, RGB and Clive Strong, 2 Dec. 2019.
47 the oil and gas business: police debrief 12 Dec. 2019.
47 'this BS element to him': Méridien recording.
48 'People won't listen': police debrief 12 Dec. 2019.
48 he had complained that his parents: statement of Roger Howells, ZJB inquest.
48 'Sometimes it almost seems': RGB to Dr Giray Cordan, 1 Nov. 2018.
49 Dr Howells had cautioned: statement of Roger Howells, ZJB inquest.

CHAPTER 3: AN EDIFICE OF LIES

50 Paley's metal sculptures: 'Mind-Blowing Metalworks at Messums in London', *Financial Times*, 3 Nov. 2019.
51 Rachelle received an email: ZJB to RGB, 28 Nov. 2019.
51 'I don't mind as long': RGB to ZJB, 28 Nov. 2019.
52 tall Black man she did not know: CCTV footage, 29 Nov. 2019.
52 demanding to know who: RGB to ZJB, 29 Nov. 2019.
53 words seeming almost to slur: voicemail recording, 29 Nov. 2019, shared by RGB.
53 as many as fifty calls: 'How the Met Police Deals with Missing Persons Reports', *BBC News*, 13 July 2021.
53 Most of the missing: 'More than 36,000 Missing Person Reports Were Made in London Last Year', *Evening Standard*, 20 July, 2021.
54 a bushy black beard: 'Fishmongers' Hall Attacker Duped Prison Boss Over Extra-Large Coat That Hid Fake Suicide Belt', *Independent*, 29 Apr. 2021.
54 to attend a conference: 'Don't Let the London Bridge Attacks Destroy the Work of Its Victims', *Slate*, 5 Dec. 2019.
54 Khan had been convicted: 'London Bridge Stabbing Suspect Usman Khan Plotted to Attack London Stock Exchange in 2010', *ABC News*, 30 Nov. 2019.
54 But the authorities responsible: the circumstances of Khan's attendance and the events of the attack are reconstructed from a detailed account in Inquest Arising from the Deaths in the Fishmongers' Hall Terror Attack, Regulation 28 Report on Action to Prevent Future Deaths, Chief Coroner of England and Wales, 3 Nov. 2021.
55 proposed the Méridien: unless otherwise noted, details from this conversation come from a recording made by the Brettlers (Méridien recording).
56 a real estate venture: prospectus for Lion House real estate venture in Lisbon.
59 cavorting in a flurry: 'Oligarch Pays for Party That Enraged Putin', *Independent*, 16 July 2009.
61 operated a production facility in Turkey: '7 Turkish Fashion Designers in London You Need to Know', *Luxury London*, 27 Feb. 2017.
61 'You may be having': RGB to ZJB, 2 Dec. 2019.
62 stood by in silent terror: recording of a telephone call between MB, RGB and Clive Strong, 2 Dec. 2019.
63 started at the age of fourteen: this detail, which Akbar volunteered in an earlier

conversation with Rachelle, comes from Rachelle's account of that conversation in a discussion with Clive Strong and an associate of his on 2 Dec. 2019. (The Brettlers recorded the conversation.)

CHAPTER 4: MISSING PERSONS
68 decorated for Christmas: crime scene photos taken in and around Riverwalk, Dec. 2019.
68 As a Scotland Yard detective: unless otherwise noted, details related to Strong and his visit to Riverwalk are derived from an author interview with Clive Strong and from 'Meeting w Sharma', in Clive Strong's notes from 3 Dec. 2019.
70 'I have a feeling': recording of a telephone call between MB, RGB and Clive Strong, 2 Dec. 2019.
70 'If he burns every bridge': ibid.
70 'into the centre of their families': recording of a meeting between MB, RGB and Clive Strong, 2 Dec. 2019. On 2 Dec. the Brettlers spoke with Strong by phone, then went to meet Akbar at the Méridien, then went to meet Strong in person.
70 Strong had been cautioned: 'Meeting with Clients', Clive Strong's notes from 2 Dec. 2019.
70 Verinder was not wearing shoes: statement of PC Gemma Scott (witness), 6 Dec. 2019 (hereafter cited as 'GS statement').
72 Scott was a constable: ibid.
72 dressed in civilian clothes: statement of PC Judith McCabe (witness), 6 Dec. 2019 (hereafter cited as 'JM statement').
72 There were cranes: crime scene photo taken in and around Riverwalk, 3 Dec. 2019.
72 A few people were sitting: crime scene photo taken by Officers McCabe and Scott, 3 Dec. 2019.
72 Verinder had a cut: GS statement.
73 'Closed,' he said: ibid.
73 Was it really necessary: ibid.
73 His voice sounded 'quite shaky': JM statement.
74 Then suddenly she spotted: GS statement.
74 It was Zac's: JM statement.
74 purchased it at Harrods: MB and RGB, interviews by author.

CHAPTER 5: RIVER OF DEATH
76 'He is incredibly vulnerable': 'Family's Plea Over Happy Student Who Vanished on Christmas Eve', *Times*, 31 Dec. 2007.
76 Their attention soon turned: Baxter Willis, interview by author.
77 a passing bargeman: 'Missing Teenager Found in Thames', *BBC News*, 23 Jan. 2008.
77 At a subsequent inquest: 'Young Actor's Thames Death Stays a Mystery', *Evening Standard*, 12 Apr. 2012.
77 thirty or so bodies: 'Bodies Recovered from the River Thames from 2012 to 2022', Metropolitan Police, https://www.met.police.uk/foi-ai/metropolitan-police/disclosure-2023/march-2023/bodies-recovered-river-thames-2012-2022.
77 'The vast majority of these crimes': Peter Ackroyd, *Thames: The Biography* (Anchor, 2007), p. 382.
77 She came to be known: UK Missing Persons, Case 06-021036. See 'Lady in the Thames: Woman Who Drowned 45 Years Ago Linked to Leeds', *BBC News*, 1 Dec. 2022.
77 the great majority of deaths: 'Drowning Prevention Strategy', Tidal Thames Water Safety Forum, Port of London Authority, May 2019.
77 In a short story from 1853: Charles Dickens, 'Down with the Tide'. Originally published in *All the Year Round* 3, no. 62 (21 July 1860).
77 'The river is haunted': 'Watery Grave', *Guardian*, 14 Dec. 2004.
78 On the morning of Friday: unless otherwise noted, the account of Baxter Willis's discovery of Zac Brettler's body is drawn from Baxter Willis, interview by author, and Baxter Willis, statement to police, 29 Nov. 2019.
78 pale and ghostly: the description of Zac's body is based on several photos taken of the body in the moments after it was found, shared with me by Pino D'Amore.
79 He could see that: Pino D'Amore, interview by author.
79 'My patient was cold': statement of Jonathan Merryfield (witness), ZJB inquest.
80 examination by a pathologist: testimony of Dr Robert Chapman, ZJB inquest.
80 Police endeavoured to take fingerprints: statement of Detective Sergeant Alex Mallen (witness), 2 Aug. 2022.

81 'I cannot describe': RGB witness statement.
81 'I have the saddest news': RGB Facebook post, 3 Dec. 2019. (The funeral was ultimately held Sunday 15 Dec..)
82 The Paddington Wrecks, Matthew's football: MB eulogy.
83 'I think he was murdered': MB, interview by author.

CHAPTER 6: THE NIGHT IN QUESTION
84 Shamji presented himself: Akbar was subjected to a sequence of interrogations on two different dates. Unless otherwise noted, all material relating to this initial session comes from AS interrogation 1 and 2. (These interviews started on the night of 5 Dec. and continued into the early hours of 6 Dec..)
86 'I believe that Zac': statement of Verinder Kumar Sharma, 2 Dec. 2019.
86 But he refused to answer: unless otherwise noted, details from Sharma's abortive post-arrest interview come from VS interrogation 1.
89 So later that evening: AS interrogation 2.
89 At 1:25 a.m. on 29 November: the timing of Akbar's movements and the CCTV details are drawn from Akbar's police interrogations and from Rory Wilkinson's conversations with the Brettlers, in which the specific hours are noted, as well as from ZJB inquest.

CHAPTER 7: A FAMILY OF BRAVES
95 and now he vowed: '50 Years On from the Arrival of the Ugandan Asians', *Economist*, 18 Aug. 2022; 'Asians Given 90 Days to Leave Uganda', *BBC News*, 7 Aug. 1972.
95 Amin had already expelled: Mark Leopold, *Idi Amin: The Story of Africa's Icon of Evil* (Yale University Press, 2020), pp. 226–27.
95 Merchants from the subcontinent: Lucy Fulford, *The Exiled: Empire, Immigration and the Ugandan Asian Exodus* (Hodder & Stoughton, 2024), p. 29; Bert N. Adams and Mike Bristow, 'The Politico-Economic Position of Ugandan Asians in the Colonial and Independent Eras', *Journal of Asian and African Studies* 13, no. 3 (July 1978).
95 so the company imported: Fulford, *The Exiled*, p. 30.
95 Recruiting agents got to work: G. C. Whitehouse, 'The Building of the Kenya and Uganda Railway', *The Uganda Journal* 12, no. 1 (March 1948).
96 a three-year contract: ibid.
96 nearly forty thousand of these recruits: ibid.
96 laying track through swampland: H. F. Ward and J. W. Milligan, *Handbook of British East Africa* (Nairobi: Caxton B.E.A. Printing & Publishing, 1912), p. 29.
96 voracious man-eating lions: J. H. Patterson, *The Man-Eaters of Tsavo* (Macmillan, 1926), p. 20. This story is true, if no doubt subject to embellishment at the time. The lions were ultimately killed, and their hides transported to the Field Museum, in Chicago, where they reside today. In 2009, scientists tested their bone collagen and hair keratin and concluded that they were 'consistent with a progressive dietary specialization on humans'. See Justin D. Yeakel et al., 'Cooperation and Individuality Among Man-Eating Lions', *Proceedings of the National Academy of Sciences of the United States of America* 106, no. 45 (10 Nov. 2009).
96 nearly four people for each mile of track: Fulford, *The Exiled*, p. 31. Fulford puts the figure at 4 people for each mile; there were 660 miles of track, and 2,493 dead, so roughly 3.7 per mile.
96 'The Gateway to British East Africa': Ward and Milligan, *Handbook of British East Africa*, p. xxiii.
96 one account in 1912: ibid., p. 14.
96 tended to favour South Asians: Leopold, *Idi Amin*, p. 232.
96 controlled 90 per cent of: 'Ugandan Asians Dominate Economy After Exile', *BBC News*, 15 May 2016.
97 'war of economic liberation': Vali Jamal, 'Asians in Uganda, 1880–1972: Inequality and Expulsion', *Economic History Review* 29, no. 4 (Nov. 1976).
97 You could leave the country: '50 Years On from the Arrival of the Ugandan Asians'; 'From Entebbe to Stansted: The Flight of Uganda's South Asian Community', *Hyphen*, 1 Sept. 2023.
97 took possession of the grand residences: Leopold, *Idi Amin*, p. 232.
97 anxiously clutching their passports: Mahmood Mamdani, *From Citizen to Refugee: Uganda Asians Come to Britain*, 3rd ed. (Darajah Press, 2022), p. 12.
97 nearly the entire Asian population left:

the figures are frustratingly imprecise, with some accounts suggesting that the number of Ugandan Asians who left (and who were in Uganda to begin with) was lower, but it seems to have been about seventy thousand, virtually the whole population. See 'Ugandan Asians 40 Years On', National Archives (2012); and 'Ugandan Asians: 50 Years Since Their Expulsion from Uganda', House of Lords Library, 31 Aug. 2022.
97 Born 22 January 1972: AS interrogation 1.
97 two thousand people working: 'I Simply Became a Convenient Excuse for JMB's Downfall: Abdul Shamji', *India Today*, 15 Apr. 1987; 'Asian Hotelier Buys in Maida Vale', *Evening Standard*, 17 June 1982.
97 where Abdul had been born: 'Encounters', *Illustrated London News* 272, no. 7030 (May 1984).
97 to Uganda from Gujarat: ibid.
97 The Ismailis followed: see Willi Frischauer, *The Aga Khans* (Bodley Head, 1970); 'The Agha Khan IV, Wealthy Leader of the Ismaili Muslims, Dies at 88', *New York Times*, 6 Feb. 2025.
98 helped his mother in the shop: 'Abdul Shamji', *Illustrated London News*, 1 May, 1984.
98 sell ice cubes to the people: 'Empire Built on Ice Cubes', *Daily Record*, 1 Nov. 1989.
98 man offered to purchase the van: 'Abdul Shamji'.
98 textiles. Hotels. Marinas: ibid.; 'Stonefield's Exiled Saviour', *Observer*, 22 Mar. 1981.
98 a woman named Zarina: 'Upper Crust Asians', *Tatler*, Feb. 1985.
98 so overshadowed by him: Sanjiv Bhattacharya described Zarina as 'kind of an extra in that family'.
98 'everything blew up': 'Abdul Shamji'.
98 'milked the cow but did not feed it': 'Asians Given 90 Days to Leave Uganda'; Mamdani, *From Citizen to Refugee*, p. 7.
99 should think of that part of the world: Adams and Bristow, 'Politico-Economic Position of Ugandan Asians in the Colonial and Independent Eras'.
99 Amin had him thrown in jail: 'Abdul Shamji'.
99 Abdul managed to escape: ibid.
99 flights were departing: Fulford, *The Exiled*, p. 105.
99 A report from America's: 'Wider Implications of Uganda's Expulsion of Its Asians', memorandum, Central Intelligence Agency, 25 Oct. 1972.
99 There were fears: ibid.
99 erupt into cheers: Fulford, *The Exiled*, p. 116.
99 'Every colonial child': Mamdani, *From Citizen to Refugee*, p. 38.
99 twenty-eight thousand: '50 Years On from the Arrival of the Ugandan Asians'.
100 Prime Minister Edward Heath: ibid.
100 Enoch Powell had delivered: 'Rivers of Blood: The Lasting Legacy of a Poisonous Speech', *Economist*, 19 Apr. 2018.
100 'no connection with Britain': 'Asians Given 90 Days to Leave Uganda', *BBC News*, 7 Aug. 1972.
100 angry porters from Smithfield: Fulford, *The Exiled*, p. 99; 'Porters March to Stop Asians', *Kent Evening Post*, 24 Aug. 1972.
100 posters in Tube stations: untitled item, Associated Press, 9 Sept. 1977.
100 Physically assaulting Asian people: 'Britain: The Fire This Time', *Newsweek*, 13 Sept. 1976; untitled item on the Southall riots, Associated Press, 23 Apr. 1979; 'The Fire This Time for the British', *New York Times*, 14 Sept. 1980; 'Myths That Fuel the Fears', *Guardian*, 21 Apr. 1981. Also see the terrific three-part documentary *Defiance: Fighting the Far Right*, produced by Rogan Productions, GroupM Motion Entertainment, and Left Handed Films for Channel 4 (2024).
100 when a Sikh boy: *Defiance: Fighting the Far Right*.
101 (This gambit backfired): Mamdani, *From Citizen to Refugee*, p. 39.
101 'a family of braves': *World in Action*, season 23, episode 6, 'A Most Unsatisfactory Customer', part 2, investigated by Michael Gillard, aired 27 Oct. 1986, on ITV.
101 'For an Asian man': 'Indians Making It in Britain', *Chicago Tribune*, 28 Apr. 1985.
101 sixteen refugee camps: Fulford, *The Exiled*, p. 121; Mamdani, *From Citizen to Refugee*, p. xxiv.
101 In later years, Abdul Shamji would occasionally: *World in Action*, season 23, episode 5, 'A Most Unsatisfactory Customer', part 1, investigated by Michael Gillard, aired 20 Oct. 1986, on ITV.
101 England with 'virtually nothing': the phrase 'virtually nothing' is from 'Eastern

Promise of Trade', *Manchester Evening News*, 1 June 1983; he indicated to the *Illustrated London News* that he had 'little money' when he arrived; the claim is refuted in 'A Most Unsatisfactory Customer', part 1.
101 Instead, they moved: 'A Most Unsatisfactory Customer', part 1; 'Upper Crust Asians'.
101 'lost much of my empire': 'Indians Making It in Britain'.
101 crockery, cutlery and Johnnie Walker: 'Abdul Shamji'; 'Stonefield's Exiled Saviour'.
102 to play the board game Monopoly: 'Indians Making It in Britain'.
102 Within four years: 'A Most Unsatisfactory Customer', part 1.
102 'the best salesman': ibid.
102 He invested in a metalworks: 'Feeding Crocodiles to the USM', *Evening Standard*, 13 May 1983.
102 a 176-room hotel: 'Asian Hotelier Buys in Maida Vale'; 'Upper Crust Asians'.
102 'Uganda's loss was': 'Asian Hotelier Buys in Maida Vale'.
102 the economy collapsed: '50 Years On from the Arrival of the Ugandan Asians'; Leopold, *Idi Amin*, p. 2.
102 a later prime minister: Fulford, *The Exiled*, p. 1.
102 pumped £5 million: 'The Offshore World of Stonefield's Rescuer', *Observer*, 10 May 1981.
102 established commercial vehicle makers: 'Going, Going, Gomba!', *Mirror*, 12 Dec. 1983.
102 in swept Abdul Shamji: 'Stonefield's Exiled Saviour'.
102 Abdul offered to pay: 'A Most Unsatisfactory Customer', part 1.
103 In a publicity photo: 'Stonefield's Exiled Saviour'.
103 purred ridiculous questions: 'Margaret Thatcher: Cumnock Visit Recalled 42 Years On', *Cumnock Chronicle*, 23 Apr. 2023.
103 gamely climbed aboard: 'A Most Unsatisfactory Customer', part 1.
103 displayed it prominently: 'Empire Built on Ice Cubes'.
104 the party of Enoch Powell: Powell had by this point abandoned the Conservative Party because of its support for Britain's entry to the European Economic Community. He became a member of the Ulster Unionist Party.
104 Abdul hosted a dinner: 'A Most Unsatisfactory Customer', part 1.
104 'Whenever anybody swims': ibid.
104 vice president of the Small Business Bureau: ibid.
104 a 'miracle man': 'Who Is the Liar', *Daily Mirror*, 9 Nov. 1989.
104 'a prototype of the Asian immigrant': 'Empire Built on Ice Cubes'.
105 permitted to visit him at the hospital: 'A Most Unsatisfactory Customer', part 1; 'Tebbit and the Wizard of Gomba', *Mirror*, 5 Dec. 1985.
105 the Aga Khan had: 'The Story of "K",' *Vanity Fair*, June 1988.
105 six hundred horses: ibid.
105 in every bedroom: 'The Edmundsbury', real estate brochure, Coombe Residential; 'Upper Crust Asians'.
105 frugal self-restraint: Jamal, 'Asians in Uganda, 1880–1972'.
106 installed a miniature train: Larissa MacFarquhar, interview by author; Sanjiv Bhattacharya, interview by author.
106 shots of Abdul with his close friend: 'Upper Crust Asians'.
106 Alsatian dogs, and servants: John Waite, 'The Unpleasantness at the Mermaid', produced by Graham Ellis, *Face the Facts*, BBC Radio 4 (28 Sept. 1994).
106 to play Monopoly: 'Upper Crust Asians'.
106 taken him to the movies: Jack Ponti, interview by author.
106 97 Park Lane: 'Upper Crust Asians'.
106 empty apartments upstairs: 'A Most Unsatisfactory Customer'.
107 rented to the filmmakers: this is a quote from Phil Méheux, in the documentary *Bloody Business: Making the Long Good Friday* (Anchor Bay Entertainment, 2006), which is available on YouTube at https://www.youtube.com/watch?v=YUlEYELf1vY.
107 help of a jumbo mortgage: 'Upper Crust Asians'.
107 He borrowed heavily: 'A Most Unsatisfactory Customer', part 1.
108 about his lending philosophy: Anthony Sampson, *The Changing Anatomy of Britain* (Coronet, 1983), p. 313.
108 'He was entertaining them': 'A Most Unsatisfactory Customer', part 1.
108 All fifty employees: 'Going, Going, Gomba!'

108 'the ultimate patter merchant': 'Gomba Boss Shamji Jailed', *Daily Record*, 1 Nov. 1989.
108 was *itself* a subsidiary: 'Going, Going, Gomba!'; 'Offshore World of Stonefield's Rescuer'.
109 Shamji was not available: 'Move to Unravel Stonefield Plant Mystery', *Scotsman*, 31 Dec. 1983.
109 as the 'peak': 'Reversal of Fortune', *Independent*, 29 May, 1993.
109 Britain's 'Upper Crust Asians': 'Upper Crust Asians'.
109 to purchase Wembley Stadium: 'Wembley Final for Gomba', *Times*, 21 Jan. 1985.
109 the Empire Stadium: Sathnam Sanghera, *Empireland: How Imperialism Has Shaped Modern Britain* (London: Penguin, 2021), p. 7.
109 self-glorifying, privately published: 'A Most Unsatisfactory Customer', part 2.
109 'take over the business': 'Upper Crust Asians'.
109 A gang of thieves: 'The Heist', *Guardian*, 16 Nov. 2003; Neil Forsyth and Thomas Turner, *The Gold: The Real Story Behind Brink's-Mat* (Ebury, 2023), pp. 5–16.
110 Tokyo, Johannesburg and Dubai: 'Three Plead Innocent to Britain's Biggest Robbery', Associated Press, 29 Oct. 1984.
110 Black had tipped them off: 'The Heist'. Before his death, McAvoy would claim to Neil Forsyth and Thomas Turner that he had *not* been surprised by the volume of gold that day, because he'd been tipped off that there would be 'two tonnes'. But I don't find this assertion especially convincing. See 'Two Tons of Yella: First and Last Interview with Brink's-Mat Robber', *Sunday Post*, 19 Mar. 2023.
110 got his start as a schoolboy: Forsyth and Turner, *The Gold*, p. 32; Wensley Clarkson, *The Curse of Brink's-Mat* (Quercus, 2013), p. 28.
110 in used banknotes: 'The Heist'.
110 doused them with gasoline: 'Three Plead Innocent to Britain's Biggest Robbery'.
110 threatened to castrate: 'The Heist'.
111 called Johnson Matthey: 'Guard Gives Details of British Gold Robbery', *New York Times*, 18 Feb. 1984.
111 roughly twenty tonnes: Forsyth and Turner, *The Gold*, p. 14.
111 'need another van': ibid., p. 15.
111 riding dangerously low: 'The Heist'; Clarkson, *Curse of Brink's-Mat*, p. 75.
111 worth £1 million more: *Brinks Mat: The Greatest Heist*, written by Mark Hayhurst, directed by Bruce Goodison, originally aired on Channel 4 (2003). A 1983 report suggested that the amount of gold was too small to move the market before acknowledging that the price did climb, because according to traders, 'The theft seemed to have had a psychological impact on the market.' 'Bullion Stolen in Record Theft', Facts on File World News Digest, 2 Dec. 1983.
111 'The only way you're gonna': 'Two Tons of Yella'.
111 exactly what Black did: 'Guard Gives Details of British Gold Robbery'.
111 to provide a false alibi: 'Airport Bullion Raiders Given 25 Years Each', *Guardian*, 4 Dec. 1984.
112 back into the gold market: Forsyth and Turner, *The Gold*, p. 52.
112 the very company it had been stolen from: ibid., p. 78.
112 a London woman: 'Granny Launders $6M and Earns 5 Years in Jail', *Herald Sun*, 18 Aug. 1992; 'Scotland Yard Still Probes Britain's Biggest Gold Robbery', Associated Press, 16 Mar. 1987; 'Brinks-Mat Booty "Put into Property",' *Guardian*, 12 Apr. 1988; 'Docklands "Profit for Gold Robbers",' *Guardian*, 2 July 1991.
112 redevelopment of the Docklands: 'Scotland Yard Still Probes Britain's Biggest Gold Robbery'; 'Brinks-Mat Booty "Put into Property"'; 'Docklands "Profit for Gold Robbers".'
112 Brink's-Mat funds: Forsyth and Turner, *The Gold*, pp. 216–18.
112 'fucked for my money': 'Robber "Sent Death Threat from Prison",' *Guardian*, 15 Apr. 1988.
113 In 1985, a detective: 'Murdered Policeman Was Investigating $36 Million Gold Robbery', Associated Press, 29 Jan. 1985.
113 car park with an axe in his head: 'The Curse of Brinks-Mat', *Mail Online*, 5 May, 2012.
113 his home near Marbella: 'Fool's Gold', *Mirror*, 12 May 2012.

113 pulled up on a motorcycle: 'Hitman Blamed for Killing of London Businessman', *Independent*, 4 Jan. 1993.
113 yacht off Corfu: 'Avast There! Pirates Return to the High Seas', *Independent*, 27 Sept. 1996.
113 a North London jeweller: 'A Quiet Suburban Street, a Gangland Hit, and the Death of Solly Who?', *Independent*, 5 Dec. 1998.
113 making outsized loans: 'Shock Waves Rock Financial Community: Bank's Near Collapse May Put an End to Britain's Clubby Financial Regulations', *Los Angeles Times*, 22 Sept. 1985.
114 would sometimes joke: 'A Most Unsatisfactory Customer', part 1.
114 to lend him £35 million: ibid., part 2.
114 £20 million to Johnson Matthey: 'Shamji Owned Raid Vaults', *Observer*, 19 July 1987; 'Shock Waves Rock Financial Community'.
114 'appalling and bizarre record': ibid.
114 director named Ian Fraser: 'Shamji Owned Raid Vaults'; 'Shock Waves Rock Financial Community'; 'A Most Unsatisfactory Customer', part 1.
114 Sedgemore had a reputation: 'Brian Sedgemore: Obituary', *Guardian*, 26 May 2015.
115 as a love nest: 'I'm No Crook Says Banker', *Sunday Sun*, 10 Nov. 1985.
115 quid pro quo 'sex romps': 'Secrets of Women in Bank Scandal', *Sunday People*, 8 Dec. 1985.
115 'he might be a simpleton': HC Deb. (6th ser.) (27 July 1985) (83) cols. 1442–50.
115 had not been influenced: 'Shamji Says He Is "Scapegoat",' *Sunday Telegraph*, 10 Nov. 1985.
115 he described as a 'crook': 'I'm No Crook Says Banker'.
115 made a scapegoat: 'Shamji Says He Is "Scapegoat".'
116 tried to 'buy' him: 'Tycoon Denies Claim', *Evening Sentinel*, 19 Dec. 1985.
116 was a family man: 'Shamji Says He Is "Scapegoat".'
116 'corruption, fraud, and tarts for bankers': 'Fury Over "Tarts for Bankers" Attack', *Mirror*, 9 Nov. 1985.
116 interest in Wembley: 'Shamji Says He Is "Scapegoat".'

116 the house did not belong: 'A Most Unsatisfactory Customer', part 2.
116 'champagne, clothes and jewellery': ibid.
116 'neither practicable nor reasonable': HC Deb. (6th ser.) (20 Jan. 1986) (90) col. 86W.
117 Michael Hendry was interviewed: 'A Most Unsatisfactory Customer', part 1. I should note that while *World in Action* spells his last name with a 'y', certain other sources spell the last name 'Hendrie'. See for instance, 'Johnson Matthey Calls in Receiver at Gomba', *Financial Times*, 29 Oct. 1985. Despite a lot of trying, I was unable to speak with Hendry myself.
117 most famous barristers: 'Millionaire Admits Perjury Charge', *Guardian*, 31 Oct. 1989.
117 he had 'few assets': '£1,000 Fine for Businessman Accused over JMB Collapse', *Scotsman*, 13 Nov. 1985.
118 had no Swiss bank account: 'Millionaire Admits Perjury Charge'.
118 Six of them: 'Millionaire Jailed for Lying During Inquiry into Wealth', *Courier and Advertiser*, 1 Nov. 1989.
118 'You lied like a trooper': 'Gomba Boss Shamji Jailed'.

CHAPTER 8: PRODIGAL SON
119 had been diagnosed: an initial diagnosis in 1982 was confirmed in 1985. 'Ali: Still Magic', *New York Times*, 17 July 1988.
119 a million punches: 'Thoughts of Ali: Victim of Sport He Saved', *New York Times*, 23 Sept. 1984.
119 Diana Ross and Whitney Houston: 'Muhammad Ali's 50th Birthday Celebration (Full Special)', originally aired 1 Mar. 1992, on ABC, posted 12 Jan. 2024, by Clown Jewels, YouTube, https://www.youtube.com/watch?v=jzsAf3VArXA.
120 'down to Puddle Wharf': 'Oyez! Bernard Is Bringing Glitter to Puddle Dock', *Daily Mirror*, 18 Oct. 1956; deed from Henry Walker to William Shakespeare and his Trustees, 10 Mar. 1613, available at the Folger Shakespeare Library's online archive Shakespeare Documented.
120 pockmarked with bomb sites: 'Bomb Site Boy Killed as Roof Collapses', *Daily Mirror*, 15 Feb. 1958; 'Plan for Bomb Sites to Ease Car Parking', *South London Observer*,

23 Dec. 1958; Simon Jenkins, 'The Blight Around Blackfriars', *Illustrated London News*, 30 Oct. 1971.
120 a kind of junkyard: 'Thames Beachcombers', *Scotsman*, 16 Aug. 1948.
120 'It sprawls muddily': 'Oyez! Bernard Is Bringing Glitter to Puddle Dock'.
120 hallowed ground where Shakespeare: 'Mozart Brick', *Birmingham Daily Gazette*, 18 Oct. 1956.
120 he sold bricks: 'Mermaid Theatre Campaign', *The Stage*, 12 Sept. 1957; 'Mermaid Theatre Appeal', *The Stage*, 26 Sept. 1957.
121 building was finally complete: the opening of the theatre was in March 1959. 'Mermaid Theatre', *Belfast Newsletter*, 29 Aug. 1957; 'Mermaid Theatre', *East End News & London Shipping Chronicle*, 24 Jan. 1958; 'New Theatre for the New Year', *The Stage*, 25 Dec. 1957. There are conflicting reports of the exact number of seats, but in 1993 *The Times* put it at 610. 'Going for a Technical Knockout', *Times*, 9 June 1993.
121 Julie Walters to Ian McKellen: John Waite, 'The Unpleasantness at the Mermaid', produced by Graham Ellis, *Face the Facts*, BBC Radio 4, 28 Sept. 1994.
121 a tenner apiece: Waite, 'Unpleasantness at the Mermaid'.
121 their own savings: Alan Strachan, *Adventurer: Bernard Miles and the Mermaid Theatre* (Wordville Press, 2023), p. 188.
121 'The richest square mile': ibid., p. 62.
121 'more venal world': ibid.
121 Miles was desperate: 'Reversal of Fortune', *Independent*, 29 May 1993; Waite, 'Unpleasantness at the Mermaid'.
121 had outstanding debts: Strachan, *Adventurer*, p. 183.
121 Abdul was able: 'Reversal of Fortune'; Strachan, *Adventurer*, p. 185.
122 ninety-seven-year lease: ibid., p. 185.
122 His big inaugural production: 'Reversal of Fortune'.
122 He played a swindler: 'At the Theatre', *West Cambridgeshire Town Crier*, 8 Dec. 1990.
123 Akbar got around: Sanjiv Bhattacharya, interview by author.
123 Their name was Muthafunk: ibid.
123 'whistling as he strides': 'Going for a Technical Knockout'.
123 as a dire injustice: Marc Sinden, interview by author.
123 'Let me remind you that *Gomba*': 'I Simply Became a Convenient Excuse for JMB's Downfall', *India Today*, 15 Apr. 1987.
124 'his Monopoly board': 'Reversal of Fortune'.
124 trying to reclaim all the holdings: Tony Breen, interview by author.
124 hold on to the Mermaid: 'Mermaid Sits Pretty as Gomba Pays Up', *The Stage*, 28 Apr. 1988.
124 a man named Marc Sinden: unless otherwise noted, details relating to Marc Sinden's tenure at the Mermaid come from multiple author interviews with Sinden.
124 'psychology of the world of commerce': 'Reversal of Fortune'.
124 with beams and bricks: 'Upper Crust Asians'; 'The Edmundsbury', real estate brochure, Coombe Residential.
125 The champ wanted £10,000: Breen, interview. Unless otherwise noted, details relating to Tony Breen and his dealings with the Shamji family come from this interview.
125 former boxer turned businessman: Breen, interview. Breen's memory is of contributing £30,000, but according to a contemporaneous account, it was £35,000. 'Ugandan Discussions', *Evening Standard*, 17 June 1994.
126 in a white Rolls-Royce: 'Ali Still Draws Fans', *Cleveland Plain Dealer*, 18 June 1993.
126 as a fundraising gala: 'Former Boxing Champion Ali Mobbed by Fans', Press Association, 17 June 1993.
126 Akbar was beaming: photo shared by Tony Breen.
126 in a glass case: 'Ali Gloves Stolen', Press Association, 21 June 1993.
126 'feel cavernously empty': 'Going for a Technical Knockout'.
126 thieves broke into the Mermaid: 'Ali Gloves Stolen'.
127 merely a holding company: 'Mermaid Braced for Legal Onslaught', *The Stage*, 9 June 1994.
128 often failed to pay: Waite, 'Unpleasantness at the Mermaid'.
128 run to the bank: ibid.
128 couldn't purchase the light bulbs: ibid.
128 'a very psychedelic effect': ibid.

128 ran out of toilet paper: ibid.
128 Shamjis had neglected the oil bill: ibid.
129 'if you had something, you had to pay for it': *World in Action*, season 23, episode 5, 'A Most Unsatisfactory Customer', part 1, investigated by Michael Gillard, aired 20 Oct. 1986, on ITV.
129 could apply for a change of use: 'Mermaid Faces Closure Threat as City Corporation Gets Tough', *The Stage*, 10 Sept. 1987.
130 the family didn't actually pay: Waite, 'Unpleasantness at the Mermaid'.
130 the Shamjis simply dissolved: 'Beta Claims Mermaid Money Has Run Out', *The Stage*, 31 May 1990.
130 this one called Comfortcall: Waite, 'Unpleasantness at the Mermaid'.
131 Bettina Jonic, who ran: ibid.
131 fired by the Shamjis: 'Sinden Is Sacked', *The Stage*, 2 June 1994.

CHAPTER 9: SUSPICION OF MURDER

132 Thirty-two new cases: 'Chief Medical Officer (CMO) Professor Chris Whitty Statement on 32 New Cases of COVID-19', Department of Health and Social Care, 4 Mar. 2020, https://www.gov.uk/government/news/cmo-for-england-announces-32-new-cases-of-novel-coronavirus-4-march-2020.
132 panicked shoppers stockpiling: 'UK Supermarkets Draw Up Plan to "Feed the Nation" as Coronavirus Spreads', *Guardian*, 2 Mar. 2020.
132 prospect of a lockdown: 'Coronavirus: Action Plan', Department of Health and Social Care (UK Government), 3 Mar. 2020.
132 'while singing Happy Birthday': 'Boris Fails to Convince with Sanitised Take on Coronavirus', *Guardian*, 3 Mar. 2020.
132 'I don't want your coronavirus': 'Police Investigate Alleged Coronavirus-Linked Attack on London Student', *Guardian*, 3 Mar. 2020.
132 they knew he was lying: AS interrogation 2.
132 'It's a nice bit of the river': ibid.
133 cold, wet, miserable: London weather report for 4 Mar. 2020, Weather Spark.
134 'a cut and dried suicidal jump': AS interrogation 2.
134 'There are some inconsistencies': unless otherwise noted, material from Akbar's next set of police interviews comes from AS interrogation 3, which took place at Charing Cross Police Station on 4 Mar. 2020.
136 Akbar sent him a message: AS to ZJB, 27 Nov. 2019, cited in NW statement.
138 'No, bro,' Akbar replied: ibid.
138 a message to a family group: Daniela Karnuts's message from 29 Nov. 2019, cited in AS interrogation 3, and in NW statement.

CHAPTER 10: THE GREAT SHAM

140 The saxophonist of Muthafunk: unless otherwise noted, details relating to Sanjiv Bhattacharya's experiences with Akbar Shamji come from Sanjiv Bhattacharya, interviews by author.
141 most successful musicals: 'Turn Again, Gillian', *Guardian*, 7 Dec. 1999; 'London Production of *Cats* to Close on May 11', *Playbill*, 15 Jan. 2002; '*Cats* Ends Historic Run at Bway's Winter Garden', *Playbill*, 11 Sept. 2000.
141 glamorous life, with homes: 'Dancer Gillian Does the Splits', *Daily Mail*, 26 June 1997; 'I Knew from the Start He Would Leave Me', *Mail on Sunday*, 23 Jan. 2000; '"My Life Is One Big Battle",' *Daily Telegraph*, 6 Mar. 2001.
141 speculation in the press: to quote *The Guardian*: 'The marriage lasted 18 years, after which time Land left, amid press speculation about his alleged homosexuality and a mercenary attempt to wrest half her fortune from her.' 'Turn Again, Gillian'.
141 'hadn't quite found himself': ibid.
142 Peter Land would later assert: though Land is never described in any press accounts of Soulife as one of its founders, his biography on the website of the Lynne & Land Foundation asserts that he 'co-founded' the company in 1999; https://lynneandlandfoundation.co.uk/.
143 Sparks hailed from Wadesboro: 'Soulife Label Aspires to Be Motown South', *Charlotte Observer*, 13 May, 2001.
143 a loose consortium: 'Let the Sunshine In', *Soul and Jazz and Funk*, 16 Dec. 2010.
143 some forty people: 'Soulife Label Aspires to Be Motown South'.
143 Dawley told *Billboard*: 'Indie Label

Soulife Aims to Expand on Soul Legacy of Motown, Stax', *Billboard*, 21 Oct. 2000.
143 'Why's Akbar running around': Bhattacharya, interview.
143 ambitious slate of projects: 'Indie Label Soulife Aims to Expand'.
145 'like Batman and Robin': 'Soulife Records: Going Behind the Label That Brought Us Sunshine', *Gavin*, 25 May 2001.
145 a music industry veteran: Jack Ponti, interview by author.
146 together with his wife: 'Back in Step', *Daily Mail*, 14 July 2003.
147 'I am not fucking playing': AS to Mervin Sealy, 28 Nov. 2019, cited in NW statement.
147 'Shit's about to go wrong': ibid. Akbar and Mervin were using WhatsApp and alternating between voice memos and text messages. This last one from Akbar was a voice memo.

CHAPTER 11: A JIGSAW IN THE DARK
148 entering his 'anecdotage': Naomi Gryn, ed., *Three Minutes of Hope: Hugo Gryn on the God Slot* (Continuum, 2010), p. 15. The portrait of Hugo Gryn is based on his own writings and interviews he gave during his life, and on conversations with his four children: Rachelle, Naomi, Gaby and David.
148 one of Hugo's folksy parables: there are different versions of this story; in some, the man is presenting himself at the gates of heaven. See Hugo Gryn with Naomi Gryn, *Chasing Shadows: Memories of a Vanished World* (London: Viking, 2000), p. 6; Gryn, *Three Minutes of Hope*, pp. 28–29.
148 Yiddish, Czech, German or Hebrew: Gryn with Gryn, *Chasing Shadows*, p. 38.
148 culling the plums: ibid., pp. 19–20.
149 a glass of slivovitz: ibid., p. xxv.
149 prepare boiled cabbage: ibid., p. xxvi.
149 didn't have an ending: ibid.
149 muttering under his breath: Rabbi Hugo Gryn, oral history, 1986, Imperial War Museum, Catalogue No. 9280, Reel 3.
149 Géza would forfeit: Gryn, *Three Minutes of Hope*, p. 22.
149 'I suppose I got to': ibid., p. 21.
149 Hugo saw a truck: ibid., pp. 22–23.
150 Géza died of typhoid: ibid., p. 6.
150 Prestwick Airport, in Scotland: ibid., p. 31.
150 milking cows at a Scottish: ibid., p. 4.
150 'to get a place at a university': ibid.
150 aspect of Hugo's life story: see, for instance, 'Rabbi Hugo Gryn: A Childhood', *Times*, 31 July 1993; Hugo Gryn, interview by Sue Lawley, *Desert Island Discs*, BBC Radio, 10 July 1994; 'Auschwitz Survivor Hugo Gryn Is Appalled', *Herald* (Scotland), 15 Oct. 1995. A remembrance by his friend Michael Freedland in 2016 notes that at sixteen Hugo 'gained a scholarship to study maths at Cambridge'; 'Hugo Gryn: Everyone's Chief Rabbi', *Jewish Chronicle*, 26 May 2016.
150 purple-and-white Cambridge scarf: RGB, interview by author; Naomi Gryn, interview by author.
150 the historian Martin Gilbert: 'Rabbi Hugo Gryn: Obituary', *Times*, 20 Aug. 1996.
151 Gilbert telephoned Rachelle's sister: Naomi Gryn, interview.
151 popular BBC radio programme: *Desert Island Discs*.
152 is incredibly common: Christian L. Hart and Drew A. Curtis, *Big Liars: What Psychological Science Tells Us About Lying and How You Can Avoid Being Duped* (American Psychological Association, 2023), pp. 13–14.
152 once or twice a day: Bella M. DePaulo et al., 'Lying in Everyday Life', *Journal of Personality and Social Psychology* 70, no. 5 (1996); Hart and Curtis, *Big Liars*, p. 13.
152 'middle-aged' as a teenager: Gryn, *Three Minutes of Hope*, p. 20.
156 a pair of ten-pointed stars: the specific temporary tattoo set he purchased was 'Russian Prison Set', from the website Tattooed Now: https://www.tattooednow.com/products/russian-prison-set.
156 'I'm your neighbour': Zamira Ismailova's interactions were described to me by Ismailova and substantiated by the WhatsApp messages she exchanged with Zac. The description of the meeting between Rachelle and Zamira is based on interviews with both women.
157 'Chef made sushi': all of the following text messages are taken from screenshots that Zamira Ismailova shared with RGB, who shared them with me.
159 'no such thing as reproduction': Andrew Solomon, *Far from the Tree: Parents, Children, and the Search for Identity* (Scribner, 2013), p. 1.

160 called a clinical psychologist: recording of a phone call between RGB and Dr Giray Cordan, undated.

CHAPTER 12: LIGHTS OUT
161 an old friend of Rachelle's: Jeannie Lorenz, interview by author.
163 a middle-aged detective inspector: unless otherwise noted, details from this meeting are drawn from police debrief 12 Dec. 2019.
163 thirty-three thousand officers: 'The Structure of the Met', 'About the Met', Metropolitan Police, https://www.met.police.uk/police-forces/metropolitan-police/areas/about-us/about-the-met/structure.
163 six pages, single-spaced: MB notes prepared for police, Dec. 2019.
164 registered as a director: Axx Solutions Limited, Company Number 11726494, listing on Companies House, https://find-and-update.company-information.service.gov.uk/company/11726494/officers.
165 'Nick Gold pays for that apartment': Matthew related this detail to the police shortly after it happened. Police debrief 12 Dec. 2019.
165 a performance by Boy George: '"I Can Never Marry You Enough Times",' *Daily Mail*, 5 Nov. 2018.
165 more of a 'fantasy friend': police debrief 12 Dec. 2019.
166 Brettlers were also alarmed: MB notes prepared for police, Dec. 2019.
166 suspended the examination: police debrief 9 Nov. 2021; testimony of Dr Robert Chapman, ZJB inquest.
167 plunged into darkness: statement of Detective Sergeant Alex Mallen (witness), 2 Aug. 2022; VS interrogation 2.

CHAPTER 13: THE LITTLE FELLA
168 physique, once lean and strong: 'Brinks Fat', *Sunday Mirror*, 23 Nov. 2003.
168 a helicopter would land: 'Two Tons of Yella: First and Last Interview with Brink's-Mat Robber', *Sunday Post*, 19 Mar. 2023.
168 gymnasium of Leicester Prison: Neil Forsyth and Thomas Turner, *The Gold: The Real Story Behind Brink's-Mat* (Ebury, 2023), p. 268.
168 through a shell corporation: 'Brink's-Mat Robbers Sought Deal "to Stall Yard Search for Gold",' *Guardian*, 13 Apr. 1988; 'How Mossack Fonseca Helped Hide Millions from Britain's Biggest Gold Bullion Robbery', *Guardian*, 4 Apr. 2016. The property was Turpington Farm, in Bickley.
168 lead them to the missing gold: 'Treasure Hunt for Stolen Gold', *Sunday Express*, 2 Dec. 2001.
169 as many as a hundred major British criminals: Forsyth and Turner, *The Gold*, p. 188.
169 Murderers, drug runners, sex offenders: 'Crimestoppers Takes on Costa Gangsters', *Guardian*, 31 Oct. 2006; 'Britain's 10 Most Wanted Men at Large in Costa del Crime', *Guardian*, 22 Feb. 2011.
169 rechristened the area: 'Crackdown on Brits Thriving on the Costa del Crime', *Birmingham Post*, 31 Oct. 2006; 'Why Spain's Costa del Crime Is Now the Worst Place to Go on the Run', *Daily Telegraph*, 13 May 2013.
169 through Europol or Interpol: a former British law enforcement official who worked at the UK's Serious Organised Crime Agency and National Crime Agency, interview by author.
169 'a real rigamarole': Keith Butler, interview by author.
169 'cut off' from the old: 'Two Tons of Yella'.
170 'a very well-respected man': RV testimony.
170 cause blood to clot: Matthew Collin, *Altered State: The Story of Ecstasy Culture and Acid House* (Serpent's Tail, 2009), p. 22.
170 At the Starck Club: Collin, *Altered State*, pp. 29–32; Torsten Passie, *The History of MDMA* (London: Oxford University Press, 2023), pp. 99–103; 'The King of X', *Texas Monthly*, May 2025.
170 unlicensed parties in underground clubs: 'Reality of Ecstasy; Latest "Designer" Drug', *Times*, 7 Nov. 1988; 'Acid House Without the Acidity', *Guardian*, 4 Jan. 1990; 'The Acid Test for Acid House', *Independent*, 23 May 1990; Passie, *History of MDMA*, chaps. 9 and 10.
170 fully licensed nightclubs: 'The Hip List', *Sunday Times*, 24 Nov. 1991; 'Raving Madness', *Times*, 22 Feb. 1992.
171 'golden age for armed robbery': 'Where Did All the Bank Robbers Go?', *Guardian*, 4 July, 2014.

171 'I first met Dave': unless otherwise noted, material relating to Andy Baker comes from Andy Baker, interviews by author.
171 Verinder's father: birth certificate of Verinder Kumar Sharma.
172 opportunity for upward mobility: 'Indian Workers Strike Spreads', *Red Mole Reporter*, 13 Nov. 1972; 'Racism Among U.K. Workers; Indians on Strike', *Times of India*, 14 Dec. 1972.
172 white employees had protested: 'Lifting the Veil at T'mill', *Guardian*, 12 Mar. 1973.
172 Loughborough prospered: 'Industrial Output Increasing', *Financial Times*, 8 Feb. 1984.
172 a few thousand pounds: 'Asians in a British Mill Striking for Right to Better Jobs', *New York Times*, 27 Dec. 1972; 'Industrial Output Increasing'.
172 hundreds of Indian workers: 'Indian Workers Strike Spreads'; 'Racism Among U.K. Workers; Indians on Strike'.
172 a red-brick factory: 'Asians in a British Mill Striking'.
172 two older brothers: it took me a while to confirm the identities of Verinder's older brothers, but they are Vinod Kumar Sharma and Vijay Kumar Sharma, and they have a Loughborough company called Flora Designs Limited. They did not respond to my interview requests.
172 on charges of forgery: this information is drawn from confidential law enforcement files relating to Verinder Sharma.
172 running security firms: RV testimony; Baker, interview.
173 sticking an unsuspecting stranger: 'ID: Who Was the London Gangster Behind the Death of a Public Schoolboy?', *Upsetter*, 29 Feb. 2024.
173 tried to ban him: ibid.
173 a young club owner: unless otherwise noted, material related to Howard Spooner comes from Howard Spooner, interviews by author.
174 accosted him with a machete: 'A Gangland Killing, Lap Dancers Who Are Said to Sell Sex and the Criminal Past of the Man Behind the Spearmint Rhino Empire', *Evening Standard*, 16 Sept. 2002.
174 the Metropolitan Police suspected: 'ID: Who Was the London Gangster?'

175 in thirty-three different prisons: 'Jails "Ghost" Tells of Suffering', *Independent*, 3 June, 1991.
175 'what I could endure': 'Switching of Disruptive Prisoners "Inhumane",' *Guardian*, 6 May, 1991; 'Jails "Ghost" Tells of Suffering'.
175 murdered a police constable: 'Yardie Who Was Prime Suspect in PC's Murder to Give Evidence at Inquest', *Evening Standard*, 2 Nov. 1998.
175 just finished murdering somebody else: Mike Pannett and Kris Hollington, *Crime Squad: Life and Death on London's Front Line* (Thistle, 2016), p. 73; 'How a Bobby's Killer Got Away with Murder', *Daily Mail*, 5 Dec. 1998.
175 Witnesses heard him laughing: 'How Scotland Yard Helped Snitch', *Mirror*, 9 Jan. 2022; 'Touching Tribute to an Unarmed Bobby', *Mail Online*, 20 Oct. 2023.
175 citing a 'lack of evidence': 'Fury as PC Death Cases Are Dropped', *Mail on Sunday*, 6 Feb. 1994.
175 'a hold over the community': 'Gangster Jailed for PC Death "May Have Killed Four Others",' *Evening Standard*, 12 July 2016.
175 'Looks to have been suicide': 'Eight Years Jail for Road Rage Gunman', *Evening Standard*, 16 Aug. 1995; 'How a Bobby's Killer Got Away with Murder'.
175 Tyson was driving: 'Road Rage Motorist Shot at Me, Driver Tells Court', Press Association, 9 Aug. 1995.
175 festooned in bling: 'PC Murder Suspect to Walk Free', *Mirror*, 20 July 1999.
176 with a snooker cue: Pannett and Hollington, *Crime Squad*, p. 252.
176 He was transferred: 'PC Murder Suspect to Walk Free'.
176 'most dangerous man': Pannett and Hollington, *Crime Squad*, p. 197.
176 'as a killing machine': Butler, interview.
176 he was released: 'PC Murder Suspect to Walk Free'; 'He Is One of Britain's Most Vicious Gangsters', *Mirror*, 14 Aug. 1999.
176 often serve only half: new criminal justice reforms enacted in 2025 further reduced the average time served by stipulating that prisoners in England and Wales can be eligible for release after serving a third of their sentences, though officials maintained that this would not apply to the most serious offenders. 'Prisoners to Be Eli-

gible for Release After Serving a Third of Sentence', BBC, 22 May 2025.
176 new table-dancing club: 'Underdressed, Over the Top and Over Here', *Independent*, 7 Oct. 1995.
176 champagne and lap dances: 'Real Lives: Dirty Dancing', *Observer*, 17 Dec. 1995.
176 three-hundred-seat venue: 'Meet the WPC Who Threw Away Her Uniform', *Evening Standard*, 18 Sept. 1997; 'The Politics of Dancing', *Guardian*, 27 Mar. 1999.
176 emptying ashtrays and serving drinks: 'Real Lives: Dirty Dancing'.
176 just telephone the club: RV testimony.
176 they had two daughters: birth records for Dominique Elizabeth Sharma Clarke, born Dec. 1996, and Matisse Ellie Sharma Clarke, born Sept. 2000.
176 taken when Dominique was a little girl: family photograph posted by Dominique Sharma Clarke on Facebook, 1 Jan. 2016.
176 who was a dancer: Baker, interview; author interview with another longtime friend of Verinder Sharma.
176 Tara One and Tara Two: Baker, interview; RV testimony.
176 he had a son: birth record of Chanze Mosey Sharma, born Feb. 2002.
176 'not a very active parental role': testimony of Dominique Sharma Clarke, ZJB inquest.
177 spent time in prison: John Rollinson, *Gaffer* (John Blake, 2003), p. 205; 'Hoddesdon Gym Victim's Past Revealed', *Evening Standard*, 9 Oct. 2003.
177 produced a ten-inch knife: Rollinson, *Gaffer*, p. 214.
177 bodyguard for celebrities: RV testimony; 'Bodybuilder Murder Trial Jury Out', BBC, 22 Aug. 2005.
177 'this geezer came swaggering': Rollinson, *Gaffer*, p. 205.
177 had no fixed abode: RV testimony.
177 some of his belongings: ibid.
177 photo of Muscles and Verinder: the photo was published in 'Journey of AK47 from War Zone to a Killing in the Shires', *Times*, 27 Aug. 2005.
177 shipment of fourteen kilos: RV summing up; 'Murder of Muscles', *Mirror*, 24 Aug. 2005; RV case summary.
177 he would kiss a photo: Baker, interview.
177 dropping all charges: RV summing up.

178 'He's a grass!': ibid.
178 McAvoy spoke of informants: Wensley Clarkson, *The Curse of Brink's-Mat* (Quercus, 2013). p. 59.
178 all charges were dropped: RV summing up.
178 two guns used: 'Gangster Who Laughed After Shooting PC Gets 35 Years', *Guardian*, 17 Feb. 2006.
178 a black-market supplier: 'The Shield: Scotland Yard Protected Gangland Grass Who Helped Kill Cop', *Upsetter*, 8 Jan. 2022; 'Police "Highest Level" Corruption Probe Over Guns Sold to Murder Cop Killer', *Mirror*, 25 June 2022.
178 Wink was suspected: 'Curse of Brinks Mat', *Independent*, 3 July 2015.
178 later found dead in an alley: 'The Shield'; Pannett and Hollington, *Crime Squad*, pp. 258–59; Steve Richardson, author interview.
178 plant a listening device: RV testimony; Pannett and Hollington, *Crime Squad*, p. 265.
178 that sounded like a weapon: RV testimony; Pannett and Hollington, *Crime Squad*, p. 265.
179 one of the lead investigators: Butler, interview.
179 'Get out of London': 'Did King's Threat Lead to His Murder?', *Hertfordshire Mercury*, 22 June, 2005.
179 'I'd take that very serious': RV testimony.
179 a man named Graeme Hammond: unless otherwise specified, details relating to the Graeme Hammond case come from interviews with Andy Baker and with Dennis Phelan, the lead detective in the case, who testified at the trial, as well as a witness statement Graeme Hammond provided to the police on 9 Mar. 2002; a substantial file of legal documentation related to the case that was supplied by one of the attorneys involved; and 'Nightclub Boss "Taken Hostage for £150,000"', Press Association, 11 June 2003.
179 flyers for nightclubs: 'Men Cleared After Kidnap Plot', *Ipswich Star*, 26 June 2003; Baker, interview; statement of Graeme Hammond (witness), 9 Mar. 2002.
180 the services of Andy Baker: 'Club Owner Tells of Terror Ordeal', Press Association, 12 June 2003.

180 subsequent court testimony: ibid.; 'Men Cleared After Kidnap Plot'; Graeme Hammond Witness Statements, 9 Mar. 2002. 'ID: Who Was the London Gangster?' I have interviewed Andy Baker, Howard Spooner (who was in touch with Baker during the trial) and Dennis Phelan, the lead detective in the case, and the real motivations here are difficult to parse, but this was happening during a period when different nightclubs were being bundled into businesses that could be sold to publicly traded companies. So I think there were two things going on in this case: there was the immediate shakedown of Hammond — his watch, his cars, his cash — but there was also a more ambitious agenda involving the acquisition (by persuasion or by force) of what amounted to undervalued assets; underperforming nightclubs that could be bundled and flipped.
180 Baker and Verinder Sharma knocked: unless otherwise noted, the details of Hammond's ordeal are from statements of Graeme Hammond (witness), 9 Mar. 2002, and 21 Mar. 2002.
181 As Hammond said later: 'Nightclub Boss "Taken Hostage for £150,000".'
181 codefendants burst into laughter: Baker, interview.
181 To put up the surety: ibid.
181 Somebody had torched it: interviews with Dennis Phelan and another former law enforcement official.
182 to acquit all three defendants: 'Three Cleared over Imprisoning Nightclub Owner', Press Association, 25 June 2003.
182 director of a professional football team: 'Last Defendants Cleared in Q.P.R. Conspiracy Case', *Guardian*, 28 June 2006.
182 six to eight months' time: 'Anthony Arlidge KC Obituary', *Times*, 11 Feb. 2023.
182 fourteen acquittals: Baker, interview.
183 Patel had a passport: interview with a former law enforcement official.
183 'on a desert island': RV testimony.
183 a place in Cannes: Sharma's apartment was above what used to be a Diesel boutique, at 154 rue d'Antibes.
183 'over there on his own': RV testimony.
183 his other gangland nickname: ibid.

184 still very much in danger: Butler, interview; RV summing up.
184 'The Little Fella's with me': RV testimony.
184 'coast had been made clear': RV summing up.
185 Five days a week: RV case summary.
185 an armed robber from Manchester: 'Murder of Muscles'.
185 'They were twice as big': RV case summary.
185 'one-tenth of the arsehole': ibid.
185 At 7:15 the following morning: ibid.
185 few plastic chairs: Hertfordshire Constabulary, 'Operation Sphinx', undated PowerPoint presentation.
185 killed almost instantly: RV case summary.
185 cover in the footwell: RV summing up.
186 peeled off in the white van: 'Murder of Muscles'.
186 piercing blue eyes: RV case summary.
186 AK-47 variant with two handles: Hertfordshire Constabulary, 'Operation Sphinx'.
186 originated in Hungary: 'Journey of AK47'.
186 marked the first time in history: 'Two Jailed for Life for AK-47 Drive-by Murder of Gangster', *Guardian*, 23 Aug. 2005.
186 twenty-six armour-piercing bullets: 'Journey of AK47'.
186 Sharma finally returned: he returned on 28 Oct. 2003. RV summing up.
186 sentence of three months in Brixton: ibid. Interviews with friends of Sharma confirm that he served this time at Brixton.
186 detectives arrested Roger Vincent: RV case summary.
186 Ample forensic evidence: Hertfordshire Constabulary, 'Operation Sphinx'.
186 'had fallen out with an Indian man': RV summing up.
186 for an audience with Micky McAvoy: RV testimony. Prosecutors discussed a recorded phone call on 1 Sept. 2003, between Gary Nelson and Roger Vincent, in which Vincent hands the telephone to Sharma. Vincent said that he then flew from France to Spain to meet with McAvoy on 3 Sept.
187 'What about Dad?': RV testimony.
187 helicopter hung in the sky: 'Drive-by

Assassins Are Jailed for Life', *Hoddesdon and Broxbourne Mercury*, 26 Aug. 2005. Some of these details come from an author interview with someone who participated in the trial.
187 a man named Robert Magill: 'Man "Executed" Walking His Dog', *Independent*, 13 Oct. 1994.
187 Lavers made a submission: statement of Barry Paul Lavers, undated, in which he describes Vincent as a former employee at his plumbing business turned close friend, maintains that 'Roger is a completely trustworthy and honest person', and discusses taking a trip with Vincent to Tenerife in Sept. 1994, several weeks before the killing. Through an intermediary, Lavers declined my request for an interview.
187 long-standing ties to Roger Vincent: 'Mystery Files Cast Doubt Over Verdict on Robert Magill Gangland Killing', *Guardian*, 8 Oct. 2011. Detective Spackman ended up going to prison himself, in 2003. 'Murder Conviction Reviewed by Police', *Guardian*, 27 July 2003.
187 Lane always fiercely protested: Kevin Lane, interview by author. Also see his book about the long effort to clear his name: Kevin Lane, *Fitted Up and Fighting Back* (independently published, 2021).
187 pinstriped suit: author interview with someone who participated in the trial; 'Drive-by Assassins Are Jailed for Life'.
187 'I've been around crooks': RV testimony.
188 because he was at home: ibid.; RV summing up.
188 'I saw him in the morning': RV testimony.
188 'We're both mad on golf': ibid.
188 it was in Hoddesdon: Hertfordshire Constabulary, 'Operation Sphinx'; interviews with two retired law enforcement officials who were involved in the case. Vincent's rebuttal, for what it's worth, was that this discrepancy could be explained because a different friend happened to have borrowed his phone that morning.
188 three minutes after the shooting: RV testimony; Hertfordshire Constabulary, 'Operation Sphinx'.
188 'This is a tit-for-tat': 'Murder of Muscles'.
188 'Job done. He's dead': RV testimony.
189 a banner that read WANTED: 'Wanted, Hoddesdon and Broxbourne Mercury', 26 Aug. 2005.
189 In a press briefing: 'Drive-by Assassins Are Jailed for Life'.
190 'petrified about coming back': RV testimony.
190 Eventually Micky McAvoy: RV summing up.
190 'If you've got two convicted': Butler, interview.
191 to follow a trail of crosses: Pannett and Hollington, *Crime Squad*, pp. 257–59.
191 cocaine, blackmail: '10-Man Gang Behind £500K Drug Factory', *Bristol Post*, 3 Dec. 2018.
191 an old Clash song: 'Unmasking the Cornerman', episode 1 of *The Cornerman*, Bristol Cable, https://thebristolcable.org/series/cornerman/episode/unmasking-the-cornerman.
191 'bully-boy tactics': '10-Man Gang Behind £500K Drug Factory'.
192 'I want 5% of that 205 million': VS to AS, 28 Nov. 2019, cited in NW statement; also discussed in AS interrogation 3.
192 'I'm thinking fuck this little kid': AS interrogation 3.
192 'He's not allowed to run': ibid.
192 'witness protection uk': NW statement.
192 'Prove that this isn't': VS interrogation 2.

CHAPTER 14: THE CIPRIANI FIVE

197 a charismatic hustler: Heidi Blake, *From Russia with Blood: Putin's Ruthless Killing Campaign and Secret War on the West* (William Collins, 2019), p. 76.
197 as a drug dealer: ibid., pp. 29, 36.
197 On the oligarch's behalf: ibid., pp. 68, 77.
198 extravagant gifts: 'Did Scot Young and His High-Rolling Friends Really Die by Their Own Hands?', *Tatler*, 22 Jan. 2018.
198 purchased an Agusta helicopter: Blake, *From Russia with Blood*, pp. 84, 123; '"If You Find Me Dead, It Won't Be an Accident",' *Daily Mail*, 18 July 2009.
198 known as the Cipriani Five: 'Did Scot Young and His High-Rolling Friends'; 'Scot Young's Wife Calls for New Inquiry into Businessman's "Murder" in Wake of Spy Poisoning', *Daily Telegraph*, 8 Mar. 2018.
198 hiding a fortune: '"Only £20m – That's Disgraceful": Tycoon Scot Young's Wife

Reacts Furiously to Divorce Ruling – and Vows to Fight for More', *Independent*, 22 Nov. 2013.

198 an onscreen caption: *Ladies of London*, season 1, episode 1, 'My Fair Ladies of London', aired 2 June 2014, on Bravo.

199 using a fountain pen: 'Russian Spies Plot to Kill Tycoon in Britain', *Times*, 21 Sept. 2003.

199 a sudden heart attack: Blake, *From Russia with Blood*, pp. 118–19.

199 a massive fireball: ibid.; 'Life and Death of Stephen Curtis', *Sunderland Echo*, 27 Aug. 2004.

199 'If anything happens': Blake, *From Russia with Blood*, pp. 119–21.

199 ruled the death an accident: 'Jury Rejects Sabotage Theory in Helicopter Crash', *Guardian*, 2 Nov. 2005. See also 'Did Moscow Order the Death of the Oligarchs' London Lawyer?', *Independent*, 3 Mar. 2024.

199 hastily cancelled his order: Blake, *From Russia with Blood*, p. 123.

199 whisked out of Britain: 'IMO's Ponomarev, 41, Dies', *American Shipper*, 29 Oct. 2006; 'The Man Who Knew Too Much,' *BuzzFeed*, 19 June 2017.

199 laced with radioactive polonium: 'Alexander Litvinenko: Profile of Murdered Russian Spy', *BBC News*, 21 Jan. 2016.

200 two different knives: 'The Man Who Knew Too Much'.

200 police investigation concluded: 'Litvinenko Expert Took His Own Life', *Times*, 25 Nov. 2016.

200 'Britain asks few questions': Mark Hollingsworth and Stewart Lansley, *Londongrad: From Russia with Cash, the Inside Story of the Oligarchs* (Fourth Estate, 2009), p. 28.

200 carelessly exposing random hotel: Owen Dyer, 'More Cases of Polonium-210 Contamination Are Uncovered in London', *British Medical Journal*, 13 Jan. 2007.

200 One afternoon in 2010: 'Polo Playing Friend of Prince Charles Throws Himself in Front of Tube Train After Business Is Hit by Recession', *Daily Mail*, 20 Nov. 2010.

200 to carry a Geiger counter: Blake, *From Russia with Blood*, p. 114.

200 favourite cashmere scarf: ibid., pp. 273–74.

200 quickly closed the case: ibid., p. 274.

201 plunged to his death: 'Trinny Woodall's Ex-Husband, His Fatal Fall and a Doomed Circle of Friends', *Daily Telegraph*, 7 Nov. 2015; 'Family of Trinny's Ex: "We Should Have Been Told of Suicide Attempts",' *Evening Standard*, 12 Nov. 2015.

201 he phoned the police: Blake, *From Russia with Blood*, p. 249.

201 telephoned his daughters: ibid., p. 283.

201 nothing to investigate: ibid., p. 282.

201 had been not a suicide: Young's girlfriend Noelle Reno was more ready to believe that his death was a suicide. 'Noelle Reno on Why She Believes Her Ex-Fiancé, Scot Young, Was Driven to Suicide by the Russian Mob', *Times*, 1 July 2018.

202 scrape marks left by fingers: Blake, *From Russia with Blood*, p. 284.

202 identifying fourteen men: 'From Russia with Blood: 14 Suspected Hits on British Soil That the Government Ignored', *BuzzFeed*, 15 June, 2017.

202 Half of the police stations: 'This Is Why Scotland Yard Is in Disgrace: Bad Policing and Penny-Pinching Politicians', *Guardian*, 29 June 2022.

202 failing in almost all work areas: 'Met Failing in Almost All Work Areas', BBC, 15 Aug. 2024; HMICFRS, *Police Effectiveness, Efficiency and Legitimacy, 2023–25: An Inspection of the Metropolitan Police Service*, 15 Aug. 2024.

202 investor in Russia's energy sector: Blake, *From Russia with Blood*, p. 16.

202 One national security adviser: ibid.

203 extending carte blanche: Duncan Allen, *Managed Confrontation: UK Policy Towards Russia After the Salisbury Attack* (Chatham House, 2018), https://www.chathamhouse.org/2018/10/managed-confrontation-uk-policy-towards-russia-after-salisbury-attack.

203 a nerve agent in the English city: 'A Spy Story: Sergei Skripal Was a Little Fish. He Had a Big Enemy', *New York Times*, 9 Sept. 2018.

203 'looked expensive': 'Novichok Victim Found Substance Disguised as Perfume in Sealed Box', *Guardian*, 24 July 2018; 'Novichok Inquiry: Who Was Dawn Sturgess and How Was She Poisoned?', *BBC News*, 29 Oct. 2024.

203 That same year, another Berezovsky ally: 'Murder of Kremlin Critic in London

"Was Made to Look Like Suicide",' *Guardian*, 9 Apr. 2021.
203 Zac Brettler had been fascinated: recording of a telephone call between MB, RGB and Clive Strong, 2 Dec. 2019.
204 Verinder was the only person: police debrief 9 Nov. 2021.
204 citizens in Putin-era Russia: Blake, *From Russia with Blood*, p. 10.
205 'Akbar the family man': police debrief 25 Nov. 2020.
206 'There was no chance of Zac': ibid.
207 Safiya posted a picture: Safiya (@safiyashamji), photo, on Instagram, 29 Nov. 2020.
207 'that will go down in history': 'Why Meghan Markle's Final Evening Look "Exuded Power" – and Takes After Another American Royal', *People*, 10 Mar. 2020.
207 'languid tunics': 'Daniela Karnuts of Luxury Fashion Brand, Safiyaa', *Forbes*, 10 May 2021.
209 Wilkinson began by: unless otherwise noted, dialogue and details from this conversation are from police debrief 9 Nov. 2021.
210 There was talk of a 'football agent': these details are mentioned by Wilkinson but also cited in NW statement.
211 'on suicide watch': NW statement.
213 'sceptical about this 205 million': AS to VS, 28 Nov. 2019, cited in NW statement.
213 'Ask him how much': VS to AS, 28 Nov. 2019, cited in NW statement.
213 'not speak to him at all': AS to ZJB, 27 Nov. 2019, cited in NW statement.
213 'fifty per cent of everything': VS to AS, 29 Nov. 2019, cited in NW statement.
213 internet search for 'what to do with skin burns': NW statement.
214 a younger sister, Sonia: details about the life and death of Sonia Troop (née Selby) are from author interviews and text exchanges with RGB, Naomi Gryn and Gaby Massey.
215 on the 1984 thriller: *The Evil That Men Do* is Sonia's lone IMDb entry.
216 doctors who saw Young: Blake, *From Russia with Blood*, p. 149.

CHAPTER 15: PRIVATE INVESTIGATIONS
219 sat down with the proprietor: the reconstruction of this meeting is based on MB, interview by author, and Pino D'Amore, interview by author.
219 Matthew had received an email: John Sweeney to MB, 17 Nov. 2021. In a subsequent conversation with me, Sweeney initially denied asking for £20,000, but upon reflection he did acknowledge having done so. 'I would need as a freelance journalist to earn a living,' he explained in an email. 'My thinking was something like £2,500 for a thorough report which tackled gangsters and the Met. If they wanted more, say, a podcast or a book, which they would control, then that might cost something like £20,000. Those numbers reflect my estimate of my time, a month at the low end, a year, more at the top. They were abstract, based on my experience as a freelance and a podcaster, and only ever conditional.' John Sweeney to PRK, 6 June 2025. (The Brettlers have no memory of the smaller £2,500 figure being mentioned.)
220 boxes of Cipriani pasta: this description is based on author's visit to the café and on photos shared with the author by Pino D'Amore.
221 Nunes had only just: statement of Ana Nunes, 2 Mar. 2020, subsequently presented in ZJB inquest.
222 'I would like not to get involved': text from Bogdan to MB, 7 Feb. 2022.
222 Tibor, from Hungary: the account of the meeting with Tibor is based on MB and RGB, interviews by author. Tibor did not respond to requests for comment.
222 in Akbar's telling, that he: AS interrogation 1.
222 The doormen 'all knew him': AS interrogation 3.
223 'He did not give me any reason': statement of Ana Nunes, 2 Mar. 2020.
223 Gold had been banned: 'Four Jockeys Banned', *Daily Telegraph*, 15 Dec. 2011; 'TV Chef Aldo Zilli's Daughter Laura Is Divorcing Her Businessman Husband Nick Gold Who's Gone Bust with Debts of £22 Million – Just Two Years After Their Star-Studded Miami Wedding', *Daily Mail*, 8 Dec. 2020.
224 cheap road salt was fraudulently:

'Freeze! Briton Accused of Swedish Ice Melting Con', *Times*, 3 Nov. 2018.

224 an infamous erotic cabaret: 'Harry and the Den of Debauchery', *Daily Mail*, 19 Feb. 2011.

224 He was famously partial to cocaine: though Gold did not respond to this characterization specifically in a fact-checking query that was put to him, he did generally dispute the tenor of my questioning. But his fondness for cocaine and gambling was attested to by multiple people who know him in interviews with me. In a 2023 article in *The New Yorker*, Ben Taub wrote of Gold:

> [He] did lots of cocaine and dazzled guests with card tricks... 'I used to go up to Oxford Street when I was seventeen and I would hustle people,' he told me. 'Some sucker would come, like you, and you'd lose.' In the decades since, he has been banned from casinos for counting cards.

Elsewhere in the article, Gold tells Taub, of himself: 'I'm doing coke, I'm off my mind, I'm going drinking like a lunatic.' 'The Price of Belief', *New Yorker*, 6 Mar. 2023.

224 Nick Gold had been friends: Nick Gold, interview by author.

224 'are sort of best friends': Méridien recording. He also said this to the police: AS interrogation 3.

225 as much as £22 million: 'TV Chef Aldo Zilli's Daughter Laura Is Divorcing'.

225 spending time on the Côte d'Azur: 'Wirecard and Me: Dan McCrum on Exposing a Criminal Enterprise', *Financial Times*, 3 Sept. 2020.

225 Zac's phone records indicated: NW statement.

225 'Oliver is a pussy': VS to AS, cited in AS interrogation 3. Met detectives, having reviewed the communications of Zac, Akbar and Verinder, noted that 'it may be the case that Oliver Harris was involved in the business deal with Zac and Verinder', but they could not say so conclusively. NW statement.

225 'I didn't know he': AS to VS, cited in AS interrogation 3.

226 'put some force on him': AS interrogation 3.

226 recently been robbed: 'Meeting with Clients', Clive Strong notes, 2 Dec. 2019.

227 between Indian Dave and the death of Robbie Curtis: I have subsequently been able to confirm that Robbie Curtis owed money to Verinder, and Verinder did send men to dangle him off a building. I spoke to somebody who was present. He emphasized that Curtis owed money to numerous people and specified that Verinder had nothing to do with his death, which this person blamed squarely on 'the Russians'.

227 Verinder had instructed Oliver: VS to Oliver Harris, 29 Nov. 2019.

228 'He doesn't acknowledge him': interestingly, during the fact-checking of this book, Joe maintained that the brothers did acknowledge each other in some fashion. If this is the case, then it must have been a subtle enough exchange to not register on the CCTV.

232 *The Times* ran a report: 'Dirty Cash Pays Fees at Top Private Schools', *Times*, 19 Feb. 2022.

232 'The halcyon days of the oligarchs': 'What the Russian Oligarchs Did Next', *Daily Telegraph*, 13 Jan. 2023.

232 Even Roman Abramovich: Foreign, Commonwealth and Development Office (UK), 'Abramovich and Deripaska Among 7 Oligarchs Targeted in Estimated £15 Billion Sanction Hit', press release, 10 Mar. 2022. After receiving a special licence to complete the transaction, Abramovich sold the team to a consortium of American investors in May 2022, for £2.5 billion. There was a stipulation by the UK government, however, that the funds should be directed to Ukrainian humanitarian aid. Abramovich has resisted this, saying that the money should go to 'all victims of the war in Ukraine'. As of this writing, the UK government has threatened legal action against the oligarch and the funds remain frozen in an account pending resolution of this impasse. 'UK Threatens to Sue Abramovich to Release Frozen Money from Chelsea Sale', Reuters, 3 June 2025.

232 with a rowdy chant: 'Chelsea Fans Chant Roman Abramovich's Name During Ukraine Tribute at Burnley', Sky Sports, 6 Mar. 2022.

232 In a sequence of letters: MB and RGB to the CPS London, 4 Feb. 2022; Lisa Mayne to MB and RGB, 14 Feb. 2022; Christian Meikle to MB and RGB, 22 Feb. 2022.

232 'Sadly, a meeting cannot be': Lisa Mayne to MB and RGB, 14 Feb. 2022.
232 Wilkinson expressed his sincere: all dialogue from this meeting with Wilkinson comes from a transcript of the meeting, with MB, RGB, Rory Wilkinson and Phil Lane, on 16 Feb. 2022.
235 arranged for a maid service: statement of Detective Sergeant Alex Mallen (witness), 2 Aug. 2022.
236 the special pathologist: ZJB inquest.

CHAPTER 16: POCKET DIAL
238 One day in December 2022: ZJB inquest. The reconstruction of the inquest is based in part on interviews with MB, RGB, David Gryn, Andrew Fingret and one other person who attended. David Gryn also took notes during the proceeding.
240 to the University of Exeter: details of Dominique Sharma Clarke's educational and professional background are from 'Dominique Sharma Clark', LinkedIn profile (since deleted).
241 a family meal on Sundays: this detail is from VS inquest.
241 a gangster and club owner: this characterization of Trevor Floyd Smith is based on interviews with Andy Baker and Howard Spooner, both friends of his.
241 convicted cocaine trafficker: 'ID: Who Was the London Gangster Behind the Death of a Public Schoolboy?', *Upsetter*, 29 Feb. 2024.
241 an all-terrain vehicle in New Zealand: 'Two Men Killed in Ranfurly Quad Bike Crash Identified', *New Zealand Herald*, 2 Apr. 2019.
244 'She's Sharma's daughter': David Gryn, interview by author.
247 'arrest more criminals than': 'Sir Robert Mark Obituary', *Guardian*, 1 Oct. 2010.
247 Operation Tiberius identified: 'Operation Tiberius', Strategic Intelligence Report, Metropolitan Police, March 2002.
248 'about to expose a south London': 'Daniel Morgan: How a 30-Year-Old Murder Still Haunts Britain's Powerful', *Guardian*, 10 Mar. 2017.
248 establishing that 'institutional corruption': *The Report of the Daniel Morgan Independent Panel* (House of Commons), June 2021, https://www.gov.uk/government/publications/daniel-morgan-independent-panel-report.
248 no suspect has been: 'No Officers Will Face Punishment, Says Police Watchdog', *Guardian*, 3 Aug. 2022.
248 'could have been a police informer': transcript of meeting with MB, RGB, Rory Wilkinson and Phil Lane, 16 Feb. 2022.

CHAPTER 17: A DIFFERENT LIGHT
250 as Verinder had explained to: police debrief 25 Nov. 2020.
251 going to Land's home: 'The Dead Teenager, the Lying Suspect and the Black Box That Proves It', *Sunday Times*, 6 Apr. 2024. After arriving at 1:58 p.m., Akbar stayed for two and a half hours.
251 'Sending you lots of love': the following text messages between AS and Peter Land are cited in NW statement and discussed at length in AS interrogation 3.
252 with a 'No comment': VS interrogation 2.
253 'Is someone coercing him': David Gryn, interview by author.
253 a single sperm: police debrief 9 Nov. 2021.
253 'Was it like "Daddy"': ibid.
254 Wilkinson noted gingerly: ibid.
254 produced a document: 'Zachary Brettler iPad Summary', Appendix 83 in Metropolitan Police investigation of the death of Zachary Brettler.
257 Dylan was barely out of his: 'Sixty Years Ago Today, Bob Dylan Kicked Off His Career with a Made-up Backstory for WNYC', *Gothamist*, 29 Oct. 2021; 'Birthday Boy', *New Yorker*, 6 May, 2001. For the actual details of Dylan's childhood, see Robert Shelton, *No Direction Home: The Life and Music of Bob Dylan* (Backbeat Books, 2011), chap. 1.
257 'I don't know my parents': 'A Lighter Side of Bob Dylan', *Independent*, 24 May, 2021.

CHAPTER 18: HORNET'S NEST
258 'I now call Akbar Shamji': ZJB inquest.
258 'chief vision officer': a website that Akbar Shamji previously maintained said that he was Bitzero's founder and chief vision officer: CPEC (website), https://cpec

.io/visionary (website no longer available). His LinkedIn profile suggests that he was 'Founder, Chairman and CEO'.

258 'We're torn between Fargo': 'Bitzero Data Centers Planned in North Dakota: "Data Is the New Oil",' *InForum*, 1 June 2022.

258 raised nearly $100 million: ibid.

258 'Data is the new oil': ibid.

259 runway shows in Milan: as he explained on his Instagram, @akbarshamji, 'When I was 16, Tom Ford was my first major casting. Now two years later, very grateful to walk the #TOMFORDSS23 show to end @nyfw – my first fashion week', Instagram post, 15 Sept. 2022.

259 posed in the fragrance aisle: Instagram post by Akbar Jr, 4 Sept. 2023.

259 showrooms in Hong Kong: 'Daniela Karnuts of Luxury Fashion Brand, Safiyaa', *Forbes*, 10 May 2021.

259 training at the Lee Strasberg Institute: Safiya Shamji actor profile, Backstage (website), https://www.backstage.com/u/safiya-shamji.

264 Grieving families frequently: Jessica Jacobson, Lorna Templeton and Alexandra Murray, *'I Needed More than Answers': Bereaved People's Expectations of the Coronial Process*, project report, Institute for Crime and Justice Policy Research, University of Birkbeck, and Centre for Death & Society, University of Bath, May 2024.

265 'Coroner falling asleep': David Gryn notes taken during ZJB inquest.

266 A startled, naked Akbar: this account is based on interviews with five witnesses: MB, RGB, David Gryn, Andrew Fingret and one other person who attended the inquest.

CHAPTER 19: A CHANCE ENCOUNTER

271 At Leeds University: unless otherwise noted, details relating to Andrew Fingret come from multiple author interviews with Fingret and with MB and RGB.

272 celebrated her fortieth birthday: this account of Daniela Karnuts's birthday is based on the video and photos posted on Instagram by Safiya Shamji (@safiyashamji) on 14 Jan. 2023, and on an interview with a confidential source.

273 Oswald's was a fashionable venue: the account of Oswald's is based on 'Party Central', *Guardian*, 1 Feb. 2025, and 'Join the Likes of Guy Ritchie...', *Tatler*, 5 Dec. 2024, and on an interview with a confidential souce.

273 'Brexit sex dungeon': 'How 5 Hertford Street Became the Most Influential Members' Club in London', *Evening Standard*, 12 Dec. 2019.

273 Daniela stood, her face aglow: Safiya Shamji posted photos and a video of this scene on her Instagram account, with the caption 'very special birthday ♥'. Akbar Jr commented, 'I surprised mum by coming from Milan for the night when I told her the day before that I wouldn't be able to.' Safiya Shamji (@safiyashamji), Instagram post, 14 Jan. 2023. (This account was subsequently made private.)

277 ripping up hundred-dollar bills: 'Peter Thiel Shreds $100s and Mocks the Unwashed Masses at Crypto Conference', *Gizmodo*, 7 Apr. 2022.

277 'the new kid on the block': 'Bitcoin's Next Evolution Is to Become a Reserve Currency – Akbar Shamji', interview by David Lin, posted 21 Apr. 2022, by Kitco News, YouTube, https://www.youtube.com/watch?v=FknB5ilpoV8.

277 missing progress benchmarks: author interview with an executive who was involved with Bitzero during AS's tenure.

277 'big announcement': Marc Sinden, interview by author.

278 Bitzero's board asked Akbar to resign: Interview with Carl Agren (who was appointed interim CEO).

278 'Shamji has a history of': Due Diligence Investigation: Akbar Abdulhamid Jamal Shamji, prepared by TD International, 30 Oct. 2023.

278 this one called DarkByte: 'AI Meets Renewable Energy: DarkByte Teams Up with Hewlett Packard Enterprise to Deliver an AI Cloud', PR Newswire, 15 Nov. 2023.

278 'after my daughter': 'Exclusive: Meet Meghan Markle's German Designer!', *RTL Today*, 25 Oct. 2018.

278 a woman named Megan McLaughlin: I was able to gather some of Megan McLaughlin's family background from the obituary of her mother, Bette Jean McLaughlin, on the website of the Champion Funeral Home, Sheridan, Wyoming,

https://www.championfh.com/obituaries/bette-jean-mclaughlin. My efforts to speak to Megan were unsuccessful.
278 'She was white. She was American': François Pham-Quang, interview by author.
278 ended up getting sued: *Coomes v. Shamji*, U.S. District Court for the Central District of California, 05-CV-3483. The musicians were Erick T. Coomes and Erick Walls.
278 Akbar skipped town: Allen Hyman, interview by author.
278 According to Jack Ponti: Jack Ponti, interview by author.
279 posted a snapshot: Megan Mclaughlin Shamji, Facebook post, 19 May 2018.
279 entered a default judgment: the judge in *Coomes v. Shamji*, Percy Anderson, found for the plaintiffs in a default judgment entered 3 Mar. 2006, ruling that Coomes was entitled to a judgment of $378,977 and Walls was entitled to a judgment of $338,563, 'for breach of contract and fraud'. Judgment, *Coomes v. Shamji*, U.S. District Court for the Central District of California, 1 Mar. 2006. Shamji's appeal was denied. *Coomes v. Shamji*, 260 F. App'x 988 (9th Cir.), 26 Dec. 2007.
279 could not identify any assets: Erick Coomes, Allen Hyman and Adrian Davies, interviews by author.
279 because he was 'broke': AS to Sarah Cato, 23 Feb. 2014.
279 'Shamji's position was': Davies, interview.
279 formally declared bankruptcy: in the Matter of Akbar Abdulhamid Jamal Shamji, Bankruptcy Order in the High Court of Justice, Business and Property Courts of England and Wales, 5 Feb. 2019.
280 'That's my wife's address': AS interrogation 1.
280 'Zac had built an extraordinary': AS to PRK, email message, 12 Dec. 2023. This was the first response I had from Akbar, and it was followed by a sustained back-and-forth via email over the next several weeks. I won't cite each date individually, but all of the quotes from Akbar that come from correspondence with me were part of this ongoing exchange.
281 been friends with Akbar for years: John Connies-Laing to PRK, 13 Dec. 2023.
281 'Last thing I need is': AS interrogation 3; AS to JCL, 4 Dec. 2019, cited in NW statement.

281 'Mark was well connected': John Connies-Laing to PRK, 13 Dec. 2023.
282 'he concurs completely': John Connies-Laing to PRK, 14 Dec. 2023.
282 'I just called him Zac': John Connies-Laing to PRK, 26 Jan. 2024.
282 In 1890, a group of artists: 'Our Story', Chelsea Arts Club (website): https://chelseaartsclub.com/about-the-club/history.
282 a creaky old place: this account of the Chelsea Arts Club is based on author's visit to the club and interviews with multiple longtime members.
283 one of the guests was Mark Foley: Mark Foley, interview by author.

CHAPTER 20: THE BLACK BOX

288 ran a typical headline: 'Police Failed Us, Say Parents of Public Schoolboy After Mysterious Balcony Death', *Daily Telegraph*, 8 Feb. 2024.
289 new UK law passed in 2022: the Economic Crime (Transparency and Enforcement) Act of 2022 requires any overseas entity that invests in UK property to file information on beneficial ownership with a publicly accessible register.
289 It was a Saudi princess: Flat W504 belongs to a company called Riverwalk Exquisite Residence S.A., which is registered in the British Virgin Islands and which purchased the unit in October 2016 for £4,782,500. Riverwalk Exquisite Residence registered with Companies House, in accordance with the new 2022 regulations, in Feb. 2023. But on 7 Feb. 2024, an accountant named Shahid Javed filed an update to Companies House, applying for 'protected status'. This kind of exemption to the standard disclosure requirements is granted very rarely, generally when an applicant might be somehow put at risk if the information were public. But in this case the request was granted and the company's true owner is now listed as 'withdrawn'. There are other ways to obtain this information, however. The business information provider Endole continues to list the Ultimate Beneficial Owner of Riverwalk Exquisite Residence: Her Royal Highness Princess Abeer Bint Sultan Bin Abdulaziz Al Saud. See https://open.endole.co.uk

/insight/company/OE024854-riverwalk-exquisite-residence-s-a. Princess Abeer's name also appears in paperwork associated with the lease for Flat W504, which was filed with the Land Registry. I should say: none of this impressive reportorial legwork is my own. It was Emanuele Midolo of the *Sunday Times* who made these discoveries and generously brought them to my attention.

289 at least ten wives: 'Crown Prince Sultan Bin Abdul-Aziz: Obituary', *Guardian*, 23 Oct. 2011.

289 mansion on The Bishops Avenue: Princess Abeer is listed, along with her mother, Nawal Al-Khaimi, as Ultimate Beneficial Owners of another BVI company called 40A Bishop Avenue Exclusive Residence S.A. According to the Land Registry, Abeer bought the property in her own name in Oct. 2010, for £8,950,000. (She transferred it to the BVI company in 2015.)

289 'I was paying for it': Nick Gold, interview by author.

290 reached Oliver Harris: I traded calls and exchanged texts with Oliver Harris on 9 Dec. 2023. He maintains that he did not know Zac or Verinder well, that he did not know Akbar Shamji at all, and that he was not involved in any business deal with any of them.

292 a small black box: unless otherwise noted, details relating to the evidence from the black box of Akbar's Mercedes come from 'The Dead Teenager, the Lying Suspect and the Black Box That Proves It', *Sunday Times*, 6 Apr. 2024, and from the interpretation of the underlying dataset, which was provided to me by Pogrund.

292 'I will remember him': Gabriel Pogrund to MB and RGB, 7 Feb. 2024; Gabriel Pogrund, interview by author.

292 to 'arrange a meeting' with Zac: VS to AS, 27 Nov. 2019, cited in NW statement.

294 'I just don't remember. I really don't': AS interrogation 3.

294 a Belgian American businessman: unless otherwise indicated, details related to Pham-Quang and his relationship with Akbar come from François Pham-Quang, interview by author.

294 as a 'financial leader': 'Music Veteran and Financial Leaders Announce Formation of New Record Label', *Business Wire*, 24 July 2003.

295 was featured prominently: image of Akbar Shamji and Narendra Modi, CPEC (website), https://cpec.io/visionary. This website appears to have been taken down in 2024 or early 2025, but the photo was previously displayed alongside a biography of Akbar. (The 'visionary' was presumably a reference to Akbar.)

296 found a video: a good fact-checker would point out that *I* wasn't actually the one who found this video. It was a *New Yorker* fact-checker, Yinuo Shi. Watch for yourself: 'PM Modi Inaugurates RE-Invest 2015, the First Renewable Energy Global Investors' Meet and Expo', posted 15 Feb. 2015, YouTube, https://www.youtube.com/watch?v=dZ9QjVbCxaA. Shamji appears at the 21:27 mark.

CHAPTER 21: UNDERTOW

297 a scandalous report: 'Love Child Names TV Rabbi as Her Dad', *News of the World*, 11 Sept. 1988. I tried to speak with Angela, informing her in advance, in writing, that I would be including the truth about Hugo and Ester in this book and seeking any input, clarification or concerns she might be willing to share. She did not respond.

297 told his wife and children: this account is based on author interviews with RGB, David Gryn, Naomi Gryn and Gaby Massey.

297 hour-long documentary: *The Sabbath Bride*, directed by Naomi Gryn, See More Productions, originally aired on Channel 4 (1987).

298 as Ester grew up: details about Ester are drawn from a short biographical sketch on the website of the Separated Child Foundation, an organization that was created in part to honour her memory, at https://separatedchild.org/about-us/our-inspiration, and from recollections of her posted on the blog *Ester the Purple Princess*: https://esterthepurpleprincess.blogspot.com.

299 jumped in front of a moving train: 'Where Did My Daughter Spend Her Last Ten Hours?', *Camden New Journal*, 12 July 2007. In an echo of Zac's story, Ester's mother, Angela, was not fully persuaded that

her daughter had committed suicide. But in this case the man who had been driving the train described witnessing the moment in which she jumped onto the tracks.
299 blared, comprehensively: 'Did This Public Schoolboy and Grandson of a Celebrity Rabbi Jump to His Death to Escape Being Tortured with Hot Knives by a Gangster He Thought Was His Friend?', *Daily Mail*, 9 Feb. 2024.
300 posted the photograph: John Sweeney (@johnsweeneyroar), post on X (formerly Twitter), 5 Feb. 2024. The tweet, which has since been deleted, contained a photograph of Zac's dead body, along with the text 'Who Killed Zac Brettler? In 2019, the body of a young man washed up on the foreshore opposite MI6. The murder mystery poses big questions for figures in organized crime in London – and the Metropolitan Police. Full story to follow.' (He never followed up.)
300 Matthew texted Sweeney: MB to John Sweeney, 5 Feb. 2024.
300 Sweeney refused: John Sweeney to MB, 5 Feb. 2024.
300 'I can't imagine you': RGB to John Sweeney, 5 Feb. 2024.
300 Sweeney took the image down: John Sweeney to RGB, 6 Feb. 2024.
300 a Turkish artist: Alper Yesiltas (@alperyesiltas), Instagram page.
301 published a report: Dame Margaret Hodge, *Losing Our Moral Compass: Corrupt Money and Corrupt Politics*, Policy Institute, King's College London, 2022. The quotes used here are from a new foreword to the report that was released by Hodge in 2023.
301 named Mohamed Amersi: 'Tory Donor Accused of "Bribery and Blackmail" by Conservative Grandee', *Independent*, 30 June 2023; 'Tory Donor Accused of Using Bullying Legal Threats to Suppress a Report', *Guardian*, 3 July 2023; 'The Millionaire Tory Party Donor Who Used the Law to Silence Critics', *Sunday Times*, 26 Oct. 2023. For much more on Amersi, see Tom Burgis, *Cuckooland: Where the Rich Own the Truth* (William Collins, 2024).
302 'We are, bluntly, concerned': Oliver Bullough, *Butler to the World: How Britain Became the Servant of Tycoons, Tax Dodgers, Kleptocrats, and Criminals* (Profile Books, 2022), p. 201.
302 gave an interview in 2023: 'Transcript: Candy Says Property Buyers Want Dubai Luxury, Not London Crime', *Bloomberg News*, 27 Apr. 2023.
302 'The oligarchs today are': Trevor Abrahmsohn, interview by author.
302 Roman Abramovich was reported to be selling: 'Roman Abramovich Hastily Selling UK Properties, MP Claims', *Guardian*, 1 Mar. 2022. I should note that it is not entirely clear that he actually *did* end up selling these properties.
302 On the eve of Russia's: 'Leak Reveals Roman Abramovich's Billion-Dollar Trusts Transferred Before Russia Sanctions', *Guardian*, 6 Jan. 2023.
302 was *herself* a non-dom: 'Rishi Sunak's Wife Claims Non-Domicile Status', *Guardian*, 6 Apr. 2022.
302 she committed to pay: 'British Chancellor Rishi Sunak's Wife Agrees to Pay UK Tax on All of Her Income', *Politico*, 8 Apr. 2022.
302 in 2024, the government announced: 'What Does Non-Dom Mean and How Are the Rules Changing?', BBC, 23 Jan. 2025.
303 dire warnings of a 'wealth exodus': 'London's Wealth Exodus', a report by Henley & Partners and New World Wealth; 'UK Families "Seize Moment" to Buy Exclusive Luxury Homes as Non-Doms Retreat', *FT*, 10 June 2025.
303 Pugachev once observed: Belton, *Putin's People*, p. 13.
303 'suggest you go to Annabel's': 'What the Russian Oligarchs Did Next', *Daily Telegraph*, 13 Jan. 2023.
303 In 1967, Otto Frank gave: he gave this interview for *The Eternal Light*, 'The Legacy of Anne Frank', produced by the Jewish Theological Seminary of America and NBC, originally aired 24 Dec. 1967, on NBC. I first saw this extract at the Anne Frank House, in Amsterdam, where it plays on a loop. It is also available on YouTube: 'Otto Frank Talks Anne's Diary', posted 23 Sept. 2009, by Anne Frank House, YouTube, https://www.youtube.com/watch?v=AWRBinP7ans.

CHAPTER 22: THE KID'S HOME SAFE

306 'Can you explain this?': PRK to AS, 15 May 2025.
306 suggested without prompting: Clive Strong, interview by author.

307 man named David McKelvey: for background on David 'Mac' McKelvey, see Michael Gillard, *Legacy: Gangsters, Corruption and the London Olympics* (Bloomsbury, 2021), in which he features prominently.
307 When I reached him and brought: David McKelvey, interview by author.
307 retired under a cloud: 'Murder Caught on Victim's Own Camera but Motive Unclear', *BBC News*, 31 Mar. 2010.
307 'dissolute and wholly treacherous': Gillard, *Legacy*, p. 239.
307 after thirty years: ibid., pp. 236–39.
308 he had never known: Chris Cubitt to PRK, 26 June 2025.
308 much postponed virtual proceeding: unless otherwise noted, information related to the inquest comes from VS inquest. Note that there was initially some confusion over the date of the earlier overdose, with some saying it occurred on the thirtieth. In fact it was the twenty-ninth, as recorded in the contemporaneous notes of Dr Grace Walker, who treated Sharma that day.
311 old gangster associate: Andy Baker, interview by author.
313 following 'the success of Bitzero': Akbar Shamji (website), https://www.akbarshamji.com/about.
313 the Princess of Wales: 'Kate Middleton Steps Out in Purple Safiyaa Dress for Wimbledon Finals 2024', *Women's Wear Daily*, 14 July 2024.
313 spoke to Akbar's friend: John Connies-Laing to PRK, 13 Dec. 2023.
314 'People often say "time is a great healer"': Gryn with Gryn, *Chasing Shadows*, pp. 256–57.
315 Hugo Gryn wrote a short story: the story is described in a document titled 'HUGO GRUEN DP 488', prepared by L. Wallentin, a caseworker, and dated 3 Nov. 1947. This document is part of an archive preserved by Naomi Gryn. She shared a photocopy with me but believes that the original is held in the archives of World Jewish Relief.

EPILOGUE

319 preface to the British edition: Mark Twain and Charles Dudley Warner, *The Gilded Age* (George Routledge and Sons, 1874).

ABOUT THE AUTHOR

Patrick Radden Keefe is a staff writer at *The New Yorker* and the author of the international bestsellers *Empire of Pain*, winner of the Baillie Gifford Prize for Non-Fiction and named one of the 20 Best Non-Fiction Books of All Time by *The Telegraph*, and *Say Nothing*, which won the Orwell Prize for Political Writing, was named one of the 20 Best Books of the 21st Century by *The New York Times* and is now an award-winning limited series on Disney+. He has also written the bestselling *Rogues*, a collection of his *New Yorker* articles, as well as two earlier books, *The Snakehead* and *Chatter*. He is the writer and host of the eight-part podcast *Wind of Change*, which *The Guardian* named the No. 1 podcast of 2020, and the recipient of the National Magazine Award for Feature Writing and the National Book Critics Circle Award for Nonfiction. He lives in New York.